Dictionary of Abstract Painting

Translated from the French
Dictionnaire de la Peinture Abstraite

(FERNAND HAZAN ÉDITEUR, PARIS)

by LIONEL IZOD, JOHN MONTAGUE
and FRANCIS SCARFE

First published in 1957

DICTIONARY
OF
ABSTRACT PAINTING

with a
History of Abstract Painting

———————

MICHEL SEUPHOR

TUDOR PUBLISHING COMPANY
NEW YORK

THIS DICTIONARY
WAS FIRST PRINTED
IN PARIS IN 1957
ON THE OFFSET PRESSES OF
LA PHOTOLITH
UNDER THE DIRECTION OF
RENÉ MAZURIER.
THE PLATES WERE MADE BY
CLICHÉS UNION
UNDER THE DIRECTION OF
CHARLES FONTAINE.
THE PAPER IS A WOVE
MADE IN THE MILLS OF
ARCHES JOHANNOT MARAIS.

FOREWORD

Although a great deal has been written about abstract painting, there is no one work available which gives a comprehensive historical survey of the subject for all countries in which this new development has manifested itself. The study published by Michel Seuphor some years ago was confined in its historical scope to the first ten years of abstract art and hence gives little indication as to what happened after 1920.

The present work does not pretend to list the name of every abstract painter—obviously an impossible task—nor to make a final critical selection. It will however, we venture to think, provide the general public, students of art and artists themselves with a source of information which has been lacking up to the present time.

This book may be used in three ways: it may be read as a historical work, it may be perused from time to time as an album, or it may be kept at hand as a reference work full of accurate and ample information.

The illustrations have been chosen so as to give the widest possible view of the subject, although this concern has not been allowed to take precedence over such important considerations as the quality of the work illustrated or the proven value of the artist.

The chronological chart given on pages 106 to 113 provides an ever-present guide to the reader who wishes to place a particular development in its historical context as he reads, or to take in at a glance the whole history of abstract art from 1910 to 1956.

THE PUBLISHER

CONTENTS

PART I

History of Abstract Painting

PRELIMINARIES. A DEFINITION. THE IMPRESSIONISTS' AWARENESS
OF ABSTRACTION. ABSTRACT ART AND NATURE.
FREEDOM AND DIFFICULTY OF ABSTRACT ART.

It is by no means easy, at this stage, to give a generally acceptable
definition of abstract art. From one standpoint it is evident that its
authority and range have so widened in recent years that there are few or
no young artists, however great or slight their ability, who have no share
whatever in its development, at least through some particular aspect of
their work. On the other hand we must not overlook the fact that certain
artists, and by no means the least important, are suspicious of the term
'abstract' art, if not of the thing itself, and that they try to adopt a non-
committal position in order to safeguard their own individualism, seeing
present-day 'Abstract' painters as mere offshoots or hangers-on of the
earlier abstractionists. Thus critical jargon falls back on terms like *content*
and *legibility* or *readability* as if a human work could possibly be devoid of
content, and as if a painted work could conform to the same requirements
as a written text. But even in literature the readable is not necessarily
good, any more than what is unreadable.

But no amount of painting with 'content' or more readable content
can save artists from inevitably belonging to their own time. However
much they recoil from the term, the painted object which is carried out of
their studio shows them to be just as 'abstract' as those whom they denounce
as a clique. Their arguments are of no avail, because, in the mid-twentieth
century, in matters of art the spirit of the age has firmly lodged itself in
abstraction. This is so much the case that we now automatically approach
and interpret all works of art, whether ancient or modern, according to
abstract data and principles. Faced with some Old Master, the mind of
1955 man tends to interpret in terms of composition, points of technique,
psychological details, and we try to penetrate into the character of the
man himself by revealing, through a minute analysis of the work of art,
the reservations and discoveries, the hesitations and audacities of the
painter. Our admiration swings between a synthesis effected on broad
schematic lines and an analysis of craftsmanship, while we tend to forget
at the same time that the spectator of a few centuries ago was concerned

with nothing but the 'subject' in the proper sense of the term, the *what* and not the *how*.

For some of us the *Sistine Madonna* is one of Raphael's finest works because of its outstandingly powerful composition. For the painter's contemporaries this sense of power no doubt lay in the expressive faces of the Virgin and Child. But nowadays we are less attracted by things in themselves than by the way in which they are presented: we find a man's manner of walking more revealing than his objective. The hundreds of little strokes criss-crossed and juxtaposed in bewildering variety on the back of Rembrandt's *Recumbent Negress* afford us more visual pleasure than the woman's back itself, for there are better specimens to be found in albums of photographers' nudes, while we are delighted to find an amplification of Rembrandt's strokes in an abstract by De Staël. This seems to bring an understanding of Rembrandt within the layman's reach and at the same time to demonstrate De Staël's greatness as a draughtsman. In the simplest possible terms, we are looking at art through glasses appropriate to the century we are living in, and not through those we inherit from previous generations. Whether people like it or not these modern 'glasses' exist and are nothing more nor less than *abstraction*. However bitterly the schools and dealers might wrangle over the word's possible meanings, we see all art in terms of its abstract qualities, regardless of its degree of figurativeness or non-figurativeness, representation or non-representation, objectivity or subjectivity.

In any case it is thanks to these squabbles and barrages of apparently futile arguments that abstract art has extended its influence wherever young artists are trained all over the world, as well as penetrating the circles of dealers and amateurs. We need not worry unduly over the historical errors brought about through hasty journalism, nor over half-baked definitions, quibbles over terminology, nor even the bullying and anger that accompanied this change: all this creates a stir and serves to draw the attention of a 'general' public impervious to everything but shouts and posters. After the sandwich-boards comes the show itself, and something positive remains which is gradually sifted and shaped in the mind. It is then time for the historian and the detached interpreter to begin their work.

Let us first try to offer some definition of the material to be dealt with in this book. We shall take as our antinomies figurative painting (or *figuration*) and abstract painting (or *abstraction*) (1).

2

A painting is to be called abstract when it is impossible to recognize in it the slightest trace of that objective reality which makes up the normal background of our everyday existence: in other words, a painting is abstract when the absence of any other form of sensible reality compels us to regard it purely as painting and as nothing else, and to judge it according to values that have nothing to do with representation or with the imitation or reproduction of some other thing. It follows that a transposition of nature, even when it is very far-fetched, remains figurative and is *figuration ;* but it also follows that a transposition taken to the point where nothing in the work suggests or evokes some basic naturalistic subject—a transposition, therefore, which to the naked eye does not even imply the act of transposition itself—will rightly be called abstract, *abstraction.*

Thus, even in cases when some representation or transposition of shapes has served as a point of departure, whether in the painter's mind or just on the canvas, the work is to be deemed abstract, providing that no aspect of that point of departure remains recognizable, and so long as the work, *ipso facto,* has nothing to convey to us except the pure elements of composition and colour (2).

Conversely, we shall say that any work of art which, though setting out from abstract principles or processes, either by accident or playfully embodies representational elements, however fantastic or extraordinary they appear, cannot be called abstract (3).

But even if a canvas is strictly abstract—that is to say neither representing, interpreting or transposing any reality from the external world, this cannot prevent our imagination from discerning subjects in it—such as those shapes that people fancy they see in the clouds—that had nothing to do with the painter's own intentions. The abstract painter must do all he can to avoid such representational accidents, though of course he cannot be held responsible for the spectator's whims.

Long before it existed in actual fact, abstraction was "in the air" and painters intuitively tried to grasp it, like the 'frozen syllables' of Mandeville and Rabelais. They were not so lucky as Pantagruel; the words eluded them and the most notorious passwords and incantations failed to make them sing before they were fully matured. Those passwords, however, came as so many unmistakable forewarnings of a new age. We could trot out dozens of quotations from Baudelaire to Cézanne, from Van Gogh to Seurat and Maurice Denis, all centred on the same realisation, that painting is not a matter of subject but of colour, form, sensibility, composition (4). But they felt themselves under no obligation on this account to leave out the theme altogether, and perhaps they were not far wrong, since we all admire the masterpieces they left us. But now that we can look back on it all we cannot help noticing a certain contradiction between their often extreme pronouncements and their actual behaviour as painters. This was because the theory of the abstract in art could only gradually be translated into actual works, and it had to be by a process of evolution rather than revolution. Great discoveries are made slowly, and there is no *eureka* without a long and tedious preparation behind it.

It is true that in 1841 or thereabouts Turner came so close to abstract painting that his works have no parallel in his century. They can be explained only in terms of the 'long preparation' I have mentioned. By the time he was sixty Turner had reached the end of a long evolution in the course of which he had stated the problems of representation and expression on the canvas, with an ever-increasing frankness that enables us to trace the gradual development of his bold yet calm resolve to find a solution to the paradox.

The Impressionists took a long time to catch up with the great English painter. But there are many moments of abstract beauty in some of their works, all arising from the same premonition in the artist. Whether in works that were delicate and mild, or startlingly violent, Impressionism like Fauvism and Cubism later on was a pioneer in abstract painting, and many unpretentious canvases of the period still teem with marvellous lessons for our young abstract painters. I am not thinking only of Cézanne, but of works by Van Gogh (*The wheat-field,* the *Landscape with rooks*), Renoir (*Women in a field*), Claude Monet (*The poppy-field*). In the last of these paintings, in particular, the subtle proportions of red and blue show a craftsmanship fully aware of abstract composition. There is an exquisite delicacy in the *parasol-étoile,* its ultramarine bringing out the redness of the flowers and uttering a kind of gentle exclamation in response to the diffused, soft blue of the sky. But even that is not the finest discovery made in this canvas. To my mind it is to be seen in the discreet stretch of light green just above the line of the horizon, without which the darker green of the belt of trees would be flat or would need stressing,—a solution which would have ruined the general effect which was meant to be calm and soothing. Thus everything in this work is quite simple, as is the case in every really beautiful work, yet there is nothing banal about it.

At this point I can imagine some readers asking "What more can

4

abstract art possibly offer us, than this ? Here we can enjoy non-representation and representation at the same time. What is there wrong in superimposing a real landscape on to pure art ? The truth is that this offers
not less, but more than does abstract art." To this I would reply that
Monet's first intention was certainly to paint a landscape, and that in order
to dispense with subject and paint nothing but *a painting* a certain evolution,
or call it if you like a slow revolution, had to be gone through. I would
add that art is worth exactly as much as the spectator is able to put into it,
and that the spectator at the moment is the man of 1955 and not of 1873.

I think the time has come to assert that abstraction in art does not
mean being anti-nature. There is too much of nature in us for it to be
other than an intrinsic part of our make-up. There would be no point
in trying to rid our inner field of experience of all those visions and perceptions that have impressed themselves on our minds since childhood.
It is well known, also, that the most profound visual sensations automatically
give rise to symbols which are then nourished by the subconscious, and
which cannot but exteriorise themselves in art in a fairly obvious way.

Altogether to exclude nature from our thoughts and works would
amount to a harsh form of mental repression, resulting in a kind of narrow
mental dictatorship. It cannot be denied, however, that since 1912 the

KLEE. VIBRATION OF SOUTHERN FLORA. WATER-COLOUR, 1927.
Private Collection.

5

most outstanding works and those most calculated to enrich the human mind seem to have been made in the absence of any apparent help from external nature, which incidentally, Cubism tended more and more to reduce to a *still*-life, a nature-*morte*.

Further misunderstanding may be avoided by adding that abstract art does not eliminate nature but expresses it in a different way. The Impressionist used to set up his easel in front of his subject, against the background of the external world; but the abstract painter instals himself, so to speak, in the domain of inwardness, in the inner life, or, to put it another way, he opens up this inner life before the canvas with which he then communes in secret. The mind of man is the greatest of unexplored territories, and it is there that the greatest discoveries are to be made. It is a microcosm in which dream and speculation, idealism and love flourish side by side, and it bears the indelible marks of our experience of material nature. Thus it is not surprising if some unexpected reminiscence of nature occurs in the works of an abstract painter. The artist abhors dogmatism of any kind and to ban any particular thing (black is not a colour !) causes more violent reactions in the field of the arts than elsewhere. It is undeniable that after practising abstract art for some years, certain artists finally returned to representational or figurative art, only to produce threadbare commonplaces and forfeit any claim to our interest. The protection of a few critical mandarins and magazines does nothing to soften their fall, but only makes it the more spectacular. This is because in 1955, as in 1912, the hard way, but the way along which discoveries are to be made, still lies in abstraction.

It is a long and complicated task for any young painter to find his own personal voice and keep it intact and natural. It is a painful triumph over the self, and when it is carried out sincerely and profoundly, in depth, it is bound to be an heroic undertaking.

Even from the outside it looks like a wager, a wild undertaking. Everything seems to have been done already: there are now abstract painters all over the world, every possible form has been invented. For a sensitive person, strict, uncompromising abstraction might well look like a kind of hit or miss. All drawing leads to the ideogram. Everything suggests an image to the fertile imagination: a square is a house, a wavy line a river, a circle the moon, a few dots are the starry sky. If you let the pen doodle on a sheet of paper it is not long before it suggests a human or other figure. Join up a few lines at the foot of the page and you have a tree, a plant, a flame or a fan. Whether you accept these suggestions or dismiss them in

6

KANDINSKY. DRAWING FOR COMPOSITION NO. 2. INDIAN INK, 1910.

your search for something more unusual, you are returning to the figurative world and rediscovering the delights of childhood. The greatest of such enchanters is Paul Klee. He covers a sheet all over with horizontal lines, then adds a few vertical strokes and creates a palace, a village, a fairy-like tower. The towers are turned upside-down and Klee only has to write the word 'rain' under his drawing to suggest cloud-castles slowly pouring down on to the earth. A profound humorist, gifted with a light touch, full of poetic surprises and forever flirting with the absurd, Klee has produced few works that do not contain some allusion to external nature.

The abstract work, on the other hand, is one in which not the slightest suggestion of an image is voluntarily accepted by the artist.

PERSISTENCE AND VITALITY OF ABSTRACT ART.
A UNIVERSAL LANGUAGE.   HISTORY AND THE LAW OF CHANGE.
AN ART CORRESPONDING TO OUR AGE.   THE DISCOVERY OF THE SELF.

Those who have followed the course of abstract art over the past 20 or 30 years will have been struck by its persistence.   When the *Cercle et Carré* exhibition was held in April 1930, the Parisian press informed us that such painting was "the mere ghost of an experiment which we thought had died long ago," and that "all this has nothing new to offer."   In 1955 the same outbursts of weariness and boredom, if not anger, can be heard at any exhibition of abstract art: "about time the joke was buried. . . same old bag of tricks. . . poor old public. . . "

Maybe.   But things become entirely different if we are patient enough to take a closer look.   Then we see that abstract art has never stopped adding to its range and means of expression, never faltered in its search for greater depth.   If the ABC of this language was firmly established in the 'heroic' phase by Kandinsky, Mondrian, Delaunay and Malevitch, this does not mean that everything has been said in the same language. The critics' ignorance and the public's sophisticated grumbling were unable to prevent it from branching out into the remotest corners of the western world, where it has won over intelligent collectors and gained a hold, even a considerable hold, in civic museums and galleries.   Kandinsky and Mondrian, both of whom lived to a good age, thanks to their long working life were able to show their successors what a range of values can be drawn out of such simple elements; Kandinsky stressing inventiveness and Mondrian the importance of increasing depth.

The other movements or schools which sprang up in such great numbers all over the world in the past hundred years all enjoyed a much shorter span of life.   At the moment of writing (1955), abstract painting has flourished for forty years and shows no signs of slackening vitality. Those critics who began by encouraging it but who now pull a long face at some geometrical composition by Vasarely or some colour-composition by Riopelle, remind me of Zola when, throwing over his former Impressionist friends in 1896, he voiced his disillusionment in a notorious article in the *Figaro* which does not stand to his credit: "Not a single artist in this

KANDINSKY. SKETCH 1912.
Joseph Slifka Collection, New York.

group," wrote the author of *L'Œuvre,* "has succeeded in translating into paint, with the slightest power of finality, the new formula which is to be observed in snippets on their various canvases. . . They are all forerunners. The genius is yet to be born. . . They are all unequal to the task they have set themselves, they can't talk, they stutter." At the Jeu de Paume Museum (for example) we can now go and see exactly what stuttering meant. No oracle is needed to predict that fifty years hence some other Jeu de Paume will be showing an astonished public those masterpieces of abstract art that are being painted at the present time and which we are treating with contempt.

But those who have been keeping a close watch on art during the past twenty or thirty years will have also noticed that in the twentieth century every form of art has evolved in the direction of abstraction. Thus the term abstract art cannot be used to single out any school, nor any movement however widespread. It is a universal phenomenon, a universal language.

Abstract art has lasted too long for it still to be put down to snobbery, while its styles and its types of expression are too numerous and different for it to be in any danger of being called academic. It would be more accurate as well as simpler to regard it as a fresh departure, setting out from a new principle or datum, to wit *the free expression of the self,* regardless of any laws but those invented by the artist or which his chosen material imposes on him. As for such formulas as "a new basis for a more direct expression of man" or "a healthier foundation for the life of the mind", I am disinclined to speak in terms of 'bases' or 'foundations' in referring to abstract art in general, for such words imply the concept of a plan or theory, and therefore of some system or method. There are twenty different systems or methods of abstract art, and if at times some look more valid than others, that is because the success or otherwise of systems depends entirely on the talents that exploit them at any given moment, or the stature of the genius who thrusts them aside.

Abstract art is art itself, the art of all time, but grasped in its most intimate substance, I mean the apprehension of whatever it is which determines that art is art and not just illustration or education or propaganda or a substitute for literature or religion. It is perhaps a dangerous and certainly a shocking venture. I am not likely to be found saying that abstract art is easy art. There is no abstract art without an awareness, however dim or hard to express in words, of the profound nature of art, or without a secret union between the artist and art integrally itself, to the exclusion of any other alliance. Not a philosophy but a clairvoyance, an insight. And that insight could not possibly express itself in any other way than the very act of creating. From now on man's mind will express itself by the creator's direct action on passive material, without passing, as formerly, through the medium of such external forms as are already generally admitted as being 'beautiful' or 'suitable for pictures'.

A new departure in art, then, but one to which there is no need to presuppose any base or foundation: it strikes out and radiates in every direction, without any particular direction being the dominant one.

This upsets many values which people thought were permanently assured, and that is why abstract art arouses almost as much hostility half way through the century as it did thirty years ago. But its arrival was foretold in the logical progression of the life of art itself. We can be sure that mockery, jibes, violence (cries of 'degenerate art') nor even the shrugged shoulders of the indifferent can never long prevail against the organic evolution of things.

Even within the ranks of these new artists, the various tendencies and their spokesmen are waging a merciless war. Listening to some of them, anyone might take abstract art to be an endless process of destruction, or imagine that nobody has the right to paint unless he is forever in a state of hypnotic trance, or who does not find his daily thrill in a kind of frenzy of painting which is bound to end in some form of aggressiveness. According to others, abstract art, which they assert alone deserves to be called art, cannot be anything but a series of exercises in construction, a matter of clever scaffolding and blueprints put out by somewhat bashful architects. So we must take our stand outside all that and take no part in such squabbles, if we are to see that abstract art is simply the stage that has now been reached in the general evolution of the arts, the multiform style of twentieth-century art.

Life is change.

Like man in the course of his personal existence, societies undergo a transformation of the mind or spirit, as well as of their outward appearance. The universe is a continuous creation, a bearing or 'bringing forth' in Biblical terms, and all its elements are subject, like the world, itself, to the great law of mutation or change. It might be said that history is only an analytical account of the transformation of mankind of which art is the direct and synthetical expression. The essence of successive societies is embodied in the divers forms of art which have been left to us over the centuries. It is an explicit statement, complete in itself and in need of no commentary: for instance the XIIIth century can be read more easily in the statuary of Chartres cathedral than in the most learned history-books. The tedious, futile series of battles and political upheavals seems to have crawled out of the yellow press, when compared with those tangible witnesses we find in works of art. And what other conceivable evidence for the XIIIth century could there be, than those anonymous illustrations of the Scriptures, made by those sculptors and glass-makers who were as humble as they were effective ?

Our century, also, has its own face, its own look, which is reflected in an art made in its own image. It is a century of chain-invention, of short-lived freaks, confused aspirations, violent sensations, accompanied by all the diseases of a society whose institutions are crumbling and in which the very conditions of life are fragile, constantly threatened by a cycle of crises. These features are all to be observed in block letters in the evolutions or revolutions that have occurred in art since the dawn of the century.

There is, however, one dominant idea that permeates the apparent disorder of our time, an idea that determines its spiritual outlook and controls all its reactions whenever they show the slightest hint of seriousness. That is the idea of liberty. I cannot think of a more appropriate word to convey the fundamental characteristic of modern art as a whole. Not only does it define it according to its underlying psychological basis, but the word encloses and sums up all its visible manifestations. There is freedom to say everything, to invent everything, to create a style for its own sake, to prefer discord to harmony, to choose the rule and set limits to it, a freedom from both constraint and licence.

It is the most normal thing in the world for liberty to have its opponents at the best of times, always slandering and failing to understand it. There is a mystery of freedom for every individual, but some are perhaps

ROBERT DELAUNAY. WINDOW NO. 2. 1912.
S. D. Collection, Paris.

MONDRIAN. COMPOSITION. 1913
Kröller-Müller Museum, Otterlo.

not mature enough to cleave to it, or else they are inadequately prepared by a misguided education. In any case we know now, after half a century of experiments, that freedom is the best of masters in all that concerns art.

It is a master who by no means condemns the disciplines, easy though that might be to believe. The very opposite is true, for more surely than any other master, liberty teaches restraint and measure through trials and errors of every kind. It alone can enable a personality to discover itself and open out. That is why modern art owes to liberty its discoveries, its infinite variety and freshness.

The same fifty years of experiment has proved that the traditional images—nudes, landscapes, still-lives—have all lost their substance and have nothing essential to offer man to-day. Or, rather, the landscape, fruit-dish or mandoline can only be accepted in so far as they are pretexts for the *real subject*—which however has now come to the forefront—that is to say, painting in itself and for itself.

Thus it has been only logical to take cubism to its natural conclusions, and to cut out the traditional subject and give final expression, in a clear style and in absolute liberty, to the values of pure art as they appear to the artist.

Abstract art came into being when, at almost the same time and in different parts of Europe, there appeared a number of fearless creators who saw, at a glance, both the evidence of an existing problem and evidence of how it could be solved.

This happened between 1910 and 1917. The centres in question were Paris, Munich, Moscow, Florence, Zurich and Amsterdam. The main protagonists were Kandinsky, Larionov, Kupka, Picabia, Mondrian, Delaunay, Malevitch, Magnelli and Arp. Others followed quickly in their wake. A hundred men presented themselves to replace those who practically stopped painting (such as Larionov), or who for varying periods returned to figurative painting (Picabia, Delaunay, Magnelli). It gradually became obvious that there were as many new styles as there were truly creative artists. The greatest of these had their usual band of slavish imitators whose mediocrity did not long pass unnoticed, since an art freed from subject implies and enforces the absolute necessity for creativeness. Thus, under the cheerful finery of 'liberty', obligatory invention has become the new tyrant of art. Henceforward any artist failing to invent himself and become the happy prospector of an autonomous world, was to be condemned out of hand. The object of art became and is now more than ever, to find a personal and inexhaustible mode of expression, the image of our profound inner being.

This put an end to the harlequins, ray-fish, stuffed tomatoes and such-like trifles. Subject in itself only serves to lull the conscience of the uncreative artist, as he basks in sweet oblivion in the arms of short-term art which can offer the amateur nothing but wallowing in shallow enjoyment.

It is in the manifold tendencies of abstract art that modern man, who is equally manifold, can recognise his own being and find once more some substantial nourishment. I mean that he finds in it some response to his own distinct sensibility, the sensibility of the town-dweller involved in the rhythm and technics of present-day life, as well as an answer to his need for harmony and novelty, equilibrium and surprise, the complex and the simple. It is not surprising, then, if abstract art, in spite of all that tries to stand in its way, is finding a world-wide and ever-increasing favour, for it is the only art that really coincides with the age we live in.

Every man is a complete world in himself, full of astonishing poten-tialities; but every man is also a member of a spiritual family whose well-being he shares. The twentieth century is such a 'family'. It has already bequeathed us an infinitely precious legacy, though so many eyes refuse to see and so many ears refuse to hear it.

Once we have learnt to admire the Fauves and the great Cubists, it behoves us to try and understand those who, having learnt from those predecessors and from the canvases they painted in their days of struggle, have each in his own way invented an independent art of painting.

It so happens, by a sort of miracle, that this intensely individualistic art sums up again and again the whole art of painting, whenever it is grafted on to some richly-endowed sensibility which is both honest with itself and capable of giving and communicating itself.

Thus the key to abstract art lies in the discovery of the self and the exploitation, by a suitable technique, of that hidden store of virgin material which we all carry within us, and to which we must find a path—and this is perhaps the hardest aspect of the artist's work—before it can be brought to light.

The next important question is to consider every work in its proper order, watching its apparent tendencies and seeking its autonomous laws. The greatest pleasure for those who care for art is no longer, as it used to be, a matter of penetrating into the represented object by way of a temperament; but to uncover whatever it is in the depths of the artist that dictates the intentions of his work: that is to say, to follow the very process of composition step by step, apprehending it from the inside, much as an orchestra interprets music. The sensitive critic or the informed lover of art can determine where and by virtue of what the artist has remained or failed to remain faithful to himself. And it is precisely at the points where he is unfaithful that we perhaps come closest to the crucial moment of discovery, the enlarging of the self, the shedding of past selves.

3

KANDINSKY AND MONDRIAN.

The immediate forerunners of abstract art, as we know, were Fauvism and Cubism. The influence of the Fauves was decisive in the case of Kandinsky, while Mondrian's formation was completed by that of the Cubists. 1906 and 1912 are two important dates here. The first was not only the year of the death of Cézanne, whose influence on early Cubism has been fully explored; it was also the year when Bergson's *Creative Evolution* appeared, and when Kandinsky spent a long spell in or near Paris. There he sustained the full shock of the Fauves and Gauguin (through the Gauguin retrospective exhibition at the Autumn Salon, showing 227 exhibits). It was after that year's stay in Paris (or rather Sèvres) that Kandinsky emerged from the New Secession style that characterised his previous work, and began to assert an independent personality. (5) As for the year 1912, it found Mondrian in Paris, unreservedly submitting to the influence of Cubism which was to lead him very soon to works that were remarkably mature in their abstraction, and whose originality was at once noticed by Apollinaire.

Both Kandinsky and Mondrian were older in years than the Cubists and Fauves. What the latter discovered—apparently by accident—found a ready soil in the Russian and Dutch painters, both arduously prepared

MONDRIAN. COMPOSITION IN RED, BLUE AND YELLOW. 1930.
Bartos Collection, New York.

16

KANDINSKY. BLACK POINT. 1937.
Jucker Collection, Milan.

by their earlier technical experiments as well as by a certain amount of philosophical speculation. Braque, Picasso, Léger, Delaunay and Matisse were first and foremost painters. Kandinsky and Mondrian were both painters and thinkers, for whom the problems of art could not be approached apart from the other problems facing man. They aimed not only at renewing painting, but thought that man must transform himself and that the whole of mankind is moving towards an age of material and spiritual betterment. The artist appeared to them the person best qualified for preparing and announcing the golden age. That is why the painted work and the painting man must be identical. The evolution of art is unthinkable without a parallel internal development in man himself. Fauves and Cubists are painters and have no intention of being taken for anything else, whereas Kandinsky and Mondrian are prophets.

17

In Russia, Kandinsky had at first embarked on a career as a scientist. He only turned to painting when he was approaching thirty, impelled by a genuine 'inner necessity' which he had repressed for some years. In his writings on the philosophy of art during his Munich period the term 'inner necessity' constantly recurred, and had an important part to play. It was on this that he based the whole aesthetic justification of his work, after it had already served to justify his career as a painter. After the necessary preliminaries (studies in Munich academies, some instructive travelling) and once he had completed his philosophy of art, (6) Kandinsky flung himself into an orgy of production. A baffling world of forms and colours teemed from his apparently delirious brush. Was it delirium or ecstasy? This dramatic phase in Kandinsky's abstraction still amazes us by its surging overflow, its resonant lyricism, its Wagnerian violence full of clarion-calls. It is the 'Durchbruch', a breaking-through or more precisely a demolition, the battering of the ram on the walls of traditional painting. After a few years this generous strength gradually calmed down. In about 1921 Kandinsky came to accept the geometrical studies of Malevitch and the Russian Constructivists. His painting then progressively changed outwardly but its inventiveness lost nothing of its richness, density and warmth. For a time the presence of Klee could be felt in his work, which began to show touches of humour, and we are not suggesting that this was the least satisfactory part of his output. After 1933 he moved to Neuilly, living in a bright and comfortable flat on the banks of the Seine, where he painted pictures which for the most part are brilliant variations on themes to which he had long been partial. This period has often been called that of the "great synthesis", which is accurate enough so long as it is not taken to include the dramatic period, which finds no echo in it.

Mondrian's period of preparation lasted much longer. Between taking his first art-teaching diploma and his arrival in Paris some twenty-three years slipped by, but they were fruitful years. Rather later than Kandinsky he worked out his own philosophy of art, and the *Stijl* movement was founded on it. At the opposite pole from Kandinsky's, his painting was the pursuit of simplification, of essential measure and economy, at least once Cubism had shown him his way. From Cubism he drew an unexpected lesson, which was that pure rhythm may be reduced to a horizontal-vertical movement. There was only a step from that to the right-angle. He took several years in making that step, painting and meditating, then he laid the first stone of his system, which is that the whole language of painting (and the language of life itself) may be condensed into the dualism of the rectangular tension of two straight lines set in a horizontal-vertical relationship. That and that alone makes construction possible. This was the birth of Neo-Plasticism. Till the end of his life, that is to say for another thirty years, Mondrian never diverged from this principle, slowly advancing towards an imaginary perfection which was always within arms'-reach yet always a bit farther on. That was his own expres-

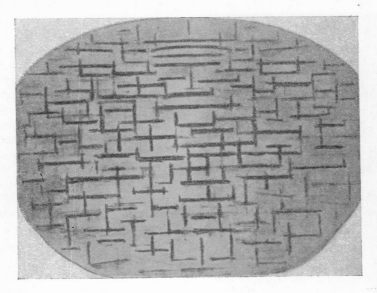

MONDRIAN. THE SEA. DRAWING. 1914.
Bally Collection, Montreux.

sion. "Don't you think, all the same, that it's just a little bit farther on ?" he asked a friend as he showed him the latest canvas, which, as ever, must surely be a progress on the one before. Perhaps it was precisely in the last canvas he ever painted, the unfinished *Victory boogie-woogie,* that he came closest to this imaginary perfection. The very least we can say before his work is that we feel ourselves to be in the presence of a wonderful synthesis, fully alive yet denying nothing of the fundamental neo-plastic principle.

Mondrian and Kandinsky represent two different aspects of human genius, crystallised into two archetypes, infinite patience and saintly impatience. According to our temperament we will be drawn towards one or the other, or perhaps towards each in turn. If genius is something like the toil of a bee, the distillation drop by drop of some unique and all-inclusive essence, then we will favour Mondrian. But if intelligence is restless and multiple, if truth progresses in immense leaps, if creation is a crazy sparkling of treasures, the overflow

of some unfathomable primal cause, then we will choose Kandinsky and see in him the Ariel of abstract painters. Externally these two great personalities were not unlike, avoiding eccentric manners or dress and preferring the correct turn-out of the professional man to that of the bohemian. But Mondrian's threadbare smartness hid a bleak, lonely existence, while Kandinsky never wanted for money, comfort or recognition. They were both gentlemanly and distinguished-looking and had a certain reserve that hinted at a timid childhood. But they had little in common and met rarely, though politely, in Paris during 1930 and after 1933.

Kandinsky's merit lay in showing what marvels can be wrung from genuine freedom, and that the limits of the canvas allow of no excess. Mondrian's lay in his lesson of discipline and humility. Reducing his art to the simplest data ever used, he showed how spiritual stature grows with self-denial and how the poorest means are the purest, often the strongest.

MACDONALD-WRIGHT. SYNCHROMY. 1916.
Earl Stendhal Gallery, Los Angeles.

ROBERT DELAUNAY.   SIMULTANEOUS DISC. 1912.

Tremaine Collection, U.S.A.

4

ROBERT AND SONIA DELAUNAY. MORGAN RUSSELL AND MACDONALD-
WRIGHT. KUPKA. PICABIA. PARIS AND MUNICH, 1912.

Between Mondrian's strict economy and Kandinsky's ebullience there
was room for some restraining, conciliatory element.   This place was filled
by Robert Delaunay for a short time, just long enough for him to leave a
few works of incomparable beauty, by which I mean his *Windows* of 1912.

We are constantly reminded of that exceptional year, 1912.   1912
is increasingly recognized as the peak year of this century's painting, a year
of transition in which everything was begun afresh although the old disciplines were neither consciously nor finally cast aside; a year from which
the main tendencies of abstract art have radiated and to which we can always
turn in our search for origins, for the seed of invention.   One of the most
valuable and fertile of these was the gay, fresh painting of Delaunay, who

named his canvases after an expression of Eugène Chevreul's, *Simultaneous Contrasts*.

Delaunay was born in Paris, in the rue de Chaillot, not far from the present Musée d'Art Moderne. He was the jovial type of Frenchman, or rather a typical Parisian, with a ready tongue and those quick blue eyes which seem to dwell on nothing but look straight through everything. He always spoke his mind without mincing words, while his round, pink face made him the picture of health. For him life meant happiness, a sensual, physical happiness and he approached painting in the same spirit. It was in 1908 or 1909 that he read Eugène Chevreul, the physicist's, theory of simultaneous colours (7) which had already had such an influence on Seurat thirty years earlier. This confirmed the conclusions he had already reached intuitively. In the next few years his natural lyrical gifts found expression through the channel provided by these ideas. His main undertaking was in breaking down the prism and reassembling its elements on the canvas by a discreet though thorough division of surfaces. What Braque and Picasso did with a mandoline, fruit-dish or nude, Delaunay did with light itself, cutting it up and piecing it together again in a new way. This 'new way' implies personal research into the basic laws of painting. Apollinaire had already written "I like contemporary art because I love light more than anything: all men love light more than anything, having invented fire." Delaunay's work between 1911-1914 is a striking illustration of this thought. Like a child with its favorite toy he took the rainbow to pieces and improvised with the separate parts, but without ever going too far or betraying the rainbow's essence. He turned it into the very song of light, both airy and powerful.

Delaunay's works of that period are astonishing achievements. Form and idea are so closely united, the utterance so fused with the style, that in the forty years after him there was no painting capable of conveying such a sensation of physical joy, innocent serenity and strength combined—unless it be the painting of his wife, less candid and spiritually less spontaneous though it is.

In 1910 Delaunay married Sonia Terk, a Russian by birth, who was also a painter, and former wife of the German art-critic Wilhelm Uhde the discoverer of the 'Douanier' Rousseau. She gave him unfailing moral support and I have heard Delaunay say that but for her many a canvas would have remained unfinished. Delaunay was highly-strung, easily discouraged but just as easily stimulated to further effort.

Sonia Delaunay, whom Arthur Cravan so sharply but brillantly attacked in his pamphlet-review *Maintenant* is a remarkably gifted painter. Her large canvas *Electric Prisms,* painted in 1914 is one of the major works of that period. Like her husband she gave up abstract art while living in Portugal during the first World War. It was some years before they returned to pure painting; he in 1930 and she in 1937.

Much as Kandinsky set out from Fauvism and Mondrian from early synthetic Cubism (1912), Delaunay's abstract painting has its roots in Impressionism. The work of all three artists demonstrated well before 1914 that all forms of art are bound to move towards abstraction.

There were two American artists frequenting the same circles as Delaunay in 1911 and 1912. These were Morgan Russell and Stanton Macdonald-Wright, the former being of predominantly French extraction, and the latter, whose real name was Van Vranken, of Dutch parentage. They came to Paris in 1906 and 1907 respectively in order to study painting. Russell, who was the elder of the two, already has a good background as a painter, while Macdonald-Wright, less advanced technically, was trying to train himself through a scientific study of colour and reading—like Delaunay—the works of Eugène Chevreul and other physicists. Shortly after making each other's acquaintance they began to feel sufficiently sure of themselves to launch a movement of their own and founded Synchronism. Synchromism was a departure from the Orphism led by Delaunay. (8) The Synchromists were particularly active in 1913. In this one year they held a large exhibition in Munich, another at Bernheim Jeune's gallery in Paris, as well as sending canvases to the Salon des Indépendants and the Armory Show in New York which were both landmarks in the history of modern painting. But only one of their numerous works shown that year—and it was one of Russell's—can be regarded as abstract in the proper sense of the word: the other canvases are only secondary abstractions of subjects taken from nature, however advanced they might be. It was at this point that Russell's career really began, for at the Salon des Indépendants in the following year he showed his vast *Synchromy in Form* which, over thirty years later, was one of the key items in the exhibition of American abstract art held in the New York Museum of Modern Art in 1951.

Macdonald-Wright was not so quick to develop. The *Synchromatic Piece in Orange-Yellow* of 1915 and the *Synchromy in Red* of 1916 are undeniably abstract works, as was his *Nude or Synchromy in Blue* which was also painted in 1916. The Whitney Museum in New York owns one of his finest canvases, the *Oriental Synchromy in Blue-green* of 1918.

Morgan Russell and Macdonald-Wright are the real founders of American abstract art. They made a public and genuine profession of faith in abstract painting in the catalogue of their exhibition at Bernheim jeune's, but unfortunately they both gave up what they had so vigorously defended and returned to figurative art. This is mentioned as a matter of historical fact, and by no means in order to detract from their pioneer achievement.

Although they set out with the same principles these two Synchromist painters both managed to remain highly individual in their expression. The works they turned out during the 'heroic' period of their movement are historically very important for American culture and also show that they had very little influence on each other. Russell was the more temperamental painter of the two. His brushwork is thick and rich and his forms

MORGAN RUSSELL. TO THE LIFE OF MATTER. 1925.
M. S. Collection, Paris.

KUPKA. VERTICAL PLANES IN RED AND BLUE. 1913.
Louis Carré Gallery, Paris.

massive and violently set one against the other. His great composition of 1914 (*Synchromy in Form*) has affinities with some of Picabia's works of the previous year, notably the famous *Udnie* and *Edtaonisl* which are of much the same dimensions as Russell's work. But Russell's canvas is more elemental, like some Cyclopean wall.

Macdonald-Wright is a little closer to Delaunay. His canvases are as rich in colour as the Parisian painter's, though far less luminous, while his treatment is less firm. He seeks blurred effects, with submerged outlines, while producing an unusual kind of transparency, with a suggestion of a floating haziness corrected by a few clear, free strokes which impose some kind of order on the composition as a whole. This is in contrast to Russell, who always stresses the underlying skeletal structure, with a characteristic emphasis and a vigour that threatens to overflow the too narrow framework he imposes on it.

At about the same time another American, Patrick Henry Bruce, showed a few works at the Salon des Indépendants which also had some relationship to Delaunay's Orphism and some of Picabia's canvases. I met him much later, in about 1930 in his gloomy flat in the Place de Furstenberg, where he showed me a few coolly coloured pieces which he seemed very worried about. He himself was dispirited and disinclined to talk, and yet his painting radiated happiness and reasonableness. He died a few years later after destroying a large number of his paintings. Nevertheless a number were saved by Henri-Pierre Roché.

Frank Kupka was born in Czecho-Slovakia and came to Paris in 1895, where he made his name as an illustrator (*The Erynnies, Lysistrata, Prometheus*). He also painted portraits and a large *Nude* (1910) which is marvellously bright and fresh in its colouring. In 1911 he suddenly have up representational painting of nature, and in the 1912 Autumn Salon exhibited a *Fugue in two colours* and a *Chromatique chaude* which aroused much comment in the press. At the Salon des Indépendants in the following year he showed his *Vertical Planes, Brown Line Solo,* and at the Salon d'Automne his *Localisations des Mobiles graphiques*. After that he remained faithful to abstraction, except for the illustrations he made for the *Song of Songs* and a few other illustrated works which he published under a pseudonym.

We cannot consider Kupka's production since 1911 without our admiration being tinged with embarrassment, for his work seems to contain something of every style. This painter passes with disconcerting ease from the highly-coloured spherism of his *Newton's Discs* (1912) and their reminiscence of Delaunay, to a rectilinearism expressed in dull tones or a narrow range of colours (*Vertical Planes*, 1912 or 1913). After that he indulges in baroque impressions or nagging reminiscences of the 'Modern style' which made a name for his friend and compatriot Alphonse Mucha, first in Paris in 1900 and afterwards in New York and Chicago. However a very careful selection would show Kupka to have produced a number of works of the first order, which could be classified in two groups: the dionysiac or, rather, orphic, as Apollinaire might have put it, in which the composition is held together by the curved line alone (*Study on a Red Ground,* 1919; *The Fair,* 1921), and secondly those canvases in which only straight lines are used, with a marked preference for verticals, as in *Blue and Red Vertical Planes,* 1913, *Blue in Planes* of 1945, and *Vibrant in Lines,* 1948. In his most simplified works Kupka shows himself to be a romantic in his constant efforts to transcend painting through some literary preoccupation. In a word he is a kind of Gothic artist, either constructing solid but highly imaginative cathedral naves, or pouring out his exaltation in what might be called polyphonic paintings, evoking the lights of stained glass through their obsessional, echoing quality.

Picabia is even more disconcerting, for if Kupka went too far by trying to give everything at once, the Spanish painter has offered us a surfeit of both the worst and the best. In 1912 or 1913 he could be counted among the four or five best painters of his time, after which he blundered into every passing fashion so that the art to which he had contributed some undeniable masterpieces might easily have been misjudged as a phase in his careerism. His outstanding canvases were *Procession in Seville, Udnie, Edtaonisl, Remembrance of my beloved Udnie, New York, The Spring, Dances by the Spring, Star Dancer and her School,* all painted in 1912 or 1913. Picabia cannot be blamed, for after all no man can give more or other than what there is in him to give. It is no secret that he enjoyed the frills and small-talk of social life, but that does not mean that he was not capable of brilliant demonstrations of wit in his painting. His machine-portraits are certainly examples of this, as well as his compositions with anti-aesthetic objects such as combs, sardine-tins and matches, which are in the best Dadaist spirit. His later productions however were not so successful. At Cannes, where he delighted in organizing the festivals, he returned to figurative painting for a number of years, much of it of a disappointing level. It was only in 1945 that Picabia was moved, like many others, by the post-liberation revival and began to paint in the spirit of the age. His natural reaction was to return to abstract art, while still continuing to run it down, producing a series of very personal canvases which were somewhat aggressive in colour and in every case full of surprises in their composition (*First seek your Orpheus, Awareness of Misery, Black Eye, The Third Sex,* all of which belong to 1948). Then in 1949 he made a series of pictures consisting of nothing but dots, which are surely among the oddest works that have been produced in abstract art. I admit that I greatly enjoyed them when they were being painted, and was responsible for encouraging Picabia to produce so many of them.

While Delaunay, Kupka, Picabia, Mondrian and others made Paris the capital of abstract art, Kandinsky was working on his own in Munich. Despite his efforts to attract, round his *Blue Horseman,* all the best talents he knew of in the world of art, the fact remains that his own were the only genuinely abstract works in the exhibitions of the famous group in the course of 1912. While Franz Marc and August Macke, his young German colleagues, painted a few completely abstract canvases in 1913 or 1914, they were not recognized until much later, after both these outstanding

PICABIA. LANDSCAPE. 1912.
Simone Collinet Collection, Paris.

representatives of their generation in Germany had lost their lives in the trenches, on the Western Front.

Kandinsky was harshly treated by the critics when he exhibited his first abstract works. Jibes, insults and slander are often the price to be paid for courage and sincerity. But encouragement was not slow to follow. His works were published by Piper; Herwarth Walden took his part in his review *Der Sturm,* while in New York Alfred Stieglitz was attracted by Kandinsky's contributions to the Armory Show and gave the then considerable sum of 800 dollars for one of his canvases. This was the first one to find a buyer in America, and it subsequently caused a sensation at Chicago and paved the way for Kandinsky's success. The Solomon R. Guggenheim Museum in New York now contains the richest collections of Kandinsky's works that is to be found.

5

FUTURIST INFLUENCE. SEVERINI. RUSSIAN 'RAYONISM'.
MALEVITCH. SIMULTANEOUS BEGINNINGS OF ABSTRACT GEOMETRISM.
ARP AND SOPHIE TAÜBER. DADA. THE REVIEW *DE STIJL*.

The most sympathetic are likely to have misgivings about Futurism, for such a mixture of bluff and self-advertisement is hard to reconcile with our lofty conception of the work of art or the artist's mission. But I believe there was something compelling, something that went deeper than it realised, beneath the loud-mouthed huckstering of *futur-fascismo*. Indeed a reading of the first Futurist Manifesto of 1909 is enough to make us aware that the bloated rhetoric embodied an idea of genuine value.

Stripped of its trappings, Futurism can be seen to have been inspired by the generous ambition of bringing life into art, of bringing about a

BALLA. AUTOMOBILE IN MOTION. 1915.
Joseph Slifka Collection, New York.

closer union between them, while rejecting all dead art in favour of living life itself, the natural creator of new forms. Futurism also has other claims to our gratitude. By making such a noise, such a stir in so many countries and exciting critics and journalists in so many capitals of Europe, it did more than any other single movement to free art from the traditional forms of the past and, as a result, to open the public's mind, all over the world, to a totally new art.

Here again, abstract art was proclaimed in various statements to be found in a number of manifestoes. The painters were demanding *lines of force* and Boccioni wrote "We must assert that the sidewalk can find its way on to the dining-room table, that your head can cross the road all by itself, and that at the same time your own reading-lamp can weave a huge spider's web from one house to another with its chalky beams. We must assert that the whole visible world must make its impact on us, fusing itself with us and creating a harmony dictated by creative intuition alone." He also said "We must open up the figure or shape and fill it full of the environment in which it has its being." But it was Severini rather than Boccioni who was to come closest to abstraction, with his manifesto written in Rome during the winter of 1913-1914. It was never published till now, when it can be read in the *Appendix A* of this book.

Futurism has left few works of any importance by way of giving a plastic justification of its programme. Perhaps its real creativeness lay in its influence on men's minds. However Severini's work prior to 1914 deserves close attention, especially his series of *Dancing-girls* painted in 1913. These are abstract compositions made up of graceful lines and delicate colours, usually applied in the pointilliste manner favoured by the Post-Impressionists. He gave up his abstraction only in order to revert to a kind of academicism which might perhaps be Italian but has nothing modern about it. He returned to abstract art only after 1945, in the same way as Picabia and others. He is now painting compositions in which harsh, abrupt lines are set against flat stretches of skilfully modulated colour. These canvases are also called *Dance* or *Dancing-girls,* though they are very unlike those of the pre-1914 phase.

Among the remaining Futurist painters mention must be made of Balla, who began painting abstracts in 1913, and of a few works by Carlo Carra and De Soffici, and especially of the later canvases by Boccioni, the great hope of Futurist painting and sculpture, who died after falling from a horse in 1916. Later, when Futurism degenerated into 'Aero-painting', the only one to continue on abstract lines was Prampolini.

The many exhibitors at the Blue Horseman included a few Russians, of whom Michael Larionov and Nathalie Gontcharova are worth recalling for their share in the first stirrings of abstract painting in Russia.

In 1909 Larionov, in Moscow, was as close to abstraction (viz, *The Glass*) as Braque and Picasso were to be three or four years later. He gave his first lecture on Rayonism at the A. Kraft Studio in Moscow in 1910. (9) Two Rayonist canvases were exhibited at the same time, namely Larionov's *The Boulevard* which was mainly in greens and yellows, and Gontcharova's *Cats,* mainly yellow and black. In the following year both of them painted a long series of works the dominant characteristic of which was in a large number of straight lines either parallel (Larionov, *The Beach,* 1911), or meeting (Larionov, *Portrait of Gontcharova,* 1912) or else flying off in every direction. These represent the zenith of Rayonism, which was destined to be a short-lived movement. (10)

Larionov was a restless artist, and Goncharova was equally versatile. In Moscow at that time artists were expected to invent a new form of art every 48 hours. Larionov painted soldiers and flowers, and even anecdotal paintings with inscriptions on them, while Goncharova excelled in many different fields, painting cavases covered with numbers, as well as street-scenes that anticipated Dr. Caligari. In 1914 all these Russian experiments were shown in Paris at Paul Guillaume's, a laudatory preface being written for the catalogue by Apollinaire. We are now concerned only with the Rayonist canvases. These are among the very first abstract paintings ever made and for this reason they are of considerable importance. (11) After 1914 Goncharova and Larionov, who were great friends of Diaghilev, did most of their work for the ballet and thus fell outside the main movement in painting. Nevertheless an exhibition of the two painters' Rayonist works was held in Rome in 1917, when an explanatory brochure entitled *Radiantismo* was produced for the occasion. Alfred Barr found an unexpected ancestor of Rayonism, in Leonardo da Vinci. In his remarkable work *Cubism and Abstract Art* he quoted, in this connection, a sentence of Leonardo's: "The air is full of an infinite number of radiating straight lines, which cross and weave together without ever quite coinciding; it is these which represent the true form of every object's essence."

One painter who was to be of considerable importance emerged from the Larionov group, namely Casimir Malevitch.

Nothing could look easier: all you have to do is to take a ruler, draw a square on a sheet of paper and black in its surface area with a pencil. To offer this 'discovery' as a work of art is obviously meant as a joke? By no means: it was an act of faith which was to have unforeseen consequences. It was an end and a beginning, the end of one form of painting and the beginning of a new art.

According to Malevitch art is an additional, extraneous element which thrusts itself into life and thought and evades all dialectical reasoning. This element used to be unconscious and was diffused throughout the world and in man himself, always mingled with many other elements. That is why there was never any pure art. But the time has come for making it visible and independent and ridding it of all its parasites. For half a century this eventuality had been prepared for by Impressionism and

SEVERINI. DANCING-GIRL. 1912.
Estorick Collection, London.

LARIONOV. RAYONISM. 1910.
Artist's Collection.

Cubism: all that remained was to learn how to read shapes and how to interpret and analyse them.

The book he wrote with the help of the advance-guard Russian poets and which was published in Moscow in 1915 was nothing more nor less than an attempt to isolate the datum or element of *art* itself. For such an operation to be successful the simplest element had to be found. Malevitch saw that element to be the geometrical square, patiently blacked in with a pencil.

Why the perfect square ? Because it is the clearest assertion of man's will, the epitome of his mastery over nature.

Why should it be blacked in with pencil ? Because that is the humblest act the sensibility can perform.

Active nature and passive nature thus find themselves brought together and reconciled.

Malevitch gave the name *Suprematism* to this new art and exhibited the first Suprematist drawing, the famous square, at the *Target* exhibition in Moscow in 1913. In the same year he produced a series of other drawings of elemental forms, all in pencil. The first form to emerge from the square was the circle, then came the placing of two rectangular planes in

33

the form of a cross. Progressively more complex compositions were developed in which there appeared the trapezium, the triangle, then the broken line, the curve, and finally the blurred, shaded-off line. This took four years.

Malevitch had to evolve quickly in order to reach that point. He was born at Kiev in 1878, and began painting in the post-Impressionist manner and after that as a Fauve. He soon came under Picasso's influence and became the leader of the Russian Cubists who included Pevsner, Puni, Alexandra Exter, Lyubov Popova and Udalzova. After 1911 cubo-futurist elements were to be seen in his work, which in other respects showed striking affinities to that of Fernand Léger (*The scissors-sharpener, Woman carrying buckets,* both painted in 1912). It was from that stage that he made the leap into Suprematism. When abstract art fell politically into discredit in 1922, Malevitch left Moscow and became Professor at the Academy in Leningrad. He contrived to go to Germany in 1926, and at the Bauhaus made arrangements for the publication of his book *Die Gegenstandslose Welt* (The Objectless World). This remarkable work is the only existing source of information on his art and thought. As it has not yet been translated, extracts from it are given at *Appendix B.*

Although Malevitch was the first painter in the world to use pure geometrical forms, it must be admitted that the Cubists had made everyone vaguely conscious of the idea, even if it was still undefinable. Without having even heard of Malevitch, in 1915 Hans Arp at Zürich and Magnelli in Florence were both making abstract compositions based entirely on geometrical forms.

In the following year Sophie Taüber, also at Zürich, composed a number of smallish works—drawings in coloured crayon—based on a strictly horizontal-vertical movement, thus anticipating Neo-Plasticism.

At the same time, behind the lines in Holland, Mondrian and Van Doesburg came together and began preparing their review, *De Stijl.*

Thus at the very same time, in four different parts of the world which were separated by frontiers that were closed on account of the war, very dissimilar artists who had all heard of Parisian Cubism were reaching exactly similar conclusions.

At Zürich the beautiful experiments of Sophie Taüber and Arp were soon overwhelmed by the Dadaist uproar, which was unlikely to favour such a pure and semi-religious art. Sophie Taüber, who was too retiring and modest to assert or defend herself, carried on working almost in secret until her death in 1943, always leaving the limelight to Hans Arp, whom

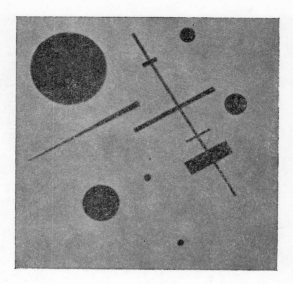

MALEVITCH. SUPREMATIST COMPOSITION. 1913.

she married in 1921. Few people knew or appreciated Sophie Taüber's work during her lifetime. One had to know the Arps well before one was admitted to Sophie's studio, in their house at Meudon where they lived after 1928. She rarely exhibited anywhere, although she took part in *Circle an Square* and helped Arp and Van Doesburg with the decorations for the various rooms in the 'Aubette' in Strasburg, a fine achievement which has since been destroyed. Sophie Taüber's works has grown in prestige since her death, revealing as it does such an inner store of honesty, candour and quiet strength. Her work has an extraordinary variety, but is always sober and full of integrity.

In 1918 and 1919 Arp, together with Sophie Taüber, made some horizontal-vertical *collages* out of paper which they cut with a bookbinder's guillotine. Then he went off in another direction and began exploiting a curved, supple line, that seemed to come as naturally to his hand as the fruit to a tree.

The contribution of Zürich Dadaism to abstract art lies mainly in the 'woods' by Arp which appeared in the review *Dada* or were used as illustrations for books by Hülsenbeck and Tristan Tzara.

GONTCHAROVA. THE CATS. 1910.
Artist's Collection.

Marcel Janco made abstract reliefs in a very personal style, most of which are now lost. Finally, Viking Eggeling in 1917 and Hans Richter in the following year produced some drawings which can also be credited to Dadaism. Late in 1918 Richter took Eggeling with him to Germany. It was there, in 1919, that Eggeling composed his famous strip-drawings on simple themes, which he called *Horizontal-Vertical Mass,* followed in 1920 by the strips for his *Diagonal Symphony,* a rather more complex theme of which he made a film in 1921.

Richter's output ran parallel with that of Eggeling who was seven years his senior. In 1919 he made his *Prelude,* the orchestration of a theme which was developed in eleven drawings. In the same year as Eggeling he also produced his first abstract film, *Rhythm 21, screen orchestration in time and space.* Eggeling died in 1925. After that Richter at first turned to more practical activities, and later to Surrealism, his *Dreams that money can buy* (1947) containing some beautiful abstract sequences.

It was in Holland, the last of the four great centres of geometrical abstraction, that this form of expression was to find its least compromising and best-reasoned formulation. This is not surprising, since it was in the case of Mondrian that the transition from figurative art to pure geometry took the longest to achieve, lasting from 1912 to 1917. It was only logical that he should be the one to state and explore the problem. Geometrical abstraction achieved its most complete and thorough form in a properly explained and demonstrated use of the horizontal and vertical, with only three primary colours (red, blue and yellow) supported by three 'non-colours', black, white and grey. It was left to Mondrian to work out the system as a whole, and to expound it in a few texts which have become classics thanks to their clarity of exposition. The first number of *De Stijl* was published by Van Doesburg in October 1917. This contained a long article on doctrinal lines by Mondrian, some essential parts of which are worth reproducing (*Appendix C*). This initial statement was followed by many others, notably, two years later, by a long platonic dialogue which is beyond doubt one of the most convincing essays of the 'heroic' period of abstract art. It certainly deserves a place alongside the famous works of Kandinsky and Malevitch. Mondrian continued to write almost as much as he painted for the rest of his life. In French he published *Néo-plasticisme* (Léonce Rosenberg, 1920) as well as contributing to several reviews. After his death an important collection of his English essays was published in New York (*Plastic Art and Pure Plastic Art*, Wittenborn, 1st edn. 1945, 3rd edn. 1951).

But we must not anticipate. To return to Holland in 1917, working with Mondrian and Van Doesburg were the painters Huszar and Van Der Leck (though the latter was not long in leaving the group), the painter and sculptor Vantongerloo, the poet Antonie Kok and a number of architects. Their literary contributions to the review all pointed in the same direction, all upholding the same central idea. But it was Mondrian who produced the most extensive and solidly-constructed writings during the first four years. At the same time Van Doesburg published, alongside his review *De Stijl,* several short but very interesting works which have never been translated from the Dutch. (12) But he was first and foremost a man of action, both quarrelsome and fiendishly energetic. His bustling temperament made him poles apart from Mondrian, but he was one of those individualists who can serve to complement another individualist, with the result that the two of them made an ideal team, the one slowly ruminating and gathering material which the other wanted to explode like a bomb. That

SOPHIE TAÜBER. COMPOSITION IN COLOURED CRAYONS. 1916.
M. S. Collection, Paris.

is how, through the medium of the little Dutch review, geometrical abstraction was to impose itself on a substantial part of the world, in spite of the
fact that it was in its narrowest and most meagre form, at first sight the
form which seemed most meaningless, in other words Neo-plasticism.

I was already familiar with these ideas and experiments when I happened to pass through Berlin at the end of 1922 and heard Marinetti give
a talk at the Futurist Centre there. After a few scathing remarks about
Goethe this brilliant mountebank began to expound his ideas on painting
and the arts in general. Dynamism and art, he argued, were one and the
same thing. Painting means giving life to a plane surface, and the life of
a plane surface can never be intense enough, since speed is the only criterion
by which any work of art can stand or fall. He wanted art and life to be
like the waves of the sea, clashing and struggling together, all with their

distinct individuality.   In order to understand both life and art, it would be enough to watch the waves unfolding and folding on the beach in a kind of delirious anarchy. . .   In these words I recognized the essence of Futurism, insisting that every man and every day should face a different task.   What Marinetti was proposing was the very opposite of Neo-plasticism.   That opposition is still going on around us, for everywhere we can see both directed fury and calm organization.   Style on the one hand, and a human cry on the other, will no doubt always be the two poles of art.

HANS ARP. STATIC COMPOSITION. 1915.
François Arp Collection, Paris.

6

THE SPIRITUAL URGE TO ABSTRACT ART. PAINTERS' MANIFESTOES
SHOW THE NEED FOR SPIRITUAL RENEWAL. PARALLEL BETWEEN
MONDRIAN AND VAN DOESBURG. THE SPECTATOR'S SHARE
IN THE WORK OF ART.

After defining the immediate origins of abstract art as lying in Fauvism
and Cubism, and having found one of its incidental causes to be in the
change of the social milieu thanks to the growth of mechanisation and
science, closer attention must be given to the problem itself in order to
see what went on in the minds of its main pioneers at the time when they
were passing from figuration to abstraction. One of the ways in which
this can be done is through re-reading what they wrote at that time. A
surprising fact then comes to light, which is that in most of them the need
for abstraction was based on an acute hunger for spiritual values. It
looks as though, after a century of materialist philosophy, the artists' own
intuition stressed an urgent need to re-charge the spiritual centres. A new
humanism then emerged, one which was very different from that of the
Renaissance, amounting in this case to a kind of inner humanism, the only
form of it that could possibly understand real equality because it brings
man face to face with that share of the infinite which he carries within
himself, and which seeks its reflection in his fellow-men. Thus a kind of
brotherhood of summits is created, for every man is a summit at certain
moments and in certain conditions, every man being, when considered in
the absolute, the centre and summit of the world.

Spirituality in art, the title Kandinsky gave to his first book, was highly
significant. In his conclusion he proclaimed a new era of the spirit, a period
of intense spirituality which was to find its direct expression through art.

In Mondrian's unpublished notebooks I found the words "It is the
internal life, its strength and joy, which determines form in art." On
another page I read "Art has no meaning except in so far as it expresses what
is non-material, for it is this that enables man to transcend his own being."

I find the same tendency, though less consciously expressed, in Robert
Delaunay's paintings of 1912 and 1913. They contain a semi-mystical
exaltation of light. Delaunay remarked to me one day that "Most painters
are only peeping-Toms, whereas what they really should aspire to is to be
Seers."

It might be asked whether, intellectually, it is just an easy way out to see this unexpected emphasis of spirituality in art, or at least in early abstract art, as an intuitive agreement with Bergson's attempts at revalorizing mind, in the broadest yet deepest sense of the term, after a hundred years of positivism and historical materialism. *Creative Evolution,* the first landmark in this change of values, appeared in 1906. In his remarkable lecture *Consciousness and Life,* published in 1914, I find the following remarks which could perfectly well be applied to the first generation of abstract painters: "Great men of integrity, and more particularly those whose sheer inventive heroism clears new paths for human virtues, serve to reveal metaphysical truth. Though they stand at the highest point of evolution, yet they are closest to the origins of things and make us conscious of that impulse which arises from the very depths." Yes, the impulse rising from the depths and which is nearest to the fundamental truths and to the naked origin of things, surely that is what we expect of art in general and what abstract art appears most fitted to reveal to us, without being hindered by material objects whose presence is no more than an agreable distraction from our main objective, which must be the mind or spirit. (13)

Nobody understood this better than Mondrian, no man ever penetrated it more deeply than he did in the course of a whole lifetime. Yet there seems to be some dichotomy in his thought as regards spiritual values as such, and this needs some brief analysis.

Mondrian was long interested in theosophical speculations. As late as 1916 the portrait of Mme Blavatsky hung on the wall of his studio. Yet in his writings he made no mention of his theosophical sympathies. Even in private conversation he avoided religious topics and closed up at the slightest hint of them. Only in an atmosphere of friendship and trust would he risk the slightest allusion to them, and even then he was more than cautious in his use of words. He usually took up an extreme agnostic position, while praising mechanisation and praising the Futurists for saying that they would prefer a motor-car to the Victory of Samothrace. He also asserted that the day would come when we could leave the job of making works of art to machines, on condition that the machines were controlled by artists. (14)

Vantongerloo came to the same conclusion: "Everything progresses and evolves, and the time is not far off when art and science will unite into a homogeneous whole." This notion was supported by Van Doesburg, who wrote to a friend in Holland, "My final conviction, a conviction arising from the sum-total of all my activities, is that in the future art will develop entirely on a scientific basis. Until now the artist has always been at the mercy of his feelings and has had no means of controlling them. There was nothing to distinguish his methods of work from those of the milliner or pastry-cook, who merely arrange things according to their taste or inclination." (16)

But this scientific outlook was not set up as the enemy of spirituality. On the contrary, in *Classical, Baroque and Modern* the same Van Doesburg wrote "However deep it went, mediaeval art was not a *direct expression* of the religious outlook, because it failed to find in the *means of expression itself* the correlative that was needed for expressing that outlook. It found that correlative in symbolic representation, with the aid of forms borrowed from nature. The expression of the religious outlook was, therefore, not direct but indirect."

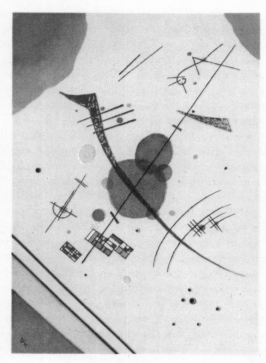

KANDINSKY. WASER-COLOUR. 1923.
M. S. Collection, Paris.

At the end of the same treatise, after speaking of a collective style of which he saw a possible fulfilment in Neo-plasticism, the author summed up his views as follows: "A style comes into being when, after achieving a collective consciousness of life, we are able to set up a harmonious relationship between the inner character and the outward appearance of life. A discontinuous development of art is the natural result of the human consciousness's discontinuous development towards truth. Over the centuries, the development of art aimed at giving reality to the aesthetic idea which consists of expressing completely, through the medium of art, this harmonious relationship between the inner life and external appearance of things, between the spirit and nature. . . Modern art's evolution towards the abstract and universal, eliminating all that is external and individual, thanks to a common effort and common idea, has made it possible to bring into existence a collective style which, transcending persons and nations, most definitely and genuinely expresses the highest, deepest and most universal requi-

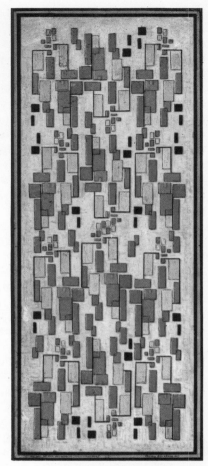

VAN DOESBURG. COMPOSITION VI. 1917.
Private Collection, Meudon.

rements of beauty." We can see or read between the lines that for Van Doesburg the terms art, spirituality, abstraction, universality and religion were identical. Neo-plasticism was an effort to bring together again the data and principles which civilisation had divorced from each other in the course of time, but which originally formed a single reality in the mind of man: that is to say, the urge to express his highest aspirations.

That, and nothing less, was the aim of the horizontal-vertical style and the "simple distribution of colours". But Van Doesburg gave up the effort in 1924 and it was left to Mondrian to work out and demonstrate the idea. The works he produced in Paris, and perhaps above all those he painted between 1925 and 1932, expressed something absolute in their strict relevance of composition, while never losing their human significance thanks to their colour and some indefinable inner resonance. Every one of his canvases embodies a pure ontology. They are the works of a man capable of expressing in paint the terse aphorisms of, say, some modern Parmenides writing a treatise on *Being as Being*. The rhomboid-shaped canvas of 1931, consisting only of two straight lines of different breadth on a uniform white ground, is in a sense the Vedanta of contemporary painting. After that he had to come down from that rarefied atmosphere and renew his contact with life. (17)

Is it possible to penetrate very far into a painter's work without having known him personally? A man is the living proof of the sum-total of his work, even when it is greater than himself. I am aware that some distinction has to be made between morality and art, but I believe there is some interchange between art and the highest forms of thought. I have observed that every artist contains a hidden mystic, sometimes only too thoroughly hidden. But a shrewd eye can reach the real man on slight evidence. A gesture, a silence, something in the eyes, a tone of voice, set us dreaming of the unique necessity which according to Plotinus is the most important thing in a man. For instance Mondrian's reserve never managed to mask what lay behind it, but rather made it plainer. Knowing the man, what was hidden was seen to be all the more clearly stated in the work.

In spite of his timidity as regards words, everything in Mondrian pointed to the *thing* or essence itself, I mean the mystic that was latent in him. In spite of the cogent things he wrote, Van Doesburg was the very opposite. He radiated violence, destruction, anger, the love of battle for its own sake. He was capable of spreading a seedy atmosphere even over such a noble conception as Neo-plasticism. This detracts nothing from his value as a manager, as an intelligent and energetic purveyor of ideas. However the difference between the the two, as men, goes far to explain the mysterious dissimilarities between their works.

At this point I should like to add a note on the spectator's role. It seems to me that the spectator is required to play a creative part, comparable with that of the artist, in abstract art more than in any other form of art. He is expected to have a well-informed mind and to be generous with it, never shrinking from the efforts that are demanded of him. Eugène Chevreul touched on this in well-chosen terms in a little book published in 1864. After showing (already !) that all the arts are made up of abstract elements, the physicist concluded his argument in these words: "But when I reduce the language of the fine-arts to abstractions, I have to point out that their effects, as abstractions, will be fewer in proportion as the minds to which they are addressed are less civilised or less cultured; for the more civilised or the more cultured people's minds are, the more inclined they will be to associate other ideas with the impressions evoked by these abstractions, —though I would not go so far as to say that they will necessarily be more open to impressions themselves. It is this capacity for grouping thoughts round the impression produced by a masterpiece, which explains the quality and variety of intellectual pleasure that is in reach of a mind that has been broadened by culture without any weakening of sensibility." (18) Thus a work of art is worth exactly what the spectator is worth; that is to say as much as the spectator or lover of art are capable of putting into it.

7

ABSTRACT ART BETWEEN THE WARS. CUBIST AND SURREALIST REACTIONS. THE "ART D'AUJOURD'HUI" EXHIBITION. THE CERCLE ET CARRÉ AND ABSTRACTION-CRÉATION GROUPS. ADVANCED REVIEWS IN EUROPE. THE BAUHAUS. PUBLIC GALLERIES OPENED TO ABSTRACT ART. DEVELOPMENT AND END OF STIJL. SPREAD OF CONSTRUCTIVISM. SOME PAINTERS.

Braque, Picasso and Gris came very close to abstraction in 1914, as can be seen through looking at a few histories of the art of that period. In his *Vision in Motion* Moholy-Nagy set side by side a Braque collage of 1914 and a Malevitch composition of 1921, showing a striking resemblance between the two works. This must have been accidental, since Braque never *intended* to go in for abstraction, while Malevitch had no use for figuration after 1913. For example when Braque said "Let us forget about things, and only consider relationships" (19) he was certainly far from realising how close he was to Mondrian. Words often outstrip thought: did not Picasso once remark about Juan Gris that the disciple often sees things more clearly than his master?

Léger gave much more thought and time to the claims of an integral abstract art, and for a time, between 1913 and 1919, he seems to have been very strongly tempted by it. His admirable series of *Contrasting Forms* of 1913-1914 is not abstract art in the strictest sense of the term, but comes within an ace of it. I have no idea who or what deflected Léger from what would have been his normal evolution. Towards 1924 he interrupted his usual style of painting to produce some mural compositions which were entirely abstract and, indeed, very much in line with Neo-plasticism. Two of them were given prominent places at the *Cercle et Carré* exhibition in 1930.

During the nineteen-twenties, when it was directed by Léger and Ozen-fant, the Académie Moderne turned out a large number of young abstract

LÉGER.
CONTRASTING FORMS. 1913.
Musée d'Art Moderne, Paris.

46

PICASSO. THE MAN WITH A GUITAR. 1913.
Private Collection, Paris.

artists. Thanks to their youth they were not slow in pushing Cubism to its logical conclusions, and I know that they were not discouraged by Léger in their pursuit of abstract art. He wrote some years later, "Of all the different directions in which the plastic arts have developed in the past 25 years, abstract art is the most important as well as the most interesting. It is no mere freak of experiment, but an art with its own intrinsic value. It has proved itself and also satisfies a demand, since so many collectors are enthusiastic about it. It is therefore a tendency arising out of life. Maybe future generations will class this form of art as an artificial paradise, but I do not think so. The abstract programme is governed by that desire for perfection and for complete liberty which turns men into saints, heroes or madmen. It is an extreme position in which few artists or their supporters can thrive. The very idealism of the abstract programme is its greatest danger. Modern life with all its turmoil and urgency, its dynamism and variety, has no mercy on this fragile, luminous creation rising from chaos. We should respect it and leave it alone, for it had to be done and is done and it will remain." (20) But Léger asserted in the same work that the abstract experiment was already a matter for history and that it "has given all it had to offer."

Whether that is true or not, after 1920 Cubism returned once and for all to figuration. Braque imposed the rhythm while Picasso marked the frontiers of extravagance. Thus Picasso was able to cling to his title as an experimenter while Braque became the classic of the moderns. Gris died prematurely in 1927, having also failed to take the next step into abstraction. This step would have been harder for him than for the others, since he had already chosen the opposite direction, declaring that "Cézanne turned a bottle into a cylinder, but I turn a cylinder into a bottle."

In the same way Fauvism moved rapidly towards abstraction thanks to Matisse. Quite a number of his works of his most productive period —for instance *The Piano-lesson*—were well on the way to abstract painting, but the impulse petered out and Matisse became the most elegant figurative painter in the world.

Purism also stopped on the theshold. Although Ozenfant wanted "the utmost intensity and quality obtainable through the most economical means" he remained fundamentally hostile to abstract art.

Charles-Édouard Jeanneret, better known as Le Corbusier, supported Ozenfant in his Purist programme, but drew much closer to the *Stijl* theories in his architectural works. (21)

The retrogression of the great Cubists, together with the veto from the Purists, held up the popularisation of abstract art, which was still further threatened by Surrealism.

In spite of these strong waves of opposition in Paris itself, abstraction calmly went its own way and from time to time managed to score some minor victories.

In December 1925 the Pole, Poznanski, organized a large exhibition called Art Now (L'art d'aujourd'hui) which was held at the Antiquarians' Syndicate headquarters at 18, rue de La Ville-l'Évêque. The abstract works exhibited included mural compositions by Baumeister, Brunet, Léger, Carlsund; paintings by Jean Crotti, Walter Dexel, Florence Henri; Marcelle Cahn, Francisca Clausen, Kakabadze, Reth, Sevranckx, Poznanski himself, as well as the *Simultaneous Colours* by Robert and Sonia Delaunay. Side by side with them were the Rayonists Larionov and Gontcharova; the Dadaists Arp and Janco, and the whole *Stijl* group with Mondrian, Van Doesburg, Huszar, Vantongerloo, Vordemberge-Gildewart and Domela. Futurism was represented by Prampolini and Depero; the Bauhaus by Moholy-Nagy and Klee. Finally there were exhibits by most of the Cubists (Gris, Picasso, Gleizes, Léger, Villon, Laurens, Lipchitz, Marcoussis, Metzinger) and of their sworn enemies the future Surrealists Max Ernst, André Masson, Joseph Sima, Toyen and Styrsky. Almost half of the entire exhibition consisted of abstract works. Some of the artists concerned have not exhibited since.

It was almost five years before another similar effort was made in support of abstract art. In April 1930 the *Cercle et Carré* exhibition was held at 'Galerie 23' (23, rue de La Boétie) with 130 exhibits by 46 artists. Some representational or hardly abstract paintings such as those of Torrès-Garcia and Ozenfant were admitted. The kernel of the group consisted of Mondrian, Kandinsky, Arp, Schwitters, Vantongerloo, Sophie Taüber, Pevsner, Huszar, Van Rees and Vordemberge-Gildewart, supported by a number of newcomers such as Buchheister, Pierre Daura, François Foltyn, Jean Gorin, Hans Welti, Germain Cueto, Eric Olson, Hans Suschny, Henri Stazewski and H. N. Werkman, all of whom sought expression through an integral abstraction. Among the other exhibitors were such artists as Léger, Charchoune, Baumeister, Fillia, Le Corbusier, Sartoris, Prampolini, Russolo, Marcelle Cahn and the American painter Stella, while César Domela, Otto Freundlich, Moholy-Nagy and Jean Xcéron, all members of the group, were absent.

Another noticeable abstention was that of Van Doesburg, who was invited to join the group at the outset—it soon had eighty members— but who curtly refused and decided to make a group of his own. He rallied round him Hélion, Carlsund and Tutundjan and published the one and only number of *Art concret,* a pamphlet whose main interest lies in its title. This is the first appearance of the term concrete art used instead of 'abstract' art which had been undisputed till then. As we know, the new expression was later favoured by Arp and Kandinsky, while the painter and sculptor Max Bill was also to make much of it.

In the following year (after Van Doesburg's death at Davos) Vantongerloo and Herbin got together a new group out of the ruins of *Cercle et Carré.* This group, *Abstraction-Création,* issued the first number of its Journal in 1952, the second in 1933, the fifth and last in 1936. It held its exhibitions in a hall at the back of a courtyard in the Avenue de Wagram, near the Place des Ternes.   After the second world war the *Salon des Réalités Nouvelles* was founded on the same lines and at the same premises as *Abstraction-Création,* whose traditions were now carried on by an annual publication of the same format and style as the pre-war ones.   I am tempted to smile when I recall that this series of groups and publications—*Cercle et Carré, Abstraction-Création* and *Réalités Nouvelles*—all originated in a visit paid to me at Vanves in 1929 by the Uruguayan painter Torrès-Garcia, which resulted in the founding of *Cercle et Carré.*   I claim no particular credit for that, but it was one of those small things which sometimes lead to unexpected results, like those mountain echoes which come back so magnified that they sound like avalanches.

That period from 1920 to 1930 was rich in advance-guard reviews. There was hardly a European country without one and abstract art often had a prominent place in them.   They were all in contact with each other and they exchanged contributors, so that a kind of International of abstract art came into being.   Political developments snapped all these valuable links that stretched across the frontiers, and the network was never restored.

Here are the titles of some of those reviews, all memorable for their courage and independence: *De Stijl, Mecano* and *The next call,* in Holland;

BRAQUE. HOMAGE TO J.-S. BACH. 1912.
H.-P. Roché Collection, Paris.

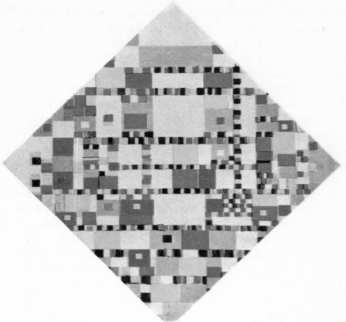

MONDRIAN. VICTORY BOOGIE-WOOGIE.　　　1943-1944. *Tremaine Collection, U.S.A.*

Het Overzicht and *Ça ira* at Antwerp; *Anthologie* at Liège; *Sept Arts* and *l'Art libre* at Brussels; *La vie des lettres et des arts, L'esprit nouveau, Les feuilles libres, Orbes, L'œuf dur, Cercle et Carré,* 391, *Le Bulletin de l'Effort moderne* and *le Mouvement accéléré,* all in Paris; *Manomètre* at Lyons; *Zenith* at Belgrade; *Contemporanul* and *Punkt* at Bucarest; *Zwrotnica* and *Bloc* at Warsaw; *Ma* at Vienna; *Merz* at Hanover; *Pasmo, Disc* and *Stavba* in Czecho-Slovakia; *Der Sturm* and *G (Gestaltung)* in Berlin; *A.B.C.* at Zürich.

　　Paris was the hub of all this activity, the centre in Paris itself being Montparnasse. It was a lively time, when on the same day, in front of the Dôme café you could meet Marinetti on a lightning visit to the capital, Gabo fresh from Berlin, Cendrars just back from America, Delaunay out for a spree, Arp trying to find somebody, Tzara and Ehrenburg sitting there with inscrutable faces; you could risk a few words with Hans Richter or argue with Van Doesburg of Kiesler, or listen to the international speechifiers making themselves drunk with their own eloquence, or you could even manage to be bored by it all.

51

At the *Sacre du Printemps,* an art-gallery which has now disappeared but which was at 5, Rue du Cherche-Midi, Paul Dermée and I used to hold exhibitions of abstract art and literary meetings in 1927. Marinetti, Walden, Kassak, Schwitters and many others had their turn at holding forth with recitations and speeches accompanied by catcalls or applause. Canvases by Werkman, Huszar, Vantongerloo, Mondrian, Arp, Sophie Taüber and others who are now forgotten were shown and eagerly discussed there. All this fertile activity, carried on in the face of hostility from the established critics of the day, was brought to an end on the eve of the second world war, though not before it had been strengthened for a time by the effects of Nazism as it emptied Germany of ther intellectuals.

One of the most important undertakings between the wars was the Bauhaus in Germany, a kind of university of pure construction and applied art which was founded by Walter Gropius at Weimar in 1919.

There has been much discussion of Van Doesburg's influence on the Bauhaus two years after its foundation (23). There is no doubt that the ideas of the *Stijl* group made themselves strongly felt in the Bauhaus, as well as those of the Russian Constructivists which were introduced by Lissitzky. From the Bauhaus these two movements spread through Germany across the whole of central Europe. But the Bauhaus was less a training-ground for abstract painters than a centre for the revival of taste, through the study of matter for its own sake, in spite of the presence of such eminent teachers as Klee, Kandinsky, Feininger, Moholy-Nagy, Albers and Schlemmer. This study and research at the Bauhaus were founded on a new vision of things, a vision purified of prejudices and conventional ideas, so that its teaching prepared the way in a high degree for an understanding of abstract art. The student as well as the general public were also enabled to share the thoughts of the Bauhaus leaders through the *Bauhausbücher,* a famous series of works published by the institution. Those dealing with painting or with art in general were written by Malevitch, Mondrian, Van Doesburg, Kandinsky and Moholy-Nagy (vide Bibliography). The Bauhaus was obliged to leave Weimar in 1925 and was set up again in the open country not far from Dessau. The new buildings, designed by Gropius, were officially opened in December 1926. The premises were beyond doubt the most rational and scrupulously functional work that the world had so far seen. I remember my amazement when I visited the Bauhaus in 1928, and my impression that I was standing before the ideas of *De Stijl,* boldly exemplified and fulfilled in an awe-inspiring

EL LISSITZKY. STORY OF TWO SQUARES. 1920.

block of buildings. The main façade was entirely of glass. The Bauhaus was closed down by the Nazis in 1933. It was certainly thanks to the Bauhaus, which had prepared the public's mind for it, that the first room or gallery was set aside in a public museum, permanently open to viewers, at Hanover in 1925. It was also the first time that any of Mondrian's works found their way into a national collection. This famous "abstract gallery", with its interior strikingly designed by Lissitzky himself, was destroyed by the Nazis in 1937.

1926 saw the first of the travelling exhibitions of abstract art which were sent on tour round the United States by the "Société Anonyme". This Society, founded in 1920 by Miss Katherine Dreier, Marcel Duchamp and Man Ray, had an outstanding influence on the teaching of art. In 1927, also in America, the A. E. Gallatin collection was thrown open to the public under the title of the Museum of Living Art; but in this case the Cubists were most strongly represented, the pure abstractionists only being introduced much later, after 1935.

To be historically exact, the second official museum to open permanent shows of abstract painting was the gallery at Lodz, in Poland. This collection was created entirely out of gifts or bequests which were mainly drawn from or arranged in Paris. I myself contributed to some extent with canvases by Baumeister, Huszar, Vordemberge and Werkman which were then my property. Arp, Sophie Taüber, Charchoune, Calder, Sonia Delaunay, Van Doesburg, Foltyn, Gleizes, Gorin, Vantongerloo, Hélion, Herbin, Schwitters and others not so well known, also gave it their support. An illustrated catalogue was issued in March 1932. The abstract rooms in the Lodz gallery are now closed to the public, but the collection itself appears to have remained intact.

In 1937 the Museum of Non-objective Painting (now the Solomon R. Guggenheim Museum) was founded in New York. Finally, in 1939, also in New York, the Museum of Modern Art opened its new premises, destined to become the most important centre in the world for the study of abstract art, thanks to its exhibitions, its well-stocked library and its own publications.

This period could be surveyed in another way, by giving an account of the main personalities involved. But let us first see what happened to the *Stijl* movement.

After being deflected from its original course by Van Doesburg himself in 1924, the famous review (*De Stijl*) was carried on without Mondrian, but with the addition of some younger artists (Domela, Vordemberge, and the scenario-writers Eggeling and Richter). It closed down in 1928, but a posthumous number was published by Mme Van Doesburg in 1932.

After Van Doesburg's death in March 1931, Mondrian's influence increased in both depth and breadth through his work in the studio.   He had fervent supporters in every country in Europe, but more especially in Germany and Switzerland. In 1934 he was visited by a very young American, Harry Holtzman, who was to be his first direct disciple in the States. (24)   In the same year Ben Nicholson, a painter of experience, came to see him and once again the studio in the Rue du Départ left an indelible memory.   As a result Nicholson became the recognized leader of abstract painting in Great Britain.

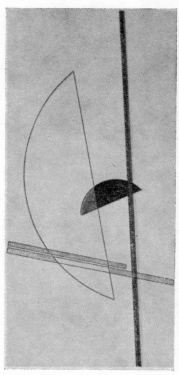

MOHOLY-NAGY. CONSTRUCTION.
LITHOGRAPH. 1923.

55

BAUMEISTER. COMPOSITION. C. 1936.
Jeanne Bucher Gallery, Paris.

George Vantongerloo, who had settled in France in 1919 (first at
Menton, then in Paris) embarked on a series of fascinating mathematical
calculations, all tending to prove by dint of figures and formulas that Mondrian's works—and of course his own—were infallibly correct. He gave
up this enterprise later to seek refuge, no less infallibly, in the curved line
and what he called "the indeterminate".

Of the rest of the *Stijl* team only the painters Vilmos Huszar and Bart
van der Leck remained in Holland. The latter gave up abstraction almost
as soon as he tried it. As for Huszar, in 1921 (three years before Van
Doesburg) he made use of the diagonal line in compositions whose theme
was often based on or intended for stage-sets, and he gradually brought
in representational elements. A flower-composition (*Fleurs,* admittedly
geometrical) was shown at the Anonymous Society exhibition in the
Brooklyn Museum in 1926.

In Holland there was an outsider, the attractive printer and painter Henry Nicolas Werkman, of Groeningen. He painted, wrote, drew and printed. Like Kurt Schwitters in Hanover, he published his own review, *The next call*. This he printed with his own hands, and often in an unusual way. One y the numbers could be unfolded so as to make a kind of poster on which the words *plattegrond van de kunst en omstreken* (a plan of art and its surroundings) were blocked out in rectangles of different colours. For a few years Werkman showed an unusual virtuosity in his creation of large monotypes in brilliant colours. The most interesting are those he painted between 1923 and 1929. After 1935 he returned to occasional suggestions of naturalism, and in the end to figuration. Werkman was very active in the Dutch resistance during the war and

SCHWITTERS. COLLAGE. 1927.
Mme Van Doesburg Collection, Meudon.

was shot by the Nazis on the night before their retreat from Groeningen. A considerable part of his work was lost in the fire.

As we have seen, the other important geometrical abstract stream came from Russia. There it went under such different names as Suprematism (Malevitch), Constructivism (Tatlin), Non-Objectivism (Rotchenko) and *Proun* (Lissitzky). When the Soviet leaders began to look unfavourably on abstraction in 1921, Lissitzky, Gabo, Pevsner and Kandinsky left Russia and went to different parts of Europe. Kandinsky went to Weimar, Pevsner to Paris, and Gabo and Lissitzky settled in Berlin. Lissitzky in particular had considerable influence in Germany. Two of his close friends were the Hungarians Laszlo Moholy-Nagy, whom he had already met at Düsseldorf in 1920, and Laszlo Peri who had spent some months as an architect in Russia. The first of these in due course achieved fame in Europe and America thanks to his manifold activities as an artist, teacher and writer; but the second is less well-known. Peri kept in the background and produced little, and as far as I know there is only one of his canvases in a public collection. Peri's constructivism is more austere and reserved than Lissitzky's, and more concentrated than Moholy's which is characterised by a lyrical handling of the medium and experiment in new techniques.

I would suggest however that the Constructivist stream found its richest fulfilment in the copious body of work so patiently and quietly produced by Sophie Taüber in Zürich and Paris over a period of thirty years.

Mention must be made of two painters in the *Stijl* tradition, the Polish artists Henry Stazewski and Ladislas Strzeminski, who painted works of exceptional purity during the 'thirties. The first of these in particular impressed me with his white canvases on which the handling of the paint alone contrived to present an extremely simple design of planes arranged in a strictly horizontal-vertical relationship. Both of them were members of the *Cercle et Carré* group in 1930. Another Pole, Henri Berlewi had already composed abstract works before them, which he called *mechanofaktur* and which aimed at a kind of alphabet of simple plastic forms.

In Germany there were also Domela (Berlin), Vordemberge (Osnabrück), Baumeister (Stuttgart) and Schwitters (Hanover). The first two of these worked at first according to orthodox *Stijl* principles, but later developed towards a more varied form of expression.

Domela settled in Paris in 1933. He is now best known for his 'object-paintings' in which the curve is most prominent and into which he introduces all kinds of themes and substances which he combines or sets off against each other with unequalled craftsmanship.

Vordemberge fled from Germany just before the war and went to live in Amsterdam. He is now teaching art at Ulm and paints very sober Neo-constructivist compositions in delicate pastel-like tones.

Baumeister attracted attention as far back as 1921 by some mural compositions of a very personal quality in which the curve is exploited in harmony with the straight line and the circle with the square. On one occasion (1922) he produced a mural relief consisting entirely of horizontals and verticals.

As for Kurt Schwitters, he is undoubtedly one of the most outstanding personalities of that period. His varied activities, full of surprises, and the unusual disinterestedness of his work and thought, have already made him something of a legend. Among his plastic productions are a large number of collages (*Papiers collés*) which can only be described as being beyond description. Everything he does has the same decisive and genuine candidness.

In Paris the fluid Hélion, as elusive as quicksilver, first flirted a little with Neo-plasticism, then invented a strong and sensitive style of his own, after which he proceeded to run wild.

In about 1930 Herbin began painting abstracts full of curves, from which basis he gradually evolved his own alphabet of geometrical features for which he is now famous.

Sergei Charchoune, a thorough romantic who is often capable of subtlety and is sometimes obscure and disturbing, composed some sober canvases between 1925 and 1935 which were painted in an ochre, maroon or olive monochrome and which he unfortunately baptised "ornamental cubism". There is nothing ornamental about them but they are moving in their gentleness, having a kind of repressed sentimentality which none the less, thanks to their transparent honesty, manages to show through their hazy indecision.

Albert Gleizes's intellectualised Cubism helped him to discover personal forms of abstraction which range from the extremely simple to the extremely sophisticated. His study of art-history afterwards led him away from that initial manner until he settled down to the interpretation or schematisation of a kind of religious painting based on the Romanesque style. Gleizes will also be remembered for restoring Robert Delaunay's faith in himself by his praise of Delaunay's intuitive work in 1912-13, and for having brought him back to abstract painting in 1930 or thereabouts.

FREUNDLICH. COMPOSITION. 1930.
Private Collection, Paris.

Alfred Reth, one of the 'forgotten children' of Cubism along with Van Rees, Tour Donas and others, found himself driven by some inner necessity to all sorts of unrewarding experiments in new materials and themes. The results he achieved in this way were often surprising but often disappointing. It was only after 1945 that he found himself, in a monumental style which leaves no further doubt that he has a genuinely creative personality.

Henri Nouveau began as a musician, then took up plastic art in 1920 when he produced some abstract collages of miniature proportions. He led and is still leading a very secluded life, still keeping an eye on the outside world, an essentially humorous eye, like Klee's, though he almost always avoids the slightest hint of figuration. His painting is immensely amusing,

60

full of discoveries and arrangements which are often comical and always discreet and rhythmical.

Finally, another outstanding personality was Otto Freundlich, a painter, sculptor and poet who began as a member of the German Expressionist school. After he came to Paris he began to paint in primary colours, laid on in flat tints. It was 1919 before he broke away from representation. In the twenty years that followed Freundlich painted a series of large canvases composed of rectangles of unequal size painted in lively hues, in which the darker areas were balanced with lighter areas. His works are impressive in their concentrated strength and there is something exhilarating in their controlled lyricism.

MAGNELLI. PAINTING NO. 0530. 1915.
Artist's Collection.

8

ABSTRACT PAINTING IN FRANCE SINCE KANDINSKY'S DEATH. MAGNELLI.
THE 'FOUNDERS OF ABSTRACT ART' EXHIBITION AT THE MAEGHT
GALLERY. 'LES RÉALITÉS NOUVELLES'. THE MAY SALON. HARTUNG,
DE STAËL AND WOLS. SOME OUTSTANDING PAINTERS. 'TACHISME'
AND 'UNIFORMISME'. WOMEN PAINTERS.

We are now coming to the present time, when the works to be discussed are so recent that some errors of assessment are bound to occur.
I shall do my best to be generous, as understanding is out of the question
unless one keeps an open mind. However it is hard to be generous in
the 'jungle' of art, in which we sometimes meet people who put us on the
defensive instead of arousing our admiration.

The second world war, in which millions lost their lives, also thinned
the ranks of artists of all kinds. It was not survived by Delaunay, Freundlich, Mondrian and Kandinsky. Delaunay died in 1941; Freundlich in a
concentration-camp in 1943; both Mondrian and Kandinsky in 1944, the
first in New York at the beginning of that year, the second in Paris three
months after the liberation. The war and the German occupation sent
art underground in France. Fear was the dominant factor. But as soon
as 'degenerate' art was able to come into the open it was seen that the
artists had carried on their work in secret. At the first important exhibition of abstract art after the war—it was called Concrete Art (*Art concret*)
and was held at the Drouin gallery in the Place Vendôme in June 1945 —
works painted during the war by Kandinsky, Herbin, Magnelli, Gorin,
Pevsner, Freundlich, and Domela were shown together with pre-war
canvases by Robert and Sonia Delaunay, Arp, Sophie Taüber, Mondrian
and Van Doesburg.

The most important event immediately after the war was the immediate
success of Alberto Magnelli. Thanks to him Italy was able to make up
lost ground in abstract art, in which her painters had so far made only a
mediocre showing. As is well known Alberto Magnelli had painted a
few geometrical abstracts in Florence in 1915 after a short stay in Paris.
After those first attempts he returned to figuration, and for about ten years
produced mainly artificially-constructed landscapes and monochrome
seascapes. He returned to Paris in 1933, where he painted broken pieces
of rock and thus made his way back towards abstraction. During the war

Magnelli fled to Grasse in the south of France where he met Arp, Sophie Taüber and Sonia Delaunay. The four of them worked together as a team, producing drawings and designing lithographs which were later published in Paris. (25) Magnelli's fame grew by leaps and bounds after the war, and he was soon the most important abstract painter in Paris. With the strong support of the critics in Paris, Switzerland and Italy (who called him 'Kandinsky's disciple of genius') he held an unforgettable exhibition at the Drouin Gallery in 1947. He is a hard worker with great reserves of strength. He is, of course, a disciple of Kandinsky, but is more robust and massive than the Russian painter. You can feel behind his work the background of the sturdy Florentine palaces of his native city, and it has sometimes the sober green and white lyricism of the famous Baptistery near which he was born. Magnelli has tirelessly strengthened and refined his style. One of his most successful discoveries is the multi-coloured line which acts like a kind of transparent skin, surrounding or even sectioning his forms and subtly changing whatever area it penetrates while respecting the values it finds there.

While the return to liberty in France was marked by the death of Kandinsky and the sudden rise of Magnelli, perhaps the main contribution of the immediate post-war period lay in the sudden inrush of a host of new painters who brought every kind of talent to the service of abstract art. The crowd of young artists who spontaneously turned to abstractions as though it represented the main tradition of art fully justified the founding of a separate Salon which would be devoted exclusively to the various forms the new plastic language has taken. That is how *Réalités Nouvelles* came to be founded by Fredo Sidès, though oddly enough he was an antique-dealer. (26)

Altan, Boumeester, Bryen, Chesnay, Coulon, Dewasne, Deyrolle, Engel-Pak, Folmer, Gorin, Hartung, Kosnick-Kloss, Lardeur, Leppien, Malespine, Ney, Piaubert, Poliakoff, Quentin, Marie Raymond, Schneider, Villeri, Vajda, Warb, Wendt, Wols, Léo Breuer, Jeanne Coppel, Duthoo, Fleischmann, Gœtz, Loubchansky, Lhotellier, Mathieu, Evelyn Marc, Néjad, Soulages, Smadja, Vasarely, Vulliamy, Davring, Del Marle, Dufour, Gœbel, Germain, Maria Manton, Nina Negri, Pillet, Pons, Bott, Closon, Dumitresco, Istrati, Koskas, Montlaur, Hella Guth, Fahr-el-Nissa Zeid, Neuberth, Marcelle Cahn, Nemours, Staritsky, Tsingos, Lapoujade—the above is a list of only a few of the painters, and to name them all would be impossible, who represented the French contingent at the *Réalités Nouvelles* shows. The same Gallery also did good work in showing exhibitions by foreign artists, some of which were of great interest, such as the Swiss and Swedish sections in 1948.

At the same time the other Salons became increasingly willing to make room for abstract art. The May Salon in particular drew some of its best contributors from Réalités Nouvelles in 1949. The same May Salon brought together the widely different abstract talents of Lanskoy, Estève, Palazuelo, Singier, Manessier, Le Moal, Bazaine, Hosiasson, Tal Coat, Gischia, de Staël, Riopelle, Lutka Pink, Chastel, Diaz, Lapicque, Lombard, Messagier, Pallut, Springer, Szobel, Rezvani, Léon Zack, Vieira da Silva, Geer van Velde, Ubac, Szenès and many others. Details of all these painters will be found in the Dictionary section of this book.

It was also in 1949, in April, that my book 'Abstract Art, its origins and founders' was published, while at the same time the accompanying exhibition of 'Founders of Abstract Art' was held at the Maeght gallery from April to June.

Then André Bloc brought out the first number of the review *Art d'aujourd'hui* (June 1949-December 1954) which served to amplify the book and exhibition already mentioned, and which was the first review in the world entirely given to a defence of abstract art. It contained important studies of the principal abstract painters, and special numbers appeared on America, Italy, Germany, and the Scandinavian countries. The complete collection of thirty-six parts, notwithstanding occasional errors, provides a unique documentation of abstract art in France and indeed all over the world.

Among the numerous painters mentioned above there are a few who stand out and deserve closer attention. First of these are Hartung, de Staël and Wols.

These three are all intuitive painters. The line together with spots or patches of paint make up Hartung's medium, while most often de Staël uses only the patch and Wols the line. The latter's painting is a display of spasms. His work gives off a sort of mental electricity, full of involuntary references and unconscious perversity. Wols died in 1951, leaving behind him an enormous number of strange scrawls which provided a nervous outlet for a somewhat indolent character, as well as some large canvases in which his over-cerebral intellectual dream is directly expressed through the act of painting in itself, without the slightest interpretation or process being allowed to come between him and the work.

De Staël, on the other hand was a completely conscious, deliberate painter. His first aim was to bring the canvas to life, and this he did with

the energy of a virile temperament.   He used to give everything he had
to the canvas, coming back to it again and again till he achieved the finish
and subtlety he wanted.   Often enough he would wring the neck of his
own painting, as Verlaine talked of wringing the neck of eloquence, and
this gave de Staël's work its intimate warmth, its own personal accent, its
eloquence.   The painter ended his life by hurling himself from his studio
window at Antibes in March 1955.

The eldest of the three, Hartung, is also the richest.   His work
as it stands at present is the most restrained and yet there is no stiffness
about it, nor are there any signs of a wilful self-discipline.   Hartung's
apparent ease is a discipline in itself.   He anticipates the very gesture of

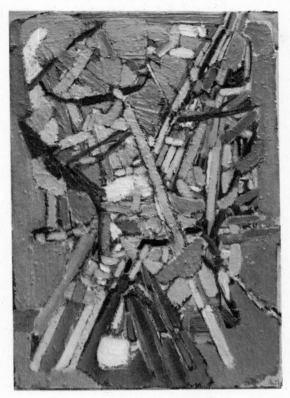

DE STAËL. COMPOSITION: HARMONY IN GREY, BEIGE,
RED PATCHES. 1940. *Private Collection, Paris.*

painting, breaks it up into its natural parts and renews it at the level of direct action, with a studied slow sincerity which heeds only a few faint echoes of what was decided in advance and has already joined the deep reserves of the unconscious mind. Painting thus becomes a religious act, an act of faith. And religion implies revolution, though in his case, however deep it may be, the revolution is bloodless like those of Beethoven or Gabriel Fauré.

Schneider, Soulages and Hosiasson will, I trust, not object if I count them among the spiritual family of Hartung. This is not to suggest that they are in any way his followers, but that there is a certain affinity between them.

Gérard Schneider's style is much less smooth than Hartung's. He has a liking for black shapes, which are stretched and roughly hacked out, looming threateningly from their lighter ground. There is more sorrow than joy in his work, in which an obvious anguish seems to be furtively craving for elegance.

Soulages has the gift of a simple and natural strength. His dark canvases, with pale wisps of colour that seem to lurk or survive in the half-light, are successful dramatic works. His strength is in the kind of discoveries he makes, in the way the amplified structure or framework is enough to make the whole composition. He gives this something like a soul, and out of a terse gesture of the brush he evokes a monument or a temple. No other contemporary painter has such a calm, reliable strength.

Hosiasson works in mud—but there are no work or mud equal to his, which strive after and achieve the pure quality of tonal harmony with an underlying wave-like movement. The wave springs from the obscure depths of the consciousness, and loses nothing of its immensity even in his smallest works.

Mathieu owes some of his symbols to Hartung, as well as something of his private apprenticeship to freedom, but otherwise the resemblance goes no further than a few external features. Their technique is just as different as their minds. Mathieu takes refuge in himself, his passion is deliberately intense and short-lived, and perhaps its impulse lies in contempt. He shows no signs of remorse: the harm is done and is better left as it is. He is a painter who has no scruples about squeezing a whole tube of bright red over a surface of twenty square centimetres, or brushing over an enormous canvas in two hours.

Manessier, Singier and Le Moal, the worthy trinity of the Galerie de France are much more serious painters. They are close friends and have

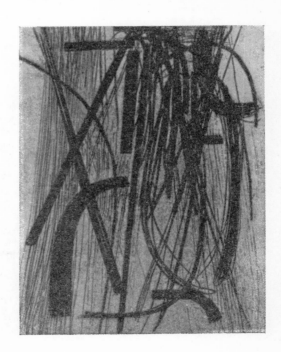

HANS HARTUNG.
ENGRAVING. 1953.

obviously influenced one another, though there are marked differences between them. Manessier is as grave as Le Moal is fresh and lively, while Singier holds the balance as a scholarly and sometimes precious painter. The work of all three is typically French, with its love of order and restraint and unadorned gracefulness. They have created an abstract art of their own, related to the tradition that goes back to the stained glass of Chartres and the Arras tapestries.

The same French lyrical use of colour which found its great champion in Delaunay, has new exponents in Bazaine, Estève, Lombard, and Germain, while it is also noticeable in the work of such oriental artists as Néjad and Rezvani. The most popular is Bazaine, who writes as well as paints. Rezvani is from Persia and produces work as rich and urbane as a Persian carpet. Néjad's characteristically broken shapes can be disturbing and often irritating, but they spring from a genuine painter's temperament in that they have no use for grace and facility alone. His mother is Princess Fahr-el-Nissa-Zeid, well known for her very large compositions executed in bright colours, again something like oriental carpets and redolent of the pungent perfumes of Asia Minor.

BEN NICHOLSON. PAINTED RELIEF. 1939.
Museum of Modern Art, New York.

Let us turn now to geometrical abstracts. The first names to suggest themselves are Vasarely, Dewasne and Pillet. Vasarely prefers a refinement of forms which is enhanced by his sober colour. Dewasne on the contrary is more concerned with colour for its own sake and the interplaying contrasts he can get out of it. He is at his best in ambitious mural compositions in which he seems more at home than with the easel. Pillet's often linear compositions are governed by his pursuit of subtle inflections of colour.

Davring and Leppien are two painters of German origin who have been settled for a long time in the south of France. They both have a very linear style which reconciles the straight and curved line. Leppien is the more light-hearted of the two and perhaps the more consistent, but although Davring is occasionally disappointing he is much more resourceful. Davring was at one time the youngest of the German Expressionists, and went under the name of Davringhausen.

Jean Piaubert is another geometrical painter who is known for his very severe canvases and for the remarkable lithographs he made for Jean Cassou's *33 Sonnets*. Sergei Poliakoff's geometrical designs have something unpolished about them which is not without admirers, and sometimes his touches of awkwardness are successful in their effect.

Geer van Velde is of Dutch origin and is a painter of exceptional crafstmanship. He was slow in his approach to abstraction and has shown no haste in his exploration of it since. Every one of his work has behind it the weight of a painter's training and experience, and the brush offers us a selection of his rich powers which are painstakingly conveyed on the canvas. His canvases are worked up slowly in a polished economical style in which the colour is always discreet. His restrained undertones are modulated in a polytonality in which the ryhthm is marked by a rectilinear stress which never degenerates into stiffness.

Geer's brother Bram van Velde has an engaging temperament which nevertheless is full of smouldering revolt and denial. His few canvases seem to be painfully drawn from an undecided personality, fluid and frameless, which together with their cold lucidity makes them all the more expressive.

Much has been said in Paris in the last year or two about *Tachisme*. This term is used to describe a movement which runs parallel with abstract Neo-Expressionism, originating in America. Its immediate ancestors are Henri Michaux (whose works are always closer to figuration than to abstraction because they are full of literary allusions) and Hans Hartung, whose painting has been strictly abstract over the past twenty years. Its more distant origins lie in the work Kandinsky produced in his so-called dramatic period of 1910-1912. The real *tachistes* are Bryen, Mathieu, Greta Sauer, Lee Hersch, Bogard, Riopelle and a number of others. Under Riopelle's influence there has developed a certain uniformity which enables painters to avoid the slightest problem of composition and to reduce the act of painting to a physical gesture. The American, Pollock, prepared the way for this in 1950. In Paris, Chelimsky and Sam Francis have taken this up, and more recently Wendt, Istrati and Nallard.

Meanwhile a number of painters who rely on pure colour-sensibility are going their own way between all these extremes, though they do no go so far as to cut out all content from their 'dialogue' with the canvas. They are thus continuing a tradition of finesse and adaptability which is always a pleasure to the eye. These painters include Vulliamy, Kolos Vary, Lagage, Debré, Van Haardt, Bott and Szenès.

Women painters have made a contribution to the phenomenology of abstract art which must not be underestimated. Berthe Morisot and Mary Cassatt were the only female Impressionists, while Marie Laurencin, Maria Blanchard and Tour Donas were the only women of note among the Cubists. After Sonia Delaunay and Sophie Taüber there has been no lack of women painting on abstract lines. It might be asked whether they are less creative than the man, whether they are inferior in strength or invention, or whether they show less restraint. My own sincere opinion is that this is not so. It cannot be denied that the greatest painters are men, and the same goes for the other arts. But such men are few and can be counted on one hand. If we carry on counting on the other hand the women find their place as equals with the men. Some of them, such as Evelyn Marc and Christine Boumeester paint with more delicacy than the men; others such as Jeanne Coppel, Marcelle Cahn, Nathalia Dumitresco and Aurélie Nemours are their equals in restraint and discipline; some are in no way inferior in their creative improvisation, such as Vieira da Silva, Karskaya and Staritsky, while others equal the men in their energy, for instance Sonia Delaunay and Nina Tryggvadottir. The part women have to play is not always easy. Their work is examined with the same aggressive suspicion by feminists and anti-feminists alike, the former expecting them to prove more than they are capable of and the latter pouncing on the slightest pretext for running them down. There is no such thing as sex where sensibility is concerned, and I know many a highly-regarded canvas which would meet with derision if it were signed with a woman's name.

9

ABSTRACT ART IN OTHER COUNTRIES.

The first artist to turn to abstract art in Belgium was Victor Servranckx. His works are made up either of rounded shapes like fragmentary worlds (*Éventration,* 1919) or sometimes of more orthogonal, rectangular features. The latter are related to the aesthetics of the machine of which the Futurists made so much (*Le règne de l'acier poli* or Polished steel kingdom, 1923). Servranckx later abandoned abstraction but gradually returned to it after 1946. In 1920 a painter from Antwerp, Joseph Peeters, began working in the abstract geometrical style. At the end of the following year he held an exhibition which attracted some notice and he was then asked to become co-editor of the advance-guard review *Het Overzicht*. In it he published several articles on his idea of 'community art' in which he took a stand against the views of *De Stijl* which he thought were too narrow. Apart from works by Delaunay, Juan Gris, Kandinsky, Moholy-Nagy, Huszar,

JOSEPH PEETERS. LINO-CUT. 1920.

Larionov and others, *Het Overzicht* reproduced abstract works by such Belgian artists as Peeters, Servranckx, Karel Maes, Edmond van Dooren, Prosper de Troyer, Jos Leonard and Paul Joostens. Within a few years they had all returned to figurative painting or, as in the case of Peeters and de Maes stopped painting altogether by 1926. During the next twenty years abstract art was almost totally neglected in Belgium. On the other hand a number of Belgian painters have been making abstracts in France for some years now, particularly Engel-Pak, Closon, Lempereur-Haut, Orix, Alechinsky. In Belgium itself at the present time the abstract group consists mainly of Delahaut, Bury, Jan Saverys, Van Lint, Anne Bonnet, Kurt Lewy, Meerbergen, Mendelsohn and Gaston Bertrand.

Almost the same thing happened in Holland as in Belgium: the *Stijl* group was left without successors. The young painters emigrated and became known, much later, as advance-guard artists of repute in their country of adoption. There were, of course, a few isolated exceptions such as Werkman who has already been discussed and who was the only abstract artist in Holland between 1925 and 1930, and a little before him but for a very short period A. C. Willinck. This is another case in which abstract art came to the fore after the country was liberated. The principal abstract painters now working in Holland are Sinemus, Van der Vossen, Willy Boers, Rooskens, Frieda Hunziker, Ouborg, Will, and Alkema.

In Germany abstract art has never been very lucky. Its two best representatives Franz Marc and August Macke both lost their lives in the first world war. Not long after his rise to power Hitler condemned and forbade all advance-guard art. Many artists and intellectuals left the country. Baumeister was one of the few who remained behind, but he had often combined figuration and abstraction and could hardly be considered as a pure abstractionist. Now there are quite a number of abstract painters in Germany, of whom the most outstanding are Ernst W. Nay, Theodor Werner, Fritz Winter, Julius Bissier, Karl Otto Götz, G. K. Schmelzeisen. Worth mentioning among the younger generation are Schultze, Sonderborg, Schilling and Fath Winter.

In Scandinavia the Swedish painter Carlsund and the Dane Francisca Clausen introduced abstract art in about 1930. However in Sweden at present I can see no more than two painters who seem genuinely drawn towards abstraction: these are Ollé Baertling, a disciple of Herbin, and

Ollé Bonnier, a much freer painter but one who has come under various influences.

There is a group of abstract painters in Iceland, notably Thorvaldur Skúlarson, Svavar Gudnason, Valtyr Petersun and Sverrir Haraldson. One of the most powerful of them, Nina Tryggvadottir, has been working in Paris for some years now.

England has Ben Nicholson, who has already been mentioned, and a few painters who work with or near him at Saint Ives in Cornwall. A fairly large group has gradually gathered in London, among whom Victor Pasmore is definitely the most significant. This painter has a completely personal style in which a Celtic, linear element comes to terms with rectangular geometrical features. The same group contains Anthony Hill, Terry Frost, Adrian Heath, Kenneth Martin, Roger Hilton and Sven Blomberg. The two women painters Marlow Moss and Paule Vézelay belong to the preceding generation. For many years the former of these was a keen disciple of Mondrian, in Paris, and she has a definite talent which she puts at the service of that doctrine of extreme caution. Paule Vézelay clearly owes most to Hans Arp, yet she has her own manner. She can express great tenderness and gentle shyness through the medium of her neutral greys and fragile, graceful shapes.

In Italy, as we have already noted, the Futurism of Boccioni, Carrà and Soffici often approached abstraction. But Balla and Magnelli are the only painters since then to have produced works of a radical and deliberate abstraction. Before 1914 Severini painted a few abstract works in Paris. A large number of abstractionists have appeared in Italy since the war, including Vedova, Corpora, Bertini, Burri, Guerrini, Bozzolini, Savelli, di Salvatore, Capograssi, Prampolini, Soldati, Dorazio, Righetti, Reggiani, Santomaso. Some of these are well known in Paris and New York. Pettoruti, who was for many years keeper of the Museum of Fine Arts in Buenos-Ayres and who is known in America for his Cubist works which are sometimes similar to those of Gris, returned to abstraction in 1953, having already tried it in Italy when he was a young man.

As for Switzerland, having had the benefit during the 1914-18 war of the presence of many foreign intellectuals, then of the beginnings of Dadaism, none the less it remained more or less indifferent to advance-guard art of every kind, so that there were no immediate developments there.　It was not until 1936 that a public exhibition (at the Zürich Kunsthaus) drew attention to an abstractionist who was both of Swiss nationality and resident in Switzerland.　He was Max Bill.　Apart from that, Switzerland did much to make up lost ground after Léo Leuppi founded the *Die Allianz* group.　This led to important exhibitions being held in Zürich, Basel (1938), the publication of a throughly documented guide or yearbook in 1940, then further exhibitions at Basel in 1944 and Zürich in 1947. The last of these had a particularly large number of exhibitors.　Apart from Bill and Leuppi mention should be made of Eble, Eichmann, Lili Erzinger, Graeser, Lhose, Spiller, Tiravanti, Fischli, Bodmer, Vreni Lœwensberg, Hinterreiter.

After the *Cercle et Carré* venture, Torrès-Garcia returned home to Uruguay, where he ran an art-school in Montevideo until his death in 1949. This school had a large number of students and spread its influence all over Buenos-Ayres.　However, what Torrès-Garcia was teaching in the same of abstract art was in reality a form of figurative art which had deep roots in the native primitive art of South America.　This led to some misunderstanding, and it is not hard to see why the first really abstract painters in Argentine preferred the term "concrete art" which had been favoured by Max Bill.

There are quite a number of abstract painters in Argentina.　To name a few of these: Hlito, Ocampo and Villalba are all related to Vordemberge and the Swiss painter Eichmann; Mele produced Neo-constructivist paintings with an element of relief in them; Vardanega has made some interesting experiments, using glass; Maldonado often comes close to pure Neo-plasticism.　But Argentina also has an indigenous tendency which has been called *Madi,* and which is led by Arden-Quin, Rothfuss and Kosice.　This movement became known in Paris through its frequent contributions to the *Réalités Nouvelles* salon.　Among its innovations are the use of a non-orthogonal frame, pictures composed of several separate or detachable parts, and suchlike.　Arden-Quin lived in Paris from 1948 till 1953, where his art became more refined.　A Parisian *Madi* group soon gathered round him which included Sallaz, Roïtman, Marcelle Saint-Omer, Alexandre and Neyrat.　In Argentina itself the Madi movement runs a profusely illustrated review edited by Kosice.　Madi art also has a follower in Cuba, namely Sandu Darie who was born in Rumania.　Darie is the simplest and most level-headed of the Madi artists.　His works are strictly geometrical, create a very pleasant effect and are marked by a certain coolness.

74

GAKUI OSAWA. CALLIGRAPHIC PAINTING.

There is a school of abstract painting in Brazil, at the Flexor studio in Sao Paulo.

Mexico is socially hostile to abstract art, but it has a young painter whose canvases, full of crystalline shapes and strange effects of light, are certainly impressive. He is Gunther Gerzso.

The abstract painters are working in isolation in Australia (Grace Crowley and Ralph Bason) and in South Africa (Nel Erasmus).

There is a considerable group of abstractionists in Jugoslavia, the nucleus of which is formed by Picelj, Kristl and Rasica.

Spain has had a group, for some time now, which exhibits in Madrid at the Galeria Fernando Fé. Some of these are Canogar, Delgado, Feito, Luque, Rodriguez Zambrana and Luiz de la Orden.

Many Japanese artists have reached abstraction through calligraphic art. (27) The reviews *Bokubi* and *Bokuzin* edited by Siryu Morita give generous space to Parisian and New York artists who have influenced such calligraphic painters as Yoshimichi Sekiya, Toko Shinoda, Futoshi Tsuji, Bokushi Nakamura, Gakiu Osawa, Youichi Inoue, Sogen Eguchi and above all the monumental manner of Siryu Morita himself. Exhibitions of Japanese calligraphy held in New York, Amsterdam, Brussels, Basel and Paris show parallels between Eastern and Weestern experiments. Tobey, Kline, Tomlin, Alcopley in America; Hartung, Soulages, Schneider, Mathieu and Alechinsky in France; Götz and Bisser in Germany are calligraphers in the modern oriental sense. The same expressiveness and liberty of style are achieved in colour in the West—except for Kline—and in black and white in the East.

ABSTRACT ART IN THE UNITED STATES.

The United States' contribution to abstract art is now almost as large as that of France, and this means that in the past few years Paris has begun to share with New York the supremacy she had in the advanced arts. New York has become an important centre for manifestations of abstract art through the shows held at the Museum of Modern Art, the Whitney Museum and the Salon of American Abstract Artists. Numerous galleries (Janis, Kootz, Fried, Willard, Parsons, etc.) have either allowed or invited American abstractionists to show their work and made them known to the public.

Some outstanding exhibitions of European abstract art have been held in the States, following the one organised by Katherine Dreier at the Brooklyn Museum in 1926. However the first official recognition of American abstractionist painting came in the form of a show at the Museum of Modern Art in New York in January 1951, which coincided with the publication of Andrew Ritchie's book *Abstract painting and sculpture in America*. A few days after the varnishing the same Museum held a series of talks in the form of a symposium, in which statements were made by the five best qualified representatives of American abstract art, Morris, de Kooning, Calder, Glarner and Motherwell. Nervous and uneasy, de Kooning was mainly negative in his opinions, and left the impression that he was fundamentally hostile to both Neo-plasticism and any form of purely geometrical art. On the other hand Glarner gave a short and quiet demonstration of what he calls "relational painting", meaning by that a painting of relationships or a relative painting. I happened to be present at that meeting. When Glarner was asked a question about Mondrian, in the course of the discussion which followed his talk, he answered simply "He was my friend and my master." Glarner is generally considered, on the other side of the Atlantic, as the only successor to Neo-plasticism worth taking seriously. This summary judgment implies some injustice towards painters of such quality as Diller, Kelly, Charmion von Wiegand, Cavallon and Bolotowsky. Yet there is no doubt that the supporters of Neo-expressionism outnumber the Neo-plastic artists and are better known in America. The leaders are Hofmann, Pollock, de Kooning, Kline, Clifford Still and Rothko, others being Tworkow, Stamos and Newman.

Somewhere between the two movements I have already mentioned (Neo-plasticism and Neo-expressionism) come two others, one abstract stream deriving from Cubism and represented by Davis, Morris and Gallatin, and the other originating in Surrealism (Gorky, Motherwell and Baziotes).

A central position among all four tendencies should be given to a fifth class of painters who are fairly numerous and whose work points to a new type of experiment, whether rhythmical or arhythmical, which sometimes reaches the monumental. Tobey and Tomlin are characteristic of this movement.

Mondrian's presence in New York in the last three years of his life was very important for America and for art in general. He arrived there in October 1940 and died on the first of February 1944. In those last years he painted some of his most remarkable works, of which the most famous are the two *Boogie-woogie* canvases. He also took part in numerous art events, publishing essays and holding two exhibitions at the Valentine Gallery. After spending his life almost as a recluse in Paris, followed by two years of obscurity in London, Mondrian was at last able to lead a happy and almost brilliant existence. He found himself surrounded by friends and everywhere held in the highest respect, even by those whom he had formerly believed to be his enemies: he had some pleasant meetings with Max Ernst and André Breton. However financial success only came after his death. Overnight he was praised and publicised in the newspapers and magazines which had hitherto been most scornful of abstract art, and he became rich when he lay in his grave. Designers made 'Neo-plastic' dresses, art-dealers scoured the world in search of his works, his life became a legend and his name a symbol, he was credited with hundreds of witty sayings and all the schools in America started explaining what Neo-plasticism really meant.

The exaggeration was such that some reaction was bound to take place sooner or later. A handful of artists went to the opposite extreme and founded the Abstract-Expressionist movement, with Pollock and de Kooning at its head. American critics tend to regard this as being an authentically American movement and regard the continuation of Neo-plasticism as being no more than a second-hand form of European art. I would suggest that those who assert this have forgotten about Kandinsky: no more is needed than to visit the Solomon R. Guggenheim Museum and see a dozen canvases painted by Kandinsky between 1912 and 1918, to grasp the fact that Abstract Expressionism was and is just as European, since it was born in Munich.

American abstract art undoubtedly has its roots in Europe. This is not my personal wish or decision: it is history's. But whatever the roots, a tree can be grafted and yield extraordinary flowers.

Two strong personalities in the States are Arshile Gorky and Marc Tobey. Gorky was born in Armenia at the beginning of the century and

BOLOTOWSKY. BLACK AND WHITE. PAINTING. 1948.

emigrated to America in 1920. His life was full of surprises. After certain tragic accidents and disappointments in his private life, he committed suicide in 1948 at the very time when he was achieving fame. Gorky was influenced for a long time by various European painters. A considerable part of his work shows a striking parallel with the experiments of Picasso and Miró, as well as, for a time, those of Léger. His abstract compositions painted in 1933 and the years immediately after were still very close to Picasso. After all these adventures and trials and errors Gorky was destined to find his own genius at last, and this happened in about 1940. The works of his last years are of the highest standard and full of meaning. Almost at once he found a personal style in which a fluid use of line gave perfect expression to a refined, erotic sensuality. This style has left a mark on Matta and de Kooning, though in different ways.

Marc Tobey has had an even longer evolution than Gorky, and was born ten years earlier than he. After travelling about in Europe and Asia he went to live in Seattle near the Pacific coast. At Seattle during the last ten years he has produced a body of work, for the most part abstract, which owes some of its unusual rhythmic qualities to a study of Chinese calligraphy. One of his earliest abstract paintings, *Broadway norm,* dating from 1935, consists of a network of white lines on a neutral ground. But it was only after 1943 that he began painting abstract compositions to which he gave all his personality. His rhythm is abrupt yet continuous and he spreads an equal intensity of vision over the whole surface of the canvas: these two characteristics have had a quiet but deep influence on other artists. Nobody can deny that he laid the foundations for Pollock and Tomlin and many others. Large mural panels of 'direct writing' are now a common feature in America, but there has been no finer 'writing' than Tobey's.

Clifford Still, who was for many years a teacher of art in California and who still has a great influence there, became the centre of the idea on

FRANZ KLINE. HIGH STREET. PAINTING. 1950.

which the "Pacific School" or "West Coast School" is based. Much has been said and written about this in recent years, but quite recently the American critic Hubert Crehan did much to this rather pretentious bubble. (28) None the less, Still is an astonishing painter. Late in 1950 I saw an exhibition of his work in New York which leaves me no doubt as to this painter's personality, which is out of the common. He is a kind of cartographer or map-maker who works on large black surfaces cut into unequal sections, strangely animated and dramatised by means of a single trail or drag of bright red, or which he contrasts with ochres and greys.

There are also a number of women painters whose personality cannot be denied. To mention only a few, attention should be given to the paintings on glass by Pereira, the free compositions of Buffie Johnson, Edda Sterne and Suzy Freilinghuysen, or the rhythmical canvases of Ronnie Elliott, the collages of Hilda Rebay and Beate Hulbeck, as well as Alice T. Mason's and Charmion von Wiegand's geometrical experiments and the luminous, hazy effects of Pearl Fine.

Now as always, Paris has quite a large contingent of American painters. Among the abstractionists there are Pfriem, one of Gorky's followers; Sam Francis who, with a deliberate monotony, works in little spots or patches placed side by side; Alcopley, a master of calligraphic improvisation; Jenkins, subtly poetic with his mysterious glimpses of light; finally Chelimsky, Levée, Childs and Malina.

Perhaps I might also count among the Americans the Austrian-born but naturalised Mexican, Wolfgang Paalen. This painter at first gravitated among the surrealist group, but after seeking further experience in his research into ancient Mexican art, discovered an art of his own which is powerfully expressive and has an exhilarating sense of colour. In 1951 Paalen organised an exhibition at the San Francisco Museum of Modern Art in which, apart from his own work, he introduced some abstracts by Lee Mullican and Gordon Onslow-Ford, two exceptionally lyrical painters. The first of these is obsessed by the theme of the sun which gives his canvases a dynamic, expansive movement, while the second is calmer and is enamoured of the glittering effects to be obtained from juxtaposing little spots of colour or vertical lines, producing some interesting optical impressions.

This rapid accumulation of names will no doubt leave the reader somewhat confused. I have tried to keep to the main lines of my inquiry in order to avoid further bewilderment, but this has more than once obliged me to over-simplify and make a rather arbitrary choice among the numerous artists concerned. Present-day art is so rich and varied that it might well seem a glory-hole in which treasures and baubles become indistinguishable. Time will perhaps give greater stature to what at first sight looks commonplace. Like mountains, paintings are more beautiful when seen from a distance.

CONCLUSION

Taking a bird's-eye view in an attempt to summarise all the activity that has been described so far, it might be said that the field of abstract art is at present divided into two camps, into geometry and algebra, or, to put it another way, into style and emotional outcry. In some countries such as Germany, the United States and Japan the algebraists are in command, while in others such as Italy, England, the Scandinavian countries, Belgium and Argentina the power is in control of the geometricians. Paris becomes a kind of arena in which the two sides are in combat and where the odds are fairly even. Points are marked up for each side from day to day. Each side has its artists of unquestionable value, great painters who are small-minded and small painters who have a certain greatness in them. Let us not, however, forget the no-man's-land lying between them, the domain of pure sensibility in which style and cry come together and sometimes produce something like ecstasy.

If contemporary abstract art is rich in every kind of experiment, it is still as alive and as tensed towards the future as it was thirty or forty years ago. We still see every artist at grips with his own conception of the world and of man, and with all the problems that accompany the laws and means of self-expression. This daily drama, this cool struggle for the conquest of truth or of plastic purity represent the essence of the artist's vocation. These problems only became acute in our century, and were hardly noticeable before the advent of abstract art.

Abstract art's function has been and is to reflect the face and being of our century. I wrote at the beginning of this book that living is change, and it is thanks to change that we become what we are. Through the evolution and constant changes of art mankind is able to discover, however slowly, its most profound concern and its truest unchanging quality, which is the tireless inquiry of the human mind, the advance of mind towards self-knowledge despite the apparent frivolity of every style and every love.

All art is metaphysical.

Whether we consider the time-worn works of prehistory, Greco-Egyptian sculptures, Byzantine mosaics, Romanesque painting, Gothic sculpture or even the superb pagan outburst of the Renaissance, every art points to a religion, every art is full to running over with ideals and admirations. Surely any active admiration is already a form of adoration? There is no difficulty in pointing out a religious tropism in the shadows of a Rembrandt, or the razor-edge of ascesis in El Greco. But on the other hand did not Raphael and Michelangelo bring a naturally mystical mind to rest, the former by virtue of a kind of supernatural tenderness, the latter through a cosmological anguish, a Maelstrom which draws us inwards towards art like a great whirlpool of hidden loves?

None the less it has been through a long abandonment of the religious theme in the proper sense of the term that abstract art, in our time, came to reveal the metaphysical nature of all art. Not that the support of naturalism strips art so that nothing is left but pure spiritual adoration, or that the artist effaces himself before some evidence or other of the absolute. In that case we could no longer speak of art as such, for it is the nature of all art to love itself with a carnal affection, so fanatical and exclusive that very often the artist becomes numb to other kinds of beauty, or even regards it and them as spurious imitations of the one true beauty, which is beauty as created by himself.

But it is precisely this absolutism of art, it is precisely this power of total love which proves that man is now brought face to face with realities that are beyond his understanding. After thousands of years of being a meditation on the ineffable, and regarding the support of man's intellect as a sign of intellect itself, in our century art has become a meditation on itself, that is to say a meditation on the relativity of the "ineffable". Thanks to abstract art, every artist finds himself faced with the problem of terms of expression, which implies a technique, and secondly with the problem of his own inner life, which implies a dialectic. All the creative artists who have advanced abstract art since it first began have demonstrated that success and undeniable originality depend on a perfect harmony between a developed technique and a state of mind. Perhaps it is that harmony itself, even in a latent state, which brings the artist to raise his hand towards the paint or the canvas, and which determines the embodiment of his thought or his will in a work of art.

If to live is to change, it is also to feel oneself being, to feel that one exists in spite of all changes within or without. There again, it seems to me that art brings fresh succour to the consciousness, an irrefutable test or ordeal which determines a universal constant by means of as many soundings as there are valid works. Thus every artist becomes a unique witness of the life of the mind, the life of the spirit. And oddly enough, the more exceptional or unique he appears, and the more odd or unusual the work itself, the greater will be the number of people who recognise themselves in it.   It is as though what is most rare is fundamentally the most universal. Thus it is that if I may illustrate my argument through a commercial image, the most unsellable picture is precisely the one that becomes most 'quoted' or sought after.

Abstract art is the *style* of our century in the same way as, generally speaking, Naturalism was the style of the Nineteenth.   Naturalism takes about twenty forms, and in the same way there are some twenty branches of abstract art.

If the two terms now seem to be at opposite poles from one another, it is not for any lack of long and painful discrimination as regards naturalism even in the very first phases of abstraction.   The transition stages which ran from the later works of Cézanne up to synthetic Cubism in 1914, rank among the finest manifestations in the whole history of art.   Periods of transition, not only in the lives of individuals but in history as a whole, are often charged with greater sensibility because of the uneasiness that goes with breaking things down, as well as the hesitations in creating new things and the effort to establish novelty.   This sensitive instability, however, has no meaning except when we relate it to the higher significance of the classicism we are always aspiring towards, in which all struggles come to an end in peaceful contemplation.

Thus the history of art, like the history of every man, is an endless movement between two opposite poles, the uneasy desire for rest and then rest itself which prepares some fresh creation.   If living is to feel oneself being, the most profound identity of being is no doubt a perpetual state of birth and beginning.   In the artist, who is perhaps the acutest though even then not fully conscious witness of his age, this state of birth expresses itself directly in his work.   In the best of cases, it is undistinguishable, because it has no intermediary, from creation itself.   But this 'best of cases' is, precisely, given every help by abstract art, because, as it puts an end to the tyranny of naturalistic representation, it allows of a direct communication of a certain inner density or intensity, without any parasitical medium intervening.   Once the instrument has become familiar and prepared for its task, the expression of successive states of birth becomes as simple and as fluent as writing, or at least just as unified or concerted. Like handwriting it can be stable or changeable, clear or obscure, orderly or irregular.   But the work of art, like writing, will always be a direct grasping and effusion of the self, with no intervening substance to pervert it.   There is no closer relationship than that between the artist and his work, and no union is more jealous, more entire and exacting or capable of being blinder to all that lies beyond possession.

If it is true that there is no substance without energy, there is no mind without rest. The body seeks its development and continuity in time, but the mind begins by a pause. To live spiritually means contemplating and finding pleasure in the self, welcoming what comes from without and rejoicing in what lies within. To live physically is to swarm like bees: matter must conquer, but spirit must bide its time.

Art, then, is a spiritual act committing body and spirit together. It is man expressing himself at his highest but most fragile level where matter and the unknown unite. In art the striving of substance and the concentration of the spirit are inseparable. The words 'spiritual act' imply an insoluble contradiction in terms, showing what a mystery underlies art, why it refuses all philosophical analysis. Any dialectical approach to art is blocked by paradox.

Art is the only moment when mind, without ceasing to be mind, is converted into physical expansion, and when matter submits to the mind's transcendence and is converted into speculation, non-contingency.

If this is so, we can understand how art withers away beneath social compulsion, why it eschews social power. Pure disinterestedness, it leads man away from wordly success.

By means of a pure expression of the mind through the submission of matter, the human being makes himself a place or finds himself in a world which is not the everyday world of weights and measures, a world of complete gratuity or disinterestedness which can be called mystical.

The result of this complete gratuitousness is that the work of art is not often recognisable when it is newly born: by definition it eludes all conventional ideas of what it ought to be.

Art is a creation which offers no guarantees. The artist is a man walking into space, and we cannot know by what miracle the solid earth rises up to support his feet.

All that an artist makes or does has the power of law, however upsetting this might appear. Almost as upsetting is the fact that those who follow him along his newly-made path appear more or less insignificant: they are coiners, forgers. The first alone is a creator, and those who follow him have nothing to say or do. Art is elsewhere, where others are travelling onwards, losing the way, losing themselves.

NOTES

(1) There is also a dispute over terminology which has caused much ink to be wasted. Van Doesburg was always starting hares or looking for trouble, and began it in 1930 when he suggested *concrete,* instead of *abstract* which until then had been considered satisfactory. For a while Hans Arp also preferred the term *concrete,* and Kandinsky came out in its favour in 1938. Max Bill became its greatest advocate and through his influence it was adopted in South America and Italy.

Some years ago in New York Miss Hilla Rebay somewhat fanatically insisted on the expression *non-objectivism.* This inevitably caused some confusion in the outlook of some of the young American painters, especially as some American critics apply the term abstract to works which are not so (see Thomas B. Hess, *Abstract Painting*).

Even in Paris there are painters who make a specious distinction between the words *abstract* and *non-figurative.*

We have no intention of being caught up in these quibbles. On the authority of the first abstract painters we have adopted the simplest and most generally accepted term.

(2) In making this distinction no attention should be paid to the title given by a painter to his work. An obvious still-life can easily be called *composition* or even *abstraction* without the title making it any less figurative, while an abstract canvas can be called *Joie de vivre* or *Trafalgar Square* without containing the slightest hint of a story or a landscape. A boy can be baptised *Marie* without being turned into a girl.

(3) This is true of Klee, Miró and often Picasso. Sometimes Picasso will add to his abstract forms—rather casually, according to all accounts—a few brush-strokes which suggest a face or figure. We know that for Picasso "there is no abstract art". He ought to say or perhaps means "there ought not to be any abstract art".

(4) Baudelaire in *L'Art romantique:* "There is no line or colour in nature. It is man who creates line and colour. They are two abstractions whose dignity comes from a common origin. . . Line and colour both make us think and dream; the pleasures resulting from them are of a different nature, though equal to ordinary nature, and absolutely independent of the picture's subject."

Flaubert, *Correspondance,* 1852: "Perhaps beauty will become a sentiment for which mankind has no further use, and art will be something half-way between algebra and music."

(5) I have been told that in his research into abstraction Kandinsky was influenced by a Lithuanian painter, M. K. Ciurlionis, who died in 1911. This painter composed, from 1904 onwards, abstract paintings which are often characterised by arabesques being used together with geometrical shapes. He also painted some dream-landscapes or dreamscapes, full of symbolic references, which have certain affinities to Kandinsky's more romantic works. A substantial exhibition of Ciurlionis' paintings was held in Moscow in the year of his death. In 1916 W. Ivanov published a book in Russian about Ciurlionis, published by Mussaget, Moscow. Mme Charmion von Wiegand regards Ciurlionis as the first abstract painter (*Encyclopaedia of Art,* New York 1946).

(6) *Uber das Geistige in der Kunst* (Spirituality in Art) was published in Munich in 1912, thanks to Franz Marc's intervention with Piper's firm. The work was written in 1910 but was rejected by several publishers.

(7) Michel-Eugène Chevreul: *De la loi du contraste simultané des couleurs* (The law of simultaneous colour-contrast), Paris 1839, and *Des couleurs et de leurs applications aux arts industriels à l'aide des cercles chromatiques* (Colours and their application in the industrial arts with the help of chromatic circles), Paris 1864. Chevreul's theories have found their fulfilment outside the scientific field, thanks to their influence on two great painters. The germ of an idea can have astonishing results in domains for which it was not intended, nor, at first sight, appropriate.

(8) It is well known that Apollinaire gave the name *Orphism* to a group of painters whose free-expression and lively colour had nothing to do with what the Cubists were aiming at. The three main painters of the group were Delaunay, Kupka and Picabia. In this connection he also spoke of 'cubisme écartelé' (quartered or dispersed Cubism). His definition of Orphic Cubism was as follows: "the art of painting new unified compositions (ensembles nouveaux) the elements of which are not drawn from visible reality but are entirely created by the artist, who endows them with powerful reality."

(9) At the same Studio, Larionov also demonstrated what could be done with shades of the same colour and the effects produced by varied handling of the same colour: 1) white upon white—imposing on a polished, glossy white surface, a particular shape in rough, lustreless white: 2) black upon black—imposing on a black porous surface, a particular shape in polished, shiny black: 3) similar combinations with other colours laid on in different ways. These details were provided by M. Larionov.

(10) A Rayonist Manifesto was drawn up by Larionov in June 1912 and appeared in Moscow in the following year (*Luchism,* pubd. by C. A. Munter, Moscow 1913). But by then Rayonism seems to have been already given up by its two inventors.

(11) Much has been said about the influence of Futurism on the work of Larionov and Gontcharova. The two painters deny this and claim that their work was completely independent. The allegation is that Marinetti went on a propaganda mission to Russia in 1910 and exerted considerable influence there. Some critics have denied that the visit was ever made, and I have made inquiries which so far have yielded only negative results. If the journey did take place it seems to have left no trace whatever in the Russian press, whereas Marinetti's visit to Russia in the winter of 1913-1914 certainly did.

(12) *De nieuwe beweging in de schilderkunst* (*The new movement in painting*) published at Delft in 1917, and *Drie voordrachten over de nieuwe beeldende kunst* (Three lectures on recent plastic art), published at Amsterdam in 1919. These two short books are abundantly illustrated: the illustrations of the second work are accompanied by commentaries which are often very much to the point. These were excellent introductory works for the general reader, written in a lively and enthusiastic style.

(13) The aim was "to raise art into those impersonal, disinterested regions beyond time, place and space, where mathematics, poetry, and the higher arts, all come together with all that is purest and freest in man's mind and heart." (Ozenfant and Jeanneret, *Modern Painting,* p. 164). We find everywhere the same desire to create in art a kind of new quadrivium or union of the liberal arts.

(14) This brings to mind the 1918 *collages* of Arp and Sophie Taüber, which they made out of bits of paper, all cut the same size with a bookbinder's guillotine. Arp gave further information about this in *Jalons* in 1950: "Our researches into the static arose from essentially different aims from those of most of the Constructivists. We were hoping for pictures to provoke meditations,—mandalas, guide-posts. Our rods of light, like surveyors' poles, were intended to show paths into space, depth, into the infinite."

(15) Georges Vantongerloo: *L'Art et son avenir* (Art and its future), Antwerp, 1924.

(16) From a letter to Paul Citroën (in Dutch), February 1930.

(17) Van Doesburg wrote on 13 July 1930, six months before he died, "The modern painter's studio should have a mountain atmosphere of three thousand metres above sea-level, with everlasting snow; height kills off microbes." (*De Stijl,* posthumous number).

(18) M. E. Chevreul: *De l'abstraction considérée relativement aux beaux-arts et à la littérature* (Abstraction considered in its relationship to the fine arts and literature), Dijon, 1864, p. 35.

(19) *XXe siècle,* No. 3, Paris 1952.

(20) In *Fernand Léger, la forme humaine dans l'espace* (*Fernand Léger, the Human Form in Space*), Montreal 1945, pp. 73-74.

(21) In *New World of Space,* New York 1948. Le Corbusier called Mondrian "an heroic pilgrim", whose "tragic destiny" was to show the younger generation the right direction in architecture.

In his numerous writings Le Corbusier has often found some impressive literary approaches to Neo-plasticism. For example: "I am in Brittany. That pure line in the distance is the limit of the ocean and the sky: a vast horizontal plane stretches towards me. This sovereign repose fills me with a voluptuous pleasure. . . There are a few rocks on the right. The undulating sandy beaches enchant me with their most gentle modulation on the horizontal plane. Suddenly I stop walking. A sensational event has taken place between the horizon and the eye: a vertical rock, a slab of granite is standing erect like a menhir, its verticality making a right-angle with the sea's horizon. It crystallises and fixes the whole area. This is the place where a man must stop, because there is a total symphony, there are wonderful relationships, nobility. The vertical fixes the sense and direction of the horizontal. The one comes to life because of the other. Here are synthetic powers. I pause to reflect: why am I so disturbed ? Why has the same emotion occurred in my life in other circumstances and in other forms ? I visualise the Parthenon, its sublime entablature with all its overwhelming power. I think, by way of contrast or comparison, of other works full of sensibility but which are so to speak aborted, unfulfilled, such as the Butter Tower at Rouen, or flamboyant arches in which so much thinly-spread genius was sacrificed without achieving brilliance, for instance the brilliance of the bronze pendentives of the Parthenon on the Acropolis. Then, with nothing but two strokes I draw this *place of all measurements* and say to myself 'There, that's enough: such poverty, such want of means, and yet what sublime limits they are. Everything is there, the keys to poems of architecture. Nothing but distance and height, and they are all that is needed.' " (*Cercle et Carré,* No. 3, 30 June 1930).

(22) *Abstraction-Création* at one time had over 400 members, half of whom were in Paris.

87

(23) "In 1919, through Feininger, the influence of the Dutch *Stijl* group began to permeate through the Bauhaus. Two years later Doesburg, the leader of the *Stijl*, began to divide his time between Weimar and Berlin. His presence at Weimar brought about a veritable revolution: from the mysticism and transcendentalism of the Expressionists the Bauhaus turned towards clarity, discipline and the desire for a consciously developed style in architecture and the allied arts which the Dutch movement had already initiated.

Within a few months, Gropius, who had been engaged in designing a picturesque wooden block house with Cubist decorations, remodelled the theatre at Jena under the influence of the *Stijl* and sent to the Chicago Tribune competition a skyscraper project of extreme simplicity." (Alfred H. Barr jr.: *Cubism and Abstract art,* p. 156.)

(24) For a few years Mondrian already had two other direct disciples in Europe: the Englishwoman Miss Marlow Moss and the French artist Jean Gorin. An important date in Mondrian's life was when Miss Katherine Dreier visited him early in 1926. It was thanks to her that his work was introduced to America. In the same year Miss Dreier wrote in the illustrated catalogue of the 'Société Anonyme', "Holland has produced three great painters who, although they were a logical expression of their country, managed to rise above it by their strength of personality. The first was Rembrandt, the second Van Gogh, the third is Mondrian. We can realise Rembrandt's powerful personality by comparing him with other men of his time, with men as great as Franz Hals. In the same way Van Gogh stands out in strong contrasts to Mauve, Israëls and other quite good painters of his epoch. And now we have Mondrian, starting off from a strongly individualistic expression and achieving a clarity which was never reached before him."

(25) *Album de dix lithographies originales en couleurs,* edited by Jacques Goldschmidt, Paris 1950.

(26) A previous exhibition entitled *Réalités Nouvelles* had already been held in 1939, at the Charpentier gallery in Paris. This was organised by Mme Van Doesburg and Fredo Sidès.

(27) Of course writing, in China and Japan, has always been regarded as one of the fine arts. In the 11th century Kuo Hsi stated categorically that there is no difference between the study of writing and that of painting. It is generally thought in China that the art of painting subjects from nature was invented by Wang Hsichih, who is regarded as the greatest of calligraphers. (See S. Macdonald-Wright, *Magazine of Art,* New York, Oct. 1919.)

(28) *Is there a California School?* in "Art News", New York, January 1956.

Appendices

Among his papers Severini has kept the manuscript copy of the following manifesto, written during the winter of 1913-1914 and originally intended for publication in the review *Lacerba*. It is here printed for the first time and clearly shows how close Futurism, as indeed was also the Cubist movement of the same period, then was to a purely abstract conception of art: *Objects no longer exist. . . The important thing is not to represent the speeding motor-car, but to represent the speed of the motor-car.*

NEO-FUTURIST PLASTIC ART

Analogies.

In achieving that higher type of Impressionism summed up in the expression : object + atmosphere, Futurist painting and sculpture have brought the illustrious wheel of Impressionism full circle.

A plastic art that is both quantitative and qualitative should succeed an art that is qualitative only, and hence completely dynamic.

THE WHOLE UNIVERSE MUST BE CONTAINED WITHIN THE WORK OF ART. OBJECTS NO LONGER EXIST.

We must forget external reality and our knowledge of its integral values, in order to CREATE those new dimensions whose order and extent in the universe are to be determined by our regenerate sensitivity.

We shall thus be able to express not only those plastic emotive responses which are relative to an EMOTIVE ATMOSPHERE, but also those which are bound up with the whole universe, since reality considered as a TOTAL

FORCE (or a dynamic absolute) encloses the universe within an infinite circle ranging from affinities, analogies and resemblances to opposites and specific differences.

Thus, the sensation produced in us by a reality which we recognise as being square in shape and blue in colour may be expressed plastically by its complementary shapes and colours, in other words by rounded shapes and shades of blue.

For henceforth, external reality and our perception of it no longer determine plastic expression.   As for the action of memory on our sensory faculties, only the memory of the feeling subsists and not that of the cause which engendered it.

The effect of MEMORY in the work of art will thus be not only that of an AGENT OF PLASTIC INTENSIFICATION but also that of a DIRECT EMOTIVE CAUSE independent of any *unity of time and place.*

(Since 1911, in my painting "Souvenirs de Voyage"—the first Futurist composition in Paris, February 1912—I have envisaged the possibility of widening the horizon of plastic sensitivity to the infinite by totally destroying the unity of time and place with a painting of memory which embraced in a single plastic entity realities perceived in Tuscany, on the Alps, in Paris, etc.).

But it should not be thought that memory, either as an agent of plastic intensification or as a direct emotive cause, should be a morbid and sentimental exaltation of things far off in time and space.   All these old nostalgic trappings we leave to the literature enamoured of the past, and go on to consider MEMORY from the point of view of PHYSICAL AND EMOTIVE SENSATION.

In any case it would be impossible to separate emotion from memory without arresting the fleeting continuity of matter.

Since both living beings and things by equal right go to make up universal motion, it is impossible to envisage any reality as separate from its wider dynamic implications which are perpetuated precisely by the memories, affinities and contrasts that it arouses SIMULTANEOUSLY within us.

These memories, affinities and contrasts are so many analogical realities or qualitative continuities directing our sensory awareness towards the universal dynamic totality of the reality in question.

Thus the spiral forms and contrasts of yellow and blue that our intuition may have discovered one evening as we felt ourselves carried away by the movements of a dancer, may be rediscovered later, either by affinity or by contrast, in the spiral flight of an aeroplane or the glinting reflections of the sea.

In the same way, certain shapes and colours which express the sensations of sound, smell, light, heat, speed, etc., relative, for example, to the reality: "transatlantic liner" may also express by plastic analogy the same sensations aroused in us by the far-removed reality: "Galeries Lafayette".

The reality "transatlantic liner" is thus linked to the reality "Galeries Lafayette" (and each reality linked to its *specific difference*) by its qualitative continuities which travel throughout the Universe on the wireless waves of our sensibility.

Here then is a complex realism which TOTALLY does away with the integrality of matter—the latter is now considered SOLELY at its MAXIMUM vitality and may be expressed thus : dancer = aeroplane = sea; or Galeries Lafayette = transatlantic liner, etc.

This system of complementary images which I intend to use is not designed to result in the "metaphor", i.e. the designation of one thing by comparison with or opposition to another thing.   My intention is to create a new reality: out of the DANCER and the AEROPLANE is engendered the SEA.

To arrive at a desired reality through the comparison or contrast of two other realities is one of the techniques proper to poetry; in the same way, through the use of *two complementary colours,* a third colour—the colour desired—may be obtained.

In music also, fifths, fourths and thirds are simply juxtapositions of notes designed to produce a given chord or harmony.

Through this purely qualitative and universal approach to reality, and by these "appropriate means", both matter itself and its volition may be simultaneously expressed at the maximum of their intensive and expansive activity.

This, moreover, brings the plastic emotive response back to its physical and spontaneous origin: LIFE, from which any intellectual consideration as such would tend to separate it.

In this interpenetration of planes and simultaneous representation of atmosphere as used in Futurist plastic art, we have shown the reciprocal influence of objects and the vitality-atmosphere of matter (intensity and expansiveness of the object-atmosphere).   With qualitative Neo-Futurist art I extend to the infinite the field of these influences, continuities, volitions and contrasts of which the SINGLE FORM, CREATED by my sensibility, is the expression of the absolute vitality of matter or of universal dynamism.

It is difficult to establish laws for the various means of expression relative to the individuality of each artist. Nevertheless, these are the technical bases, already partially employed by us, but intensified and developed in relation to the UNIVERSAL PLASTIC SENSIBILITY OF NEO-FUTURIST ART.

With Regard to Form.

1. Simultaneous contrast of lines, planes and volumes. Contrasts by groups of analogous forms arranged in spherical expansion. Constructive interpenetration.

2. Rhythmic arabesque-type construction, consciously ordered so as to point to a new qualitative architecture, composed exclusively of quantitative qualities.

3. Dynamic composition open towards space in all directions, vertically, or of rectangular, square or spherical form.

4. Rejection of the straight line, which is static and dead unless it is duly vitalised by contrasts. Rejection of parallel lines.

With Regard to Colour.

1. Exclusive use of pure prismatic colours in simultaneously contrasting zones, or in groups of analogous colours, either separately or in sequence.

(The system of complementaries in general, and the divisionist use of analogous colours, constitute the colour analogy technique. Through these analogies is obtained the *maximum intensity of light, heat, musicality and constructive and optical dynamism*).

2. The use, as means of *realistic intensification,* of onomatopoeic signs, of unattached verbal expressions and of all possible kinds of matter.

My need for absolute realism has led me to model shapes in relief on my pictures and to colour my plastic compositions with all the colours of the prism arranged in spherical expansion.

All sensations, when they take on plastic form, are expressed concretely in the sensation *light*—they can therefore be expressed only by *all the colours of the prism*.

To paint forms other than with all the colours of the spectrum would mean that one of the most important motions of matter, that of *irradiation,* would be arrested.

The coloured expression of the sensation *light,* within the context of

94

spherical expansion in Futurist painting, can only be centrifugal or centripetal in relation to the organic construction of the work. Thus, for example, the plastic entity: Dancer = Sea, would for preference be expressed with light irradiation (forms and colours, and light) moving outwards from the centre towards the surrounding space (centrifugal irradiation).

This is also relative according to the plastic sensibility of each individual artist, but it is of essential importance to destroy the principle of using light, localised tones and shadow to show the action of light on natural objects—a principle which belonged to the relativity of momentary and accidental light phenomena.

I have given to this new plastic expression of light the name: SPHERICAL EXPANSION OF LIGHT IN SPACE.

The spherical expansion of colour may thus be obtained, in perfect harmony with the spherical expansion of forms.

For example, if the centre of a group of forms is *yellow,* the colours will follow outwards in sequence (in spherical expansion), from colour analogy to colour analogy, until the complementary colour *blue,* or even if necessary, until *black* (absence of light) is reached, or vice versa.

Obviously it is possible to have, in the one picture or plastic entity, several centrifugal and centripetal groups in simultaneous and dynamic competition with one another.

One of the most important scientific advances which have contributed to the transformation of our sensibility and its canalisation towards our Futurist conclusions is no doubt that which has given rise to the conception of SPEED.

Speed has given us a new notion of *space* and *time,* and consequently of *life* itself. The plastic art of our time must therefore be *characterised* by a STYLISATION OF SPEED, which is the most immediate and most expressive manifestation of our modern way of living.

Naturally, what we have said with regard to *motion* in general, is equally true with regard to *speed ;* in other words, the important thing is not to represent the *speeding motor-car,* but the *speed* of the motor-car.

In the interests of identifying the work of art to the greatest possible extent with modern life, I consider it desirable that, just as we rejected the nude in our first manifesto of Futurist painting, the HUMAN BODY, STILL LIFE SUBJECTS and RURAL SCENES should be rejected AS CENTRES OF EMOTIVE INTEREST.

For it is my opinion that a complex of realistic and dynamic elements such as: aeroplane in flight + man + landscape; speeding tramcar or motor-car + boulevard + travellers; or underground railway carriage + station-posters-lights + crowd, etc. and all their qualitative prolongations and specific differences, constitute infinitely vaster and more interesting sources of emotion and plastic lyricism.

But, in addition, the age-old and academic distinctions of pictorial form and sculptural form must also be done away with.

Plastic dynamism, the *absolute vitality of matter,* can only be expressed by *form-colour entities* at a *maximum degree* of relief, depth, intensity and light irradiation, that is, by painting and sculpture united in a single plastic creation.

I therefore predict the *end of the picture and the statue.* These art forms, even employed in the most genuine innovating spirit, limit the creative freedom of the artist. They have within themselves their own destinies: museums and collectors' galleries, in other words, cemeteries.

THE PLASTIC CREATIONS OF THE NEO-FUTURISTS WILL LIVE AND WILL COMPLEMENT ONE ANOTHER IN ARCHITECTURAL ENTITIES, AND ALONG WITH THESE THEY WILL TAKE PART IN THE COOPERATIVE ACTIVITY OF THE EXTERNAL WORLD OF WHICH THEY REPRESENT THE SPECIFIC ESSENTIAL.

GINO SEVERINI,
Rome, 1913-1914.

.

THE NON-REPRESENTATIONAL WORLD

By "Suprematism" I mean the supremacy of pure sensibility in art.

From the point of view of the Suprematists, the external appearances of nature are of no interest whatever; the essential thing is the artist's sensibility as such, regardless of the surroundings which brought it into being.

The so-called "concretisation" of sensibility signifies, in actual fact, the "concretisation" *of the reflection* of a particular sensibility by a natural representation.   A representation of this sort is of no value in Suprematist art, and not only in Suprematist art but in any form of art; for the lasting and authentic value of a work of art (to whatever "school" it owes allegiance) lies solely in its expression of sensibility.

Academic naturalism, the naturalism of the Impressionists, "Cézann-ism", Cubism, etc.—all these approaches are to a certain extent only a variety of dialectic methods which, in themselves, have no determining influence whatever on the real value of the work of art.

The representation of an object (that is, the object regarded as the raison d'être of the representation) is something which, as such, has nothing at all to do with art.   The use of an object in a work of art, however, may not preclude that work from having a high artistic value.

Nevertheless, for the Suprematist, the means of expression will always be that given element which makes it possible for the sensibility to express itself as sensibility in all its fullness, without any reference to conventional representationalism. For him, the object in itself means nothing.

Sensibility is the only thing that counts, and it is by this means that art, in Suprematism, arrives at pure expression without representation.

All that has gone to make up the representative structure of life and art—ideas, notions, images—has been rejected by the artist so that he may give his undivided attention to pure sensibility.

The art of the past which, at least judging by its outward appearance, owed it allegiance to Church and State, must awaken to the pure (non-applied) art of Suprematism to find a new life and to build a new world, the world of sensibility.

When, in 1913, I made my desperate attempt to deliver art of the dead weight of the object, I sought refuge in the shape of a square and I exhibited a picture which showed nothing else but a black square on a white ground. The critics, and with them the public, burst into lamentations, crying: "All that we loved is lost—we are in a desert, faced with a black square on a white ground !"

They tried to find destructive words to blot out the symbol of the *desert* and to see in the "dead square" the loved image of representative reality and sentiment.

The perfect square seemed to both critics and public incomprehensible and dangerous. What else could one expect ?

The ascent to the summit of non-figurative art is difficult and full of torment—yet it is satisfying just the same. Accustomed things fall away gradually, and at every step objects fade further and further into the distance, until finally the world of pre-conceived notions—all that we loved and all that we depended on for life—completely disappears from sight.

No more images of reality, no more idealised representations—nothing but a desert !

But this desert is full of the spirit of non-objective sensibility pervading all.

I too was filled with a kind of timidity and I held back to the point of anguish when the time came to leave "the world of will and representation" in which I had lived and created—when the time came to leave the authenticity in which I had believed.

But the feeling of satisfaction which I experienced as a result of my liberation from the object drew me further and further on into the desert to the point where there was no other authenticity but that of sensibility alone—and so it was that sensibility came to be the very substance of my life.

The square that I had exhibited was not an empty square—it was the sensibility of the absence of any object.

I realised that the object and the representation of it had been held as identical with sensibility and I understood the falsehood of the world of will and representation.

Could the milk-bottle be the symbol of the milk?

Suprematism is the rediscovery of pure art which, in the course of time, had become hidden by the accumulation of objects.

It seems to me that the painting of Raphael and Rubens and Rembrandt, etc., is no longer, for contemporary critics and contemporary society, more than the "concretisation" of the innumerable objects which hide its value real, i.e. its causal sensibility. People admire in these works only the virtuosity of the figurative accomplishment. If it were possible to abstract from the works of the great masters the sensibility expressed therein—i.e. their true artistic value—and to conceal it completely, society (including the critics and the connoisseurs) would not even be aware of its absence.

It is thus not surprising that my square seemed empty to such a society.

When a person claims that a work of art may be judged according to the virtuosity of the figurative accomplishment—or according to the accuracy of the illusion—and when he believes that the symbol of the causal sensibility is to be seen in the object represented, that person will never be able to partake of the truly beneficent content of the work.

Society as a whole thus remains convinced that art is bound to disappear once it turns its back on the representation of that so dearly loved reality. And it is with a presentiment of disaster that society watches the widening assertion of that execrated *element of pure sensibility,* that is, of the principle of abstraction.

Art is no longer content to be the servant of Church and State, it is no longer content to be the illustrator of customs and costumes, it is no longer willing to have anything to do with objects as such, and it believes that it is capable of existing of itself and for itself independently of the object, independently of " that source of life which has so long stood the test of time".

Casimir MALEVITCH.

(From *Die Gegenstandslose Welt.* Albert Langen Verlag, Munich, 1927, pp. 65-72).

THE NEW PLASTIC APPROACH TO PAINTING

(*Note.*—This introduction gives only a brief outline of several ideas which I hope to deal with later and in more detailed fashion in a series of articles.   P. M.)

The life of a cultivated man in our time is gradually being divorced from natural objects and is becoming more and more an abstract existence.

Since natural (external) phenomena are becoming more and more automatic, the vital attention turns increasingly to the things of the inner life.   The life of the truly modern man is neither purely materialistic nor purely sentimental; it appears rather as a more autonomous existence of the human mind in the process of achieving a greater degree of consciousness of itself.

Modern man—although one in body, mind and soul—shows a change in consciousness: all the expressions of life appear in a new light, a more positively abstract light.

The same is true in the world of art.   Art is to become the product of another duality in man: the product of a cultivated exteriority and of a more conscious and deepened interiority.   As a pure representation of the human spirit, art will express itself in a purified aesthetic form, i.e. in an abstract form.

The truly modern artist is consciously aware of the abstractness of a feeling for beauty; he consciously recognises that a feeling for beauty is cosmic and universal. The inevitable corollary of this conscious recognition is the adoption of an abstract plastic approach—man clinging solely to that which is universal.

This new plastic approach cannot therefore take the form of natural or concrete representation, although it must be admitted that this type of representation does always show, or at least conceal within it, some indication of the universal. The new plastic approach cannot appear clothed in those things which are characteristic of particularisation, that is, in natural form and colour. It should, on the contrary, find its expression in the abstraction of all form and colour, in other words in the straight line and clearly defined primary colours.

These universal means of expression were discovered in modern painting by the gradual and logical development of the abstraction of form and colour. Once the solution was found, there appeared, as if spontaneously, the exact representation of pure relationships, and in these relationships the essential, fundamental factor of all plastic feeling for beauty.

The new plastic approach is thus an aesthetic relationship perfectly represented. The artist of today constructs this plastic approach, in painting, as a logical consequence of all the plastic theories of the past—and I say in painting advisedly because painting is the art form least tied up with contingent factors. The whole of modern life, as it becomes increasingly profound, may find its true reflection in the picture. In painting—painting that creates a picture, and not decorative painting—the naturalistic plastic approach itself, and also its means of expression, are "interiorised" by their adoption of the trend towards abstraction. Decorative painting, however, has never been able to achieve more than a generalisation of natural form and colour.

Thus, through creative painting, the sensitive quality of the aesthetic plastic appreciation of relationships finds its lucid expression.

In this art of painting—which embraces within itself existing decorative art, or rather, which becomes the true decorative art—the free expression of relationships will no doubt still remain relative and limited. However unique and at one with itself the real nature of all art may be, however clearly the sensibility of the aesthetic plastic appreciation of relationships may be expressed in all the arts, not all the branches of the arts can express this clear relationship with equal effectiveness.

For, though the content of all the arts is one and the same, the possibilities of expression in each art are different. These possibilities of expression should be found in each branch of the arts within the specific context of that branch and should remain one with that context.

Each art has its own particular accent and its own means of expression, and it is in this that the existence of the different branches of art finds its justification. The particular accent of painting may be defined as the most logical and most rational expression of pure relationships. For it is the peculiar privilege of painting to be able to express these relationships *freely*. This means that these means of expression (as the outcome of their own inherent logic) make it possible for the extreme "one" and the extreme "other" to be made explicit by their positional relationship alone, without adopting any form or any semblance of enclosed form, as is seen in architecture.

In painting, the duality of the relationship may be expressed by isolated positions, which is not possible in architecture or in sculpture. And it is for this reason that painting may be said to be perhaps the purest of the plastic arts.

The untrammelled autonomy of the means of expression is the particular privilege of painting. The liberty of the sister arts, sculpture and architecture, is more restricted. The other branches of art are even less at liberty to exercise a predetermining influence on the means of expression.

Painting, without going beyond the limitations of the means of expression proper to it, is still capable of determining clearly, and even of interiorising these means of expression.

Despite all this, the new plastic approach still remains strictly within the realm of pure painting—its means of expression still remain form and colour, although these are completely interiorised; the straight line and flat colour are still purely pictorial means of expression.

Whatever its method of expression, each art tends to become, through the gradual cultivation of the human mind, an exact representation of balanced relationships. For the balanced relationship is, in fact, the purest representation of that universality, that harmony and that unity which are the essential qualities of the mind.

If then we concentrate all our attention on the balanced relationship, we shall be able to *see* the unity which exists in natural objects. This unity is not however obviously apparent. But even if no exact expression can ever be given of this unity, all representation can at least be reduced to its terms. Thus the exact representation of unity can be expressed; it must be expressed since it is not visible in concrete reality.

In external nature it can be observed that all relationships are subservient to a single primordial relationship: that of the *extreme one* vis-à-vis the *extreme other*. The abstract plastic approach to these relationships represents the primordial relationship specifically by the positional duality which constitutes the right angle. This positional relationship is the most balanced of all since it provides a perfectly harmonious expression of the relationship of the extreme one and the extreme other, and at the same time incorporates within itself all the other relationships.

If we conceive of these two extremes as being the manifestation of interiority and exteriority, we shall see that in the new plastic approach the link between spirit and life is unbroken; thus, far from considering this approach as a negation of the essential vitality of life, we shall see in it the reconciliation of the duality between matter and spirit.

If, through contemplation, we come to the realisation that the existence of any one thing is aesthetically defined for us by a series of equivalences, this is possible because the idea of this manifestation of unity is already potentially present in our consciousness. And our individual consciousness is simply a particularised aspect of universal consciousness, which is one.

If the consciousness of man is moving away from the indeterminate towards what is positive and determined, the sense of unity in man will also be moving towards what is positive and determined.

If unity is contemplated in a precise and determinate manner, the attention will be drawn solely towards the universal, with the result that the particular in art will disappear—as has already been shown in painting. For the universal can only be expressed purely when the particular is no longer present to obstruct it. It is only then that universal consciousness (i.e. intuition), which is the basis of all art, can be rendered directly, giving birth to a purified type of artistic expression.

This expression, however, cannot be expected to come into being before its time. For it is the consciousness of the time which determines the nature of artistic expression which, in turn, reflects the consciousness of the time. The only truly living art form of the present time is that which gives expression to the consciousness of the present—or of the future.

The new means of expression (employed in pure plastic art) bear witness to a new vision. Though it may be said that the aim of all the arts is the plastic appreciation of relationships, it is only now that, through a more conscious vision, we have been able to attain to a clearer expression of this aim, and it is precisely because of the new attitude to the plastic means at our disposal that this has become possible.

The plastic means of expression should be in complete harmony with what they have to express. If they are called upon to be a direct expression of the universal, they themselves cannot be any other than universal, that is, abstract.

In composition, the artist has complete liberty, for as long a time as may be necessary, so that his subjective consciousness may express itself in a certain measure.

The rhythm of the relationships between colours and measures brings out what is absolute in the relativity of time and space.

Thus the new plastic approach is dualistic in composition. By virtue of its exact plastic appreciation of cosmic relationships it is a direct expression of the universal. By virtue of the rhythm and the material reality of its plastic technique it is an expression of the subjective consciousness of the artist as an individual.

It is thus a revelation of universal beauty, without however implying any negation of the general human element.

Piet MONDRIAN.

(*De Stijl*, No. 1, October, 1917. From the French translation of the original Dutch by M. S.)

Chronological table of abstract art

	FRANCE	RUSSIA	GERMANY
1910	Analytical Cubism.		Kandinsky's first abstract wat colour. *Der Sturm* founded by Walden.
1911	Delaunay's first *Windows*.	"Rayonnisme" (Larionov and Gontcharova).	Friendship of Franz Marc a Kandinsky. *Der Blaue Reiter*.
1912	Mondrian in Paris. Delaunay: Simultaneous Rhythms. Kupka's works at the Salon des Indépendants.	Cubo-Futurism (Malevitch).	Kandinsky: *Uber das Geistige der Kunst*. Arp's visit to Kandinsky.
1913	Notable abstract works by Picabia. The American Synchromists. Léger—Contrasting Shapes.	Advent of Suprematism (Malevitch) and of Constructivism (Tatlin). Lecture tour by Marinetti.	Kandinsky: *Rückblicke*. *Herbstsalon* of "Der Sturm".
1914	Synthetic Cubism. Larionov and Gontcharova Exhibition.	Return of Kandinsky to Moscow.	Death of Macke on the West Front.
1915		Suprematist manifesto.	
1916			Death of Franz Marc on the We ern Front.
1917		Return of Gabo and Pevsner to Moscow.	
1918	Death of Apollinaire.		
1919	Freundlich's first abstract works Return of Mondrian to Paris.	Lissitzky: *Proun*. Kandinsky teaching at the Moscow Academy.	Founding of the Bauhaus at W mar. Dada demonstrations in Colog and Berlin.

SWITZERLAND	HOLLAND	U. S. A.	
in Weggis.	Mondrian working in Zealand—exhibition in Amsterdam with Sluyters.		**1910**
	Mondrian—departure for Paris in late December.		**1911**
			1912
		Armory Show. Picabia and Marcel Duchamp in New York.	**1913**
	Return of Mondrian to Holland in July.	Publication of *291*.	**1914**
p in Zurich—first abstract works.	Mondrian—large abstract drawings; meeting with van Doesburg.	W. H. Wright: *Modern Painting, Its Tendency and Meaning.*	**1915**
vent of Dadaism. phie Taeuber—first abstract works.	Mondrian—meetings with van der Leck in the village of Laren. First abstract works of Huszar and van Doesburg.		**1916**
da publications. nco—polychromatic reliefs.	October: first number of *De Stijl* published. First abstract works of Vantongerloo.	MacDonald-Wright—exhibition at Stieglitz gallery.	**1917**
p and Sophie Taeuber—jointly executed "collages". ara—lecture on abstract art at the Kunsthaus, Zurich.	Abstract works of Mondrian in the Kröller collection at The Hague.		**1918**
cabia in Zurich. da demonstration in the Kaufleuten, Zurich.	Mondrian—essays in *De Stijl*. Van Doesburg—essays printed by various Dutch publishers.		**1919**

	FRANCE	RUSSIA	GERMANY
1920	*L'Esprit Nouveau* founded by Paul Dermée. *Néo-Plasticisme* published by Mondrian. Arp and Tzara in Paris.	Cabo and Pevsner: *Realist Manifesto*.	Klee teaching at the Bauhaus. Publication of Marc's letters drawings.
1921	Dadaist demonstrations in Paris.	Constructivist exhibition. Abstract art discredited. Exodus of artists.	Van Doesburg at the Bauhaus. First abstract works of Moh Nagy. Abstract films of Eg ling and Richter.
1922			Kandinsky teaching at the B haus. Marinetti in Berlin.
1923	Pevsner in Paris. *De Stijl* exhibition shown by Léonce Rosenberg.		Schwitters—publication of periodical *Merz*. *G* (Gestaltung) published by Ri ter and Lissitzky.
1925	"L'Art d'Aujourd'hui" exhibition. Katherine Dreier—visit to Mondrian.		Mondrian: "*Neue Gestaltung*" Opening of abstract art sect at the Hanover Museum.
1926	"Cahiers d'Art" founded. Arp in Paris. *La Chatte* produced by Diaghilev.		Bauhaus moved to Dessau. Kandinsky: *Punkt und Linie Fläche*.
1927	Vantongerloo in Paris. Dermée and Seuphor: *Documents Internationaux de l'Esprit Nouveau*.		Malevitch: *Die Gegenstands Welt*.
1928	Completion of the "Aubette" in Strasbourg (Arp, van Doesburg and Sophie Taeuber).	Return of Lissitzky to Moscow.	
1930	Seuphor and Torrès-Garcia: *Cercle et Carré*. Van Doesburg: *Art Concret*. Kandinsky exhibition.		
1931	Delaunay—new abstract rhythms. Cahiers d'Art: *De l'Art Abstrait*.		Kandinsky exhibition in Berlin
1932	First album of *Abstraction-Création* Group.		
1933	Kandinsky and Domela take up residence in Paris.		Bauhaus closed. Abstract art in disfavour ("dege erate" art). Exodus of artis

SWITZERLAND	HOLLAND	U. S. A.	
		Société Anonyme founded by Katherine Dreier, with Duchamp and Man Ray.	**1920**
	Van Doesburg: *Classique, Baroque, Moderne.*		**1921**
	Schwitters in Holland. *Mecano* published by van Doesburg.		**1922**
		W. H. Wright: *The Future of Painting.*	**1923**
rp and Lissitzky: *Les Ismes de l'Art.*	"Élémentarisme" (Van Doesburg). Withdrawal of Mondrian from *De Stijl.*		**1925**
Die Neue Welt" published in "*Das Werk*".	*The Next Call* published and abstract monotypes composed by the painter-typographer H. N. Werkman.	Exhibition of abstract art at Brooklyn Museum.	**1926**
	The periodical *I 10* published by Müller-Lehning.	*Gallery of Living Art* (Gallatin Collection) opened to the public at New York University.	**1927**
			1928
			1930
eath of van Doesburg at Davos.			**1931**
			1932
		Hélion: *The Evolution of Abstract Art* (Gallatin).	**1933**

	FRANCE	RUSSIA	GERMANY
1935	Delaunay: *Les Rythmes Sans Fin.* Reth Exhibition.	Death of Malevitch in Leningrad.	
1936	Magnelli—return to abstract art.		
1937	Periodical *Plastique* published by Arp and Sophie Taeuber.		
1938	Freundlich Exhibition. Departure of Mondrian for London. Zervos: *Histoire de l'Art Contemporain.*		
1940			
1941	Death of Delaunay.	Death of Lissitzky in Moscow.	
1942			
1943			
1944	Death of Kandinsky.		
1945	*Art concret* Exhibition.		
1946	Salon des Réalités Nouvelles inaugurated.		
1947	Magnelli Exhibition. Retrospective exhibition of Delaunay's works shown by Carré.		Domnick: *Abstrakte Malerei.* Baumeister: *Das Unbekannte in d Kunst.*

PART II

Dictionary of Abstract Painting

A

ABNER Raymond (b. Cairo, 1924). Educated in Cairo. Works exhibited at Cairo Salons of 1941 and 1942. Private exhibition, Aladin gallery, 1948. Worked in London in 1945 and Paris in 1946. Began studies at the Beaux-Arts but left, on the advice of Matisse, to study under Othon Friesz and Fernand Léger. Took up abstract art in 1952. Works shown in various Salons in Paris, and also in Yugoslavia and Venezuela. Private exhibition, Galerie Denise René, Paris, 1956. Believes himself to be the only non-figurative Egyptian painter. Lives in Paris.

ACCARDI Carla (b. Trapani, Italy, 1924). Took part in group exhibitions in Florence and Milan, and also at the Biennale in Venice in 1948. Private exhibition, Galerie Stadler, Paris, 1956. Graphic signs inscribed direct on black ground. Now living in Rome.

ACHT René-Charles (b. Basle, 1920). Studies at Basle Academy. First private exhibition Galerie Moos, Geneva, 1947. Lived in Scandinavia 1947-1950. Visited France, Italy, Holland. Abstract works since 1948. Took part in Salon des Réalités Nouvelles, Paris, 1951 and 1952. Work exhibited Basle (1940), Helsinki (1947), Copenhagen (1951), Zurich (1951) and Milan (1952). Now living in Basle.

ACKERMAN Paul (b. Jassy, Roumania, 1908). Came to France at the age of 4 years. Studies, Faculté des Lettres, Faculté de Droit (University of Paris). Doctor of Laws. Began painting at Fernand Léger's Académie Moderne. Encouraged by Bonnard. Several private exhibitions at the Galerie Creuze, Paris, since 1947. Series of abstract works painted in 1944 but never exhibited. New phase of abstract art (large polychromatic fantasies) in 1955. Private exhibition, Galeria dell' Grattacielo, Milan, 1956. Lives in Paris. In giving his talent full rein after a long apprenticeship, Paul Ackerman has proved himself to be a painter of astonish-

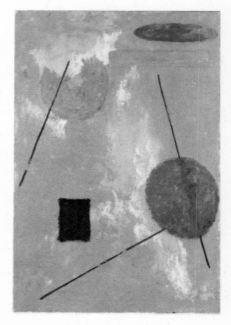

ABNER. ESCAPE. 1955.

ingly fertile inspiration. One is frequently reminded of the more unusual compositions of Klee. Has succeeded in combining graphic line (reminiscent of Chinese calligraphy) and plastic texture.

ACKERMANN Max (b. Berlin, 1887). Studied under Henri van de Velde at Weimar. Further studies at the Academies of Dresden and Munich, and under Adolf Hölzel at Stuttgart. In Paris and Normandy in 1926. Professor at Stuttgart in 1930. Debarred from exhibiting and (in 1936) from teaching under the Nazi regime. Numerous exhibitions in Germany after 1945. Now living in Stuttgart. Ackermann calls his art "absolute painting".

AFRO. GOUACHE. 1955.
Private Collection.

Is a very cultivated painter and seems to wish to found a personal style on the laws of music; is haunted by the ideas of theme, counterpoint, movement, melody and accompaniment. "The beginning and the end of Ackermann's painting is the quest for laws which make possible the composition of colours within order and ordered movement" (Kurt Leonhard). — *Bibl.* Dominck: *Abstrakte Malerei* (Stuttgart 1947).

AFRO Basadella (b. Udine, Italy, 1912). First exhibition, "Il Milione" gallery, Milan, in 1920. First influenced by Cubism. Gradually turned to abstract art which he now practises with a vigorous feeling for colour and a suppleness of form typical of the cultivated painter. Visited New York in 1950 and exhibited at the Viviano Gallery. Now living in Rome.

AGAM Jacob Gipstein (b. Israel, 1928). Son of a country Rabbi. Studied at "Bezabeel" Art School, Jerusalem, and later (in 1951) at the Atelier d'Art Abstrait in Paris. Visited Italy, Holland, Belgium, Switzerland. Private exhibition, Galerie Craven, Paris, 1953, with pictures with movable sections. Took part in the "Mouvement" exhibition at the Galerie Denise René, Paris, 1955. During the same year he produced a number of experimental abstract films. A further exhibition of his work was held in 1956, at the Galerie Denise René. He is now living in Paris. Agam is at the same time artist and inventor—his works with sliding or pivoting sections are remarkable both for their ingenuity and freshness of colour. The shapes used are geometrical but extremely varied. He also produces paintings on wood with triangular facets which change colour (and warmth of tone) as they are viewed from left, right or centre. All these experiments (or divertissements) might be used to good effect in architecture.

AGAM. PICTURE WITH ADJUSTABLE
MOVEMENT. 1954.
Galerie Denise René, Paris.

AGUAYO (b. Sotillo de la Ribera, Spain, 1926). Has been painting since 1945. Arrived in Paris in 1952. Exhibition Galerie Jeanne Bucher (Paris) 1955, with heavily impasted abstract works. Now living in Paris.

ALBERS Josef (b. Bottrop, Westphalia, 1888). Berlin Academy 1913-1915, then in Essen and Munich. Student at Bauhaus, Weimar, then professor at Bauhaus when transferred to Dessau (1925-1933). From 1933 to 1950 professor at Black Mountain College, N. Carolina, U.S.A. Since 1955 professor at Yale University, New Haven. Has stayed long periods in South America and Mexico. Numerous exhibitions in the United States. Now living in New Haven, U.S.A. The dominant feature of Albers' art is his surprise effects gained with the use of the most pure and tranquil means. Demonstrates the infinite variety of motifs which can be obtained from rectilinear geometry. — Bibl. *American Abstract Artists* (New York, 1946); *Collection of the Société Anonyme* (New Haven, 1950); "*Spirale 5*" (Berne, 1955).

ALCOPLEY Name adopted by Dr. Alfred L. Copley (b. Dresden, 1910). Went to the United States in 1937. Became American citizen. Numerous exhibitions in New York, Germany, Switzerland, Holland. In Paris since 1952. Took part in the Salon des Réalités Nouvelles, 1953-1955. Exhibitions of drawings at the Rose Fried Gallery (New York) in 1955, in company with Sebro Hasegawa and Michel Seuphor. Work shown in Amsterdam (Stedelijk Museum), Brussels (Palais des Beaux-Arts) and Paris (Galerie Bing). Alcopley's work belongs to the great calli-

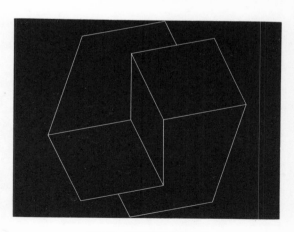

ALBERS. COMPOSITION. 1955.
Max Bill Collection, Zurich.

graphic movement which originated in the East but which counts among its exponents such American artists as Tobey, Kline and Tomlin. His drawings, often of very small format, have a graphic quality that is at the same time substantial and delicate and of undeniable charm. — Bibl. *Bokubi* No 16, Sept. 1952 (Kyôtô, Japan); Seuphor: *Écritures, Dessins d'Alcopley*, "Les Nourritures Terrestres" (Paris 1954); Seuphor: *Deux Peintres Américains,* Galerie Bing (Paris 1956).

ALECHINSKY Pierre (b. Brussels, 1927). Studied at the School of Architecture and Decorative Arts, Brussels. Took part several times in a group exhibition at the Galerie Maeght, Paris. Founder of the "Cobra" movement and the review of the same name in Brussels. Worked with S. W. Hayter at *Atelier 17.* Private exhibitions at Amsterdam, Paris (Galerie Nina Dausset, 1954) and Brussels (Palais des Beaux-Arts, 1955). Visited Japan in 1955. Now living in Paris. Alechinsky's best canvases are surfaces covered with a compact conglomeration of abstract signs packed one

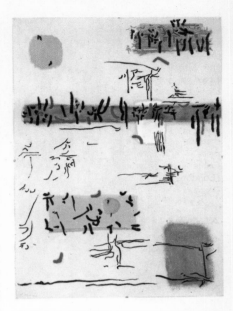

ALCOPLEY. PAINTING WITH COLLAGE. 1955.

against the other, all of equal force and giving an overall effect of discipline without excessive severity.

ALVA (b. Berlin, 1901). Studied music at the Berlin Conservatorium. Worked for some time as a typographer. Began painting while on his first visit to Paris in 1928. Took part in the Salon d'Automne, 1932. Visited Palestine and gave his first individual exhi-

ALECHINSKY. SWIMMING. 1955.
Colette Allendy Collection, Paris.

bition in 1934. First abstract work *(Dynamic Composition)* in 1945. Exhibitions in London (Leicester Gallery), New York (Meltzer Gallery), Jerusalem (Artists' House) and Brussels (Palais des Beaux-Arts). Lived in England from 1935 to 1955, then moved to Paris. Since 1935 has produced ideogrammes, sometimes abstract, sometimes figurative, always reduced to only a few lines. Colours used are evidence of a constant search for extremely refined harmonies. — *Bibl.* Herbert Read and Maurice Collis: Alva, *Recent Paintings and Drawings* (London, 1951); R. van Gindertael: *Alva* (Paris, 1955).

ALVAREZ Manuel (b. Buenos Aires, 1923). Began painting in 1942. Turned from figurative to abstract art in 1951, finally developing, two years later, a pure geometrical abstract style. Numerous exhibitions in Buenos Aires since 1949. Work shown at the Galerie La Roue (Paris) in 1954-1955

ANNENKOV Georges (b. Petropavlovsk, Kamchatka, 1894). Son of an exiled politician. In St Petersburg in 1898. Was in Paris in 1911, remaining till autumn 1913 in which year he exhibited at the Salon des Indépendants. Returned to Russia and joined the Cubo-Futurist movement of Tatlin and Malevitch. Work shown at the Dobytchina Salon and the Union of Youth. In 1918 he illustrated Alexander Blok's poem *The Twelve*. Was responsible for the open-air settings for the *Spectacles de Masses* in Petrograd in 1920. The following year in the same town, he published his famous manifesto "Le Théâtre jusqu'au Bout" (which was reproduced under this title by the review *Cimaise,* January 1955, Paris). He then exhibited, at the Institute of Pictorial Culture in Petrograd, large non-figurative group compositions with various metals, some of which were polychromatic. These works remained in Russia and it is not known what has become of them. Returned to Paris in 1925 as a representative of the U.S.S.R. at an International Congress on Drawing. After the Congress he settled in France and exhibited figurative works at various Salons. Returned to abstract principles in 1946 with a series of large compositions executed in an impetuous manner, for which he used supplementary thicknesses and

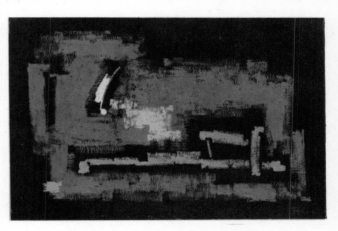

ALVA. DUO. 1955. *M. S. Collection, Paris.*

various materials (string, etc.) in relief. Now living in Paris.

APPLEBY Theodore (b. New Jersey, U.S.A., 1923). Studied with John Corneal 1938-1939. Became acquainted with Japanese engraving in Yokohama, 1945-1946. Frequently at Fernand Léger's studio in Paris, from 1950 to 1953. Took part in group exhibitions at Paris, New York, and in Portugal, and also in the Salon des Réalités Nouvelles (1950 and 1951). Now living in Paris.

ARCAY Wifredo (b. Havana, 1925). Studied painting and sculpture at the Havana Academy of Fine Arts (1943-1945). Came to Paris in 1949. Associated with Dewasne and Pillet's studio of abstract art (1950-1952). Work shown at several Salons and group exhibitions. Private exhibition at the Galerie Arnaud, Paris, 1952. Numerous serigraphy reproductions of the works of masters of abstract art executed in his studio, including those in the two albums published by *Art d'Aujourd'hui* in 1953 and 1954. Now living in Paris.

ARDEN QUIN Carmelo (b. Rivera, Uruguay, 1913). Studied under Marist brothers in Brazil. In 1930 travelled in the virgin forests of Brazil and Argentina. In Montevideo in 1935 first heard of abstract art at the lectures given by Torres-Garcia on his return from Europe. In Buenos Aires in 1938. While travelling to Rio de Janeiro in 1941, made the acquaintance of Vieira da Silva and her husband, Arpad Szenes. In January 1944 he published the sole number of the review *Arturo* and a manifesto setting in embryo all the ideas of the Madi movement. Acquainted at this time with Vincent Huidobro, Torres-Garcia, Rothfuss, Maldonado and Kosice. First exhibition of "Irregularly framed" works in 1945. In 1946, with several friends, launched the Madi movement at the Buenos Aires Institut des Études Françaises, and published several declarations of the principles of the movement. In 1948, exhibition of *Arte Madi* in the studio of the painter Martin Blaszko. Came to Paris in 1948 and in 1950 founded a scientific

Madist movement. Exhibitions in various galleries (Colette Allendy, Suzanne Michel) and regularly took part in the Salon des Réalités Nouvelles. In South America from 1953 to 1956. Now living in Paris.

Arte Madi, of which Arden-Quin is one of the leading exponents, seeks to emphasise the mobile quality of art, hence the practice of presenting pictures in irregularly shaped frames, and sometimes even in several pieces. But this is not the movement's only preoccupation—Arden-Quin writes: "Until my arrival in Paris I understood neither Mondrian nor Malevitch, least of all the Malevitch exponent of *white on white*. It was the work of Vantongerloo which made me conscious of this problem for the first time. Now, with the creation of scientific Madism, I consider white as the plastic basis of this new experiment. For me, white is not a relationship as it is for Mondrian, nor is it a void as it is for Vantongerloo—it is the plastic essence, light and space, function and creation".

ARNAL François (b. La Valette, France, 1924). Educated at the Lycée de Toulon and the Faculty of Law at Aix-en-Provence. Began painting in 1944 and took it up as a full-time activity. Has lived in Paris since 1948. Exhibitions at the Galerie Drouant-David (1950), Galerie Craven (1953). Designed immense abstract tapestries for a public building in Sarrebrück.

ARP Jean or Hans (b. Strasbourg, 1887). Immediately attracted by modern painting when he saw examples in Paris in 1904. Academy of Weimar in 1907. Académie Julian, Paris, 1908. In 1909 settled in Weggis (Switzerland), where he met Klee. In contact with Kandinsky in 1912, and joined the Blue Rider group, Munich, 1912-1913. In Paris in 1914. In December 1915 showed his first abstract works at the Galerie Tanner in Zurich. Experiments in "papier collé" with Sophie

Taeuber. In 1916, with Tzara, Ball, Hülsenbeck, Janco, founded the Dada movement. With Max Ernst in Cologne in 1920. Married Sophie Taeuber in 1921. Settled at Meudon in 1926 and became a member of the Surrealist group (1926-1930). Decorations for the "Aubette" café (Strasbourg), with Sophie Taeuber and Theo van Doesburg (1928). Member of the "Circle and Square" group in 1930, and of the "Abstraction-Creation" group (1932-1934). Worked with Sonia Delaunay and Magnelli, at Grasse, during the Second World War. His wife killed in an accident in Switzerland in 1943. Visited America in 1949 and 1950, Greece in 1952 and 1954. Large retrospective exhibition (with Schwitters) in Berne, 1956. Now lives part of the time in Meudon, part of the time in Basle. Arp is more sculptor than painter but some of his best work has been done in "papier collé" and wood engraving. His influence, since the beginnings of Dadaism, has been immense. But his personality is so simple that it remains inimitable—inimitable and inexplicable—like the art of children. The development of his work shows how, under an artist's hand, an elementary shape can become richer and progressively more profound without losing its elementary quality.

Bibl. Arp and Lissitzky: *Les Ismes de l'Art* (1925); Arp: *On my Way,* Poems and Essays (New York 1948); Seuphor: *L'Art Abstrait, ses Origines, ses Premiers Maîtres* (Paris 1949); *Collection of the Société Anonyme* (New Haven 1950); Seuphor: *Arcadie d'Arp,* La Hune (Paris 1950); *Derrière le Miroir,* No. 33, Galerie Maeght (Paris 1950); *Témoignages pour l'Art Abstrait* (Paris 1950); *Dada Painters and Poets* (New York 1951); Seuphor: *Arp,* "Sidney Janis Gallery" (New York 1949); *Onze Peintres vus par Arp* (Zurich 1949); Arp: *Dreams and Projects,* "Kurt Valentin" (New York 1952); Seuphor: *Mission Spirituelle de l'Art,* Galerie Berggruen (Paris 1953); *Dictionary of Modern Painting* (Methuen, London 1956); Marcel Jan: *Jalons d'Arp,* "Les Lettres Nouvelles" (Paris, February 1956). Arp has illustrated with abstract wood engravings, a number of collections of poems by his friends, including:—Hülsenbeck: *Phantastische Gebete* (1916), *Die Newyorker Kantaten* (1952); Tzara: *Vingt-cinq Poèmes* (1918), *Cinéma Calendrier du Cœur Abstrait* (1920), *De Nos Oiseaux* (1923); Bryen: *Temps Troué* (1952); Frey: *Kleine Menagerie* (1955).

ATLAN Jean (b. Constantine, Algeria, 1913). "I am of Judeo-Berber stock, like most of the folk in those parts, in that town, old as Jugurtha, which was once the capital of Numidia and which is *built* of rocks and ravines, eagles' nests and cactus. Despite all that, the pictures that hang in the museum of the town where I was born were scarcely any incentive to me to discover painting in my youth. So, one fine day I arrived in Paris to take a degree in philosophy at the Sorbonne. And my vocation as a painter? I think it was

ARP. WOODCUT. 1948.

ATLAN. PAINTING. 1951. *M. S. Collection, Paris.*

the Galerie Maeght and participation in numerous exhibitions in France and other countries. My work is represented in several French and foreign museums and in private collections. Michel Ragon has written an original study of me and my work: *L'Architecte et le Magicien.*" (Atlan). Now living in Paris.

"Like Chagall, Atlan has the gift of using successfully certain impossible colour tones. His orange shades are as strange as Chagall's purples—as pathetic, as heart-rending, and as sentimental. Like Soutine his expression frequently comes through a kind of formal violence, distorting lines and planes; he loves colours and delights in sombre incandescent effects." (Léon Degand).

a direct result of the fact that my studio was in the Rue de la Grande-Chaumière... I would rather not talk much about the war years (my wife and family were imprisoned by the Nazis, my brother killed as a commando, myself in prison in one place and another, including Sainte-Anne's, the lunatic asylum). In 1944, first exhibition in a little gallery in the Rue de Sèvres, shortly afterwards a new pictures shown at the Salon des Surindépendants (canvases now in the Gertrude Stein collection) and an exhibition at the Galerie Denise René. In 1945 I worked in Mourlot's studios on black and white lithographs, to illustrate Kafka's *Description of a Battle.* In 1947 one-man show at

AUGEREAU Claude (b. Chartres, 1927). Studied in Chartres and then for three years at the École des Arts Appliqués in Paris. Spent a year at the Académie Frochot under the direction of Metzinger and Audebès. Later influenced by Magnelli and Vasarely. Has exhibited at several Paris Salons and group exhibitions. Now living in Paris.

B

BÆRTLING Olle (b. Halmstad, Sweden, 1911). Began as an Expressionist and then became a portraitist under the influence of Matisse. Visited Paris frequently and travelled widely in Europe. Studied under André Lhote in 1948 and then under Fernand Léger. Influenced by the latter and by the work of Mondrian, he began to make his way as an abstract painter. His work has been exhibited in Stockholm, Copenhagen and Paris. Bærtling's painting, which is frequently characterised by large surfaces of black, reaches an extreme degree of simplification and of power. Now living in Stockholm. — *Bibl.* Tage Nilson: *Olle Bærtling* (Stockholm 1951); Eugen Wretholm: *Olle Bærtling*, Den Unga Konsten (Stockholm 1951); *Bærtling, Jacobsen, Mortensen,* Liljevalchs Konsthall (Stockholm 1956).

BALLA Giacomo (b. Turin, 1871). One of the five painters—the others were Boccioni, Severini, Carra and Russolo—who signed the Futurist Manifesto of 1910. He had come to Paris at the beginning of the century and had later been the teacher of Boccioni and Severini whom he instructed in the Divisionist technique as practised by the Neo-Impressionists. Considering that his work was not yet ready, he did not take part (despite the fact that his name figured in the catalogue) in the exhibitions of Futurist painting held in Paris in 1912. It was in 1912 however that he painted a number of typically Futurist works (*Dog on the Leash, Swallows in Flight and Interpenetration of the Eaves*). A little later he painted *Abstract Speed, Plasticity of Light and Speed* and *Atmospheric Thicknesses*—all of which, apart from the titles, are incontestably abstract works. The basic structure of linear design is a dominant feature of these works. However in 1914 he showed a marked preference for massive scrolls which recreate the illusion of depth and give a sense of lofty grandiloquence in space. At the same time he painted what might be described as cosmogonic visions (*Mercury Passing in Front of the Sun,* is an example). Balla is beyond doubt the most resolutely

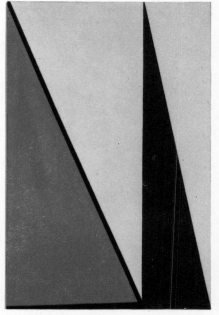

BÆRTLING. RED, YELLOW, BLACK AND WHITE TRIANGLES. 1955. *Lars Holmberg Coll., Sweden.*

BALLA. RHYTHM OF THE VIOLINIST. 1914. *Collection Estorick, London.*

a deeper philosophy of abstract art. The only great influence on me has been Mondrian. I believe him to have been the only really abstract painter. Recently I have been interested in the works of certain painters in New York and in their colourist technique which seems to open up infinite possibilities for abstract art. I believe that painting should penetrate deeper and deeper into the mystery and rhythm of the spectral, which means digging into existence itself." Ralph Balson is now living in Sydney.

abstract of all the Futurist painters. He is moreover the only one who has remained faithful to abstract art. It is true that later he also painted some figurative subjects, apparently under some external compulsion. He is now living in Rome. The work reproduced here is typical of the 1912 period and shows the characteristic Futurist endeavour to express bodily movements—a type of expression in which both Balla and Russolo particularly distinguished themselves in works which are now classics of their kind. — *Bibl.* Carrieri: *Pittura e scultura d'avanguardia in Italia* (Milan 1950); *Dictionary of Modern Painting* (Methuen, London 1956); Seuphor: *Le Futurisme... Hier,* " *L'Œil* " (Paris, February 1956).

BALSON Ralph (b. England, 1890). In Australia in 1913. Did not begin painting till about 1922. Studied at the Sydney Art School. Through his reading and associating with artists who had been abroad he got to know modern art. An exhibition of his work was held in Sydney in 1940—the first exhibition of abstract art in Australia. "Since then", he said, "I have kept on in the same way trying to work out

BARTA. PRAYER. MOSAIC. 1945.

BANDEIRA Antonio (b. Fortoleza in the northwest of Brazil, 1922). His first work was done in common with a group of young painters in his native province. In Rio de Janeiro in 1945, he was offered a bursary by the French cultural attaché to study in Paris. Studied drawing, painting and engraving at the Beaux-Arts and at the Académie de la Grande-Chaumière. Friendship with Wols and Bryen. Exhibited with them at the Galerie des Deux-Iles in 1940. Took part in the Venice and Sao Paulo Biennales and also in the Salon des Réalités Nouvelles in 1953 and 1954. Exhibitions of his works have been held in Rio de Janeiro, Sao Paulo, Paris (Galerie du Siècle) and London (Obelisk Gallery). Now living in Paris.

BARNS-GRAHAM Wilhelmina (b. St. Andrews, Scotland, 1912). Studied at the Edinburgh College of Art (1931-1936). Work exhibited in London in 1948 and 1952. Took part in an exhibition of English abstract art in New York in 1951. Now living at Leeds.

BARRÉ Martin (b. Nantes, 1924). Studied at Nantes. Came to Paris in 1943. Abstract painter since 1950. One man exhibition at the Galerie La Roue, Paris, 1955. Has taken part in the Salon des Réalités Nouvelles and the Menton Biennale. Now living in Paris. His paintings are of monochromatic shapes on a light ground with very simple straight-line variations.

BARTA Lazlo (b. Nagykoros, Hungary, 1902). Studied at the Budapest School of Fine Arts. Has been in France since 1926. Illustrated numerous books and had his work shown at the Salon d'Automne. Turned to abstract art in 1948. After learning directly from the craftsmen at Ravenna, he became a mosaicist. Showed some remarkable examples of mosaic work at the Galerie Arnaud in Paris in 1954. Now living at Saint-Tropez.

BARRÉ. PAINTING. 1955.
Michel Ragon Collection, Paris.

BAUDINIÈRE Robert (b. Cluny, Saône-et-Loire, 1919). After working at a number of different occupations, took up painting in 1942. Took part in the exhibition held at the Galerie Maeght ("Les Mains Éblouies") in 1947. Received official awards in 1950 and 1951. Is a convinced but intelligent disciple of Albert Gleizes. Now living at Saint-Tropez.

BAUER Rudolf (b. Lindenwald, Poland, 1889; d. U.S.A., 1954). Studied in Berlin. Began as a caricaturist, then became member of the "Sturm" group. In

1929 founded "Das Geistreich", a private museum of Abstract Art, in Berlin. In 1939 went to America where his work had already been introduced some years earlier by the Société Anonyme and the Guggenheim Foundation. Died near New York in 1954. — Bibl. *Art of Tomorrow,* S. R. Guggenheim Collection (New York 1939).

BAUMEISTER Willi (1889-1955). Born in Stuttgart. Was apprenticed to a house painter at the age of sixteen, but worked at the time as an independent student at the Stuttgart School of Fine Arts. Made his first visit to Paris in 1912 and exhibited in Zurich in the same year. The following year took part in the first German Autumn Exhibition (Herbstsalon) in "Der Sturm" Gallery in Berlin. Spent some time with Oscar Schlemmer in Paris in 1914. After being influenced by Lautrec, Gauguin and Cézanne, Baumeister gradually developed from 1919 to 1931 a highly personal style of his own embracing both Cubist and Constructivist elements.

Made frequent visits to Paris where he showed his work a number of times and mixed with the leading figures in the world of art. Appointed professor at the School of Fine Arts in Frankfort in 1928. In 1930 was a member of the "Cercle et Carré" group and exhibited with them. Belonged to the "Abstraction-Creation" group in 1932. Dismissed from the Frankfort School of Fine Arts by the Nazis in 1933, and officially disqualified as an artist. All his canvases were withdrawn from German museums and galleries. Continued painting clandestinely while working for a printing firm. In 1938 sent some sixty paintings to Switzerland for safety. Among the thousand "degenerate" works of art burnt in Berlin were a number of Baumeister's pictures. During the Second World War he was obliged to work in a paint and varnish factory. Unable to continue painting, he produced drawings to illustrate several Biblical books and Shakespeare's "The Tempest". Once the war was over he returned to Stuttgart and took up his former activities again. Has now a very great influence on the younger generation, and it is largely thanks to his example that art in Germany has so quickly been set back on the road to complete freedom of expression. In 1946 began teaching at the Stuttgart School of Fine Arts. Numerous exhibitions of his work in Germany. Published *Das Unbekannte in der Kunst (The Unknown in Art)* in 1947. Several exhibitions at the Galerie Jeanne Bucher in Paris. A very full retrospective exhibition of his work was held in Stuttgart in 1954. Since 1930 the development of Baumeister's art has been marked by the

BAUMEISTER. SAFER WITH PIPE. 1953. *Galerie J. Bucher, Paris.*

BAZAINE. THE CLEARING. 1949.
Cavellini Collection, Brescia.

presence of two apparently divergent trends which however occasionally combine to produce a curious mixture of themes—one, rough and almost bristling, is an attempt to give formal order to certain amorphous and intuitive perceptions, the other is a continuation of his earlier geometrical tendency, crystal-clear and precise. Typical of his work are the *Afrikanische Bilder (African Pictures)* series and the brightly-coloured *Montaru* and *Montari* series. — Bibl. *Sélection*, special number on Baumeister, with articles by Will Grohmann, Waldemar George, Arp, Zervos, Le Corbusier, Seuphor and others (Antwerp 1931); Domnick: *Abstrakte Malerei* (1947); Grohmann: *Willi Baumeister* (Stuttgart 1952); *Dictionary of Modern Painting* (Methuen, London 1956); Roh: *Willi Baumeister* (Baden-Baden 1954); Seuphor: *Exit Baumeister,* "Aujourd'hui" No. 5 (Paris 1955).

BAYER Herbert (b. Haag, Austria, 1900). Studied architecture at Linz. At the Bauhaus (Weimar) in 1921 where he was in Kandinsky's painting class. Taught typography at the Bauhaus from 1925 to 1928. Paintings exhibited in several centres in Europe, including London and Paris, between 1929 and 1937. Was in New York in 1938. Now living at Aspen (Colorado). — Bibl. Alexander Dorner: *The Way Beyond Art—The Work of Herbert Bayer* (New York 1947).

BAZAINE Jean (b. Paris, 1904). Studied sculpture at the École des Beaux-Arts. Graduated Licencié-ès-Lettres. Exhibition at the Galerie Jeanne Bucher in 1941. Works exhibited at the Galerie Carré and various foreign museums and galleries from 1942 to 1948. Took part in the Venice Biennale in 1948 and 1952. Stained-glass windows for church at Assy in 1950. Large ceramic mural for church façade at Audincourt (Doubs) in 1951. Published *Notes sur la Peinture d'Aujourd'hui* (Publ. Floury, Paris 1948). One-man exhibitions at the Gallery Maeght in 1949 and 1954. Took part in the "Four Walls" exhibition at the same gallery in 1951, along with Braque, Chagall, Léger, Matisse, Miró, Picasso and Rouault. Visited the United States in 1952. Now living in Paris.

"Each time I begin a new canvas, it is as if I had never painted before, and there is a kind of inescapable logic in the way the shapes and colours develop—in the way certain colours and certain shapes literally impose themselves on me at certain periods. It is never the result of clear deliberate calculation, it is an inner obligation from which I cannot escape, and it is often against all my inclinations, against my mood, my taste and my considered opinion. As Braque says, the canvas must kill the idea" (Bazaine). Bazaine's works are calm, harmonious compositions embracing the whole canvas with an equal delight in painting, an equal intensity of feeling and an equal continuity in colour. — Bibl. P. Courthion: *Peintres d'Aujourd'hui* (Geneva 1952); *Jean Bazaine*, Galerie Maeght (Paris 1953).

BAZIOTES William (b. Pittsburgh, Pennsylvania, 1912). Studied at the National Academy, New York, till 1936. Work developed slowly, becoming entirely abstract about 1940. His first ona-man exhibition was organised by "Art of this Century" (New York) in 1944. Numerous exhibitions of his work at the Kootz Gallery (New York) from 1944 to 1955. Took part in an exhibition at the Galerie Maeght in Paris in 1947. Is now a professor at New York University. Lives in New York. The highly unusual, though simple, shapes he invents tend to create a feeling of hallucination which often comes chose to Surrealism. — *Bibl.* Hess: *Abstract Painting* (New York 1951).

BELLEGARDE Claude (b. Paris 1927). Studied drawing and sculpture at a private studio, then began working independently. Has taken part in group exhibitions since 1946, in Paris, Buenos Aires, Madrid, Dusseldorf and elsewhere. Special exhibitions devoted to his work have been held in Paris at the Centre Saint-Jacques (1953), Galerie Arnaud (1954) and the Studio Facchetti (1955). Now living in Paris.

BENNER Gerrit (b. Leeuwarden, Holland, 1897). Is a self-taught artist. Since 1945 his work has been shown in Indonesia, the United States, Copenhagen, Berlin and Milan. He has also taken part in the Sao Paolo Biennale. Now living in Amsterdam.

BÉRARD Marius Honoré (b. Salindres, Gard, France, 1896). Studied at Alès. Has been experimenting with painting of musical inspiration since 1921. In 1927 left his position in the postal administration. Exhibited at Cannes, Paris and Boulogne-sur-Mer. In 1946 became a member of the organising committee of the Salon des Réalités Nouvelles. From 1950 onwards has travelled and exhibited in South

BERGMAN. PAINTING NO. 6. 1955.

America — among these an exhibition of French religious art. Bérard's abstract compositions usually originate from a musical theme. Greatly influenced by the music of Claude Debussy and J. S. Bach.

BERGMAN Anna-Eva (b. Stockholm, 1909). Studied in Oslo and Vienna. Abstract painter since 1947. Numerous exhibitions in Scandinavia, Germany and at the Galerie Ariel in Paris. Married to the painter Hans Hartung and living in Paris. Her paintings are characterised by large solid blocks of a single colour often isolated in the middle of the canvas. They are almost hypnotic in their effect. Has produced many engravings all marked by this same individual style. — Bibl. *Art d'Aujourd'hui* (Paris, February 1954).

BERKE Hubert (b. Buer, Germany, 1908). Studied history of art and philosophy at Königsberg and Münster. Pupil of Paul Klee in Düsseldorf (1932-1933). Exhibitions at Cologne, Duisburg, Bochum, Berne, Zurich, Basle, Paris and Brooklyn. Has had work shown at the Salon des Réalités Nouvelles in Paris. Is a member of the "Zen" group. Now living at Alfter, near Bonn.

BERLEWI Henri (b. Warsaw, 1894). Studied at the Warsaw School of Fine Arts, and later at the Beaux-Arts in Antwerp (1909-1910) and Paris (1911-1912). After a period during which he underwent various influences, mostly in the manner of Cézanne, he met Lissitzky, van Doesburg, Eggeling and Richter in Berlin in 1922. Exhibited with the Novembergruppe. In 1924, influenced by the Russian Constructivists and the Dutch Neo-Plastic school, he developed a type of abstract painting which he called *Mechanofaktur* and which he wished to bring as close as possible to the processes of machinery. Also in 1924, he published a manifesto in Warsaw under this same title, and held an exhibition of his works (Mechano-Faktur Gestaltungen) at "Der Sturm" Gallery in Berlin. In 1926, however, he returned to figurative painting. He now lives in Paris. — *Bibl.* Berlewi: *Mechano-Factur,* "Der Sturm", Drittes Vierteljahrheft, Berlin 1924.

BERTHOLLE Jean (born Dijon, 1909). Studied at the Écoles des Beaux-Arts at Saint-Étienne and Lyons. Work shown at various Salons in Paris and at the Galerie Jeanne Bucher. Now living in Paris. "Life must no doubt be lived in the context of what exists at a given time, and Bertholle is fully conscious of the existence, only recently recognised, of paintings as objective phenomena in themselves. But one must also be conscious of those forces which subsist from other times and still have their echoes in our time, and Bertholle has elected to be with all those for whom painting is a magical means of discovering the world, of going beyond outward appearances to reach the essence and the heart of things. He has a feeling for the delicate plastic properties of paint, a taste for such colours as blue and black, which call up deep emotional responses, and for sequences of subtle beauty" (Jean-Jacques Lerrant). — *Bibl.* Descargues: *Bertholle,* Presses Littéraires de France (Paris 1952).

BERTINI Gianni (b. Pisa, 1922). Specialised studies in mathematics. Since 1947 many exhibitions in Italy and at the Galerie Arnaud in Paris. His *Epilogo per un'Arte Attuale,* with wood engravings, was published in Venice in 1951. Lives in Paris.

BERTHOLLE. COMPOSITION. 1955. *Musée d'Art Moderne, Paris.*

131

BERTRAND Gaston (b. in the village of Wonck in Belgian Limburg, 1910). Began the study of classics in Brussels but was obliged to interrupt his studies to earn his living. Worked as carpenter, clerk, mechanic, and at the same time attended evening classes in drawing. Enrolled at the Brussels Académie des Beaux-Arts in 1933. Spent a short time in Paris in 1938. First exhibition devoted entirely to his work held at the Galerie Dietrich (Brussels) in 1942. Work characterised by a predilection for odd truculent figures (1947). Shortly afterwards moved towards an entirely abstract form of art, highly individual and remarkable for its extremely refined geometrical style. Exhibitions in Brussels,

Antwerp, Liège, New York (Stable Gallery) and Milan (Il Milione Gallery). Has often exhibited in Europe with the " Jeune Peinture Belge" group. One-man exhibition at the Galerie Colette Allendy, Paris, in 1956. Lives in Brussels. — *Bibl.* R. L. Delevoy: *Gaston Bertrand*, De Sikkel (Antwerp 1953). Same author: *Gaston Bertrand,* Brient (Paris 1955).

BERTRAND Huguette (b. Écouen, Seine-et-Oise, France, 1925). First exhibition in Prague, 1946. Has taken part in group exhibitions at the Galerie Maeght and at various Salons in Paris. Several individual exhibitions at the Galerie Arnaud (Paris). Showed work in New York in 1956. Now lives in Paris. "My aim is to dismember and at the same time to reconstitute space, to render it, paradoxically, cut up into pieces, set in motion by a linear process which though it wrenches at the form is not a negation of form itself, thus making it possible, in a sense, to go into and out of the canvas freely in a back-and-forth movement — in short, the canvas becomes a choreographic argument".

BIEDERMAN Charles (b. Cleveland, Ohio, 1906). Of Czech parentage. Studied at the Art Institute, Chicago (1926-1929). Attempted, without success, to work in Czechoslovakia in 1932. Returned to Chicago and began painting in the Fauve manner. Then underwent the influence of Cubism and gradually moved towards abstract art. In Paris in 1936-37 he unconsciously began painting in the Neo-Plastic manner, though his original intention had been simply to use the Neo-Plastic technique as a means of experimenting with relief effects. In New York in 1938 he made a close study of the work of Mondrian which proved to be the starting point of a voluminous work published ten years later—*Art as the Evolution of Visual Knowledge.* Two exhibitions of his abstract works in Chicago in 1941. Now living at Red Wing, Minnesota.

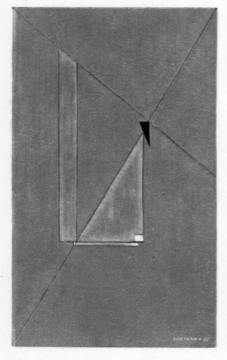

G. BERTRAND. YELLOW LANDSCAPE. 1955.

BILL Max (b. Winterthur, Switzerland, 1908). Studied at the Zurich School of Arts and Crafts and at the Bauhaus in Dessau. From 1929 onwards a variety of occupations as painter, sculptor, architect and publicity artist. His opposition to the concept of "abstract art" and his advocacy of the cause of "concrete art" (as propounded by van Doesburg in 1930) dates from 1935. From 1928 he took part in numerous exhibitions throughout Europe and also in North and South America. Was the organiser of the international exhibition of "Konkrete Kunst" (Concrete Art) at the Kunsthalle in Basle in 1944. Took part in an exhibition at Stuttgart in 1948, in company with Arp and Albers. In 1949 he showed more than fifty of his works at the Zurich Museum along with Vantongerloo and Pevsner. In the same year he organised the "Zürcher Konkrete Kunst" exhibition which travelled throughout Germany. A retrospective exhibition surveying the whole of his work was held at the Sao Paulo Museum in Brazil

in 1951. In the following year he was appointed Rector of the "Hochschule für Gestaltung", at Ulm (Germany), a kind of university of plastic techniques which tended to fill the position formerly occupied by the Bauhaus. This school was officially opened in 1955. Max Bill resigned his rectorship the following year. He now lives in Ulm and Zurich. He has had a marked influence on many young painters both in Argentina and Italy and has been responsible for the founding of various "Concrete Art" groups in these two countries. He is a firm admirer and defender of Mondrian and Kan-

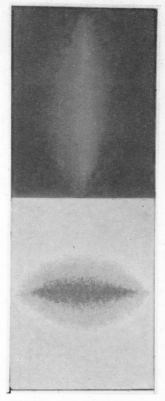

dinsky. His main source of inspiration is mathematics. — *Bibl.* Maldonado: *Max Bill* (with comprehensive bibliography on the work of the artist, Buenos Aires 1955).

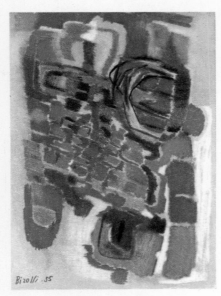

BIROLLI. GOUACHE. 1955.
Private Collection.

BIROLLI Renato (b. Verona, 1906). His work was influenced first by Ensor and van Gogh. Well known as an anti-Fascist, he was persecuted by that régime and suffered imprisonment. After the war he first followed the lead given by Pignon and Picasso but gradually turned away to an entirely free Expressionism. His work, which has been abstract since 1952, sometimes shows affinities with that of Bazaine. Now living in Milan.

BISSIER Julius (b. Freiburg-im-Breisgau, 1893). Studied at the University and Academy of Karlsruhe. Turned to abstract art in 1929. Friendship with Baumeister and Schlemmer. Has lived in retirement at Hagnau, Lake Constance, since 1939. — *Bibl.* Kurt Leonhard: *Julius Bissier* (Stuttgart 1948); *Das Kunstwerk,* Baden-Baden, Heft 8-9, 1950.

BISSIÈRE Roger (b. Villeréal, Lot-et-Garonne, France, 1888). "When I came to Paris about 1910, I did all kinds of jobs to earn a living. Up to the outbreak of war in 1914 I was attached to the staff of several newspapers. Towards the end of the war I made the acquaintance of Lhote and Favory and exhibited my work in company with them at the Salon d'Automne and the Salon des Indépendants up till 1918. My meeting with Braque in 1922 was the beginning of a long friendship. After a brief excursion into Cubism, I turned away from it, feeling that it was already outdated. From 1925 to 1938 I taught at the Academie Ranson, which for me was a somewhat unexpected departure as I have always been convinced that nothing can be taught. In fact, I used to persuade any pupils that really interested me to leave the Académie since I felt that the only effect it would have on them would be to get them into disastrous habits. In 1939 I left Paris to live in the country and settled down in the Lot country in the house where I had lived as a boy. For five years I did absolutely no painting whatever. Then I took it up again and had an exhibition at the Galerie Drouin in 1946. I showed quite a number of paintings and some tapestries made from little pieces of material sewn together. After this exhibition I went back to the country and began to work for myself, at first without any idea of exhibiting. It was then that I came to know Jaeger (manager of the Galerie Jeanne Bucher) and it is to his friendship and understanding that I owe my return to the land of the living." — *Bibl. Dictionary of Modern Painting* (Methuen, London 1956); Max-Pol Foucher: *Bissière,* Le Musée de Poche (Paris 1955); Lassaigne: *Bissière,* Galerie Jeanne Bucher (Paris 1956).

BITRAN Albert (b. Turkey, 1929). Came to Paris 1949 to study architecture. In 1950 suddenly took up painting on Constructivist lines. Since then he has often changed his style but without abandoning pure abstract art. Has exhibited at the Salon des Réalités Nouvelles, at the Galerie Arnaud and at the Galerie Denise René. Now lives in Paris.

BISSIÈRE. PAINTING. 1955. *Galerie Jeanne Bucher, Paris.*

BLASZKO Martin (b. Berlin, 1920). Of Polish - Jewish parentage. Was in Paris in 1939 and then went to Argentina. In 1945 he made the acquaintance of Arden Quin from whom he took lessons. In the following year he joined the Madi movement and took part in all the "Arte Madi" exhibitions at Buenos Aires where he now lives.

BLOCH Pierrette (b. Paris 1928). Her work has been exhibited in various Salons since 1949. Individual exhibition at the Galerie Mai in 1951, after which she visited New York and exhibited there. Her work has a vigorous individual style and also a marked dramatic tendency which owes much to the influence of Soulages. Is now living in Paris.

BLOW Sandra (b. 1925). Studied at St. Martin's School and the Royal Academy Schools, London, and in Italy in 1947, in Spain in 1949 and France in 1950. Has held one-man exhibitions in London in 1952 and 1954.

BOCCIONI Umberto (b. Reggio, Calabria, Italy, 1882; d. 1916). Was in Rome in 1901 where he met Severini and Balla who encouraged him to take up painting. In 1909 in company with them he founded the Futurist movement and

BISSIER. VARIATION. INDIAN INK. 1947.

135

published the famous Manifesto in the following year. Visited Paris in 1911 and 1912 at the time of the important Futurist exhibition. Later turned to a more dynamic style of painting which opened the way to abstract art. Work on similar problems in sculpture. Ardent "Interventionist" from the beginning of the first world war. He died in 1916 when he fell from his horse during artillery exercises near Verona. — *Bibl.* Carrieri: *Pittura e Scultura d'Avanguardia in Italia* (Milan 1950); *A Dictionary of Modern Painting* (Methuen, London 1956); Seuphor: *Le Futurisme... Hier*, "L'Œil" (Paris, February 1956).

BODMER Walter (b. Basle, 1903). Studied in Basle, Paris and in Spain. Was a member of the "Allianz" and in the exhibitions of this group exhibited abstract paintings, and more particularly, wire reliefs. Is now living in Basle.

BOCCIONI. ELASTICITY. 1912.
Private Collection, Milan.

BOGART Bram (b. Delft, Holland, 1921). Work shown for the first time at the Bennewitz Gallery at the Hague in 1940. Took part in group exhibitions at the Hague, Amsterdam, Rotterdam, London and Paris. Individual exhibitions of this work were held at the Galerie Creuze in Paris in 1954 and 1955. Is now living in Paris. Bogart paints in the Neo-Expressionist manner but with a subdued range of colours.

BOLOTOWSKY Ilya (b. St. Petersburg, 1907). Studied at Bakou in the Caucasus and then at a French school in Constantinople. First visited the United States in 1923. Was at the New York National Academy from 1924 to 1930. Travelled through Europe, visiting France, Italy, Germany, Scandinavia and England, in 1932. Adopted an abstract style of painting in 1933. Has exhibited various murals in the United States. Was a member and co-founder of the "American Abstract Artists" group (1936). Taught at Black Mountain College 1946 to 1948 and then at the University of Wyoming. Numerous one-man exhibitions of his work have been held in America since 1930, mainly at the New Art Circle in New York. Now living at Laramie, Wyoming.

BONNET Anne (b. Brussels, 1908) of Walloon parents. Studied at the Academies of Brussels and Saint-Josseten-Noode, and founded the group under the name of "La Route Libre" in 1939 in company with Louis van Lint and Gaston Bertrand. In 1941 was a foundation exhibitor at the "Apport" Salon. In 1945

BONNET. ASTRAL INFLUENCES. 1954.
Fr. Delcoigne Collection, Italy.

1947 he has taken part in many exhibitions in Sweden, in Copenhagen and Paris, and in the United States. His first abstract works were produced in 1943. Has shown a Constructivist tendency since 1947. Is now living at Storangen, near Stockholm.

BOTT Francis (b. Frankfort-on-the-Main, 1904). Started out as a kind of European vagabond and later became a journalist. Began painting in 1936 following the advice of Kokoschka. Came to Paris in 1937 where he joined the Surrealist movement and gradually developed towards completely abstract art. Exhibitions of his work have been held in Paris and in Germany and Switzerland. In 1953 he was responsible for the remarkable stained glass windows in the chapel of the Château de

was one of the founders of the Jeune Peinture group in Belgium. Her work has been shown many times since 1941 at the Palais des Beaux-Arts, Brussels, and at other centres in Belgium. The Galerie de Verneuil (Paris) has exhibited her paintings along with those of Louis van Lint. Exhibition also at the Springer Gallery in Berlin. Took part in the Venice Biennale in 1948 and 1956 and in the Biennale in Sao Paulo in 1954. Is living in Brussels. Anne Bonnet's first abstract works date from 1950. Since then she has developed a thematic plastic manner, both substantial and sensitive, which has earned for her the reputation of being one of the best of the Belgian artists painting at the present time. — *Bibl.* Walravens: *Anne Bonnet en de Abstracte Schilderkunst,* Bulletin des Musées Royaux (Brussels 1953); Davay: *Anne Bonnet,* De Sikkel (Antwerp 1954).

BONNIER Olle (b. Los Angeles, 1925). His family is of French origin. Went to Sweden in 1930. Studied at technical college and art school from 1940 to 1946. Travelled extensively in Europe and in Africa from 1946 to 1951. Since

BOTT. COMPOSITION IN RED. 1955.

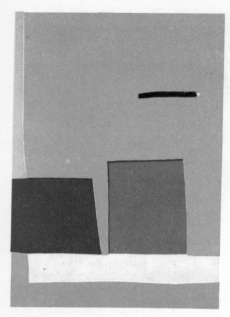

BREER. COMPOSITION IN BLUE AND RED. 1955.

drawing in 1925. Arrived in Paris in 1935 and married the painter Henri Goetz in the same year. Numerous exhibitions of her work have been held in Paris, in Holland and in Switzerland. Is a regular exhibitor at the principle abstract Salons in Paris. Has illustrated many books. Lives in Paris.

BOZZOLINI Silvano (b. Fiesole, near Florence, 1911). Studied at the School of Fine Arts in Florence. First abstract paintings in 1947. Produced a number of woodcuts both in Switzerland and in Copenhagen. His work has been exhibited in Paris, Sofia, Milan, and Lausanne. Is now living in Paris. His paintings are geometrical compositions of shapes in motion with cleverly devised gradations of colour. — Bibl. *Témoignages pour l'Art Abstrait* (Paris 1952).

BRAZZOLA Donato (b. Lausanne, 1905). Studied philosophy. Art studies at the Académie des Beaux-Arts, Lyons, and later at Lausanne. Has exhibited his work in Berne, Basle and Lausanne. Has also taken part in the Salon des Réalités Nouvelles in Paris. Lives both in Paris and Lausanne.

BREER Robert C. (b. Detroit, 1926). Studied at Stanford University, California, Came to Paris in 1949. Has exhibited at the Salon des Réalités Nouvelles and at the Galerie Denise René. Has also taken part in exhibitions in Stockholm and in Cuba. Has produced abstract films. Now living in Paris.

BREETVELT Adolf (b. Delft, 1892). Studied at the School of Fine Arts at the Hague. From 1920 to 1937 was a teacher in Indonesia. His work developed from Expressionism to a new type of Realism and then from 1945 onwards turned to abstract art but with the colours of his earlier manner. Now living in Holland.

Reux, Calvados. Is now living in Paris. Bott works with a combination of plane shapes and sharply angled lines thus obtaining a restless topographical effect on which the composition as a whole exercises a pacifying influence, frequently with obvious success. — Bibl. Seuphor: *Francis Bott,* "Kunsthaus" (Zurich 1955).

BOTTENBURG Hendrik van (b. Amsterdam, 1911). His first exhibition was held in Amsterdam in 1948. Visited France for the first time in 1934. After receiving a grant to study, came for a second time in 1956. Paints in an energetic style and also works as a fabric designer.

BOUMEESTER Christine (b. Batavia, Java, 1904). In Holland in 1921. Graduated as teacher of

BRENSON Theodore (b. Riga, Latvia, 1893). Studied architecture in Riga. Later lived in Rome and in Paris. Went to the United States in 1941 and became an American citizen. Many individual exhibitions of his work have been held in America, in Paris, Italy and Switzerland. Now living in New York.

BREUER Léo (b. Bonn, 1893). Studied at art schools in Cologne and Kassel. His work has been shown in many towns in Germany. Lives in France since 1940. Is a regular exhibitor at the Salon des Réalités Nouvelles. Now living in Paris.

BREUIL Georges, real name Adrien Dubreuil (b. Quevillon, near Rouen, 1904). Began painting in a prison camp in Germany during the years 1940 to 1945. Individual exhibition of his work in 1954 at the Galerie Colette Allendy. Now living in Rouen.

BRIELLE Roger (b. Malicorne, Sarthe, 1899). Spent his childhood in Paris. Education at the Collège Chaptal. Up to 1930 wrote art criticisms for many papers and reviews. At the same time published poetic and literary essays. Then began painting in a style not unlike Surrealism. Joined the Surrealist movement in 1947 and took part in several group exhibitions in Paris, Prague, Rio de Janeiro and Brussels. Later turned to abstract art, and his works in this style display a spirit of fantasy comparable to that of Paul Klee. Took part in the Salon des Réalités Nouvelles in 1955 and in the same year exhibited at the Galerie Michel Warren in Paris. Now lives at Blois.

BROOKS James (b. St. Louis, Missouri, 1906). Studied at the Southern Methodist University, and at the Art Students' League, New York. Individual exhibitions at the Peridot Gallery, New York, in 1950 and 1951. Now living in New York.

BRUCE Patrick Henry (b. Virginia, 1880; d. New York, 1937). Of Scottish parentage. Studied in New York with Robert Henry. Came to Paris in 1907. Worked in Matisse's studio, and exhibited at the Salon d'Automne. Later joined up with the Orphist movement led by Robert Delaunay. Exhibited at the Armory Show in 1913. Showed abstract works at

BRUCE. COMPOSITION. *c.* 1933. *H.-P. Roché Collection, Paris.*

the Salon des Indépendants in 1914. From 1920 onwards was invited by Miss Katherine Dreier to take part in the exhibitions of the "Société Anonyme". In a fit of melancholia in Paris in 1933 he destroyed the greater part of his paintings. Those remaining have been collected by Henri-Pierre Roché. "His constant endeavour was to create works which, by reason of their structural qualities, could be looked at from four sides. The absence of these qualities in the works of other modern painters was, rightly or wrongly, a constant source of anguish to him. For several years he exhibited at the Salon des Indépendants, but later gave up because no one understood the problem with which he was grappling and because people considered his works simply as pleasantly coloured decorative panels." (Henri-Pierre Roché). — *Bibl.* Wright: *Modern Painting* (New York 1915); Dreier: *Western Art and the New Era* (New York 1928); *Collection of the Société Anonyme* (New Haven 1950); Seuphor: *La Peinture aux Etats-Unis,* "Art d'Aujourd'hui" (Paris, June 1951); Ritchie: *Abstract Painting and Sculpture in America,* Museum of Modern Art (New York 1951).

BRYEN. APOCALYPSE. 1953.
Galerie Colette Allendy, Paris.

BRYEN Camille (b. Nantes, 1907). Has written poetry and produced drawings and paintings. Is very active in the artistic coteries of St.-Germain-des-Prés and Montparnasse. Has exhibited his work in Paris since 1932. Took part in the first three Salons des Réalités Nouvelles. Exhibited in company with Arp in Basle in 1946 and in Zurich in 1950. Individual exhibitions of his work have been held at the Galerie Pierre and at the Galerie Colette Allendy. Has also taken part in numerous exhibitions of 'informal' art. Is now living in Paris. "Painting is the expression of the inner life, and its nature is that of a cosmic function. Far from being a simple product of sensory excitation, it should, in its proper capacity, act like a magical phenomenon making itself felt not only through the optical, but also through the para-optical perception, not only through the dimensions of shapes and colours present, but also through what is not present, through memory and the ambivalences of the physical and psychical personality". (Bryen).

BUCHHEISTER Karl (b. Hanover, 1890). Studied at Hanover and Berlin. After the first world war, in company with Kurt Schwitters, founded an association of Abstract painters in Hanover. Member of the "Sturm" group and the "Novembergruppe". Took part in the "Cercle et Carré" exhibition in Paris in 1930. Was also a member of the "Abstraction-Création" group. Work exhibited at the Galerie Creuze in Paris in 1954. Since 1945 has been a professor at the Hanover Academy. Lives in Hanover.

BUCHHOLZ Erich (b. Bromberg, Germany, 1891). Son of an illiterate shepherd. Despite the poverty of his youth he became a school teacher, but gave up this calling in 1917 to become a painter. Was a member of the "November-gruppe" after the first world war. His first abstract works, which showed a geometrical tendency, were produced about 1919. Paintings exhibited at the Sturm Gallery in Berlin in 1921. Was a friend of Lissitzky. His career as an artist was interrupted by the Nazi régime but he returned to painting after the second world war. Retrospective exhibition at the Rose Fried Gallery, New York, in 1956. Now living in Berlin. "Buchholz's affinity with the Suprematists and with Mondrian is obvious in his relief paintings produced during the 1920s. These severely geometrical works with white, black, red and gold might be described as twentieth century icons". (R. Hülsenbeck).

BURRI Alberto (b. Citta di Castello, Italy, 1915). Studied medicine at Citta Perugia. Began painting in 1944 while a prisoner of war in Texas. From 1945 onwards has lived in Rome and concentrated entirely on painting. Individual exhibitions of his work have been held in many centres in Italy and also in Chicago.

Took part in the Venice Biennale and the New Decade exhibition at the New York Museum of Modern Art in 1955. Now living in Rome. Burri's works are composed of pieces of cloth sewn together and of oil colours—their unity is due to the characteristic climate created by the artist himself who has the gift of combining an apparent awkwardness of manner with absolute perfection of taste. — Bibl. *Art News* (New York, Dec. 1954).

BURSSENS Jan (b. Malines, Belgium, 1925). Studied at the Ghent Academy. Travelled in England, Holland, Italy and France. His work has been shown in various centres in Belgium and also in London and in Norway. Is now living at Mariakerke near Ghent.

BURY Pol (b. Haine-Saint-Pierre, Belgium, 1922). Studied at the Beaux-Arts in Mons. From 1947 exhibited with the "Jeune Peinture Belge" group, and in 1955 took part in the Mouvement exhibition at the Galerie Denise René, Paris. Is now living at Haine-Saint-Paul, Belgium.

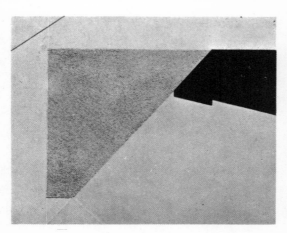

BUCHHEISTER. BLACK AND WHITE. 1932.
Yale University, U.S.A.

C

CADORET Michel (b. Paris, 1912). Studied at the École des Beaux-Arts, Paris, and the School of Decorative Arts, Dusseldorf. Visited America and Egypt. Was mobilised in September 1939 and taken prisoner in June 1940. Escaped from France and joined the army again at Casablanca. Took part in the Normandy campaign and then served in Germany. From 1947 onwards he illustrated books and took part in various exhibitions, including the exhibition "France Comes to You" which travelled through the United States. Spent three years in Mexico where he worked in the village of Erongaricuaro, Micheacan. Individual exhibitions in New York in 1953 and 1954, and at the Galerie Furstenberg in Paris in 1955. Lives either in New York or in Paris.

CAGLI Corrado (b. Ancona, Italy, 1910). First worked on large-scale mural painting. Spent some time in the United States continuing his training and then took up abstract art. Has exhibited in the main centres in Italy and also in Paris, Zurich, New York and San Francisco. Now living in Rome.

CAHN Marcelle (b. Strasbourg, 1895). Early training in Strasbourg. Was in Berlin during the first world war and associated with the artists of the Sturm group. Came to Paris in 1919. Met Munch a number of times in Zurich in 1922. Was associated with the studio of Fernand Léger in 1925, and took part in the "Art d'Aujourd'hui" exhibition. Exhibited at the 1926 exhibition of the Société Anonyme at the

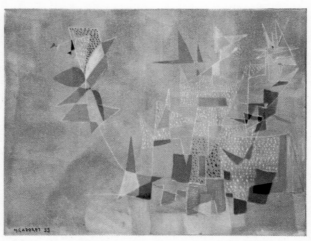

CADORET. THE JOYOUS CITY. 1955. *Galerie Furstenberg, Paris.*

CALLIYANNIS. BLACK AND WHITE. 1954.
Galerie Mouradian-Vallotton, Paris.

Africa he returned to Paris and in 1955 his work was shown at the Studio Facchetti. Exhibition also held at the Martha Jackson Gallery in New York. His painting owes a great deal to the influence of Pollock and Rothko. His latest works show the maturing of his personality. P. Restany wrote: "It was in Paris that Calcagno found his true personal style which he worked out from the chaotic tyranny of over-exacting natural vigour".

Brookland Museum. In 1930 was a member of the "Cercle et Carré" group and made the acquaintance of Mondrian and Arp. A regular exhibitor at the Salon des Réalités Nouvelles. Now living in Paris. Her works are subdued in manner with little variation of colour and generally of simple geometric design.

CALCAGNO Laurence (b. San Francisco, 1916). Self-taught artist. Travelled in the East and in Mexico. Individual exhibitions in New Orleans in 1945, San Francisco in 1948, and Florence in 1950 and 1952. Spent some time in Paris in 1952 and 1953 when he took part in several group exhibitions. After visiting North

CALLIYANNIS Manolis (b. Lesbos, Greece, 1926). Served in the R.A.F. during the war. Began painting at the age of 15 and at the same time continued his architectural studies which he completed in 1947 at the University of Johannesburg, South Africa. Came to Paris in 1948. Has exhibited at the Galerie

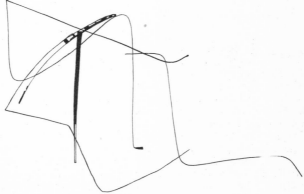

MARCELLE CAHN. INK DRAWNING. 1952.

Arnaud in Paris, at Gimpel's in London, and also in Belgium and at Amsterdam. His palette is sober, but he skilfully organises his rich material in solid compositions. Now living in Paris.

CARLSTEDT. COMPOSITION. 1955.

CALMIS Charlotte (b. Aleppo, Syria, 1918). Came to Paris at the age of 17 and frequently visited the studios of Lhote, Gromaire, Lurçat. Was advised by her friend Jacques Villon. Took part in the "Les Mains Éblouies" exhibition at the Galerie Maeght in 1947. Individual exhibition at the Galerie Arnaud in 1953. Visited Cairo and showed her work their in 1956. Now living at Saint Tropez. Effusive style of painting with violent colours which in 1955 became more disciplined without, however, losing its warmth.

CAPOGROSSI Giuseppe (b. Rome, 1900). Completed his studies in law before devoting himself to painting. Lived in Paris from 1927 to 1932. Founded the "Gruppo Romano" in Rome in company with the painters Cagli and Cavalli, and then the "Origine" group to which he belonged up to 1951. Has taken part in the Venice Biennales since 1928. His work has been shown in numerous exhibitions in Paris, Vienna, Prague, Budapest, Warsaw, New York, Buenos Aires, London, Berne and Berlin. Now living in Rome. Capogrossi's abstract work is an endless variation on a single theme, a kind of claw or trident on which he effects the most extraordinary transformations. — *Bibl*. Seuphor: *Capogrossi*, Cavallino (Venice 1954).

CARLSTEDT Birger Jarl (b. Helsinki, 1907). Travelled and studied in France, Italy and Germany. First individual exhibition of his experimental abstract works at the Konsthallen in Helsinki in 1930. From 1936 to 1938 was special correspondent of a Helsinki newspaper in various European countries. Took part in numerous group exhibitions in Paris, Berlin, Rome, Oslo, Copenhagen and Stockholm, and also at the Salon des Réalités Nouvelles in Paris in 1951 and 1952. Now living in Helsinki.

CARLSUND Otto Gustaf (b. St. Petersburg, 1897; d. Stockholm 1948). Was brought up in Sweden. Attended the Dresden Academy from 1921 to 1922, and the Oslo Academy from 1922 to 1923. Came to Paris in 1924 to study Cubist mural painting. Entered Léger's studio and became one of his favourite pupils. Frequent contacts with Mondrian in 1927. Gradually adopted and used Neo-Plastic ideas. Met van Doesburg in 1929. Was co-founder of the "Art Concret" group in 1930 with van Doesburg and Helion. In the following year organised a notable exhibition of Cubist and abstract art in Stockholm. Discouraged by the lack of success of this exhibition he abandoned painting for some time. Became an art critic in 1931. After the death of Mondrian in 1944 Carlsund decided to take up painting again. Was elected president of the Artists' Club in 1947. Died the following year. — *Bibl.* Oscar Reutersvard: *Carlsund och Neoplasticismen,* Konsthistorisk Tidskrift (Stockholm 1949); *Hommage à Otto G. Carlsund,* Galerie Artek (Helsinki 1950).

CAPOGROSSI. GOUACHE. *Private Collection, Italy.*

CARO Anita de (b. New York, 1909). Studied drawing and painting at the Art Students League in New York with Max Weber and Hans Hofmann. First visited Europe in 1930. Travelled in France, Germany, Austria, Spain, England and Italy. Lived in Zurich from 1935 to 1938 where her first individual exhibition was held. Then came to Paris where she studied engraving with S. W. Hayter at the "Atelier 17". Work shown at the Galerie des Quatre Chemins. In 1939 married the engraver Roger Vieillard. After the war her painting became gradually more abstract. Exhibited paintings at the Galerie Jeanne Bucher, Paris, in 1950, at the Hanover Gallery, London, 1953, and at the Galerie Marcel Évrard in Lille in 1954. Has exhibited at the Salon de Mai since 1948. Now living in Paris. Intuitive type of painting, in which colour maintains a constant and delicately modulated dialogue with itself.

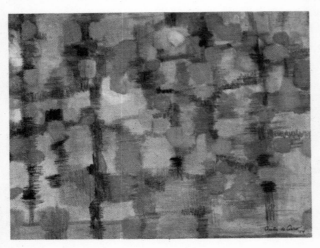

ANITA DE CARO. GOUACHE. 1954.

CARRADE Michel (b. Albi, France, 1923). Has taken part in several provincial Salons and then in the Salon de Mai and the Salon d'Octobre in Paris. Individual exhibitions at the Galerie Arnaud in Paris in 1952 and 1953, and at the Galerie Granier, Castres, in 1955. Work shown in group exhibitions in Turin, Milan, Florence, Mannheim and Offenbach (Germany) and in Vienna. Now living in Paris.

CARREY Georges (b. Paris, 1902; d. Knokke, Belgium, 1953). Studied for a short time at the École des Arts Décoratifs, Paris, then worked individually doing caricatures, posters, commercial drawings and stage settings. Settled in Brussels in 1922. Began portrait painting in 1925. His first abstract works were produced in 1946. Returned to Paris in 1948. Individual exhibition at the Galerie de Beaune in 1950. Works also shown at the Galerie Arnaud, the Salon de Mai and the Salon d'Octobre in 1952.

CAVAEL Rolf (b. Königsberg, 1898). Studied at the School of Fine Arts in Frankfort. His first exhibition, in company with Albers, was held at Braunschweig in 1933, but was suppressed by the Nazi régime. Spent two years in concentration camp in Dachau. Then lived in isolation at Garmisch-Partenkirchen, forbidden to continue painting. Since 1947 has exhibited at Basle, Cologne, Munich, New York, Paris, etc. Now living in Munich.

CAVALLON Giorgio (b. Italy, 1904). Went to America at an early age. Studied with Charles Hawthorne and Hans Hofmann. Has exhibited with the "American Abstract Artists" group since 1936. Took part in an exhibition at the Sidney Janis Gallery, New York in 1950, and in an exhibition of American abstract and at the New York Museum of Modern Art in 1951. Visited Paris and Italy in 1953. Now living in New York. Painting characterised by expanses of invitingly warm colours. — *Bibl.* Ritchie: *Abstract Painting and Sculpture in America,* Museum of Modern Art (New York 1951).

CAZIEL Casimir Zielenkiewicz (b. Poland, 1906). Studied at the College of Lodz and then at the Warsaw Academy of Art. Came to France in 1939. Has taken part in the Salon de Mai and the Salon des Surindépendants on several occasions. Now living in Paris.

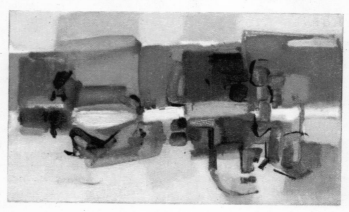

CARRADE. PAINTING. 1955. *Pierre Wurth Collection, Paris.*

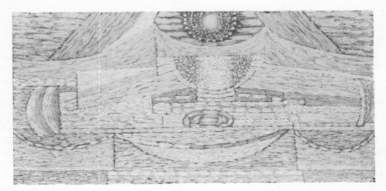

CHARCHOUNE. THE FLUTE. 1954.

CHAPOVAL Jules (b. Kiev, 1919; d. Paris 1951). Educated in Paris where he studied medicine. At the École des Beaux-Arts of Marseilles and Toulouse during the war (1939-1945). Returned to Paris after the Liberation. Individual exhibition at the Galerie Jeanne Bucher. Took part in a number of group exhibitions and also in the main abstract Salons. Was one of the most promising of the young abstract painters when he died at an early age. — Bibl. *Témoignages pour l'Art Abstrait* (Paris 1952).

CHARCHOUNE Serge (b. Bougourouslan, Russia, 1888). Refused entry to the School of Fine Arts in Kazan. Worked for several months in various Academies in Moscow. Arrived in Paris in 1912 and was associated with several independent Academies. Exhibited for the first time at the Salon des Indépendants in 1913. Spent the years 1914 to 1917 in Spain. His first individual exhibition was held in a bookshop in the Rue Dauphine in Paris in 1920. Between 1921 and 1924 he contributed to a number of reviews of the Dada movement. Work shown at the Sturm Gallery in Berlin in 1922. Has also exhibited in Barcelona, Stockholm, Brussels, New York and Prague. Several individual exhibitions at the Galerie Creuze in Paris (1947 to 1956). Now living in Paris.

The major part of Charchoune's work is abstract, but he does not hesitate to make occasional and sometimes startling excursions into figurative painting. Some of his best canvases owe their inspiration to the music of Bach or Beethoven, although this fact adds nothing to their obvious plastic qualities. It must be admitted that in his sentimental or mystical compositions Charchoune is disappointing. He is more at his ease in his Symbolist fantasy pieces. His work reaches unequalled heights of delicacy in modulations of single colour. These pictures, which are a kind of spiritual exercise for the eye, must be numbered among the best examples of pure painting. — *Bibl.* Autobiographical sketch in *L'Art Abstrait, ses Origines, ses Premiers Maîtres* (Paris 1949); *Collection of the Société Anonyme* (New Haven 1950).

CHASTEL Roger (b. Paris, 1897). Studied at the École des Beaux-Arts (Atelier Cormon) then at the Académie Julian and the Académie Ranson. Drawings and caricatures for exclusive magazines. Numerous exhibitions from 1926 onwards. Took part in the Venice and Sao Paulo Biennales. Did the illustrations for Paul

Éluard's *Bestiaire*. Drew sketches for Gobelins Tapestries in Paris. Has taken part in the Salon de Mai since its inauguration in 1948. His work is sometimes abstract but more often tending towards figurative art. Now living at Saint-Germain-en-Laye, near Paris. "The faculty of abstraction is peculiar to man, it is the specific quality of the creator... My practical objective is to attain complete abstraction, rejecting preconceived technical solutions. As the work progresses the original visual emotion, whether objective or subjective, suggests new relationships between colours and shapes which become more and more abstract as they take their place within the pattern of an inward illumination". (Chastel).

CHELIMSKY Oscar (b. New York, 1923). Studied at the Art Students League with Hans Hofmann (1946-1947). Came to Paris in 1948. Individual exhibition held at the Galerie Jeanne Bucher, Paris, 1953. Has taken part in many group exhibitions in Paris, Madrid,

Minneapolis, Amsterdam, and also in a number of Salons in Paris where he is now living. Chelimsky's painting is in a kind of calligraphic style—delicate and warm. His colours seem to float on the surface of the canvas as if reluctant to penetrate its texture. This abstract flora appears to be rippled as if by a soft breeze which, however, does not destroy its order. The artist's style changed in 1955 when he abandoned the use of mat-finish synthetic paint, and he began experimenting with shiny oils and thick mixes.

CHERMAYEFF Serge Ivan (b. Russia, 1900). Studied in London from 1910 to 1917, and then in Germany. Was appointed professor of architecture at Brooklyn College, United States, in 1952. From 1946 to 1951 was director of the Institute of Design in Chicago. Became an American citizen in 1946. Has taken part in many exhibitions in America and an individual showing of his work was held in Chicago in 1950. Now living in Chicago. His painting is rich in colour and skilful colour contrasts. His compositions are classical and frequently erudite.

CHESNAY Denise (b. Versailles, 1923). Educated in Algiers. Came to Paris in 1944. After first having experienced the influence of the earlier Cubists, then of the young abstract painters she developed a purely sensitive form of abstract art for herself. Has taken part in many group exhibitions and various Salons in Paris.

CHASTEL. DOOR TO A DREAM. 1954

CHILDS Bernard (b. New York, 1910). Studied at Pennsylvania University then worked with Kimon Nicolaides (1932) and with Amédée Ozenfant (1947). Individual exhibitions at the "Obelisco" in Rome in 1951, at the Galerie Breteau in Paris in 1953, and the Zimmergalerie in Frankfort in 1955. Has also taken part in many group exhibitions in Paris and in the Salon des Réalités Nouvelles in 1954. Now living in Paris. After first painting canvases in diffused colour sequences full of poetic fantasy, Childs adopted a more calligraphic style using a pizzicato effect of small black or grey strokes converging or dispersing.

CITRON Minna (b. Newark, New Jersey, 1896). Studied in New York. Travelled in Europe. Many exhibitions in America. Has taken part in the Salon des Réalités Nouvelles since 1947. Work shown at the Galerie Creuze, Paris, 1951. Travelling exhibition in South America in 1952. Now living in New York. — Bibl. *Minna Citron, Paintings and Graphics,* articles by Jean Cassou and others (New York 1952).

CLARK Edward (b. New Orleans, 1927). Studied for five years at the Chicago Art Institute. Began painting in 1946. Came to Paris in 1952 and took up abstract art in 1953. Has taken part in several group exhibitions. Individual exhibition at the Galerie Creuze, Paris, in 1955. His compositions are tall improvisations of very vivid colours. Now living in Paris.

CLAUSEN Fransiska (b. Denmark, 1899). Studied in Denmark and later in Berlin where she took lessons from Moholy-Nagy and Archipenko (1922). Abstract "collages" of geometrical shapes showing a marked influence of the Russian Constructivists. Worked in Paris from 1924 to 1933, first as a pupil of Léger and then independently. In 1926 she took part in Miss Dreier's International Exhibition of the Société Anonyme in Brooklyn. In 1929 she made the acquaintance of Mondrian, Arp and Seuphor, and joined the "Cercle et Carré" group with whom she exhibited in 1930. After her return to Denmark she gradually abandoned abstract art and took up portrait painting. Now living in retirement in Denmark. — Bibl. *The Société Anonyme,* Brooklyn Museum (Brooklyn 1926); *Art d'Aujourd'hui* (Paris, Oct. 1953).

CLOSON Henri J. (b. Liège, Belgium, 1888). Unsettled youth. Came to Paris after the 1914-1918 war and met Claude Monet, Mondrian and Béothy.

CHELIMSKY. PAINTING. 1955. *Galerie Jeanne Bucher, Paris.*

His studies of the reflection of colours in moving water gradually brought him to abstract art. Has regularly taken part in the Salon des Réalités Nouvelles. Now living in Paris.

COGGESHALL Calvert (b. New Utica, U.S.A., 1907). Studied art and architecture at Pennsylvania University and the Art Students League. Worked in Europe in 1937 and 1938. Individual exhibition at the Betty Parsons Gallery in New York in 1951, and in the same year his work was shown in the Abstract Painting and Sculpture in America exhibition organised by the Museum of Modern Art in New York. Now living at North Stonington, Connecticut.

COHEN Harold (b. 1928). Studied at the Slade School London, and held his first one-man shows at Oxford in 1951 and London in 1954. In 1956 was appointed Fellow in Fine Arts at Nottingham University.

COLLIGNON George (b. Liège, Belgium, 1923). Studied at the Académie des Beaux-Arts in Liège. Has produced abstract paintings since 1949. Took part in the "Les Mains Éblouies" exhibition at the Galerie Maeght in 1950 and 1951, and also in the Salon de Mai in Paris. Individual exhibitions in Liège (A.P.I.A.W.), Brussels (Galerie Apollo). Frankfort (Zimmergalerie), and Paris (Galerie Arnaud). Now living in Paris.

COMPARD Émile (b. Paris, 1900). Naturalist painter encouraged by Félix Fénéon and also by Bonnard who exchanged canvases with him. From 1946 onwards he turned towards figurative art and showed no works for almost ten years. Individual exhibition of abstract paintings at the Galerie Ariel, Paris 1955. Now lives in Paris.

CONGDON William (b. Providence, Rhode Island, 1912). Studied at Yale (New Haven), then worked with George Demetrios in Boston. Visited Italy in 1948. Individual exhibitions at the Betty Parsons Gallery, New York, in 1949, 1950 and 1952. Now lives either in New York or in Venice.

CONOVER Robert (b. Philadelphia, 1920). Studied in Philadelphia, in New York (Art Students League) and at the Brooklyn Museum School. His first individual exhibition was held at the Laurel Gallery in New York in 1950. Now lives in New York.

JEANNE COPPEL. COMPOSITION. 1955.

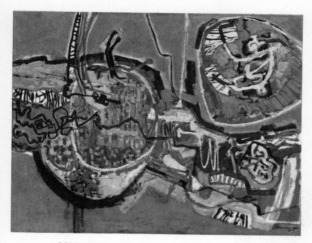

CORNEILLE. THE FLAMING SUMMER. 1955.
Galerie Craven, Paris.

CONSAGRA Pietro (b. Mozzara del Vallo, Italy, 1920). Individual exhibitions in Rome and Venice. Was one of the organisers of the Abstract Art in Italy Exhibition in Rome in 1948. Now lives in Rome.

CONTE Michelangelo (b. Spalato, Dalmatia, 1913). Formal studies in classics, but is a self-taught artist. Gradual development towards abstract art. His work has been shown in exhibitions in Naples, Rome, Venice, Berne, Vienna and Sao Paulo. Now lives in Rome.

COPPEL Jeanne (b. Galatz, Roumania, 1896). Childhood and youth spent mainly in Switzerland and Germany. Came into contact with the Sturm movement in Berlin in 1913. First abstract compositions in 1918 and 1919. Produced abstract "collages" about the same time. Settled in Paris in 1919 and worked at the Atelier Ranson with Sérusier, Vuillard, and Maurice Denis. Returned to abstract art in 1947, and has exhibited at the Salon des Réalités

Nouvelles since 1948. Individual exhibitions at the Galerie Colette Allendy (1950), and the Galerie Arnaud (1955). Lives in Paris. Jeanne Coppel's work has the same serious quality as that of Braque, the same serenity, the same discretion and the same measured tranquillity. She has a preference for mat tones and subdued colour combinations. At times she adds a vivid touch which is designed not so much to startle as to draw attention, by this apparent levity, to the underlying and hidden power in the work. — *Bibl.* Herta Wescher: *Jeanne Coppel,* Cimaise No. 5, Paris 1955.

CORBETT Edward (b. Chicago, 1919). Son of a Merchant Marine officer. Studied art in San Francisco from 1938 to 1940. In the Merchant Marine himself from 1942-1944. In New York from 1944-1946, and taught in various art schools in California from 1947-1950. Has taken part in several group exhibitions: New York 1947 ("American Abstract Artists"); Art Institute of Chicago in 1947; Henry Art Gallery, Seattle 1950; Museum of Modern Art, New York 1952 ("15 Americans"). Now living at Taos, New Mexico.

CORNEILLE Cornelis van Beverloo (b. Liège, Belgium, 1922). Of Dutch parentage. Attended classes in drawing at Amsterdam Academy from 1940 to 1943. In company with Appel and Constant founded the Dutch Experimental Group in 1948. Was co-founder of *Cobra* in Paris also in 1948. Individual exhibitions in Amsterdam (1951 and 1954), Rotterdam (1952), Budapest (1947), Copenhagen (1950), Antwerp (1953), and Paris (1953 and 1954). Has taken part in numerous group exhibitions at the Galerie Maeght, the Galerie Pierre, the Salon de Mai, and elsewhere in Paris. Now living in Paris. Painting characterised by the use of powerful arched structural motifs. Its expressive qualities are obtained by graphic effects either in black or colour, employed with both sensitivity and firmness.

CORPORA. GOUACHE. 1955.
Private Collection.

CORPORA Antonio (b. Tunis, 1909). Studied at the École des Beaux-Arts in Tunis. At the age of 20 went to Florence. Studied the Masters in the Uffizzi Gallery. Later came to Paris where his work was noticed by Modigliani's friend Zborowsky. Spent the years from 1930 to 1937 either in Paris or Tunis. His work was shown at the Milione Gallery in Milan in 1939. Has taken an active part both as a writer and lecturer in the controversy about abstract art. His main preoccupation is to combat the ideas of the "Novecento" group. Has taken part in many exhibitions in Tunis, in Italy and in Paris. Lives in Rome. — *Bibl.* Zervos: *Antonio Corpora* (Publ. Centre d'Art Italien, Paris 1952).

CORSI Carlo (b. Nice, 1879). Studied at the University of Bologna and Albertina Academy, Turin. Has taken part in the Venice Biennale since 1912 and also in many other Salons. Showed some very remarkable abstract "collages" in a group exhibition at the Palais des Beaux-Arts in Brussels. Now lives in Bologna.

COULON Jean-Michel (b. Bordeaux 1920). Studied history in Paris. Visited Picasso in 1943. Has produced abstract works since 1939. Held an exhibition of gouaches in various centres in South America in 1949. First individual exhibition at the Galerie Jeanne Bucher, Paris, in 1950. Spent a considerable time in Amsterdam. Took part in a group exhibition at the Sidney Janis Gallery, New York, in 1950. Visited Spain in 1952. Now lives in Paris.

COVERT John (b. Pittsburgh, Pennsylvania, 1882). Studied in Munich 1908-1912. Worked in Paris from 1912 to 1914. Visited England. Took part in various exhibitions in the United States. Gave up painting to go into business in 1923. Most of his work is in the collection of the Société Anonyme, New Haven. Lives in Pittsburgh. Covert was one of the first American abstract artists, and is still regarded as one of the most original figures in American painting of the period immediately following the first world war. — Bibl. *Collection of the Société Anonyme* (New Haven 1950); Ritchie: *Abstract Painting and Sculpture in America* (New York 1951).

CRAWFORD
Ralston (b. Sainte Catherine, Canada, 1906). Abandoned his career as a sailor to study art in Los Angeles and Philadelphia (1927-1933). Was in Europe in 1932 and 1933. Taught at the Cincinnati Academy in 1940 and 1941, and then at Buffalo and the Brooklyn School of Art (1948-1949). First individual exhibition in Philadelphia in 1937. Now living in New York.

CORSI. CASTLE ON THE SEA. PAPIER COLLÉ. 1954.

CRIPPA Roberto (b. Monza, Italy, 1921). Studied at the Milan Academy. Many exhibitions in Italy (since 1947) and in the United States (since 1951). Has regularly taken part in the Venice Biennale since 1948. He has developed a very calligraphic style with maze-like curved line patterns. Now lives in Milan.

CRIPPA. COMPOSITION. 1952.
Private Collection, Paris.

CROWLEY Grace (b. Australia, 1895). Studied at Sydney Art School. Spent some years in France (1927-1931). Studied under André Lhote and was influenced by Albert Gleizes. Took part in various exhibitions in Paris, but it was only after her return to Australia that she gradually gave up representational painting to become (with Ralph Balson) one of the few representatives of abstract art in Australia. Lives at Mittagong, Australia.

D

DAMIAN Horia (b. Bucharest, Rumania, 1922). Arrived in Paris in 1946. Studied under Lhote, then under Léger. Came to abstract painting in 1949. Met Herbin, and discovered neo-plasticism in 1951. Exhibited at the Salon des Réalités Nouvelles and in various group-shows, especially at the Galerie Arnaud. Lives in Paris.

DARIE Sandu (b. in Rumania, 1908). Educated in France. In Havana since 1941; a naturalized Cuban. One-man shows in Havana (The Lyceum) in 1949 and 1950. Included in exhibitions in New York and Japan. Since 1946, his work has been abstract. Sandu Darie uses panels of a simple geometrical design presented in frameless compositions. His favourite figure appears to be a triangle within which the neo-plastic elements, horizontal and vertical, are lightly and elegantly inscribed.

DAVIE Alan (b. Grangemouth, Scotland, 1920). Studied at the College of Art in Edinburgh and at the Royal Scottish Academy. Travelled and studied in France, Switzerland, Italy, and Spain. First exhibition in Edinburgh, 1946. Exhibited in Florence and Venice in 1948, in London in 1950 and 1952. Included in the *Jeunes Peintres* exhibition organized by the Congress for Cultural Freedom in Rome and in Paris in 1955, and also in an exhibition at the Galerie Bignou in 1956. Lives in London. Agonised abstractions derived, sometimes, from expressionism.

DAVIS Stuart (b. Philadelphia, 1894). Studied in New York. Exhibited five water-colours at the 'Armory Show' (1913). First one-man show in 1917. A cartographer in the army in 1918. In Paris, 1928-1929. Taught at the Art Students League, New York, 1931. Government post from 1933 to 1940. Then taught at the New School for Social Research, New York. Retrospective exhibition at the Museum of Modern Art, New York (1945).

STUART DAVIS. SALT-CELLAR. 1931.
Museum of Modern Art, New York.

154

Lives in New York. Among American painters, Stuart Davis is the one whose training was most influenced by cubism. From that point, his work slowly developed towards abstraction, more especially since 1938. Davis's style is generally forceful, but because of the very fresh colours, never harsh; there is always something of a joyous circus atmosphere. — *Bibl.* Hitchcock: *Painting toward Architecture* (New York 1948); Ritchie: *Abstract Painting and Sculpture in America* (New York 1951); *Art d'Aujourd'hui* (Paris, June 1951); *Art News* (New York, summer 1953); *50 Ans d'art aux États-Unis,* Musée d'Art Moderne (Paris 1955).

DEBRÉ. STILL LIFE. 1954.

DAVRING Henri (b. Aachen, 1900). Studied at Dusseldorf Academy and then under the painter Eckstein. He was famous in Germany under his real name, Davringhausen, having precociously exhibited at Flechtheim's, Dusseldorf, and been a member of the 'Novembergruppe' in Berlin. Took part in numerous exhibitions in Germany up to 1933. Emigrated when Hitler came to power. His work was included in the 'Degenerate Art' exhibition. Spent a few years in Spain and in Switzerland, came finally to France. One-man shows at the Galerie des Deux-Iles, Paris, 1949 and 1950, the Galerie Verneuil, Paris, 1955. Lives in Cagnes-sur-Mer (Alpes-Maritimes, France). Almost all of Davring's canvases are variations on a simple theme : two or three straight lines intersected by one or two curves. This movement details the opposition of two principles, their fusion in a composition being celebrated variously, in delicate or crude colours,

according to the mood of the painter. The theme develops in a complete calm with no hint of tragedy, like a cloudless sky.

DEBRÉ Olivier (b. Paris, 1920). After matriculation, he travelled in Italy and studied architecture for a year at the École des Beaux-Arts, Paris. Spent a year as a student in England (1939). Became more and more interested in painting. Met Othon Friesz, Segonzac, and Picasso (1941). Took part in the Salon des Surindépendants and the Salon d'Automne. One-man show at the Galerie Bing, Paris, 1949. Visited Holland, 1950. Included in various group-shows in New York and Paris. Exhibited with Germain at the Galerie Warren, Paris 1957. Lives in Paris. He composes with planes of dulled colours very cleverly combined. He makes one think of the best of De Staël, whom he seems to have already excelled.

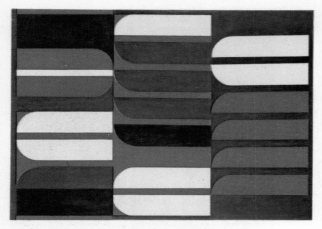

DELAHAUT. ASTRAL. 1953.

timentality, anchored to the pedestrian conclusions of sensual perception, was not done in a day. But now it is an accomplished fact, and Degottex, at the helm, can guard the spoils" (André Breton).

DEGOTTEX Jean (b. Sathonay, Ain, France, 1918). Self-educated. Came to Paris in 1933. His first paintings, done during a stay in Tunisia (1938-41), were in the Fauve manner. On his return to Paris, took part in various exhibitions. His first non-representational canvases exhibited at the Galerie Denise René in 1949 and 1952. Included in the Salon de Mai and the Salon d'Octobre. Took part in the exhibition 'Tendances', Galerie Maeght, Paris, 1952; in many exhibitions at the Galerie Kléber, Paris, 1954 and 1955, and also in the 'Younger European Painters' exhibition at the Solomon R. Guggenheim Museum, New York, 1953-4. One-man show at Étoile Scellée, Paris, 1955. Lives in Paris. Through his exploration of the possibilities of a highly coloured line, Degottex developed, about 1955, a powerful style; the projection of a self-sufficient personal vision which seeks to reveal itself spontaneously in every work. "In art, this quest for eternal verity, necessarily at odds with immediacy, has, during the last three-quarters of a century, become more and more urgent. To loosen the bonds which hold us, by habit as much as by sen-

DELAHAUT Jo (b. Liège, Belgium, 1911). Studied at the Académie des Beaux-Arts, Liège. Doctorate in Archaeology and Art History (1939). Made his debut in 1940 under the Fauve banner. First abstract paintings in 1944. Exhibited every year at the Salon des Réalités Nouvelles. Organised, 1952, the Belgian 'Art Abstrait' group, of which the first members were Bury, Collignon, Plomteux, Saverys, Burssens, Carrey, Milo. After submitting to the influences of Pignon and Gischia, Delahaut turned toward mathematical abstraction and became friendly with Herbin. One-man show at the Galerie Arnaud, Paris, 1952. Taught design at the Athénée of Shaerbeek. In 1956, exhibited in Brussels 'plastic mobiles' and 'spatial reliefs'. Lives in Brussels. His painting is restrained and geometric, in swathes of undiluted colours. — Bibl. Séaux: Delahaut, De Sikkel (Antwerp 1955).

DELAUNAY Robert (b. Paris, 1885; d. Montpellier, 1941). At 17, worked in a scene-designer's in Belleville. Began painting in Brittany during holidays, under the influence of the Pont-Aven School. Devoted himself entirely to painting in 1905; neo-impressionism. Friendly with Metzinger, then with Douanier Rousseau.

Romantic painting (*Église de Laon, Intérieur de Saint-Séverin*) in 1909. In 1910, began the lyrical series of the *Tour Eiffel,* the *Villes,* the *Fenêtres.* Included in the "Blaue Reiter" exhibition in Munich, 1912. Friendship with Apollinaire and Albert Gleizes. Travelled to Berlin with Apollinaire in 1913, when his one-man show was being held at the Der Sturm Gallery. Met de Macke in Bonn. Was travelling in Spain in 1914, when the war broke out. Stayed for some time in Lisbon. Met Diaghilev for whom he designed the decors of the ballet *Cleopatra.* Returned to Paris 1921. Retrospective exhibition at the Galerie Paul Guillaume, 1922. His house became a favourite meeting-ground for the poets of the avant-garde. In 1930, incited by Gleizes, he returned to

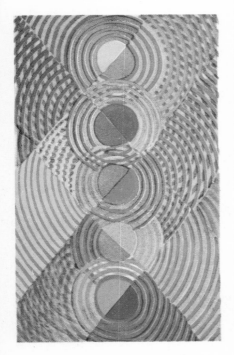

abstract themes abandoned in 1912 and began the series of the *Rythmes sans Fin* and paintings in relief. Met Kandinsky in 1938. Included in the "Réalités Nouvelles" exhibition at the Galerie Charpentier, Paris, 1939. During the 1940 invasion of France, he took refuge in Auvergne, then in Mougins, near Cannes. Died in Montpellier.

To Delaunay fell the task of maintaining the continuity of the French contribution to pure abstraction, never breaking with the lyrical tradition and rationality representative of the Paris School. In estimating the evolution of painting since 1911, his merit cannot be overstressed. Without departing radically from recent tradition, he was instinctively more influenced by his senses than by his reason, although finally always holding the senses within limits: he thus revealed a highly individual approach, never tired of trying new resonances of colours, of experimenting with new rhythms, which always, as though spontaneously, blended into an absolute harmony. The man himself was disarmingly frank, and if he sometimes dreamt of the impossible with excessive fervour, he can be forgiven for his art; one can nowhere find the slightest hint of exasperated revolt, of a too brutal solution of continuity. Delaunay's art is exalting, and yet not boundlessly so. He is the most eminent French representative in the emerging movement of abstract art. This is why he should be ranked with the great pioneers of abstract art, Mondrian, Kandinsky, Malevitch; neither beneath them nor apart from them in reputation. The work of Delaunay from 1912 to 1913 is as rich and pregnant as theirs. Important retrospective exhibition of Delaunay's work in Paris at the Musée d'Art Moderne in 1957. — *Bibl.* Jean Cassou: préface pour l'exposition à la Galerie Carré (Paris 1946); Seuphor: *L'Art Abstrait, ses Origines, ses Premiers Maîtres* (Paris 1949); Gille de la Tourette: *Robert Delaunay* (Paris 1950); "Art d'Aujourd'hui" (Paris, October 1951; studies by Degand and Seuphor; March 1950: article on *Orphisme,* by Seuphor);

SONIA DELAUNAY. COMPOSITION. 1955.

A *Dictionary of Modern Painting* (Methuen, London 1956); George L. K. Morris: *Dialogues with Delaunay.* Art News (New York, January 1955). Catalogue of the Musée d'Art Moderne exhibition; Degand: *Robert Delaunay,* "Aujourd'hui", nº 12, Paris 1957; *Art Abstrait, les premières générations,* Musée de St. Étienne, 1957.

DELAUNAY Sonia Terk (b. Ukraine, 1885). Studied in St. Petersburg, then in Germany. Travels to Paris and Finland in 1905. Settled permanently in Paris the following years. First married to the German critic Wilhelm Uhde, in whose gallery she exhibited in 1907. Then married Robert Delaunay in 1910. In 1913, she illuminated Cendrars's *La Prose du Transsibérien* and painted large abstract canvases (Simultaneous Rhythms), which represent a serious contribution to the evolution of abstract art. Her stimulating presence played an important role in the development of her husband's art. Lived in Spain and Portugal, 1914-1919. Back in Paris in 1920, she devoted herself mainly to fashion-

designing and decoration. For a number of years, she held a very lively salon, Boulevard Malesherbes, in which she tried to renew the trends of fashion, or better to give fashion a new spark by challenging it with the plastic arts. She published printed materials, which she exhibited in a famous stand at the Arts Décoratifs exhibition in Paris. Took part in the 'Réalités Nouvelles' exhibition, Ga-

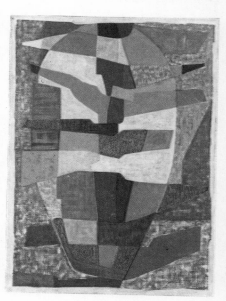

DEYROLLE. SULTANAH. 1955.
Private Collection, Brussels.

158

lerie Charpentier, 1939, and helped to organize the 'Art Concret' exhibition, Galerie Drouin, 1945. Since 1946, exhibited at the Salon des Réalités Nouvelles. Took part in exhibitions in London, Vienna, Belgium and South America, as well as in *Premiers maîtres de l'Art abstrait,* Galerie Maeght, Paris 1949. These last years, Sonia Delaunay has resumed her painting with brilliant results. Her art, which at the beginning, inclined more towards the Fauves and Gauguin, than Cézanne and Cubism, has retained its warmth and an exuberant lyricism befitting the "orphic" powers of the Delaunays. One-man show in Paris, Galerie Bing, 1954, in New York, Rose Fried Gallery, and Liège (A.P.I.A.W.) in 1955. Took part with her husband in the exhibition *Art Abstrait, les premières générations,* Musée de St. Étienne, 1957. Lives in Paris. — *Bibl.* Seuphor: *L'Art Abstrait, ses Origines, ses Premiers Maîtres* (Paris 1949); *Témoignages pour l'Art abstrait* (Paris 1952); *A Dictionary of Modern Painting* (Methuen, London 1956).

DEWASNE Jean (b. Hellemmes-Lille, 1921). Began to paint at the age of 12, whenever he could find time free from school and music lessons. After matriculation, studied architecture for two years, but only to prepare himself better for painting. He sketched every morning for five years, from still and life models. Performed many kinds of manual labour, often more out of curiosity than necessity. Then, in turn, professor of perspective, assistant in films, journalist. Abstract painting since 1943. A member of the Galerie Denise René group, from its formation (1945) up to 1956. Directed the Academy of Abstract Art with Pillet (1950-2). One-man show at the Galerie Denise René. Was included in the great abstract Salons in Paris and in numerous group-shows in the main European countries. Lives in Paris. Dewasne excels in great mural compositions. In his

DEWASNE. BADIA. 1954.

easel works, the striking colours in vehement opposition seem sometimes to leap out from the frame, despite the solid structure of the composition. — *Bibl.* Pierre Descargues: *J. Dewasne* (Paris 1952); *Témoignages pour l'Art abstrait* (Paris 1952); Léon Degand: *Dewasne,* 'Art d'Aujourd'hui' (Paris, December 1953).

DEYROLLE Jean (b. Nogent.s.Marne, 1911). Childhood in Brittany. Studied advertising in Paris, then began painting, without instruction. Travelled in Morocco and in Spain from 1932 to 1937. Returned to Brittany in 1938. Influenced by Sérusier and then by Braque. Came to Paris in 1942. Increasingly influenced by the cubists until he met Domela who launched him into abstraction. Jeanne Bucher bought his first non-representational canvases. In 1948, met Wilhelm Uhde who encouraged his work. A number of stays in Denmark (where he drew two albums of lithographs) and in Germany. Exhibited regularly in the Galerie Denise René from 1946 on. Took part in a number of group-shows and in the abstract Salons of Paris. Lives in Paris. Deyrolle composes free structures in shaded tones, sometimes discreet and sometimes subtle. His work seems dominated by a patient and wise analysis of values. "To touch many levels of meaning, square, bird, warmth, friendship, through multiplicity and formal combinations, is that what I am looking for? How can I know? When vision becomes so multiple, one naturally ceases to attach importance to the so-called object. Besides it is only when the painting is completed that one can discuss colours, forms, dynamism. But during the work, reason is not called upon constantly, everything seems intuitive. One should not be overmuch concerned about theory: most painters play fast and loose with theirs. This is no irony, even less a criticism. For me, this cheating is a phenomenon of permanent inventiveness; it is, in the end, this very cheating which nurtures the evolution of the artist and keeps the art from sclerosis". (From conversations of Deyrolle, noted by Julien Alvard). — Bibl. *Témoignages pour l'Art abstrait* (Paris 1952).

DIAS Cicero (b. in Pernambuco, Brazil, 1908). School of Architecture in Rio de Janeiro. First exhibition in Brazil in 1928. Taught drawing and painting in Pernambuco. 1937, moved permanently to Paris. 1938, shows at the galleries Jeanne Castel and Caputo. 1943, exhibitions in Lisbon and London. Painted his first abs-

DIAS. COMPOSITION. 1954.

tract compositions the same year. Included in exhibitions at Denise René's and the Galerie Drouin. Biennale of Venice in 1950 and 1952. An attaché at the Brazilian Embassy in Paris. — *Bibl.* 'Art d'Aujourd'hui' (Paris, Sept. 1954).

DIEBENKORN Richard (b. Portland, U.S., 1922). Studied at Stanford and the University of California (1940-3), then at the California School of Fine Arts (1946). Many one-man shows in California since 1948. Included in the *Younger American Painters* exhibition at the Solomon R. Guggenheim Museum in New York, 1954, and in the *Jeunes Peintres* exhibition at the Museum of Modern Art, Paris, 1955. Was a professor at the University of Illinois. Lives in Berkeley, California. Diebenkorn's work is a supple plastic universe which can be placed in the tradition of Motherwell and Hans Hofman. He seems one of the most assured young talents in American painting.

DILLER Burgoyne (b. New York, 1906). Began to paint at the age of fourteen and studied for many years in various academies. Held various practical jobs related to the fine arts; was a professor of industrial design. After being successively interested in expressionism and impressionism, he turned to Cézanne and cubism, and then, logically launched into neo-plasticism. He has been a disciple of Mondrian (1934) longer than anyone in the United States. He was intimate with Harry Holtzmann, who travelled to Paris for the sole purpose of meeting Mondrian. One-man shows at the Rose Fried Gallery in New York in 1946, 1949, 1951. Exhibited with the "American Abstract Artists". Included in the "Abstract Painting and Sculpture in America" show at the Museum of Modern Art, New York, 1951. Lives in New York. Diller is the only American painter to apply in a thorough way the principles of pure neo-plasticism: horizontal-vertical composition and primary colours. Although the influence of Mondrian is obvious, the painting does not lack a distinctive character, springing from the personal vision of the painter. "Diller is one of the most imaginative of the neo-plastic painters. It is impossible te realize the richness and possibilities of this form of art unless one has seen the hundreds of studies which Diller has made in pencil, crayon, pastel and watercolor on white paper." (Kath. S. Dreier). — Bibl. *Collection of the Société Anonyme* (New Haven 1950); Ritchie: *Abstract Painting and Sculpture in America* (New York 1951); *Diller paints a picture,* Art News, New York, October 1952.

DMITRIENKO Pierre (b. Paris 1925). Studied architecture at the same time as painting. Has devoted himself completely to painting since 1947. Took part in various exhibitions in a number of important galleries in Paris, and in exhibitions of French Art in Madrid, Edinburgh, as well as at the Salon de Mai. One-man show at the Galerie Lucien Durant, Paris 1953 and 1954. Lives in Paris.

DOESBURG Theo van (b. Utrecht, Holland, 1883; d. Davos 1931). His real name was Küpper. He wrote also under the pen-names of I. K. Bonset and Aldo Camini. Studied in Holland. First thought of becoming an actor. First paintings in 1899. First exhibition in The Hague, 1908. Published articles and a collection of poems (1913). Met Mondrian in 1915 and planned the review *De Stijl* with him. The first issue of it appeared in October 1917. Collaborated with the Dutch

DMITRIENKO. DIVES-SUR-MER. 1955. *Galerie L. Durand, Paris.*

architects Oud and Wils from 1916 on; painted his first abstract canvases the same year. Went on a propaganda tour around Europe in 1920-1921, to publicize the ideas of *De Stijl*. Introduced dadaism in Holland in 1922 and published the *Mecano* review. Friendship with Kurt Schwitters who accompanied him on a 'dadaist tour' of Holland. 1923, invited by Léonce Rosenberg to organize a *De Stijl* group-exhibition at the Galerie de l'Effort Moderne, Paris. Collaborated with the Dutch architect van Eesteren. Abandoned neo-plasticism in 1925 and published the 'Elementarist' manifesto (*De Stijl* no. 75-76). Decorated the 'Aubette' *café-dansant* in Strasbourg in collaboration with Arp and Sophie Taeuber (completed in 1928). In Paris 1929-1930. Published *Art Concret* with Hélion, Carlsund and Tutundjian.

Principal works of Theo van Doesburg: *De Nieuwe beweging in de schilderkunst* (Delft 1917); *Drie voordrachten over de nieuwe beeldende kunst* (Amsterdam 1919); *Grundbegriffe der neuen gestaltenden Kunst* (Munich 1924); *Classique, baroque, moderne* (Paris 1921); *Wat is dada?* (The Hague 1923); *L'Architecture Vivante* (Paris 1925). — Bibl. *Prisma der kunsten,* Zeist (Holland, May 1936); Barr: *Cubism and abstract art* (New York 1936); *Art of this Century* (New York 1942); *Painting toward Architecture* (New York 1948); Seuphor: *L'Art abstrait, ses Origines, ses Premiers Maîtres* (Paris 1949); *Collection of the Société Anonyme* (New Haven 1950); Raynal: *De Picasso au Surréalisme* (Geneva and Paris, 1950); Catalogue of the *De Stijl* exhibition (Amsterdam 1951); *The dada painters and poets* (New York 1952); 'Art d'Aujourd'hui' (Paris, Dec. 1953); *A Dictionary of Modern Painting* (Methuen, London 1956).

DOMELA Cesar (b. Amsterdam, 1900). Began to paint at the age of 19. Lived in Switzerland from 1922 to 1923. Abstract paintings included in the 'Novembergruppe' exhibition in Berlin, 1923. Friendship with Mondrian, Paris, 1924; he joined the *De Stijl* movement. Exhibition in The Hague in 1924. In Berlin from 1927 to 1933. Then settled in Paris. One-man show at the Galerie Pierre in 1934. Co-publisher of the review *Plastique* with Arp and Sophie Taeuber in 1937.

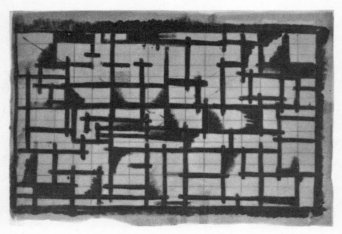

VAN DOESBURG. DESIGN. 1916.

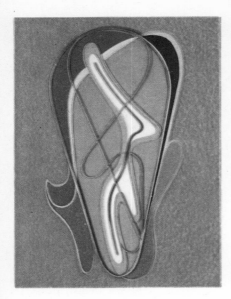

Included in the "Réalités Nouvelles" exhibition, Galerie Charpentier, 1939. Founded the 'Centre de Recherche' group in 1946. One-man show at Denise René's, Paris 1947, and the Galerie Colette Allendy in 1949 and 1951. Took part in the great abstract Salons in Paris as well as in exhibitions in London, Amsterdam, Stockholm, etc. Travel to Brazil and an exhibition there in 1954. Since 1928, Domela constructs "tableaux-objets", paintings which are also things, composed of various materials. He lives in Paris. "I feel certain that meditation, before and after work, will play an immense part with the majority of abstract artists. Before beginning their painting, they already have, as a result of this meditation, a more or less precise foresight of their composition. The fact that a painting should be an organization and not an arrangement, obliges them to know their theme thoroughly in order to attain full resonance. In abstract art, com-

pletely liberated from all narration, there remains only one link with the other arts: rhythm. Since the sanskrit root for *charm* is the same as *to pray* and *to paint*, couldn't one conclude, that a painting, especially an abstraction, is the crystallization of a painted prayer? Couldn't a painting be the basis for a meditation, a sort of yantra for the western soul?" (Domela). — Bibl. *Art of this Century* (New York 1942); *Französische Abstrakte Malerei* (Stuttgart 1948); *Témoignages pour l'Art Abstrait* (Paris 1952); *Domela*: Six reproductions in colour, préface by Kandinsky (Paris, no date); Brion, Sibert: *Domela,* Museo de arte moderna (Rio de Janeiro 1954).

DONATI Enrico (b. Milan, 1909). In Paris from 1934 to 1940, and then in the U.S. Friendly with Breton and the Surrealist group. Numerous one-man shows in New York, Paris, Milan, Venice, Rome. Took part in the Venice and Sao Paolo Biennales. Lives in New York. For some time past, Donati's art has developed toward the analysis of the material *per se,* which causes him to lose the taste for complexity and leads him to simple values which are impressive in their austere nudity. — Bibl. *Donati,* Ed. el Milione (Milan 1954); *Donati* (Cavallino, Venice 1954).

DORAZIO Piero (b. Rome, 1927). Studies in Rome and Paris. Since 1947, one of the exponents of abstract art in Rome. Travelled to the U.S. in 1954; one-man show at the Rose Fried Gallery. Other individual exhibitions : Galleria Apollinaire, Milan 1955, Galleria del Cavallino, Venice 1956, Galleria La Tartaruga, Rome 1957. Has taken part in many group exhibitions, in Italy, Switzerland, France and the Scandinavian countries. Occasional contributor to the leading Italian art reviews. Lives in Rome, where he published in 1954 *la Fan-*

tasia dell'arte nella vita moderna (Ed. Polverani e Quinti).

DORFLES Gillo (b. Trieste, 1910). Co-founder with Munari and Monnet of the Milanese 'Arte Concreta' group. Included in the first exhibition of Italian abstract art, in Milan, 1945. One-man shows since 1949. Included in many group-shows. Dorfles is also an art critic. He has published a number of articles on abstract art in specialized reviews in France and in Italy. Lives in Milan.

DOUCET Jacques (b. Boulogne.s.Seine 1924). Friendly with Max Jacob who encouraged him to paint. Influenced by Picasso's 'Blue Period'. After the Liberation, he discovered colour through the work of Matisse; stark plasticism through the work of Miro and Klee. Various one-man shows at the Galerie Colette Allendy, Paris, since 1948. Takes part in the "Les Mains Éblouies" exhibition, Galerie Maeght, 1949. Travels, accompanied by exhibitions, in Central Europe, Italy and Switzerland. One-man show at the Galerie Ariel, Paris, 1954. Lives in Paris.

DOUCHEZ Jacques (b. Mâcon, 1921). Academic mission in Brazil. Studied abstract painting under Flexor, in Sao Paolo, from 1948 on. Took part in the Abstraction Workshop in Brazil. Included in the Sao Paolo Biennales. One-man show at the Museum of Modern Art of Sao Paolo in 1955. Lives in Sao Paolo.

DOVA Gianni (b. Rome, 1925). Studied at the Brera Academy in Milan. One-man shows in Milan, Venice, Rome. Included in a number of group-shows in Paris, more especially at the Galeries Craven and Rive Droite (1954). Lives in Rome.

DOVE Arthur G. (b. Canandaigua, U.S.A., 1880; d. Huntington, U.S.A., 1946). Began to study art at the age of nine. Worked as a book-illustrator, then, about 1908, travelled in France and in Italy. First exhibition at the 'Stieglitz Gallery 291' in 1910. As early as 1912, starting from naturalistic subjects, he developed towards abstraction. — Bibl. *Collection of the Société Anonyme* (New Haven 1950); Ritchie: *Abstract painting and sculpture in America* (New York 1951).

DOWNING Joseph Dudley (b. Kentucky, 1925). Studied at the Art Institute of Chicago. After a one-

DOUCET. PAINTING. 1955.
Prince J. Troubetzkoy Collection, Paris.

man show in Chicago, he came to Paris where he took part in a number of group-shows, his painting developing all the while towards a completely abstract art, finally attained in a one-man show at the Studio Fachetti, in 1955. "The artist expresses himself like a medium communicating to us the secrets revealed to him. Sometimes we are summoned to bright feasts, sometimes we hear gentle lays." (Herta Wescher).

DREIER Katherine S. (b. New York, 1877; d. Milford, Conn., 1952). Studied art privately and at the Art Students League. Came to Paris in 1907. Periods in London, Munich and Holland. Returned to New York in 1913. Took part in the "Armory Show". Founded, in 1920, with the direct collaboration of Marcel Duchamp and Man Ray, the Société Anonyme. In China, 1921-1922. Met Mondrian in Paris, 1925. Bought one of his paintings for the Société Anonyme, the first Mondrian in America. A member of "Abstraction-Création". Marcel Duchamp's famous *Nude descending the staircase,* which was the sensation of the 'Armory Show' in New York, 1913, opened her eyes to the merits of creative abstraction. But her work as a painter is much less important than her influence as an *animateur.* The travelling exhibitions across the States, containing the works of Malevitch, Mondrian, Brancusi, Kandinsky, Schwitters, and many others, which she organized to publicize the new art, cleared the way for the full development of abstract art in the United States. Her *Portrait de Marcel Duchamp* (1918) is at the Museum of Modern Art, New York. — Bibl. *Katherine S. Dreier,* Academy of Allied Arts (New York 1933); *Collection of the Société Anonyme* (New Haven 1950).

DUFOUR Bernard (b. Paris, 1922). Intended to be a Forestry Inspector, but was sent on compulsory duty

DOWNING. KAYFER QUEENISH. 1955.

in German factories in 1943. It was there he discovered modern painting through reproductions. Came back to France in 1945. Agricultural Engineer in 1946. At the same time, he frequented the studios of Montparnasse and the École des Beaux-Arts. Exhibited in various salons from 1949 on, at the Galerie Jeanne Bucher and at the Galerie Pierre. Lives in Paris. "I notice in my study of nature, that completely different landscapes often provoke almost identical feelings, and I wonder then what can be this special, secret language, of which I perceive fragments almost accidentally. Seeing nature in that light, I sense that there must exist a series of constants which I perceive through their reflections in my soul, reflections constantly identical, in so far as a sensitive instrument like the soul can respond in the same way under all circumstances. It seems possible therefore, that from natural events, from the subjective and the objective, one may one day deduce something like an intimate and fundamental law." (Dufour).

DUMITRESCO. PAINTING. 1954.
Pierre Wurth Collection, Paris.

DUMITRESCO Natalia (b. Bucharest, Rumania, 1915). Matriculated in 1934. Degree in Fine Arts in 1939. Included in various group-shows and official Salons in Bucharest. Came to Paris in 1947. Travelled in Holland and Italy in 1948, in Spain in 1953. Took part in many Paris exhibitions, as well as in the Salon des Réalités Nouvelles. After a number of years working in black and white, she prudently tackled the problem of colours, showing undoubted originality and a great freshness of colours in her recent compositions. Married to the painter Istrati. Lives in Paris.

DUSTIR Wilma (b. Baku, Russia, 1914). Abstract painting since 1948. Has taken part in group-shows in Buenos Aires where she lives.

E

EGGELING Wiking (b. Lund, Sweden, 1880; d. Berlin, 1925). From 1900 to 1908, travelled and studied in Switzerland and in Italy. Paris in 1911. Met Modigliani and Arp. Back in Switzerland again in 1915, where he met Tristan Tzara. Composed abstract drawings in 1917, becoming a member of the dada movement in Zurich. Became friendly with Hans Richter in 1918; accompanied him to Germany, in Klein-Koelzig. Created in Berlin, 1919, the famous *rouleau* he called *Messe Horizontale-Verticale* and, in 1920, the *Symphonie Diagonale* rouleau, which he filmed the following year. — *Bibl.* 'Plastique nᵒ 2' (Paris 1937); Seuphor: *L'Art abstrait, ses Origines, ses Premiers Maîtres* (Paris 1949); *Wiking Eggeling*, National-museum (Stockholm 1950); *The Dada Painters and Poets* (New York 1951).

EGUCHI Sogen (b. Japan, 1919). Exhibited at the Japanese Institute of Calligraphy as an Art-form (1949-1951). A member of the Bokusin-Kai School since 1952. Contributed to the Japanese reviews of abstract calligraphy *Bokubi* and *Bokuzin*. Included in exhibitions in Osaka and in Tokyo, as well as in the two exhibitions of Japanese abstract calligraphy at the Museum of Modern Art, New York (1954); at the Galerie Colette Allendy, Paris, 1955; at the Stedelijk Museum in Amsterdam; at the Kunsthalle in Basel; and at the Musée Cernuschi in Paris (1956). Lives in Japan. — *Bibl.* Seuphor: *La Calligraphie Japo-naise,* 'Art d'Aujourd'hui' (Paris, Dec. 1954); Catalogue de l'exposition au Musée Cernuschi (Paris 1956).

EICHMANN Heinrich (b. Fluhi, Switzerland, 1915). Included in group-shows in Zurich and Paris since 1944. A member of the 'Die Allianz' Association. Lives in Zurich.

ELLIOTT Ronnie (b. New York, 1916). First influenced by the Impressionists and Cézanne. Attracted by surrealism in 1937. Then veered towards

EGUCHI. BLACK AND WHITE. 1954.

the art of Kandinsky and Mondrian. Since 1945, her work is completely abstract. A number of exhibitions in America since 1933. Took part in the Salon des Réalités Nouvelles, Paris, from 1948 on. One-man shows at the Galerie Creuze, Paris, 1948, and Galerie Colette Allendy in 1952. Lives in New York. In her most recent work, Ronnie Elliott moves towards an abstract impressionism with a textural quality akin to Monet.

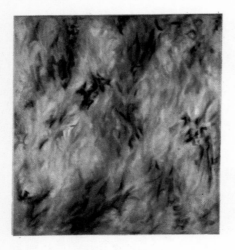

ELLIOTT. PAINTING. 1953.

ÉNARD André (b. Le Mans, Sarthe, 1926). Came to Paris in 1944. École des Beaux-Arts. Worked in the studios of Lhote and Léger. Influenced by Herbin and neo-plasticism in 1950. One-man show at the Galerie Arnaud, Paris, 1952. Lives in Paris.

ENGEL-PAK (b. Spa, Belgium, 1885). Also known under the name of Engel-Rozier. A chequered career as a young man. First exhibition at the Galerie Vignol, Paris, 1926. In 1927, after a long connection with Torrès-Garcia, he came by stages to abstraction. Lengthy stay near Toulon. Included in an abstract group-show in Paris after the Liberation and exhibited many times at the Salon des Réalités Nouvelles. Has illustrated with coloured lithographs Paul Éluard's *Objet des mots et des images* (Paris 1947). One-man show at Colette Allendy's in 1952. Lives in Southern France. Stains of bright colours almost life-like in their vividness, on a monochromatic background.

ERASMUS Nel (b. Bethal, Transvaal, 1928). Dutch ancestry. Studied Fine Arts at the Witwatersrand University in Johannesburg. Worked as a label- and letter-designer in a factory and then as a teacher. Travelled to London in 1953. In Paris (1953-1955), attended classes at the École des Beaux-Arts and the Académie Ranson. Included in group-shows and in the Salon des Réalités Nouvelles. Lives in Transvaal.

ERNST Jimmy (born Cologne, 1920). Son of Max Ernst. Studied at the Lindenthal Real Gymnasium, Cologne, and the School of Applied Arts in Altona. Came to New York, 1938. Has taught in Brooklyn College since 1951. Numerous one-man shows in the United States. Included in the 'Abstract Painting and Sculpture in America' exhibition at the Museum of Modern Art, New York, 1951, and in 'Younger American Painters', at the Solomon R. Guggenheim Museum, New York 1954. Lives in Rowayton (Connecticut). Compositions in very clear plastic language: lines predominate; frank lines and forms without ambiguity.

ERZINGER Lili (b. Zurich, 1908). Studied in Switzerland and in Paris. Worked under Lhote, Bissière, Severini, Léger, Arp (1936-1937). Taught painting for some time in the United States. Lives in Neuchâtel (Switzerland).

ESTÈVE Maurice (b. Culan, Cher, 1904). Studied at various Paris Academies. Spent a year in Spain and directed a workshop of design for a textile factory in Barcelona. Then worked until 1927 at the Académie Colarossi, Paris, and since 1928 has exhibited in the main Paris Salons. One-man shows: Galerie Yvangot (1930); Galerie Carré (1948); Galerie Galanis (1955 and 1956). Took part in a number of group-shows in Prague, Stockholm, Copenhagen, Amsterdam, etc. Collaborated with Robert Delaunay in the decoration of the Railway and Aviation Pavilions at the Exposition Universelle, Paris 1937. Lives and works in isolation in his Montmartre studio. Likes to brave colours at their most naked and exciting, showing a particular fondness for red which he can make vibrate with masculine ecstasy. "Esteve is one of those painters in whom one can best see, reduced to scale, the harmonious organization of aspects, emotions, suggestions, thoughts, even illusions, excited by contact with a theme which is at first vague, and which yet gradually attracts and centres the artist's sensations, both vivid and quiescent." (Pierre Courthion, *Peintres d'Aujourd'hui,* Geneva 1952).

EVANS Merlyn (b. 1910). Born of Welsh parentage in Cardiff. Studied at Glasgow School of Art, and at the Royal College of Art, London. In 1936 met Ozenfant, Mondrian, Kandinsky, Hé-

ESTÈVE. WATER-COLOUR. 1955.
Galerie S. Heller, Paris.

lion, Hayter and other leaders of abstract art, and began to study engraving. In 1939 went to Durban (South Africa) where he held his first exhibition. His first London exhibition was held in 1949; a large retrospective exhibition was held at Whitechapel in 1956.

F

FALCHI Ettore (b. Rome, 1913). Began as a music-hall performer. At one time was world-famous as a variety-show athlete. Began to paint in 1939. Studied at non-institutional Academies. Studied Egyptian art and the Italian primitives. First abstract painting in 1946. Exhibited in New York (1947), Paris (1948), Copenhagen (1950), Lausanne (1954); took part in the Salon des Réalités Nouvelles and in displays of the 'Espace' group. Great geometrical compositions with reliefs. Lives in Paris.

FASSBENDER Josef (b. Cologne, 1903). Studied at the Fine Arts School in Cologne. His works are in a number of museums and private collections. Took part in the German non-representational exhibition at the Cercle Volney, Paris, 1955. Lives in Cologne.

FATHWINTER (F. A. Th. Winter) (b. Mainz-Castel, Germany, 1906). At first a factory-hand. Self-educated. From 1926 to 1928, travelled through Belgium, Holland and Poland. First exhibition in 1931. From 1933 on, being under a Nazi ban, worked in seclusion in Krefeld. 1945, many exhibitions, particularly in Munich, Cologne, Hanover and Wuppertal. Stayed a few months in Paris on a French government grant. Included in the Salon des Réalités Nouvelles in 1954 and 1955. Lives in Dusseldorf.

FAUTRIER Jean (born Paris, 1898 of parents from Béarn). Educated in London. Recalled to France by the 1914 war. Campaigned for three years; was both wounded and gassed. Exhibited ten canvases in a Paris garage in 1921. For a few years, starting from 1925, Paul Guillaume encouraged him. At

FATHWINTER. ACCENT IN GREY. 1954.

the time, Fautrier kept a hotel in the Alps and gave skiing lessons. After the Second World War, exhibited at the Galerie Drouin, Place Vendôme, Paris. Fautrier paints in thick masses, using a very limited palette, grey for preference. His is pure painting, if ever there was; the titles change nothing: *fruits, nus, otages, objets* are all interchangeable. He had one-man shows at the Galerie Rive Droite, Paris, in 1955 and 1956. Lives in Châtenay-Malabry, near Paris. — *Bibl.* Paulhan: *Les objets de Fautrier,* Galerie Rive Droite (Paris 1955); Tapié: *Fautrier paints a picture,* 'Art News' (New York, Dec. 1955); Ponge: *Paroles à propos des nus de Fautrier,* Galerie Rive Droite (Paris 1956).

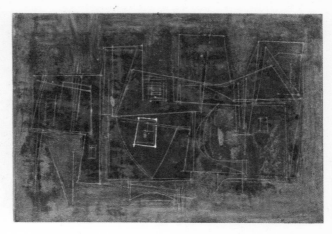

FEITO. COMPOSITION. 1954. *John Koenig Collection, Paris.*

FEITO (b. Madrid, 1929). San Fernando School of Fine Arts in Madrid. After a number of group-shows, one-man shows at the Gallery Buchholz and the Gallery Fernando Fe (Madrid 1954) followed by a one-man show at the Galerie Arnaud (Paris 1955). Lives in Madrid.

FÉLY-MOUTTET (b. Collobrières, Var, France, 1893; d. Toulon, 1953). Attended the École des Beaux-Arts (Atelier Cormon) and the School of Decorative Arts in Paris. Later became the director of the École des Beaux-Arts in Toulon. Exhibited in numerous Salons, then turned to abstraction and became one of the mainstays of the Salon des Réalités Nouvelles. Organized an important exhibition of Abstract Art at the Museum of Toulon (1952). A retrospective exhibition of his work was held in the Salon des Réalités Nouvelles, Paris, in 1954.

FERREN John (b. Pendleton, Ore., 1905). Studied in California. Self-educated. Worked first as a sculptor and a craftsman in San Francisco. Began painting in 1930. In Paris (1931-1938) he frequented S. W. Hayter's famous 'Studio 17'. Composed a series of engravings printed on plaster. Exhibitions at the Galerie Pierre and the Galerie de l'Effort Moderne. Returned to America in 1938. A number of exhibitions in the U.S., particularly at the Galerie Pierre Matisse, New York (1936, 1937, 1938); Willard Gallery (1942); Santa Barbara Museum of Art, California (1952). Lives in New York. An experimental painter whose work has passed through many stages before attaining an extreme refinement of colour and form. He writes : "Sworn enemies as they have always been, all artists nevertheless tell the same story, the same few rare things, in so far as they can make themselves understood at all." — *Bibl.* Ritchie: *Abstract Painting and Sculpture in America* (New York 1951); 'Art News' (New York, Feb. 1954); Leepa: *The Challenge of Modern Art* (New York 1949).

FICHET. PAINTING. 1955. *Galerie Arnaud, Paris.*

FICHET Pierre (b. Paris, 1927). Self-taught in matters of art. First abstract works in 1947, followed by a representational period. Return to abstraction in 1951. One-man shows at the Galerie Arnaud, Paris 1954 and 1955. Took part in the Salon des Réalités Nouvelles and a number of group-displays, especially in Stockholm and in Germany. Lives in Paris.

FIETZ Gerhard (b. Breslau 1910). Studied at the Breslau Academy and the Schlemmer Studio (1930-1932), then in Dusseldorf and Berlin. Drafted in the East German Army. Took part in the Salon des Réalités Nouvelles, Paris, 1948, and the Venice Biennale, 1950. Included in the exhibition of German abstract painters, Cercle Volney, Paris 1955. A member of the German 'Zen' group. Lives in Buchbei-Illertissen (Wurtemberg).

FINE Perle (b. Boston, 1908). Numerous one-man shows in America. A member of the 'American Abstract Artists' group. Took part a number of times in the Salon des Réalités Nouvelles, Paris, and in a few important group-shows in the United States. Lives in New York or Provincetown (Mass.) Starting from compositions with geometrical elements, Miss Fine has slowly progressed towards a more supple art, characterized, these last years, by a cloudy monochrome. Perle Fine is also known for her erudite interpretation of Mondrian's *Victory boogie-woogie* in twelve analytical charts. — *Bibl.* Hitchcock: *Painting towards Architecture* (New York 1948).

FINK Don (b. Duluth, Minn., 1923). Studied at the Walker Art Institute, Minneapolis, and at the Art Students League, New York. In Paris 1953-1954; one-man show at the Galerie Craven. After spending some time in the United States, returned to Paris in 1955 and took part in art competitions. A calligraphy of fine black lines coiled, after the manner of Pollock, against a background of monochrome.

FITZSIMMONS James (b. Shanghai, China, 1919). Educated in Switzerland, England, and New York

172

(Columbia University). At first a commercial photographer in New York (1938-1944). After 1945, he investigated the possibilities of photolithography and discovered a new way of making coloured monotypes out of photographical elements. From 1947 to 1950, exhibited his researches at the San Francisco Museum of Art, the Art Institute in Chicago, and the Pinacotheca in New York. At the same time, he developed a geometrical style of painting and exhibited at the Rose Fried Gallery, New York, 1951. A well-known critic, he has contributed to many American reviews. He is at present director of the magazine "European Art this Month" in Zurich. — Bibl. *Collection of the Société Anonyme* (New Haven, Conn., 1950).

FLEISCHMANN Adolf Richard (b. Esslingen, Germany, 1892). Attended the Academy of Fine Arts, Stuttgart, then worked in advertising. Severely wounded in the war, 1917. During his convalescence in Switzerland, was a castmaker at the University of Zurich Hospital. In 1922, first participation in the 'Neue Secession' exhibition in Munich. 1930-1933, was in Ascona (Tessin); 1933-1936 in Spain; 1936-1938 in Italy. Settled then in France where he took part in a number of exhibitions, especially at the Salon des Réalités Nouvelles. One-man shows at the Galerie Creuze (1948); the Galerie Colette Allendy (1951); the Gallery Lutz und Meyer, Stuttgart (1952). Left for the United States in 1952. One-man show at the Rose Fried Gallery, New York, in 1955. A member of the "American Abstract Artists" group with whom he exhibits regularly. Lives in New York.

Fleischmann has gradually passed from curves to straight lines; from undulating to rectilinear calmness. For a number of years, he has like Mondrian only used horizontal and vertical positions. He brings to the neo-plastic principles infinitely rich scales of tones and a great suppleness in the interplay of shades. He is one of the few disciples of Mondrian to-day who can infuse neo-plasticism with a personal vision. "Fleischmann is the Juan Gris of our time." (Will Grohmann). — Bibl. *Témoignages pour l'Art Abstrait* (Paris 1952); Dario Suro: *Fleischmann,* El Caribe, 26 de Junio 1955.

DON FINK.
RED AND BLACK COMPOSITION. 1955.

173

FLEXOR Sanson (b. Rumania, 1907). His father was an agricultural officer. Came to Paris 1924. Frequented the École des Beaux-Arts and the Académies Ranson and Grande Chaumière. Became a naturalized French citizen in 1929. Exhibited in a number of Salons and executed decorations in churches. Since 1948, when he left for Brazil, has tended toward abstract art, encouraged by the critic Léon Degand. Founded the Abstraction workshop in Sao Paolo. A number of group-shows in Brazil. Took part in the Venice and Sao Paolo Biennales. One-man shows at the Museum of Modern Art, Sao Paolo (1954) and Rio de Janeiro (1955). Lives in Sao Paolo.

FOLMER Georges (b. Nancy, France, 1899). First abstract work in 1935. Took part every year in the Salon des Réalités Nouvelles with works inclining sometimes towards a relatively simple geometrical style which seems close to neoplasticism. Numerous one-man shows at the Galerie Colette Allendy. Lives in Paris.

FONTENÉ Robert (b. Paris, 1892). Attended the École des Beaux-Arts, Paris, and a number of Academies in Montparnasse, but worked mainly in isolation. One-man show Galerie Heller, Paris 1955. Took part in a number of important Salons, and since its foundation, in the Salon des Réalités Nouvelles, of which he was elected President in 1956. Lives in Paris.

FRANCIS Sam (b. San Mateo, California, 1923). Studied Medicine and Psychology at the University of California. Abstract painting since 1947. Settled in Paris in 1950. Took part in various exhibitions in California and in France. One-man shows in Paris, Galerie Nina Dausset (1952) and Galerie Rive Droite (1955). Lives in

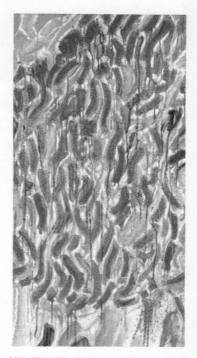

SAM FRANCIS. RED AND YELLOW. 1955.

Paris. "I believe the value of an action (painting) lies in the realm of the unintentional. For the intended necessarily has a surface which betrays us, for it conceals nearly the all. I feel the work must put one in a position of doubt." (Francis). — *Bibl*. Read: *An Art of internal Necessity*. "Quadrum" N⁰ 1 (Brussels 1956); Duthuit: *Préface à l'exposition Sam Francis*, Galerie Rive droite (Paris 1955).

FREIST Greta (b. Vienna, 1914). Came to Paris 1957; her early paintings tended toward Surrealism. Ventured upon abstract art in 1949. Took part in many Salons, especially the Salon des Réalités Nouvelles where she sent, from 1954 to 1955, large compositions in dulled colours. Lives in Paris.

FRELINGHUYSEN Suzy (b. in New Jersey, U. S. A., 1912). Started realistic painting on her own. Lived later in New York where she became known as an opera-singer; at the same time she kept on painting. Since 1936 her work has been abstract. Exhibited regularly with the 'American Abstract Artists' group. Took part in the Salon des Réalités Nouvelles, Paris, as well as in group-shows in Rome and Amsterdam. Married to the painter George L. K. Morris. Lives in New York and Lenox (Mass.).

FREUNDLICH Otto (b. Stolp, Pomerania, 1878; d. Poland, 1943). At first a shop-apprentice, then an assistant. Later on he studied Art History in Munich and Florence. Began painting and sculpting at the age of 27. Specialized from 1908 in constructive painting with swathes of pure colours. Came to Paris 1909; had a studio at the 'Bateau Lavoir', Place Ravignan, where he became friendly with Picasso. Exhibited with the cubists in Paris, Amsterdam, Cologne. Executed mosaics and stained-glass windows. Composed his first entirely abstract paintings in 1919. A member of the 'Cercle et Carré' group in 1930, then of 'Abstraction-Création'. Hitler classed him among the 'degenerate artists'; he was deported as a Jew to the concentration camp of Lublin - Maidanech (Poland) where he died in 1943. Retrospective exhibition at the Galerie Rive Droite, Paris 1954.

"The artist is a barometer of transformations. He senses them in his acts and his thoughts before they are realized in the world. When he detaches himself gradually from the generally admitted forms and truths, he is executing the edicts of a new reality. All artistic realisations have an inclination: a narrow inclination when it is the safeguard of the artist, a large one when the artist renounces himself and his work opens mental frontiers. A forcing of barriers—social, political, spiritual—begins every great historical period. Ours will for the first time accomplish the union of man with the whole earth and will thus change nostalgia and desire for far-away things into something else, certainly much greater, although everywhere within our reach." (Freundlich in *Cercle et Carré*, nº 2). — *Bibl.* Seuphor: *L'Art Abstrait, ses Origines, ses premiers Maîtres* (Paris 1949).

FREUNDLICH. COMPOSITION. 1930.

FROST Terry (b. Leamington, England, 1917). Began painting when a war-prisoner in Germany. Then studied in London and was greatly influenced by Victor Pasmore who had just turned to abstraction. One-man show in London, 1952. Lives in St. Ives (Cornwall).

FRUHTRUNK Günter (b. Munich, 1923). After five years of war-service, studied painting at a non-institutional Academy, and then under Fernand Léger (1952). One-man show at Ueberlingen, Germany, 1948. Lives in Paris since 1954 and takes part in a number of Salons.

G

GABRIELLI Louis (b. Corte, Corsica, 1901). Studied Law in Aix-en-Provence. Settled in Paris 1928. Began modelling clay and painting, 1930. One-man shows of abstract paintings entitled 'informals' at the Galerie Creuze, Paris 1949 and 1955. At the Galerie Colette Allendy, 1952, exhibited monochromatic paintings where movement and shape depend on the thickness of the paint alone. In his recent work, disintegrating forms seem to float in the air or slowly swim through a clouded atmosphere. Lives in Paris.

GALLATIN A. E. (b. Villanova, Pa., 1882; d. New York, 1952). Studied Law in New York. Began painting without instruction. Each year, from 1921 to 1938, he spent a few months in Paris where he became acquainted with the world of painters, sculptors, and collectors. It was during those years he formed his famous avant-garde collection known as the Gallery of Living Art. It contains works of the great cubists as well as of Miro, Arp, and Mondrian. This collection is now at the Museum of Philadelphia. As a painter, Gallatin progressed from the influence of Léger to an abstract art half-way between cubism and constructivism. Numerous one-man shows in New York since 1938. Took part in art-shows in the main cities of America and Europe.

GARBELL Alexandre (b. Riga, Latvia, 1903). Came to Paris in 1923 and worked at the Académie Ranson under Bissière. One-man and group-shows, since 1928, in Paris, Copenhagen, Lausanne. Lives in Paris. Garbell came to abstraction a few years ago, with a rich palette and a great elegance of expression. His untrammelled compositions suggest a painter expert in colours. They keep, even at their most lyrical, a lovely inner balance. — *Bibl.* Courthion: *Peintres d'Aujourd'hui* (Geneva 1952).

GAUTHIER Oscar (b. Fours, Nièvre, France, 1921). Studied in Paris, under Othon Friesz at the Académie de la Grande Chaumière. Travelled to the United States, 1946-1947, and to Mexico, from which he brought back expressionistic canvases. Abstract painting since 1948. One-man shows at the Galerie Colette Allendy (1950 and 1951) and Galerie Arnaud (every year since 1952). Took part in a number of group-shows. Lives in Paris.

GEAR William (b. Fife, Scotland, 1915). Studied in Edinburgh, 1932-1937. Travelled through Europe. Worked in Paris, 1947-1950. One-man shows in Paris, New York, Hamburg, Florence, and London. Took part in the Salon des Réalités Nouvelles in 1949 and 1950 as well as in exhibitions of British art on the continent. Lives in Buckinghamshire.

"Art is a living thing; the real artist contributes to the evolutionary process, expanding by his work the scope of human vision and delight. The artist like the research scientist is concerned with the discovery of new truths in nature. I regard my work not as a denial of nature, but rather as an extension of it." (Gear).

GEIGER Rupprecht (b. Munich, 1908). Studied architecture, but was largely self-taught as a painter. Travelled to Greece and Spain. Has exhibited since 1950. Member and founder of the 'Zen' group. Took part in the Salon des Réalités Nouvelles, Paris. One-man shows in 1953, Munich (Gallery Stangl) and Cologne (Gallery Der Spiegel). Took part, 1955, in an exhibition of German abstract painters, Cercle Volney, Paris. Lives in Munich. Compositions in large planes, somewhat sombre, sometimes even black, made more dramatic still by single tracks of red or blue light.

GAUTHIER. THE GRENADIER. 1954.
Private Collection, Paris.

GEORGES Claude (b. Fumay, Ardennes, France, 1929). Worked on a degree in physics. Travelled to Italy, Holland, Sweden. One-man show at the Galerie Drouin, Paris 1955. An anguished sensibility expressing itself in turbulent canvases. Inorganic nature in violent gestation. — Bibl. *Claude Georges,* Galerie Drouin (Paris 1955).

GERMAIN Jacques (b. Paris, 1915). A student of Fernand Léger at the Académie Moderne, 1931. Attended the Bauhaus (Dessau), 1932. Exhibited at the Surindépendants, 1947 and 1948. One-man show at the Galerie des Deux-Iles in

1949. Took part in the Salon de Mai in 1951 and 1952, and in a group-show at the Galerie Maeght. One-man show at the Galerie Warren, Paris 1955. Lives in Paris. To judge by his recent work, Germain seems the direct successor of Cézanne in the domain of the abstract. Richly varied greens predominate. With great subtlety, a suggestion of red, yellow, or ochre flicked on this universal green sets everything off.

GILLET. PAINTING. 1954.
Galerie Jeanne Bucher, Paris.

GERRITS Ger (b. Nieuwer-Amstel, Holland, 1893). At first a lithographer and an advertising-designer. Has painted in many styles since 1930. Exhibited in Antwerp, Chicago, Venice, Vienna, Prague, Berlin, Hamburg, Copenhagen, Stockholm, Cincinnati, Monaco, San Francisco, and took part in the Salon des Réalités Nouvelles, Paris, 1949 and 1950. Rectilinear geometry very soberly conceived. Lives in Amsterdam.

GILBERT Stephen (b. Scotland, 1910). The grandson of Alfred Gilbert, the English sculptor who was a friend of Rodin's. Spent his youth in Ireland. Was in Paris 1938-1939; in Ireland 1940-1945. Had a number of exhibitions in Dublin. Short abstract period in 1942, followed by seven years of expressionism. Took part in many exhibitions of the Dutch 'Cobra' group. Went to Denmark, 1949. Left 'Cobra' and started on a second abstract period (1950). Has since taken part regularly in the Salon des Réalités Nouvelles and, in 1952, in the Salon d'Octobre. Lives in Paris.

GILLET Roger Edgar (b. Paris, 1924). Studied at the École Boulle and the School of Decorative Arts. Took part in a number of exhibitions of 'informal' art since 1952. One-man show at the Galerie Craven, Paris 1953. Took part in the Salon de Mai, Paris 1955. Lives in Paris. Lyrical painting contained within a limited chromatic range. A whirlwind projection of ideas with powerful effects from reds, blacks, whites, in an ochre ensemble.

GISCHIA Léon (b. Dax, Landes, France, 1903). Studied Literature, Art History, Archaeology. Devoted himself to painting from 1923 on. Studied under Othon Friesz and Fernand Léger. Made a number of trips to Spain and Italy. Lived in the United States from 1927 to 1930. Stopped painting from 1927 to 1937. Included in exhibitions of contemporary French art circulating through South America, the United States, Sweden, Switzerland. Exhibited mainly at the Galerie de France, Paris. A member of the Salon de Mai committee. The author of *La Sculpture en France depuis Rodin* (in collab. with N. Védrès). Launched into abstraction about 1948, but does not mind returning occasionally to representational art. Swathes of frank colours, side by side, without blending.

GLARNER Fritz (b. Zurich, 1899). Attended the Academy of Naples, 1915-1918. In Rome and Milan, 1918-1923; then came to Paris. Took part in a number of Salons. At first influenced by impressionism, he slowly turned to abstraction. A member of 'Abstraction-Création' in 1933. In Zurich in 1935. Settled in New York, 1936 and became an American citizen. Struck up a friendship with Mondrian, New York, 1943. One-man shows: in New York, Kootz Gallery, 1945; Rose Fried Gallery 1949, 1951; in Paris, at the Galerie Carré, 1952 and 1955. Since Mondrian's death, Garner, who calls his work *relational painting,* has modified pure neoplasticism by the introduction of the *slanted line,* which is always to be found between two perpendiculars. Thus his basic form is never a rectangle, as in Mondrian, but a trapeze-rectangle. He has composed a number of circular canvases (*tondo*) and handles greys with great virtuosity.

"It was fortunate for the art world that Mondrian came to New York, and that during the few years that Mondrian lived here he was able to introduce the philosophy underlying his work to both Diller and Glarner. There were others who were fascinated by Mondrian's approach to art, but they never seemed to have absorbed his philosophy, and without the philosophy there is no continuity of thought and work. However, Diller and Glarner have absorbed Mondrian's philosophy without becoming imitators, but have instead retained their own individuality". (Kath. S. Dreier). — Bibl. *Collection de la Société Anonyme* (New Haven 1950); Ritchie: *Abstract Painting and Sculpture in America* (New York 1951); 'Art d'Aujourd'hui' (Paris, juin 1951); *What abstract art means to me* (New York 1951).

GLEIZES Albert (b. Paris, 1881; d. Avignon, 1953). Trained in his father's workshop of industrial design. At first influenced by impressionism. Exhibited in 1911, in the famous Room 41 of the Salon des Indépendants, the room where cubism started. With Jean Metzinger, a theoretician of the Movement. A friend of Robert Delaunay and Jacques Villon. Wrote a number of works where he interprets the History of Art through his own doctrines. His theories had a great influence on young painters from 1930 on; one can indeed say that the impetus for a good deal of the abstract art movement sprang from his books and his numerous lectures. Gleizes's influence brought Robert Delaunay back to abstraction in 1930. He himself painted a number of abstract canvases, though their titles indicate that symbolism is not too far off.

Principal works of Albert Gleizes: *Du Cubisme* in collaboration with Jean Metzinger (Figuière, Paris 1912); *Du Cubisme et des moyens de le comprendre* (La Cible, Paris 1920); *La Peinture et ses lois, ce qui devait sortir du cubisme* (Paris 1924); *La Forme et l'Histoire* (Povolozky, Paris 1932). — Bibl. *Collection of the Société Anonyme* (Yale University 1950);

GLEIZES. COMPOSITION. 1915.
Galerie Henri Benezit, Paris.

Raynal: *De Picasso au Surréalisme* (Skira, Paris and Geneva 1950); *A Dictionary of Modern Painting* (Methuen, London 1956); *Art Abstrait, les Premières Générations* (Musée de Saint-Étienne, 1957).

GOEBEL Gottfried (b. Vienna, 1906). Attended the School of Fine Arts, Vienna. Travelled for a time. Settled in Paris, 1936. Was at first influenced by Delaunay's orphic cubism. Turned to abstraction in 1946. Took part in numerous group-shows in France, Austria, Germany, Italy, America, as well as in the Salon des Réalités Nouvelles. First one-man show at the Galerie Colette Allendy, 1951, followed by a number of exhibitions at the Galerie Arnaud. Exhibits at Salon des Réalités Nouvelles and with Austrian abstracts, Galerie Arnaud, 1957. Goebel's painting has changed often and suddenly. His recent abstract manner consists of pure geometrical forms filled in with delicate atmospheric nuances in the impressionistic manner. Lives in Paris. — *Bibl.* Neuwirth: *L'Abstraction* (Paris 1956).

GOETZ Henri (b. New York, 1909). Studied at the Mass. Institute of Technology, Harvard, and Grand Central Art School. Came to Paris, 1930. Painted portraits. Married Christine Boumeester, 1935. Abstract painting since 1936. A naturalized French citizen. One-man shows in a number of Paris galleries since 1937 and participation in the main abstract art Salons. Illustrated books, published albums of etchings. Gave weekly lectures on painting over the French radio network, 1945. Professor at the Académie Ranson 1951, at the Académie de la Grande Chaumière, 1955. One-man show, Galerie Ariel, Paris, 1954. Lives in Paris. Henri Goetz has slowly progressed from surrealism to abstraction. His abstract work remained for some time vague and undefined, as though lost in the

GONTCHAROVA. ELECTRICITY. 1910-1911.

confusions of surrealism; but it gradually became more positive, using the delicacies of colour without sacrificing its original dreaminess of atmosphere. — *Bibl.* Lorsky: *Henri Goetz* (Paris 1952).

GONTCHAROVA Nathalie (b. Toula, Russia, 1881). Studied in Moscow. Began exhibiting in 1900. Travelled to England, Spain, Switzerland, Italy, Greece, etc. As early as 1910 she launched with Larionov into the rayonist venture. Designed many stage-decors and ballet costumes. Settled in Paris with Larionov, 1914. Formed a friendship with Diaghilev. Exhibited her rayonist and other work together with Larionov, at the Galerie Paul Guillaume, 1914 (preface to the exhibition by Guillaume Apollinaire). Practically gave up painting in order to devote herself to the ballet. Retrospective exhibition at the Galerie des Deux-Iles, Paris 1948. Included in 1952, in the 'L'Œuvre du XXe siècle' exhibition at the Museum of Modern

Art, Paris. She returned to painting in 1956 and exhibited about fifty of her works, dated 1907 to 1956, at the Galerie de l'Institut, Paris, the same year. Lives in Paris. — *Bibl.* Barr: *Cubism and Abstract Art* (New York 1936); Seuphor: *L'Art Abstrait, ses Origines, ses Premiers Maîtres* (Paris 1949).

GOODNOUGH Robert (b. Cortland, U.S., 1917). Attended the University of Syracuse. Then studied in New York under Hofmann. Was for a time assistant-professor in the Department of Painting, New York University. Exhibited with the 'American Abstract Artists' group. Included in the 'Aspects de la Peinture Américaine' show, Galerie de France, Paris, 1952. One-man show at the Tibor de Nagy Gallery, New York 1952. Lives in New York. Little touches of bright colour (commas) on a white background.

GORIN Jean (b. Saint-Émilien-Blain, Loire-Inférieure, France, 1899). Studied at the Académie de la Grande Chaumière, then at the École des Beaux-Arts in Nantes. Settled in Nort-sur-Erdre (Loire-Inférieure), 1932. Influenced by Cézanne, Van Gogh, Matisse. Gleizes's books on cubism hastened his development. After a flirtation with purism (Ozenfant), he struck out into neo-plasticism as early as 1926. First contacts with Mondrian in 1927. Included in the 'Cercle et Carré' exhibition 1930. Exhibited at the Salon des Réalités Nouvelles since its foundation. After a lengthy stay in Nice, he settled in Le Perreux, near Paris, in 1955. His long friendship with Mondrian left a strong imprint of neo-plasticism; he must be considered as one of the most typical and gifted of Europeans working in that tradition. He does not hesitate, however, to infringe the severe dogmas of neo-plasticism by using diagonals and circles, particularly in reliefs, works which yet testify to high spiritual nobility. — *Bibl.* Biederman: *Art as the evolution of visual knowledge,* Redwing (Minn. 1948); *Témoignages pour l'art abstrait* (Paris 1952).

GORKY Arshile (b. Armenia, 1904; d. New York, 1948). Studied at the Polytechnical Institute in Tiflis (Georgia). Came to the United States, 1920. Studied engineering at Brown University and painted in his spare time. In New York, 1925. Was expelled from three academies successively. Moved towards abstract art from 1929 on, being influenced in turn by Picasso, Léger, and Miro. Mastered a highly personal style of organic abs-

GORKY. THE PLOUGH AND THE SONG. 1947.

traction in 1940. Met André Breton, Calder, Matta, and Max Ernst. A fire in his studio, in 1946, destroyed thirty paintings and a number of drawings. Committed suicide after having been operated upon for cancer and having had a car accident. Important retrospective exhibition at the Whitney Museum, New York, 1950.

"Arshile Gorky's productive artistic life comprised little more than sixteen years, but within that short time he achieved a fulfillment which cannot be without effect upon future American art. Gorky's examination of nature and conquest of space were visually achieved in the fullest terms of modern experience. It is possible that this art, as much as any other individual manifestation, offers us the image of our times in one of those rare moments when art triumphs over the tragedy of living." (Hamilton) — *Bibl.* Breton: *Le Surréalisme et la Peinture* (New York 1945); Janis: *Abstract and Surrealist Art in America* (New York 1944); *Fourteen Americans* (New York 1946); *Collection of the Société Anonyme* (New Haven 1950); Ritchie: *Abstract painting and sculpture in America* (New York 1951); Hess: *Abstract Painting* (New York 1951); *Arshile Gorky Memorial Exhibition* (New York 1951).

GOTTLIEB Adolph (b. New York, 1903). Studied in Europe, 1921-1922. Carried out many decorative works, notably for the Post Office of Yerrington (Nevada) and for the Synagogue of Millburn (New Jersey). One-man shows in New York from 1930 on, especially at the Kootz Gallery. President of the United States Modern Painters and Sculptors Federation (1944-1945). His works are to be found in a number of American museums. Lives in New York. "With his friend Mark Rothko, Gottlieb has searched for the point where Mondrian and Soutine join, and Picasso can be left behind." (Hess). — *Bibl.* Hess: *Abstract Painting* (New York 1951).

GÖTZ Karl Otto (b. Aachen, Germany, 1914). 1931-1932, worked at the School of Decorative Art and became acquainted with the Bauhaus theories. After the war, had numerous exhibitions in Germany. Took part in the 'Art en Allemagne 1930-1949' exhibition in Zurich, 1949. Included in the 'Cobra' exhibition in Amsterdam and Liège. One-man shows: Galerie Creuze, Paris; Dusanne Gallery (Seattle, U.S.A.); Werthmüller Gallery, Basel; Colibry Gallery, Malmoë (Sweden); and 'Nordisk Kunsthandel', Copenhagen. Included in the 'Phases' exhibition, Salle Balzac, Paris, 1955, and in the German abstract painting show at the Cercle Volney, Paris. Lives in Frankfurt-am-Main. After a painting of symbols and themes with variations revealing the marked influence, now of Arp, and again of Willi Baumeister, Götz has progressed towards a more exuberant lyricism. His calligraphic improvisations in monochrome have the suppleness of a whirlwind filmed in slow motion.

GRAESER Camille (b. Geneva, 1892). An architect and interior-decorator. Studied at the School of Applied Arts in Stuttgart and under Adolf Hölzel. A member of the 'Sturm' and 'Deutscher Werkbund' groups. Exhibited since 1919 in various German cities and in Switzerland. A member of the Swiss 'Die Allianz' association. Lives in Zurich. Pure geometrical abstraction. — Bibl. *Almanach neuer Kunst in der Schweiz* (Zurich 1940); *Allianz* (Zurich 1954).

GREENE Balcomb (b. Niagara Falls, New York, 1904). Studied in New York, Paris, and Vienna. Self-taught in matters of art. Exhibited with the 'American Abstract Artists', 1937-1945. Took part in group-shows in Paris and in the great American museums, especially the Museum of Modern Art, New York, 1951.

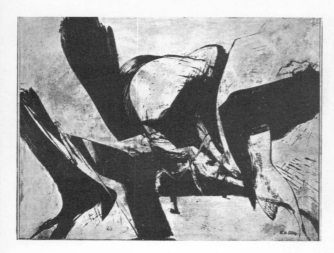

GÖTZ. COMPOSITION. 1955. *Private Collection, Paris.*

Léger. Took part in a number of exhibitions throughout Scandinavia. Included in the Salon des Surindépendants, Paris, 1950. Travelled to Rome, 1955. Lives in Reykjavik (Iceland).

GUERRERO José (b. Granada, Spain, 1914) Studied at the School of Fine Arts of Granada, then Madrid. Studied fresco-painting at the École des Beaux - Arts, Paris (1945 - 1946). Travels and exhibitions in Rome, Brussels, Paris, London, and Switzerland (1947). In New York, 1950; an American citizen since 1952. Took part in the exhibitions of contemporary Spanish painting, Schaeffer Galleries, New York, 1953. Exhibited with Miro at the Art Club, Chicago. Was included in the 'Younger American Painters' exhibition, Solomon R. Guggenheim Museum, New York, 1954. One-man show at the Betty Parsons Gallery, New York, 1954. Lives in New York or Paris. Strong contrasts of black forms compacted against light backgrounds. Guerrero has also composed murals in bricks and cement. He uses the same symbols, making massive blues and reds vibrate against grey backgrounds.

After a period of abstract art tending markedly toward the geometric, Greene swung to representational art. His recent works are mainly studies in the decomposition of the object by light: he has therefore, returned to abstraction, though from a very different angle. — *Bibl.* Ritchie: *Abstract Painting and Sculpture in America* (New York 1951); Hess: *Abstract Painting* (New York 1951).

GREIS Otto (b. Frankfurt - am - Main, 1913). Studied engineering. Devoted himself to painting in 1933. Studied painting in Frankfurt, under Bunk and Höhl, until 1938. Met E. W. Nay in 1945. Took part since 1948 in group-shows throughout Germany. Travelled to Switzerland, France, Italy, Belgium. Contributed to the Salon des Indépendants, Paris 1952. Lives in Bad Soden, near Frankfurt.

GUDNASON Zvavar (b. Iceland, 1909). Studied at the Academy of Copenhagen, then in Paris under Fernand

GUERRINI Mino (b. Rome, 1927). A co-signer of the abstract art manifesto *Forma I,* Rome, 1947. Took part in a number of group-shows in the main cities of Italy. His painting has a geometrical tendency. Guerrini is also a poet and an art-critic. Lives in Rome.

GUTH. MYSTERY FOUR. 1955.

GUEVARA Luis (b. Valencia, Venezuela, 1926). Studied at the School of Fine Arts in Caracas. A number of exhibitions in Venezuela until 1949. Then settled in Paris; was included in the Salon des Réalités Nouvelles in 1951 and 1952, as well as in numerous group-shows in various Paris galleries. A member of the 'Madi' group founded by Arden-Quin. Lives in Paris.

GUITET James (b. Nantes, France, 1925). Attended the the École des Beaux-Arts in Nantes. Taught drawing in Angers. Exhibition at the Galerie Arnaud, Paris 1954. Took part in the Salon des Réalités Nouvelles and the Menton Biennale. Lives in Angers. Free-styled compositions subtly shaded, showing an affinity with Geer van Velde's work.

GUSTON Philip (b. Montreal, 1913). Studied at the Art Institute, Los Angeles, 1930. First exhibition at Mid-town Galleries, New York, 1945. Began to paint abstract canvases in 1948. Was included in the 'Cinquante ans d'art moderne aux États-Unis' exhibition, Museum of Modern Art, Paris, 1955 and in 'Twelve Americans', Museum of Modern Art, New York, 1956. Lives in New York.

GUTH Hella (b. near Carlsbad, Bohemia, 1912). Studied at the School of Applied Arts in Vienna and the Academy of Prague. Came to London, 1939. Her early painting tended towards surrealism. Exhibited at the Czech Institute, London (1943). Has travelled to Italy a number of times since 1947. Came to Paris, 1951. Gradually abandoned representational art. Exhibited at the Galerie Arnaud and took part in the Salon des Réalités Nouvelles, 1954. Lives in Paris. Acquired British nationality in 1947. Exhibits at the Galerie Colette Allendy, Réalités Nouvelles since 1954.

H

HAARDT Georges van (b. Poznan, Poland, 1907). Bachelor in Law. Doctor in Philosophy of the University of Poznan. A magistrate from 1933 to 1939. His surname is Jerzy Brodnicki. So that his painting should not be regarded as a distraction from his official duties, he exhibited under the name of his wife, Egga van Haardt, who, until her death in 1944, was thought to be the author of his paintings. Exhibited in Poland and many other countries. Left Poland for Italy (1939), then Greece and Turkey where he

VAN HAARDT. INK DRAWING. 1953.
M. S. Collection, Paris.

volunteered in the Polish Brigade. Settled then in Palestine and worked as a painter in Jerusalem; the museum there contains paintings of his from various periods (1940-1948). Worked in Paris from 1950 on. One-man show at the Galerie Nina Dausset, 1951, and at the Studio Facchetti in 1952. Travelled and exhibited in Germany, 1954. Took part in the Salon des Réalités Nouvelles. Lives in Paris. Visited and exhibited in London in 1947.

"Painting is not a pretext. It exists in itself and does not represent anything. It presents, proposes. It is not to be understood: it is to be taken, accepted or rejected. But one has to perceive first, in order to reject. The values and the tones of the colours are co-equal. Yellow does not mean jealousy or a note of music affecting or shrill. Painting penetrates noiselessly. It is thus ridiculous to measure the temperature of colours or shades. For colours are neither warm nor cold, but simply different, as colours. The painter is not an optician. This is why it is useless to invoke the laws of complementary colours from a discipline that has nothing to do with painting. Red can be married as effectively with green, brown, grey, or red as with any other colour, according to the free choice and responsibility of the creator. The luminosity of colour in painting remains a myth" (van Haardt). After a period deeply influenced by graphism, a type of writing biting deeply into the mass of the paint, van Haardt has become more of a colorist and his work has gained in lightness, in invention, without ceasing to be a sort of writing.

HAMOUDI Jamil (b. Baghdad, 1924). Studied at the Art Institute in Baghdad. Was sent to Paris in 1947 to study the art situation on behalf of the government of Iraq. Took part in a number of exhibitions in Baghdad and in Paris. One-man show at the Galerie Colette Allendy, 1952. Lives in Paris.

HARTLEY Marsden (b. Lewiston, 1877; d. Ellsworth, Maine, 1943). Studied in New York. In Paris, 1912-1913; made contacts with the cubists. Took part in the 'Blaue Reiter' show in Munich and in the first German Salon d'Automne, in Berlin, 1913. Included in the 'Armory Show' in New York, the same year. Abstract painting in Germany, 1914-1916. One-man show in Berlin. Returned to the United States in 1916 and took part in various exhibitions. Returned to representational art after 1918. — Bibl. *Collection of the Société Anonyme* (New Haven 1950); Ritchie: *Abstract Painting and Sculpture in America* (New York 1951).

HARTUNG Hans (b. Leipzig, 1904). In Basel 1912-1914, then in Dresden until 1932. Began to paint at an early age, first under the influence of Rembrandt, then Kokoschka, Nolde, and Franz Marc. Abstract drawings and water-colours as early as 1922. Met Kandinsky in 1925. His father forced him to take classes at the Academies of Leipzig, Dresden, and Munich from 1924 to 1928. Representational paintings during that period. At the same time he studied art history and philosophy. Travelled and studied in France, Italy, Holland and Belgium. First exhibition in Dresden, 1931. In Spain, 1933 and 1934. He returned then to Berlin where he got into trouble with the Gestapo. He left Germany in autumn 1935 with the help of the critic Grohman and of Christian Zervos, and settled in Paris. In 1939, volunteered into the French Foreign Legion. In 1943, was in North Africa with General de Gaulle's forces. Wounded in Belfort in November 1944; his right leg had to be amputated. Naturalized French citizen in 1945. During the following years, Hartung took part in a number of exhibitions in Paris, in Germany, and in New York. He has become one of the most famous exponents of French abstract art. His art is both sensitive and wilful, supple and well-defined. Lives in Paris. "The more we enter within ourselves, the clearer and the more imperative the image of inner sedimentations that we can reproduce, and the more universal our expression." (Hartung). — Bibl. *Französische abstrakte Malerei* (Stuttgart 1948); Seuphor: *L'Art Abstrait, ses Origines, ses Premiers Maîtres* (Paris 1949); Madeleine Rousseau: *Hans Hartung* (Stuttgart 1950); 'Art

HARTUNG. PAINTING. 1954.
Private Collection, Paris.

HAYTER. JUNGLE. 1954.

Chicago, Brussels, etc. Lives in Paris. Painting and engraving are kindred in Hayter's work: if the line is always present in the canvases, planes of colour are often the background of the engraved work. The human figure, sketched traditionally for a long time, has little by little given way to free lines where the spectator can read what he wants. Hayter's line, with its strong inner tension, is not without influence, especially on the work of the Chilean painter Matta.

HEATH Adrian (b. in Burma, 1920). England 1925. Began to paint, 1938. Studied at the Slade School. Volunteered in the R.A.F. in 1940. Was a prisoner of war from 1942 to 1945. Returned to the Slade School, 1945-1947. Then spent one year in Carcassonne, Southern France, where he painted landscapes and portraits. Returned to London in 1948 and rapidly progressed towards abstraction through his interest in the works of Seurat, Villon, Gris, and Mondrian, successively. Exhibited abstract paintings in a group-show, 1948. Included in the 'English Abstract Art' show at the Galerie Gimpel Fils, 1951. Lives in London. — *Bibl.* Alloway: *Nine abstract artists* (London 1954).

d'Aujourd'hui' (Paris, March 1951); Seuphor: *Hans Hartung,* 'Art Digest' (New York, 1st March 1955); René de Solier: *Hans Hartung,* 'Quadrum' (Brussels 1956).

HAYTER Stanley William (b. London, 1901). Studied at King's College, London. Worked in the chemistry laboratories of the Anglo-Iranian Oil Company, Abadan (1922-1925). Studied art with his father who was a professional painter, and at the Académie Julian, in Paris. Founded the *Atelier 17* which specialized in the technical aspects of engraving, Paris, 1927. A member of the surrealist group, 1934-1940. In New York 1940-1950. Returned to Paris in 1950, re-opened his *Atelier* and resumed his researches. Published *New Ways of Gravure* (New York 1949), a major work on the technique of engraving. One-man shows, particularly at the San Francisco Museum of Art (1940 and 1948), in Paris (Galerie Carré, 1951; Galerie Denise René, 1955) as well as in London, New York,

HÉLION Jean (b. Couterne, Orne, France, 1904). Studied engineering in Lille, and architecture in Paris. In 1926, met Torrès-Garcia, who introduced him to cubism. Met van Doesburg in 1930, and collaborated in 'Art Concret'. Went to Russia, 1931. A member of 'Abstraction-Création' from 1932 to 1934. Then, in America until the war. He volunteered in the French army, was made a prisoner; he escaped and published in America an account of his adventures. After having been under the influence of Mondrian (1930), from whom he developed an undeniably personal style (1936), Hélion has returned to representational painting. Lives in Paris.

HERBIN Auguste (b. Quiévy, near Cambrai, Northern France, 1882). Attended the École des Beaux-Arts in Lille 1900-1901. In Paris, 1903; worked in isolation. Struck up a friendship with Wilhelm Uhde. Exhibited in Léonce Rosenberg's Galerie de l'Effort Moderne, from 1917 on. In 1923, he painted landscapes in brownish tones, following a period of simplified cubism where pure geometrical elements were sometimes introduced. Abstract painting since 1926. Co-founder with Vantongerloo of the 'Abstraction-Création' group in 1931. The inventor of a system of abstract painting analysed in his *Art non-figuratif et non-objectif* (Galerie Lydia Conti, Paris 1949): it borrows very much from Goethe's theory of colours. Herbin exercised a great influence upon young abstract painters, in France and elsewhere. He exhibits regularly at the Salon des Réalités Nouvelles (of which he was a director until 1955) and at the Galerie Denise René. Lives in Paris. — *Bibl.* Jakovski: *Herbin* (Paris 1933); 'Art d'Aujourd'hui' (Paris November 1949 and December 1951); *Témoignages pour l'Art Abstrait* (Paris 1952); Massat: *Auguste Herbin,* Collection Prisme (Paris 1953).

HERSCH Lee (b. Cleveland, Ohio, 1896; d. Madrid, 1953). Studied at the Cleveland School of Art and the National Academy of Design (New York). A member of the expeditionary corps in France, 1918. Numerous one-man shows in the United States. Abstract painting from 1943 on. Included in group-shows at the Whitney Museum and the Solomon R. Guggenheim Museum (New York) as well as in the Salon des Réalités Nouvelles (Paris). Retrospective exhibition at the Studio Facchetti, Paris. One room was devoted to his work in the Salon des Réalités Nouvelles in 1953. His works calmly exude generous colours. — *Bibl.* Seuphor: *Lee Hersch* (Paris 1954).

HEURTAUX André (b. Paris, 1898). Painting after Nature, 1921. First imaginative paintings, 1930; progressed towards neo-plasticism at the end of 1933. Exhibited at the Salon des Indépendants from 1925 to 1930, at the Surindépendants from 1931 on. Took part in abstract art exhibitions in Lille, Cannes and South America. Lives in Paris. Geometrical compositions with large, delicately shaded surfaces.

HILL Anthony (b. London, 1930). The son of an academic painter. Was at first interested in science. Took classes at the Central School of Arts and Crafts. Took part in 1951 in the first post-war exhibition of English abstract art. Travelled to Paris where he met Vantongerloo, Sonia Delaunay, Picabia, Seuphor. Lives in London. — *Bibl.* Alloway: *Nine Abstract Artists* (London 1954).

HERBIN. LUCK. 1953.

HOFMANN. UNDULATING EXPANSE. 1955.

HILTON Roger (b. Northwood, England, 1911). Studied at the Slade School, London, and the Académie Ranson, Paris (under Bissière). Exhibited at Gimpel Fils's, London 1952, and took part the same year in an exhibition of modern English painting at the Galerie de France, Paris. Lives in London.

HINDER Frank (b. Sydney, Australia, 1906). Studied in Sydney, Chicago, New York, New Mexico. Toured Europe in 1927. A professor at the National Art School, Sydney. One of the few exponents of abstract art in Australia. Lives in Sydney.

HLITO Alfredo (b. Buenos Aires, 1923). Studied at the Academy of Buenos Aires. Expressionistic paintings in 1943. First abstract works in 1944. A member and founder of the 'Arte Concreto' group. First one-man show, 1952. Lives in Buenos Aires. A painting emphasising planes and lines, traced with subtlety: an art stripped to the bone. — Bibl. *Grupo de artistas modernos de la Argentina* (Buenos Aires, 1952); *Acht argentijnse abstracten*, Stedelijk Museum (Amsterdam, no date).

HÖCH Hannah (b. Gotha, Thuringia, 1889). Studied in Berlin. Took part in the dada movement from 1917 to 1921. Was a member of the 'Novembergruppe'. Friendly with Schwitters, Raoul Hausmann, Van Doesburg, Moholy-Nagy, Arp. Was in Holland from 1926 to 1929. Returned to Berlin. Took part in numerous exhibitions in Holland, Germany, and New York (Sidney Janis Gallery). Both abstract and representational work. She also composed a number of photo-montages. Lives in Berlin.

HOFMANN Hans (b. Weissenburg, Germany, 1880). Studied in Germany and in France. After having followed the secessionist movement in Germany, he founded a School of Modern Art in Munich (1915) and taught in the Bavarian mountains, in Italy, and in France, successively. In 1930, he left for America to teach at the University of California, then at the Art Students League, New York. Became an American citizen and founded the Hofmann School in New York, in 1934. He has trained a number of American artists and his influence is still spreading. One-man shows: Paul Cassirer gallery, Berlin, 1910; Betty Parsons Gallery, New York,

1947; Galerie Maeght, Paris, 1949, and every year since 1947 at the Kootz Gallery (New York). Lives in New York.

Hofmann's work is densely expressionist, but sound, full of vigour and delight. It is a perpetual feast where order has but recently prevailed, and is gaining more and more room. "Art is for me the glorification of the human spirit and as such, it is the cultural documentation of its time. The deepest purpose of art is, clearly, to keep the spirit of man lastingly young in a world constantly fluctuating. Art must counterbalance the banal weight of everyday life, it must give us the constant aesthetic joy we need." (Hofmann). — *Bibl.* Janis: *Abstract and Surrealist Art in America* (New York 1944); *Derrière le Miroir* (Paris, January 1949); Hess: *Abstract Painting* (New York 1951).

HOLTY Carl (b. Freiburg, Germany, 1900). Came to the United States as a child. Studied at the Art Institute in Chicago, then in Munich under Hans Hofmann. In Europe, 1925 to 1933. First one-man show at the Nierendorf Gallery, New York, 1938. Included in the "American Abstract Artists" shows from 1937 to 1946. Friendship with Mondrian in New York. Lives in New York.

HOLTZMAN Harry (b. New York, 1912). Studied at the Art Students League (New York) from 1928 to 1933. Came to Paris in 1934 to meet Mondrian and had a number of interviews with him. Returned to America and participated in the foundation of the 'American Abstract Artists' group. It was thanks to his insistence and his financial help that Mondrian was able to go to New York in 1940. Was the sole beneficiary of Mondrian when the latter died (1944). He gave up painting almost completely then, in order to devote himself to the study of semantics and to teaching. The publisher of the review *Transformation* since 1950. Lives in

New York. — Bibl. *Collection of the Société Anonyme* (New Haven 1950).

HOSIASSON Philippe (b. Odessa, 1898). Studied law and travelled frequently in Switzerland, Austria, Germany, Sweden. Was in Italy for some

HOSIASSON. PAINTING. 1955.
Galerie Stadler, Paris.

time at the end of the First World War. First one-man show in Rome. In Berlin, 1922. Exhibited at Flechtheim's and worked as a designer for the Romantic Ballet. Settled in Paris, 1924. Was a founder of the Salon des Surindépendants where he exhibited until 1939. A number of one-man shows in France, Italy, Belgium. His painting went through many phases before reaching non-representational art in 1947. Took part in the Salon de Mai from 1948 on. Exhibited at the Galerie du Haut-Pavé, Paris 1955, and Galerie Stadler, Paris 1956. Lives in Paris.

Hossiason's work proceeds by monochromatic series. The painter lets himself be enchanted by a wave of blue, then green, then black. It is a painting of sudden eruptions, but long years of training, of spiritual decantation precede the sudden and violent impulses of creation. This art disconcerts some by its brutal and unanswerable frankness, but it persuades others by its deep humanity. "M. S. has found a formula I love: *art is anything, but with a certain style.* I think that general circumstances, in our time, have brought painting to complete autonomy through the progressive discarding of representation. But the heart of the matter remains unchanged, because non-representational paintings, as well, must be accomplished *with a certain style* to accede to the rank of art." (Hossiason).

HULBECK Charles R. (b. in Germany, 1892). Known under the name of Richard Hülsenbeck as one of the leading members of the dada movement in Zurich (1916), then in Berlin. After an eventful career, finally arrived in New York where he became a psychiatrist and took the name of Hulbeck. For some years now he has managed to paint vigorous abstract works in the intervals between interviews. His wife, Beate Hulbeck, born in Berlin in 1903, has also done some abstract painting but has mostly specialized in collages. A member of the 'American Abstract Artists' group. One-man shows: Paris, 1950 (Galerie des Deux-Iles), and Berlin, 1956 (Kunstantiquariat Wasmuth). Lives in New York.

HULL James (b. 1921). First one-man show in London, 1949. Then exhibited at the Gallery Gimpel Fils, London, 1951 and 1953, and took part in the exhibition of modern English painting at the Galerie de France, Paris, 1952. Exhibited at the Passedoit Gallery, New York, 1953. Lives in London.

HUNDERTWASSER Fritz (b. Vienna, 1928). Attended the Academy of Fine Arts in Vienna. Travelled in Africa and South West Europe. One-man shows in Vienna since 1952, as well as in Italy and Paris (Studio Facchetti). Took part in a number of group-shows in Paris and elsewhere. Lives in Vienna. An obsessive art, akin to the more bizarre and morbid aspects of surrealism. It has gained in strength in becoming abstract.

HUNZIKER Frieda (b. Amsterdam, 1908). Studied at the Institute of Design. Came to abstraction about 1945. Travelled to Curaçao, 1951 and 1952. Lyrical forms and colours influenced by her travels in the tropics. Exhibited in Amsterdam, The Hague, Paris, Antwerp, Curaçao and Indonesia. Lives in Holland.

HURTADO Angel (b. Venezuela, 1927). School of Fine Arts in Caracas. Travels in Spain and in France. Took part in a number of exhibitions in South America and in Paris. First abstract works in 1948. Lives in Paris.

HUSZAR Vilmos (b. Hungary, 1884), Settled in Holland in 1905. A friend of van Doesburg and a co-founder of the 'De Stijl' group, 1917. Composed abstract stained-glass windows and neoplastic interiors. A lecturer and an essay-writer. Attempted to bring the 'De Stijl' principles into the theatre; to that end he produced a series of remarkable sketches (1922) which are also works of art. He then returned to representational painting. Lives in Hierden (Holland). — *Bibl.* The works of van Doesburg and the complete files of the review *De Stijl*.

I

ISTRATI. PAINTING. 1954.
Galerie Craven, Paris.

IDOUX Claude (b. Lyons, 1915). École des Beaux-Arts, in Lyons. Mostly interested in fresco-painting. Renews with Lenormand the great and inspired traditions of this discipline. Took part in a number of international exhibitions: Germany, Sweden, Denmark, North America, and Sao Paolo. One-man show at the Galerie Mai, Paris, 1951. Lives in Paris.

IONESCO Nicolas (b. Bucharest, 1919). School of Fine Arts in Bucharest. Took part in a number of exhibitions there. Came to Paris in 1946; studied under Lhote and Léger. Turned to abstraction in 1949 and studied in the Dewasne and Pillet Studio. Met Herbin. Took part in the Salon des Réalités Nouvelles. One-man show at the Galerie Arnaud in 1952. Lives in Paris.

ISTRATI Alexandre (b. Dorohai, Rumania, 1915). Bachelor in Law. Studied at the same time at the School of Fine Arts, where he eventually stayed as an assistant professor for nine years. Came to Paris in 1947 on a grant from the French Institute in Bucharest. Worked at the École des Beaux-Arts, under Lhote, and then on his own. One-man show at the Galerie Colette Allendy in 1952. Took part in a number of group-shows, particularly at the Galerie Denise René and the main abstract Salons in Paris. One-man show at the Galerie Craven, Paris, 1956. Lives in Paris.

"I have investigated colour a long time: it has always attracted me and my craving to seek further brought me to abstraction. It is colour, considered not only in terms of its chromatic relations but as an *inner* resonance, that guided me toward form. I sensed form through colour." (Istrati). His recent works are usually great monochromatic panels voluptuously laden with paint, the colour feeding upon itself and yet vibrating through the subtlety of its tones or the presence of some thinly suggested complementary. — Bibl. *Premier Bilan de l'Art Actuel* (Paris 1953); Gindertael: *Istrati*, 'Cimaise' (Paris, Dec. 1953); Gindertael: *Propos sur la peinture actuelle* (Paris 1955).

J

JANCO Marcel (b. Bucharest, 1895). Studied architecture at the Polytechnic school in Zurich (1915-1916). Took an active part in the reunions at the famous 'cabaret Voltaire', the cradle of dadaism, with Arp, Tzara, Hugo Ball, Hülsenbeck and a few others. He drew and composed costumes and masks for dadaist sessions. Made painted reliefs and abstract sculptures from 1917 to 1919. He foresaw the close relationship between abstract art and architecture. In 1919, created the "Peintres Radicaux" group expressing his confidence in a social structure where art would be an integral part of life and architecture. Took part in exhibitions with Klee, Richter, Arp, Sophie Taeuber and other pioneers of abstract art. In 1920, founded a new group in Switzerland, "Das Neue Leben" (New Life), then left for Paris where he met Picabia, Ernst, Dali. After quarrelling a few times with Tzara, returned to Rumania where he created the movement and the review *Contimporanul* (1922-1940). Emigrated to Israel in 1940 where he took part in the cultural movement of the country. Since Dadaism, Janco's painting has passed through many stages. One can often sense in his work a certain pressure of anguish. His most noteworthy compositions remain the polychromatic reliefs as well as the drawings and the water-colours of his dada period. Lives in Tel-Aviv. — Bibl. *Dada Painters and Poets* (New York 1951).

MARCEL JANCO. SUN BRIGHT GARDEN. PAINTED RELIEF. 1918.

JAREMA Josef (b. in Poland, 1900). Studied at the Academy of Cracow, in Paris and in Egypt. Took part in exhibitions in Paris, Poland, Italy and the Near-East. President and founder of the Italian Art Club in Rome. The friendship and influence of Prampolini, Reggiani and Soldati converted him to abstraction in 1948. Settled in Nice in 1951 and made friends with Jean Gorin, one of the first disciples of Mondrian in France. His work then approached toward a very simple geometry without however becoming neo-plastic. Was in Paris, 1955. Took part in a number of art Salons in Paris as well as in a group-show at the Museum of Rouen (1955). Jarema is still working ardently towards art principles that would substitute universalism for individualism. Exhibits tapestries at the Galerie Mai, Paris 1956.

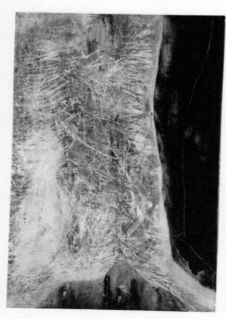

JENKINS. SOLSTICE. 1955.

JEAN Marcel (b. La Charité-sur-Loire, France, 1900). Attended the School of Decorative Arts, Paris (1919-1921). Various activities until 1924. Spent a year in the United States where he made a living as an industrial designer. Exhibited at the Salon d'Automne, 1930. Then took part in the surrealist movement with which he exhibited regularly. Was in Hungary 1938-1945: published there an illustrated essay *Mnésiques*. Essays on the pre-surrealist poets. Exhibited at the Salons des Sur-indépendants and other shows, abstract canvases where nothing remains of the literary painting dear to his fellow-surrealists. Lives in Paris.

JENKINS Paul (b. Kansas City, 1923). Studied in Kansas City and Struthers (Ohio). Was in the Armed forces, 1944-1946. Studied at the Art Students League, New York (1948-1952). Travelled to Spain and to Sicily. In Paris, 1953. One-man shows: Studio Facchetti, Paris; Zimmergalerie, Frankfurt; Zoe Dusanne Gallery, Seattle. Lives in Paris or New York. A painter full of charm and mystery. The half-colours and the flickering light of night time. " That which has been left in silence rounds off the statement and renders the unknown perceptible and clear." (Jenkins).

JOBIN Arthur (b. Yverdon, Switzerland, 1927). School of Applied Arts in Lausanne. Abstract painting since 1949. Numerous visits to Paris. Has progressed in the neo-plastic direction since 1953. One-man shows in Lausanne, 1952 and 1954. Lives in Lausanne.

JOHNSON Buffie (b. New York, 1912). Studied in New York and in Los Angeles, later at the Art Students League. Lengthy stays in Paris. Exhib-itions in Paris and in America. Took part

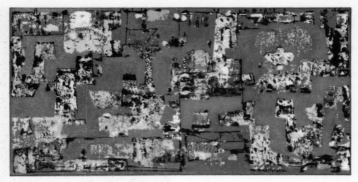

BUFFIE JOHNSON. THE GARDEN III. 1954.

in the Salon des Réalités Nouvelles in 1949. A number of exhibitions at the Betty Parsons Gallery, New York. Lives in New York and Paris. Buffie Johnson's painting is full of the the delicacies of impressionism. On a background of colour, usually mono-chrome, fragments of calligraphy merge and emerge. The French poet Pierre Emmanuel has written an appreciation of this painter comparing her with Mozart. — *Bibl.* Seuphor: *Buffie Johnson et Alcopley*, Galerie Bing (Paris 1956).

JOHNSON Ray (b. 1927, Detroit, Michigan). Studied at Black Mountain College under Albers. A member of the "American Abstract Artists" group. Lives in New York.

K

KAKABADZE David (b. Georgia, 1890). Professor of Natural Sciences in Moscow. Settled later in Paris where he published a manifesto, about 1925. Exhibited regularly at the Salon des Indépendants from 1920 on. His works are partly in the National Museum in Tiflis and partly in the collection of the Société Anonyme (U. S. A.). Whereabouts unknown.

KALINOWSKI Horst Egon (b. Dusseldorf, 1924). Academy of Dusseldorf (1945-1948). After some time in Italy, settled in Paris (1950). Attended the Abstract Art workshop of Dewasne and Pillet (1950-1952). Took part in a number of group-shows. Two one-man shows at the Galerie Arnaud, Paris. Lives in Paris. After industriously painting abstract works with precise forms and colours, so trenchant that they offended many critical susceptibilities, Kalinoswki followed the general movement towards more feeling and warmth in painting. A dramatic atmosphere now prevails, but the development of his work is certainly not yet closed.

KALLOS Paul (b. Hernadnemeti, Hungary, 1928). Spent a year in a concentration camp in Germany (1944-1945), before he had even matriculated at Kiskunhalas. Attended the School of Fine Arts in Budapest (1946-1949). In Paris, 1950; first abstract paintings the same year. One-man show at the Galerie Pierre, Paris, 1956. Lives in Paris.

KANDINSKY Wassili (b. Moscow, 1866; d. Paris, 1944.) Studied in Odessa, then at the University of Moscow (law and political economy). Was sent in 1889 on an ethnographic mission in the North of Russia. Travelled a number of times to Paris before he was appointed artistic director of a Moscow printing-press. Went to Munich in 1896 to study painting; it was there he met Jawlensky. First exhibition in Munich, 1901. Travelled to Holland and again to Paris in 1902. Was in Tunisia and Italy 1903-1904; in Dresden, 1905. Then, again in Paris 1906-1907, where he contributed wood-cuts to the review *Tendances Nouvelles*. Returned to Munich where he met Franz Marc (1910), then Macke and Klee (1911). Published *Ueber das Geistige in der Kunst* (Concerning the Spiritual in Art) and painted his first abstract works. Was a co-founder with Franz Marc of the 'Der Blaue Reiter' group and compiled with him a famous year-book under the same insignia. In 1913, *Der Sturm* published his 'Rückblicke' (Glimpses of the Past), an autobiographical essay where he carefully described his progress toward abstraction. When the war broke out, he moved to Switzerland, and then returned

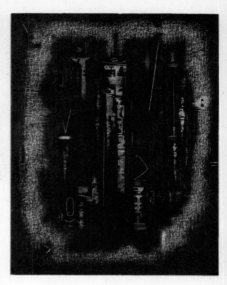

KALINOWSKI. PAGAN IKON. 1955.

to Russia through Italy and the Balkans. From 1896 to 1914, he had spent a few weeks in Russia each year. In 1916, went to Stockholm; in 1917, to Finland : he had at one and the same time an exhibition in Helsinki and Saint-Petersburg. Was appointed professor of the Fine Arts Academy in Moscow, 1918. In 1919, reorganized the Russian museums and founded the Museum of Pictorial Culture. Met Pevsner, Gabo, and Chagall. A professor at the University of Moscow in 1920: a one-man show organized by the government was held the same year in Moscow. Left Moscow at the end of 1921, and the following year, was appointed professor at the Bauhaus (Weimar), of which he soon became vice-president. In 1925, followed the Bauhaus to Dessau and formed a class of free-style painting. In 1926, he published *Punkt und Linie zu Fläche* (Point and Line to Surface) and marked his sixtieth birthday by a number of large exhibitions. Did a good deal of travelling from 1927 to 1932.

The Bauhaus having been closed by order of the Nazi government, Kandinsky left for Paris where he settled permanently, remaining in Neuilly, until his death. In 1937, about fifty of his works were confiscated by the Nazi government and classed as 'Degenerate Art'. Exhibited in London in 1938, then in Paris and in New York. He died in Paris in December 1944 as he was working on the sets of a ballet. Many retrospective exhibitions have taken place since his death, at the Galerie Drouin and the Galerie Maeght, Paris.

In his abstract work of the "Blaue Reiter" period, Kandinsky is the precursor of the 'effusionist', lyrical, and neo-expressionist styles which play a large part in abstract painting today. Later on, in 1921, he introduced into his work the geometrical elements of Malevitch. Then, probably under the influence of Paul Klee, also a professor at the Bauhaus, a new element of poetry and fantasy appears in his work. The last period of his life is characterized by balanced compositions, in sober tones, sometimes delicate. But the imaginative variety of his forms always astonishes. No artist in this century has left us as rich and varied a work testifying, once for all, to the infinite resources of abstract art. — *Bibl.* Grohmann: *Kandinsky* (Paris 1931); *Selection,* n° 14, texts by Grohmann, Zervos, Baumeister, Seuphor, Sartoris (Antwerp 1933); *Kandinsky memorial* (New York 1945); Debrunner: *Wir entdecken Kandinsky* (Zurich 1947); Seuphor: *l'Art abstrait,* *ses Origines, ses Premiers Maîtres* (Paris 1949); Raynal: *De Picasso au Surréalisme* (Paris-Geneva 1950), *The Collection of the Société Anonyme* (New Haven 1950); 'Art d'Aujourd'hui' (Paris, January 1950); Max Bill, Magnelli, Arp, Estienne: *Kandinsky,* published by Galery Maeght (Paris 1951); Barr: *Masters of Modern Art* (New York 1954); *Kandinsky, œuvre gravée,* Galerie Berggruen (Paris 1954).

KARSKAYA Ida (b. Bender, Southern Russia, 1905). "I came to France at the age of 18 to study medicine. After I married Serge Karsky, who was at that time a painter, I became tired of sitting for him, and I launched out into painting on my own. I never had any instructor, I have never attended any school. I carefully examined the vision and the technique of all the painters who influenced me, both good and bad; I had no help other than the exacting criticism of my husband and of Soutine." One-man shows at the Galerie Breteau (1949), Galerie Calligrammes (1950), Galerie Colette Allendy (1954), in Paris.

KANDINSKY. FIRST ABSTRACT WATER-COLOUR. 1910.

Took part in a number of group-shows, contributing mostly collages. To an exhibition Coppel-Karskaya-Koenig, Galerie Arnaud, Paris 1956, she contributed a number of collages, some which she called *Lettres sans Réponse,* composed solely with the bark of trees. Lives in Paris. — Bibl. *XXe siècle,* no 6 (Paris 1956).

KAUFFMANN Louis (b. in Switzerland, 1923). Began to paint in 1942 and came to non-representational art in 1945. Took part in the Salon des Réalités Nouvelles from 1949 to 1951. One-man show at the Galerie Arnaud, Paris 1951. Lives in Bienne (Switzerland).

KAYLER Richard (b. Paris, 1927). Began to paint in 1946, abstract compositions since 1952. One-man show at the Galerie de Beaune, Paris 1954. Took part in two group exhibitions at the Galerie Creuze, Paris 1957. Geometrical compositions of great sobriety, usually confined to two or three colours seeking their harmony in an elementary form. Lives in Paris.

KELLY Ellsworth (b. Newburgh, U.S.A., 1923). Studied in Englewood (New Jersey) and in Brooklyn. Then studied two years in Boston with Carl Zerbe. Came to Paris in 1948, where he at first studied Byzantine art. Then changed his manner completely and turned toward geometrical abstraction. In 1950, met Arp, Vantongerloo, Seuphor. Took part in the Salon des Réalités Nouvelles in 1950 and 1951. One-man show of paintings and polychromatic reliefs at the Galerie Arnaud, in 1951. Was twice represented in group-shows at the Galerie Maeght (1951 and 1952) by paintings with large orthogonal planes of unabashed colour. Kelly is one of the purest followers of Mondrian's neo-plasticism. Returned to the United States in 1954; exhibited at the Betty Parsons Gallery, 1956.

KENNEDY Jack (b. Otterbein, Indiana, 1922). Studied in Chicago. Began to paint in 1942. Came to Paris in 1949. Travelled throughout Europe. One-man shows at the Esquire Gallery, Chicago, 1949, and Galerie Creuze, Paris 1951. Started then on a manner of painting he calls *Formessence* on flat non-orthogonal frames. He has, therefore, in an unexpected way, an affiliation with the Argentine school of 'madism'. Kennedy's forms, generally rounded off, make one also think of Arp. Lives in the United States.

KARSKAYA. LETTER WITH NO ANSWER. GOUACHE. 1955.

KINLEY Peter (b. 1926). Studied at St. Martin's School of Art, London (1949-1953). Took part in exhibitions in London since 1951. One-man show at Gimpel's, London 1954. Lives in London.

KLEE Paul (b. München-buchsee, near Bern, 1879; d. Muralto-Locarno, Tessin, 1940). Educated in Bern. Studied art in Munich (1898 to 1901). Travelled to Italy and France. Exhibited with the Secession group, in Munich and Berlin, 1908. Met Kandinsky, Marc, Macke, Arp, in 1911. Took part in the second "Blaue Reiter" exhibition (1912) as well as in the "Sturm" Herbstsalon, Berlin 1913. Went to Tunisia with Macke and Moilliet

KLEE. AIR-TSU-DNI. INK DRAWING. 1927.

(1914). He brought back landscapes from this trip, that were almost abstract works. A professor at the Bauhaus, in Weimar, then in Dessau (1921 to 1931). Travelled to Sicily, Corsica, Brittany, Egypt. Exhibited at Flechtheim's, Berlin 1929, and at the Museum of Modern Art, New York (1930). Taught at the Academy of Dusseldorf, 1931. Under a Nazi ban in 1933; went to live in Switzerland. Retrospective exhibition in Bern, 1935. Seventeen of his works were included in the "Degenerate Art" exhibition in Munich, and a hundred and two others were seized by the Nazi authorities. Many retrospective exhibitions of Klee's work have been held since the last war, notably in Paris, Brussels, London, Amsterdam, New York, and in Switzerland, Germany and Italy.

All the lands of the spirit lie open to Klee. The free spirit transfigures everything in a ceaseless act of creation achieved through the tip of the pen, the bristles of a paint-brush. No inner call goes unanswered, no single solicitation, however strange or outlandish, remains unobeyed. Klee is incredible, stupefying. And yet he is true. He reaches more truth with a touch of his hand, than any other painter with the most strenuous efforts. This is because he does not follow Nature, but acts as she does, acts through her. His act is Nature herself, as much Nature as the blooming of a flower, the rippling of a river, the hoot of an owl. His is not an intelligence which dominates and exploits, which considers and explains, but a sensibility which mingles, submitting to the inner laws of creation, less acting than acted upon. "Art," says Klee, "does not render the visible, but renders visible". He inserts himself into nature, steeps in it, and then expresses what he feels, what he sees through this second sight, a sort of *post-mortem,* from a vantage-point where all things are equal, a pin as large as a

KLINE Franz (b. Wilkes-Barre, Pennsylvania, 1910). Studied at Boston University, then at Heatherly's Art School, London. Returned to New York in 1938. One-man shows at the Egan Gallery from 1950 on. Took part in a number of exhibitions in America as well as in an exhibition of American painting at the Galerie de France, Paris 1952. Taught at Black Mountain College and at the Pratt Institute, Brooklyn. Lives in New York. Powerful linear work. Striking tension between black, white, and grey. A large-scale calligraphy; the richness and the texture of the paint testify to the authenticity of the painter's talent. — *Bibl.* Hess: *Abstract Painting* (New York 1951); *Cinquante Ans d'Art aux États-Unis,* Musée d'Art Moderne (Paris 1955).

KOENIG. DEPARTURE FROM WEISWAMPACH.
1955. *Private Collection, Montreal.*

mountain, good and evil without significance other than movement, variety, measures and usages. — *Bibl.* Klee: *Pädagogisches Skizzenbuck* (Munich 1945); Klee: *Ueber die Moderne Kunst* (Bern 1945); *Paul Klee,* Museum of Modern Art (New York 1946); Geist: *Paul Klee* (Hamburg 1948); Read: *Paul Klee on Modern Art* (London 1948); *Paul Klee,* 'Kunst museum' (Basel 1950); Giedion-Welcker: *Paul Klee* (Stuttgart 1954); Grohmann: *Paul Klee* (Stuttgart 1954); Seuphor: *Paul Klee ou la création ininterrompue,* 'Preuves' (Paris, March 1955). Klee: *Tagebücher 1898-1918,* Du Mont Schauberg (Cologne 1956).

KOENIG John Franklin (b. Seattle, United States, 1924). After having fought in Europe during the war, he attended classes of painting and drawing at the American University in Biarritz, created for the G.I's. Returned to America

DE KOONING. PAINTING. 1948.
Museum of Modern Art, New York

in 1946. Travelled in Mexico; studied decoration, drawing and architecture at the University of Washington. Exhibited in Bellevue (Wash.). Returned to Paris in 1948. First abstract works in 1951. One-man shows at the Galerie Arnaud, Paris, 1952 and 1955. Took part in a number of group-shows and in the Salon des Réalités Nouvelles. Co-director of the Galerie-Librairie Arnaud, and editor of the review *Cimaise*. Lives in Paris. Highly sophisticated collages with scraps of paper. Monochromatic works in the abstract impressionist manner. Extreme delicacy of the colour, both in the collages and the oil-paintings.

KOLOS-VARY Sigismond (or Kolos-Vari, b. Banffyhunyad, Hungary, 1899). Attended the School of Applied Arts in Budapest. Settled in Paris (1926), where he continued his studies and became a naturalized French citizen. Travelled and studied in Italy. Exhibited in Paris, New York, Geneva, Bern, Basel, Antwerp, Amsterdam, Brussels, Milan, Tokyo. Took part regularly in the Salon de Mai. Lives in Paris. Kolos-Vary came to abstraction through long and patient examination of the possibilities of his favorite themes and the both firm and delicate character of his palette. — Bibl. *Sigismond Kolos-Vari*, 'Documents' n⁰ 14 (Geneva 1955); R. van Gindertael: *Propos sur la Peinture Actuelle* (Paris 1955).

KOONING Willem de (b. Rotterdam, 1904). Left school at the age of twelve to be apprenticed to a house-painter. Took night-classes at the Fine Arts Academy in Rotterdam, at the same time. One of his professors introduced him to the *Stijl* principles. Spent a year in Brussels where he saw the Flemish expressionist paintings which left him with a very deep impression. Came to the United States in 1926. Worked for some time as a house-painter. First abstract works in

1934. First one-man show at the Egan Gallery, New York, 1948. Took part in the 'Abstract Painting and Sculpture in America' show at the Museum of Modern Art, New York, 1951, as well as in 'Regards sur la Peinture américaine', Galerie de France Paris, 1952. Although he had reverted in recent years to a representational painting much influenced by expressionism, an exhibition at the Sidney Janis Gallery, New York 1956, showed a further return to an abstract manner. Lives in New York. — *Bibl.* Ritchie: *Abstract Painting and Sculpture in America* (New York 1950); *What abstract art means to me* (New York 1951); 'Art d'Aujourd'hui' (Paris, June 1951).

KOLOS-VARY. COMPOSITION. 1955.

KOSICE Gyula (b. on the Czech-Hungarian border, in 1924). A naturalized citizen of Argentine. Studied in the non-institutional Academies of Buenos Aires. Took part with Arden Quin in the creation of e 'Madi' movement,

(1946). Since 1947, the director of the review *Arte Madi*. A number of exhibitions in Buenos Aires with various abstract groups. Took part in the Salon des Réalités Nouvelles, Paris, 1948 and 1950. Lives in Buenos Aires.

KOSKAS Georges (b. Tunisia, 1926). Came to Paris, 1946. Attended Fernand Léger's studio. In 1949, turned toward abstraction and was included in the 'Mains Éblouies' exhibition at the Galerie Maeght. One-man show at the Galerie Arnaud, 1951, and at the Galerie Colette Allendy, 1952. Spent some time in New York in 1955 and had a one-man show at the Rose Fried Gallery. Lives in Paris.

KOSNICK-KLOSS Jeanne (b. Glogau, Silesia, 1892). Studied in Cologne and Geneva. Married the pianist and writer Henri Kosnick in Berlin. Came to Paris in 1925, and started painting the following year. Exhibition at the Galerie Billet, Paris 1927. Mett Otto Freundlich in 1929: she became his companion and collaborator. She composed with him a number of mosaics. After Freundlich's death in a concentration camp (1943), she kept on working on her own and took part in many exhibitions in Paris. Jeanne Kosnick-Kloss has created abstract tapestries dense with movement and colour. She freely lends young abstract painters Freundlich's studio for their work. Lives in Paris.

KUPKA Frank (b. Opocno, Czechoslovakia). Entered the School of Fine Arts in Prague at the age of 17. Came to Vienna 1892; studied at the Fine Arts School and exhibited portraits and landscapes at the Kuntsverein. In Paris, 1895. Illustrated books and exhibited at the Société des Beaux-Arts. A member of the Salon d'Automne in 1906. Great fame as an illustrator of rare books and as neo-impressionist painter. In 1911, suddenly turned to abstraction. Exhibited abstract canvases for the first time at the Salon d'Automne, 1912: *Fugue à deux Couleurs* and *Chromatique Chaude*. It is in connection with his works (and those of Delaunay and Picabia) that Apollinaire spoke of *orphic* painting. In 1913, contributed to the Salon des Indépendants *Plans Verticaux* and *Solo d'un trait brun,* and the same year, to the Salon d'Automne: *Localisation des mobiles graphiques*. One-man shows: Galerie Povolotsky, Paris 1921 and Galerie La Boétie, Paris 1924. There was a major retrospective exhibition of his work at the Museum of Prague in 1946, and

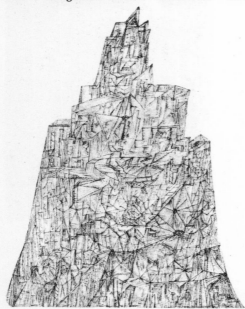

KOSNICK-KLOSS.
CRYSTALLINE ARCHITECTURAL COMPOSITION. 1929.

KUPKA. THE DECISION. 1921.

another at the Galerie Carré, New York, in 1951. Honorary president of the Salon des Réalités Nouvelles to which he contributes every year. Lives in Puteaux, near Paris.

"Almost fifty years ago, Kupka gave a memorable reception on New Year's Day in his studio on the rue Caulaincourt. Shortly afterwards, he began to *see* abstract, as one says nowadays. For, in those happy days, the word was not yet in the dictionary. Apollinaire used the word *orphism* when he spoke of these things. . . and now all the would-be fathers are tracing their rights of paternity, for none of them would admit of the polypaternity of this gigantic child." (Marchel Duchamp). — *Bibl.* Gremilly: *Kupka* (Paris 1922); Seuphor: *L'Art abstrait, ses origines, ses premiers maîtres* (Paris 1949); *Catalogue Illustré de l'exposition Kupka,* Galerie Carré (New York 1951); *Art d'Aujourd'hui* (Paris, March 1952); *A Dictionary of Modern Painting* (Methuen, London 1956).

L

LACASSE Joseph (b. Tournai, Belgium, 1894). An ordinary workman, he attended night-classes in drawing and painted in his spare time. His friends made fun of his free-style paintings and nicknamed him 'mosaic-er'. Then attended the School of Fine Arts in Tournai, and from 1919 to 1920 the Fine Arts Academy in Brussels. Travelled in Italy in 1921. Settled in Paris in 1924. He made himself a reputation, for a few years, as a painter of great religious compositions (1927-1936). Then came to abstraction. Numerous one-man shows in Belgium and in Paris. Took part in the main Belgian Salons and in the Sao Paolo Biennale. One-man show at the Rose Fried Gallery, New York 1955. Lives in Paris. "In art, the more simple the means the more powerful the form. Every true artist is always fascinated by the undefinable beauty of light. He constantly and unwittingly eliminates the visual object that bars him from the universal principle of life." (Lacasse). — *Bibl*. Bordier: *Il faut maintenant connaître Lacasse*, 'Art d'Aujourd'hui' (Paris, Nov. 1954).

LAGAGE Pierre César (b. Croix, Northern France, 1911). Studied at the School of Fine Arts in Roubaix; he attended classes in drawing, wood-cuts, and etching. Worked at painting on his own; influenced by the Flemish primitives. First exhibitions in Paris and Lille, 1932. Exhibited in a number of Polish towns, 1936-1937, then in Brussels. Settled in Paris, 1937. His work, geared at that time towards experiment in style and colour, progressed, after the Liberation, in the direction of a more mural conception of painting, and finally came to abstraction in 1950. Many exhibitions in Sweden and in Paris (Galerie Drouant-David, 1949, Galerie de Beaune, 1952). He exhibited also in Zurich and

in Los Angeles. Lives in Paris. In Lagage, the harmonies of tones are, in a sense, the real subject of the canvases. His range of reds, or yellows, or greys, underlined by a touch of ultramarine are modulated with a rare technical adroitness. It is a balanced art where nothing is left to chance. Few painters possess in such measure the art of charming by lyrical nuances of colour.

LAGO Antonio Lago Rivera (b. La Coruña, Spain, 1916). Studied art in La Coruña and in Madrid, then at the École des Beaux-Arts, Paris (1945-1946). Professor of drawing at the French *lycée* in Madrid. Came to Paris, 1951. Abstract paintings since 1952. Numerous one-man shows in Spain since 1941, particularly at the Buchholz gallery in Madrid (1945). One-man shows in Paris: Galerie Altarriba (1946), Galerie Breteau (1953), Galerie Arnaud (1954 and 1955). Took part in the Venice, Sao Paolo, and Menton Biennales, as well as in the Salon des Réalités Nouvelles. Lives in Paris.

LAGAGE. COMPOSITION. 1955.
M. S. Collection, Paris.

LANSKOY André (b. Moscow, 1902). His youth was spent in Saint-Petersburg, Kiev and in the Crimea. Came to Paris, 1921. Worked at the Académie de la Grande Chaumière; studied under Soudeikine. First exhibition in a group-show, Galerie La Licorne, 1923. One-man show, Galerie Bing 1925. Travelling exhibition in Holland, 1938. First abstract gouaches, 1939. First abstract paintings, 1944. Formed a connection with the Galerie Carré (1944), where, in 1948, he exhibited works dated 1944 to 1948. Numerous exhibitions in a number of European countries from 1948 to 1952 (Brussels, London, New York, Lausanne, Zurich, Berlin, etc. . .). Took part regularly in the Salon de Mai. Composed cartoons for large tapestries. Lives in Paris.

One of the richest temperaments among contemporary Paris painters; his colours are generally warm and his touch is deft, sometimes akin to a fluent handwriting, He has some affinities in disposition with his compatriot De Staël : there is the same disquiet in both men, the same romanticism seeking to surpass itself in each mastered style. But whereas De Staël reaches a dead end of funereal greys, Lanskoy bypasses the stage of anguish and achieves liberation in a painting of pure lyricism (with reds and yellows predominating from 1954 and 1955) where joy appears exuberantly victorious.

"Painting was always abstract, but one did not notice it. When one no longer looks for apples, trees, or young girls in a picture the word *abstract* will become redundant. It is not what enters the painter's eye which enriches a picture, but what springs from his brush. There is no progress in religion or art. But in order to remain the same man, one must develop: thus, if there were only one painter for all the periods, and he were still alive, his message would remain always the same, although worded differently. Let us paint; we shall always die alone." (Lanskoy). — *Bibl.*

Gindertael: *Lanskoy,* 'Art d'Aujourd'hui' (Paris, October 1951); *Témoignages pour l'Art Abstrait* (Paris 1952); Ashton: *Lanskoy,* 'Arts' (New York, March 1956); Grenier: *Lanskoy,* 'L'Œil' (Paris, May 1956).

LANYON Peter (b. St. Ives, Cornwall, 1918). Studied at the Art School in Penzance and at the Euston Road School in London. Worked under Ben Nicholson and Naum Gabo. Exhibited in London, 1949, and in New York, 1953. Travelled in Italy. A retrospective exhibition of his work was held in Plymouth and in Nottingham, 1955. Co-principal of St Peter's Loft Art School in St. Ives. A professor at the Bath Academy of Art in Corsham. Lives in St. Ives.

LAPICQUE Charles (b. Theizé, Rhône, France, 1898). Studied the sciences as well as art. Devoted himself totally to painting from 1943 on. A friend of Bazaine, Manessier, and Jacques Villon.

LANSKOY. GOUACHE. 1954.
Galerie Jacques Dubourg, Paris.

One-man shows in Paris: Galerie Jeanne Bucher (1929 and 1941), Galerie Carré (1946), Galerie Denise René (1949 and 1951), Galerie Galanis (1953 and 1956). After some very successful abstract works (the *Régates* series), strong in colour and audaciously drawn, Lapicque has turned toward a more narrative style akin to Dufy. Lives in Paris. — *Bibl*. 'Documents' nº 38 (Geneva 1956); Lescure: *Lapicque* (Paris 1956).

LAPOUJADE Robert (b. Montauban, France, 1921). At first held various jobs, notably that of butcher's boy. Lived alone for one year in a cave in the Alps (1941). First exhibition, Galerie Jeanne Castel, Paris, 1947. In 1949, exhibited portraits of literary celebrities. The following year, he turned to abstraction and published a book analysing the problem of form *Le Mal à Voir*. In 1952, one-man shows at the Galerie de Babylone and the Galerie Arnaud, Paris. He gave a number of lectures on painting the same year, and took part in the Salon de Mai and the Salon des Réalités Nouvelles. Travelled and exhibited in Italy and Germany, 1953. In 1955, published a new theoretical work *Les Mécanismes de la Fascination* (Éditions du Seuil, Paris). Lives in Paris.

LARIONOV Michel (b. Tiraspol, near Odessa, 1881). Attended the School of Painting, Sculpture, and Architecture in Moscow. Took an active part in the artistic events in Moscow as early as 1898. In 1909, exhibited an almost abstract composition which he called *The Glass* at the Society of the Free Aesthetic. He launched the *rayonist* (*luchism* in Russian) movement the following year. Published the rayonist manifesto in Moscow in 1913. Was a friend of Malevitch and the instructor of Tatlin, the founder of constructivism. In Paris, 1914. Exhibited at Paul Guillaume's, the same year, with his wife Na-

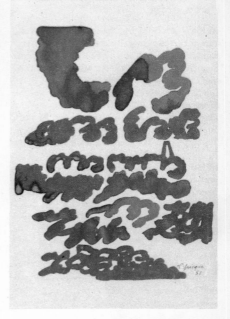

LAPICQUE. THE SEA. WATER-COLOUR. 1951.

thalie Gontcharova (cf. that name): Apollinaire prefaced the exhibition. Then he began to work for Diaghilev's Ballets Russes and almost completely gave up painting. Retrospective exhibitions of rayonism were held in Rome (1917), and in Paris (Galerie des Deux-Iles, 1948). Some of Larionov's works were included in the 'Premiers Maîtres de l'Art Abstrait' exhibition, Galerie Maeght, Paris 1949, and 'L'Œuvre du xxᵉ Siècle' at the Museum of Modern Art, Paris 1952. Also, about forty of Larionov's canvases, dated 1903 to 1915, were gathered at the Galerie de l'Institut, Paris, in 1956. Lives in Paris. — *Bibl*. Barr: *Cubism and Abstract Art* (New York 1936); Seuphor: *L'Art abstrait, ses origines, ses premiers maîtres* (Paris 1949); 'Art d'Aujourd'hui' (Paris, Nov. 1950); *A Dictionary of Modern Painting* (Methuen, London 1956).

LATASTER Gerard (b. Schaesberg, Holland, 1920). Attended the School of Industrial Art in Maestricht and the Academy of Fine Arts in Amsterdam. Took part in exhibitions in Paris, Rome, Brussels, Berlin, Stuttgart, and in the United States. Brief smears of paint freely combined with graphisms. Lives in Holland.

LAUBIÈS René (b. Cholonville, Indo-China, 1922). Has lived in Indo-China, Morocco and England. Took part in a number of group-shows in Paris, Nice, Brussels. One-man show at the Studio Facchetti, Paris 1953. Supple lines of calligraphy dissolving into subtle backgrounds.

LAUTREC Lucien (b. Nîmes, France, 1909). Attended the School of Fine Arts in Nîmes. Taught in various schools in Paris. After many different stages, his recent work tends toward lyrical abstraction, taking its departure in landscape. Took part in the Salon de Mai. Lives in Paris.

LAVIOLLE Gaston (b. Marseilles, 1906). Received a classical education. A professor of drawing from 1944 on. Took part in a number of group-shows, particularly in the Salon des Réalités Nouvelles (1953 and 1954) One-man show at the Galerie Suzanne Michel, Paris 1954. Lives in Paris.

LAZZARI Pietro (b. Rome, 1898). Educated in Rome. Drafted in the Italian Infantry during the First World War. Then came to France (on foot from Marseilles to Paris). Went to America, 1925. Painted in Greenwich Village: no affiliations. Became an American citizen. Did some large mural painting in Florida. These last few years, his inspiration seems close to the expressionist vigour of certain works of Hans Hofmann. Lives in the United States.

LECK Bart van der (b. Utrecht, Holland, 1876). Studied at the Academy of Amsterdam. He progressed slowly towards painting in swathes (1916). Met Mondrian many times in 1917. The same year, he transposed his representational works into geometrical compositions employing only the three fundamental colours. Mondrian and van der Leck have greatly influenced each other, more especially through their long theoretical discussions in Blaricum, in 1917. Worked on the first issue of *De*

LARIONOV. RAYONNISME. 1912.

207

Stijl but immediately quarrelled with van Doesburg. As early as 1918 he went back to representational painting; he only reverts to abstraction in decorative works (carpets, interior decoration), and more recently, in ceramics. Lives in Blaricum (Holland). — Bibl. *Catalogue de l'Exposition rétrospective van der Leck,* Stedelijk Museum (Amsterdam 1949); Seuphor: *Le Peintre Bart van der Leck,* 'Werk' (Zurich, Nov. 1951).

LEEPA Allan (b. New York 1919). Studied at the American Artists School, then at Hans Hofmann's Academy. Published *The Challenge of Modern Art* in 1949. In Paris, 1950 to 1951. Numerous exhibitions in America. A professor at Michigan State College, East Lansing (Mich.).

LEGRAND René (b. Nantes, France, 1923). Attended the School of Decorative Arts in Paris, 1941-1942. Worked at the Académie de la Grande Chaumière in 1943. He was encouraged by Manessier and the Argentine sculptor Vitullo who introduced him to the splendours of modern art. Took part in the Salon de Mai since 1949. One-man show at the Galerie Arnaud, Paris 1953. Lives in Paris.

LE MOAL Jean (b. Authon-du-Perche, France, 1909). Attended the School of Fine Arts in Lyons, then the Académie Ranson in Paris, where he met Bissière. Worked with a group of friends: Manessier, Bertholle, Martin. Exhibitions in Lyons and Paris. Composed many murals from 1937 on. Generally exhibited with Singier and Manessier at the Galerie de France, Paris. Designed the sets for a number of stage productions. One-man show at the Galerie de France, 1956. Lives in Paris. Le Moal's painting seems to have basic affinities with that of Bazaine on the one hand, and Manessier on the other. The diversity of the titles (*Prairie, Barques, Midi sur le Port, Floraison*) does not prevent a certain uniformity of plastic inspiration: linear tracings, mainly vertical, with dashes of bright colour regularly spaced between. — Bibl. Bourniquel: *Trois Peintres* (*Le Moal, Manessier, Singier*), Drouin (Paris 1946); Jacques Lassaigne: *Le Moal,* 'xxe siècle' nº 6 (Paris 1956).

LEPPIEN Jean (b. Luneburg, Germany, 1910). Studied under Kandinsky at the Bauhaus of Dessau (1929-1930). In Berlin, 1930-1933. Worked in Moholy-Nagy's studio. In Paris, 1933 to 1939. Volunteered for the army at the declaration of war. Was deported in Germany, 1944. All his work prior to 1944 was destroyed by the Nazis. Settled on the Riviera in 1945. Took part in the Salon des Réalités Nouvelles and the Salon de Mai.

LE MOAL. VERDURE. 1956.

One-man shows at the Galerie Colette Allendy, 1949 and 1951. Lives in Roquebrune, near Menton. Thematic compositions of geometric elements reduced to the essential. A series of canvases with crisscrossing curves and straight lines; another series of multiple and separate rectangles. — *Bibl.* Sibert: *Jean Leppien,* 'Art d'Aujourd'hui' (Paris, Feb. 1954).

LEVÉE. OCTOBER III. 1955. *Private Collection, Paris.*

LEUPPI Léo (b. Zurich 1893). Founder and President of the 'Die Allianz' society, which assembles the principal contemporary Swiss painters. Took part in numerous exhibitions in Switzerland, Italy, Paris, South America, etc. Lives in Zurich. Swathes of paint in combined transparent planes.

LEVÉE John H. (b. Los Angeles, 1924). Studied at the Art Center School, New York, then at the Académie Julian, Paris. Took part in the Salon de Mai from 1954 on. Travelling exhibition in Germany: 'Amerikanische Künstler in Frankreich'. Exhibited at the Stedelijk Museum, Amsterdam 1955, with the American painters Alcopley, Chelimsky, Fontaine, and Parker. One-man show at Gimpel's, London, in 1955. Took part in a group-show, Galerie de France, Paris 1956. Lives in Paris. After passing through a period of black and heavy graphism somewhat like Soulages, Levée found a more personal style, a brilliantly improvised painting of dull colours, which yet retains the same wilful emphasis.

LEWIS Norman (b. New York, 1909). Self-educated in art matters. Began painting in 1935. Exhibited at the Willard Gallery, New York, and took part in the 'Abstract Painting and Sculpture in America' show at the Museum of Modern Art, New York 1951, as well as in 'Le Dessin aux États-Unis' at the Museum of Modern Art, Paris 1954. Delicate compositions which seem as frail as mesh or lace.

LEWY Kurt (b. Essen, Germany, 1898). Studied at the Volkswangschule in Essen and the Staatliche Hochschule für Bildende Künste, Berlin (1919-1923). In 1924, apprentice in enamel-work in Pforzheim (Bade). Then worked in Essen (painting, enamel, graphic arts), where he taught at the Volkswangschule until 1933. In 1935, settled in Belgium. Naturalized Belgian citizen in 1951. A number of exhibitions of abstract paintings and enamels in Germany, England, Italy, notably at the Volkwang-Museum, Essen 1925, at Brussels 1952, and at Ghent 1955. Long matured geometrical fantasies suggesting nobility and inner calm. Lives in Brussels.

VAN LINT. WHITE AND BLUE. 1955.

LHOTELIER Henry (b. Calais, 1908). Received a classical education. Attended at the same time classes of painting at the School of Decorative and Industrial Arts in Calais. Took a degree in Law at the University of Lille. Abandoned a legal career in 1935 in order to devote himself to the study of stained glass at Boulogne-sur-Mer. Composed (1938) twenty four small abstract stained glass windows for the Pavillon de l'Artois at the exhibition of Social Progress in Lille-Roubaix, and (1951) nineteen abstract stained glass windows for the Little Seminary of Boulogne-sur-Mer. The following year, he constructed a 130-foot-square abstract in stained glass as a partition in an apartment house in Hardelot (Pas-de-Calais). Takes part regularly in the Salon des Réalités Nouvelles. Lives in Boulogne-sur-Mer. "The multiplicity of appearances disguises the void, but completeness of perfection dwells in stark simplicity". (Lhotellier).

LINT Louis van (b. Brussels, 1909, of a Flemish father and a French mother). Attended the Academy of Saint-Josse-ten-Noode (1924-1937). In 1939, founded the *la Route libre* club with Anne Bonnet and Gaston Bertrand. First one-man show at the Palais des Beaux-Arts, Brussels, 1941. One of the leading members of the 'Jeune Peinture' Belgian group, founded in 1945. Designed the sets for *L'Histoire du Soldat* (Stravinsky) and took part in numerous exhibitions in Belgium, Holland, Switzerland, Italy as well as in the United States and in Paris. Abstract works since 1951. Has been a long time under the influence of Bazaine. Lives in Brussels. — *Bibl.* Sosset: *Van Lint,* De Sikkel (Antwerp 1953).

LISSITZKY Eliezer (El) Markovitch (b. in the district of Smolensk, Russia, 1890; d. Moscow, 1941). Studied engineering in Darmstadt, 1909-1914. Then returned to Russia. Joined the constructivist movement of Rodchenko and Tatlin in 1919, and began, the same year, the famous series of drawings for which he invented the name *Proun*. Was a professor in Moscow, 1921. The hostility of the Russian government towards modern art forced him to leave for Berlin, where he contributed to various reviews with van Doesburg and Moholy-Nagy. In Switzerland from 1923 to 1925. There, he organized the 'ABC' group and partly directed its periodical. In 1925, published with Arp *The Isms of Art.* From 1925 to 1928, was in Hanover as the guest of the Kestnergesellschaft. It was then he composed the interior decoration of the famous abstract room in the Landesmuseum, later destroyed by the Nazis. After a short stay in Berlin, 1928, he returned to Moscow, where he specialized mainly in visual education. — *Bibl.* Kallai: *El Lissitzky,* Jahrbuch der jungen Kunst (Leipzig 1924); Barr: *Cubism and Abstract Art* (New York 1936); Dorner: *Art of this Century* (New York 1942); *The way beyond art* (New York 1947); *Collection of the Société Anonyme* (New Haven, 1950).

LOHSE Richard Paul (b. Zurich, 1902). Educated in Zurich. Travelled in Italy, France, Germany. Took part in many exhibitions in Switzerland from 1936 on. A member of the 'Die Allianz' society. Lives in Zurich. Rhythmical studies in vertical and horizontal lines, very exactly traced, in the neo-plastic tradition.

LOLO Dolorès Soldevilla (b. Pinar del Rio, 1911). First devoted herself to trade-unions activities. Then began to paint and sculpt. Exhibited at the Salon d'Automne and at the Indépendants, in Paris. Travelled and studied in Italy, Spain, Belgium, England, Switzerland, Czechoslovakia. One-man shows of paintings, objects, and collages at the Galerie Arnaud (1945) and the Galerie La Roue, Paris 1955. As the Cultural delegate of the Cuban Republic in Europe, she organized an exhibition of contemporary Cuban painting at the Museum of Modern Art, Paris, 1951, and an exhibition of Parisian abstraction in Havana, 1956. Collages and paintings starting from very simple elements and recalling the work of Sophie Taeuber or the suprematism of Malevitch.

LOMBARD Jean (b. Dijon, France, 1895). Attended the École des Beaux-Arts in Lyons and Paris. Impatient with academic teaching, he left to work on his own. Exhibited in the various major Salons from 1922 on. After 1943, he abandoned working from the model; his desire to give the plastic full play slowly brought him to abstraction. The director, since 1942, of an Academy of Painting the students and alumni of which form the "Vert-Bois" group. Lombard's canvases are scholarly transcriptions of landscapes into pure painting. The initial subject is entirely sacrificed to the composition and the lyricism. Lives in Paris.

LONGOBARDI Xavier (b. Algiers, 1923). A volunteer in the war (1942-1945). Studied literature and philosophy in Paris and took a degree in classics. Studied in various Academies. One-man shows Galerie de Beaune, Paris 1953, and Galerie Arnaud, Paris 1954 and 1955. Composed representational tapestries (commissioned by the Government). Abs-

LOMBARD. PAINTING. 1954. *Adam-Teissier Collection, Paris*

tract collages and paintings: an exceptional density of overlapping forms and colours. Lives in Paris.

LOPUSZNIAK (b. Tarnopol, Poland, 1904). Studied at the Fine Arts School in Cracow. Exhibited in Cracow and Warsaw since 1930. In Paris, 1938. Was first influenced by Bonnard, then by surrealism. Came to abstraction in 1946. One-man shows: Galerie Arnaud and Galerie Colette Allendy, Paris. Lives in Paris and in Southern France (La Turbie) where he has built his own house. Painting with large rectilinear and geometrical forms.

LOUBCHANSKY Marcelle (b. Paris, 1917). Began to paint after the Liberation of Paris (1944). Took part in various group-shows, particularly 'Younger European Painters', New York 1954. One-man shows at the Galerie de Beaune, Paris 1950, and the Galerie Kléber, Paris 1956. After a painting characterized by melting and viscous forms, rather melancholy in effect, she tackled the problem of colour, showing a predilection for bright red. She has recently launched into multicoloured cosmogony, and joined, on a larger scale, the studies of Malespine.

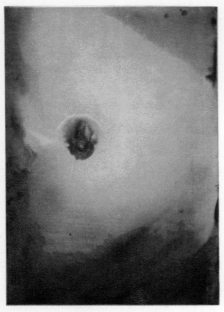

LOUBCHANSKY. GRAIN OF AMBER. 1955.
Galerie Kléber, Paris.

M

MACDONALD-WRIGHT Stanton (b. Charlottesville, Virginia, 1890). Of Dutch origin: his real name was van Vranken. In Paris, 1907. Attended the Academy of Fine Arts, the Académie Julian, and the Sorbonne. Met Morgan Russel in 1912, and founded with him the *synchromist* movement, akin to Delaunay's *orphism*. Exhibited at the Salon des Indépendants the following year. Synchromist exhibitions in Munich and in Paris (Galerie Bernheim Jeune, 1913). Took part in the 'Armory' show, New York. Returned to the United States in 1916. One-man show at the Stieglitz Gallery 291, in 1917. About 1919, he came back to representational painting. Travelled in Japan in 1937, and spent some time there in 1952-1953. Restrospective exhibition, together with Morgan Russel and Bruce, at the Rose Fried Gallery, New York 1950. Reverted to abstraction in 1954. Important retrospective exhibition in Los Angeles (County Museum), 1956. Lives in Santa Monica (Calif.) The recent works of Macdonald-Wright show a lyricism which is both brilliant and refined. — *Bibl.* W. H. Wright: *Modern Painting, its tendency and meaning* (New York 1915); Seuphor: *L'Art abstrait, ses origines, ses premiers maîtres* (Paris 1949); Ritchie: *Abstract Painting and Sculpture in America* (New York 1951); Catalogue of the Los Angeles Exhibition, 1956.

MACKE August (b. Meschede, Ruhr, 1887; d. Perthes, France, 1914). Studied in Cologne, Bonn, Dusseldorf. Travelled in Italy, Holland, Belgium, France, etc. In 1910, met Franz Marc, then Kandinsky and Jawlensky. Took part in the 'Blaue Reiter' group. In 1912, travelled to Paris with Franz Marc. They met Delaunay and Le Fauconnier. In April 1914, travelled to Tunis with Moilliet and Paul Klee. Drafted in 1914, he was killed on the front. Only a few of Macke's works can be considered abstract. He died too early to have found his own style. Letters to Franz Marc, as yet unpublished, indicate violent reaction against some of Kandinsky's abstractions. — *Bibl.* Seuphor: *L'Art Abstrait, ses origines, ses premiers maîtres* (Paris 1949).

MACDONALD-WRIGHT. TASK OF SISYPHUS. SLEEP IV. 1955.

MAC NEIL George (b. New York, 1909). Studied at the Art Students League, then under Hans Hofmann. Exhibited with the 'American Abstract Artists' group from 1937 on. Took part in the 'Abstract Painting and Sculpture in America' show, Museum of Modern Art, New York, 1951. Lives in New York.

MACRIS Constantin G. (b. Cairo, 1919, of Greek parents). Studied academic painting under an instructor who belonged to the Munich School. Exhibited regularly in Cairo. Was drafted in the Greek air force during the war. In Paris, 1948. Studied drawing in Léger's studio. Then worked on his own. His paintings, large abstract works the surfaces of which are covered with closely placed smears of paint, give the impression of walls, and show a definite affinity with the chequered compositions of Mondrian. Lives in Paris.

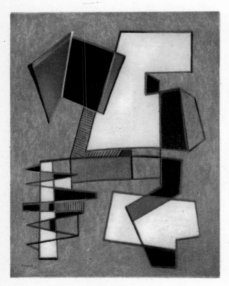

MAGNELLI. COMPOSITION. 1944.
Jucker Collection, Milan.

MAGNELLI Alberto (b. Florence, 1888). Self-educated in matters of art. Travelled many times to Paris. Frequented the futurists, in 1913, without, however, taking part in their movement. Another trip to Paris, 1914. Met Apollinaire, Max Jacob, Picasso, Léger, Gris. Representational compositions in swathes. Returned to Italy at the time of the declaration of war. In 1915, while in Florence, painted a series of abstract canvases in bright and effective colours. Reverted then to representational painting, for a period of almost twenty years. Returned to Paris in 1933, painted compositions he called *pierres éclatées* (shattered rocks), and soon was drawn back to abstraction. Numerous one-man and group-shows. Took part in the main Abstract Salons in Paris. Important one-man shows : Paris, Galerie Drouin, 1947; Brussels, Palais des Beaux-Arts, 1954; Eindhoven, Van Abbe Museum, 1954; Museum of Antibes, 1955. Lives in Paris.

"It is very easy to draw parallel or curved lines, or to draw visual or imaginary forms. But it is difficult to make them glow with fire, to make them expressive." (Magnelli). "In the years of unreal darkness 1941-1942, the reality of beauty was the sole consolation of our small group in Grasse. Sonia Delaunay, Sophie Taeuber, Susi Magnelli, Alberto Magnelli and myself were part of that group. During these years, Magnelli was rich in ideas which he now carries through with mastery. This careful work links him to the popular art of the great periods. The black, brown, blue, of Magnelli's paintings recall the colours in frescoes of the first Cretan periods. His works could well balance these august and serene decorations. They are natural ornaments, neither blatant nor exceptional." (Arp). — *Bibl.* Arp: *Magnelli,* 'Galerie Drouin' (Paris 1947); Seuphor: *L'Art abstrait, ses origines, ses premiers maîtres* (Paris 1949); *XXe Siècle,* no 1 (Paris 1951); *Témoignages pour l'Art abstrait* (Paris 1952); *A Dictionary of Modern Painting* (Methuen, London 1956).

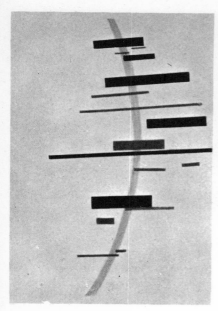

CASIMIR MALEVITCH.
SUPREMATIST COMPOSITION. 1916.

MALDONADO Tomas (b. Buenos Aires, 1922). Academy of Fine Arts in 1938. A member and founder of the 'Arte Concreto' group. Met Max Bill and Vantongerloo. First abstract paintings in 1944. Travelled to Europe in 1948. Editor of the review *Nueva Vision* (Buenos Aires). In 1955, a professor at the Hochschule für Gestaltung (Ulm, Germany). Lives in Ulm.

MALESPINE Émile (b. Lyons, 1892; d. Paris, 1952). From 1922 to 1928, published the avant-garde review *Manomètre* in Lyons. Took a degree in Science and qualified as an M.D. In 1925, founded the 'Donjon' theatrical company; has written number of plays. In Paris, 1929. In 1944, discovered a new style of abstract painting on paper. He then exhibited in the main Abstract Salons in Paris and in a number of galleries.

Malespine's plastic work is very spectacular: a fusion of worlds, a turmoil of virgin matter, a seething of potentialities. Cloudgardens where fancy can fashion what it will. One penetrates to the heart of whirlwinds, one assists at the birth of elements. Nothing human yet, but suggestions, vague presentiments of emotion everywhere in the air. — *Bibl*. Malespine: *Peinture intégrale,* 'Cahiers d'Art' (Paris 1947).

MALEVITCH Casimir (b. Kiev, 1878; d. Leningrad, 1935). At first influenced by the impressionists and the fauves. A member of the 'Jack of Diamonds' group in Moscow, 1911. Became the leader of the cubist school in Russia, after a trip to Paris (1912). Exhibited the first elements of suprematism, notably a perfect black square on a white background, in a small art gallery 'La Cible', 1913 (testimony of George Annenkow who was present). Two years later, published his *From Cubism to Suprematism* manifesto in Moscow. A professor at the Fine Arts School in Moscow, 1919, in Leningrad after 1921. Took part in an exhibition of Russian art in Berlin, 1922. Was granted the permission to go to Germany, 1926, to prepare the publication of his book *Die gegenstandslose Welt* (The world without objects). Then returned to Russia, leaving about sixty of his works to a friend who still has them today (Feb. 1956). He died completely destitute. He asked his friends to bury him with arms extended in the form of a cross. According to dependable witnesses, Malevitch must have been imprisoned after he came back from Germany, but released when his health began to fail.

Malevitch's suprematism originated in futurist and cubist influences, both of which worked powerfully on the young Russian artists of the time (the dynamic Marinetti had made a momentous lecture-tour in Russia). One knows, on the other hand, that the great collectors Stchoukine and Morosov introduced the cubist works of Braque and Picasso in Moscow, before the paint was dry on the canvases. Whatever the reasons, however, no one had proposed as radical a solution as Malevitch did with his suprematism, in 1913: works composed solely with squares, circles, triangles, and

MANESSIER. THORNS. 1955. *Galerie de France, Paris.*

crosses. Later on, he introduced other simple elements, zigzags and ovals. But presently he returned to straight lines and in 1919 painted his double white square on a white background (now at the Museum of Modern Art, New York). After 1921, when the Moscow government relegated Malevitch to Leningrad, he finished up by making applied art, exactly like his colleagues Rodchenko and Tatlin. But the compositions he painted on delf cups and beakers remain perfectly recognizable suprematist works. — *Bibl.* Barr: *Cubism and Abstract Art* (New York 1936); *Circle, international Survey of Constructive Art* (London 1937); *Art of this Century* (New York 1942); Janis: *Abstract and Surrealist Art in America* (New York 1944); Biederman: *Art as the Evolution of visual Knowledge* (Red Wing 1948); Moholy-Nagy: *Vision in Motion* (Chicago 1947); Seuphor: *L'art abstrait, ses origines, ses premiers maîtres* (Paris 1949); *Collection of the Société Anonyme* (New Haven 1950); 'Art d'Aujourd'hui' (Paris, June 1952); Barr, *Masters of Modern Art* (New York 1954); *A Dictionary of Modern Painting* (Methuen, London 1956); Seuphor: *Au temps de l'avant-garde,* 'L'Œil'

(Paris, Nov. 1955); Brion: *Art Abstrait* (Paris 1956).

MALINA Frank Joseph (b. Brenham, Texas, 1912). Studied mechanics and technology in Texas and in California (1934-1940). Carried on research work in interplanetary fuses and rockets. A professor at the Institute of Technology, Pasadena (Calif.). Composes paintings on trellis work with effects of transparency, and paintings of transformations with the aid of interior lighting. One-man shows Galerie Arnaud (1954) and Galerie Colette Allendy (1955). Took part in the Salon des Réalités Nouvelles. Lives in Paris.

MANESSIER Alfred (b. Saint-Ouen, Somme, 1911). Attended the lycée and the School of Fine Arts at Amiens. In Paris, 1931. Studied architecture at the École des Beaux-Arts. Attended at the same time classes at the Louvre and at various Academies of Montparnasse. Met Bissière at the Académie Ranson in

1935. A group was then formed around Bissière, with the painters Le Moal and Bertholle and the sculptor Martin. Numerous one-man and group-shows from 1937 on. Took part in the Salons from 1933 on. Since 1945, has been included in many exhibitions of young French painters abroad. Composed cartoons of abstract stained glass windows for a number of churches, including Bréseux (Jura), Saint-Pierre de Trinquetaille (Arles), the Chapel of Hem (near Roubaix) and the Church of All Souls (Basel). Manessier lives in Paris.

Some critics question the purely abstract quality of Mannessier's works, because the young artist gave his paintings such titles as *La Couronne d'Épines, Portement de la Croix,* which, they contend, confer a superfluous literary connotation. One should nevertheless realise that the mystical atmosphere which permeates Manessier's work expresses itself mainly in completely abstract plastic terms. No artist has done more, by the simple eloquence of his work, to introduce abstract art to large ecclesiastical circles. "Non-representational art", writes Manessier, "seems to me to give the modern painter the best chance of reaching his personal reality,

of becoming aware again of what is essential in him. Only by starting from an understanding of this point can an artist eventually regain balance and revitalize even the exterior reality of the world. If man is indeed a hierarchy of values, then his outward appearance is merely a transparent envelope, if void of spiritual content." Manessier has published many coloured lithographs. — *Bibl.* Bourniquel: *Trois Peintres (Le Moal, Manessier, Singier),* Drouin (Paris 1946); Dorival: *Alfred Manessier, artisan religieux,* 'L'Œil' (Paris, Oct. 1955); Howe: *Alfred Manessier,* 'Apollo' (London, June 1957).

MANSOUROV Paul (b. Saint-Petersburg, 1896). A friend of Malevitch and Tatlin. Exhibited with them from 1917 on. Lives in Paris since 1929. A study in very simple motifs, usually painted on lengths of plank.

MANTON Maria (b. Blida, Algeria, 1915). Studied at the School of Fine Arts in Algiers. Met Nallard in 1941. In Tunisia from 1943 to 1945. Settled in Paris 1947. Took part regularly in the Salon des Réalités Nouvelles from 1947 on. One-man shows Galerie Lydia Conti, Galerie des Deux-Iles, Galerie Colette Allendy and Galerie Arnaud, Paris. Took part in exhibitions in Italy, Germany, Switzerland, Belgium, and New York. Travelled in Italy and Yugoslavia in 1952. Lives in Paris. A painting often monochromatic and restrained in effect. Perfect poise in the

MARIA MANTON. COMPOSITION. 1954.

EVELYN MARC. INK DRAWING. 1955.

composition: simplicity and clarity. A rigor that is never hard.

MARC Evelyn (b. Angers, France, 1915). Her parents, Willy Eisenschitz and Claire Bertrand are both painters and disciples of Cézanne and Van Gogh. She spent a year in an American University (1935-6) and then attended a few Paris Academies. Dazzled by her first contact with abstract painting and surrealism. "There is a deep separation between what really impresses me and what I can learn in the schools." Exhibited many times, in Marseilles and in Paris, together with her parents who remained attached to figurative art. Took part in the Salon des Réalités Nouvelles. Blurred, melting colours and forms, sometimes fervent in feeling.

MARC Franz (b. Munich, 1880; d. Verdun, 1916). Was the son of the painter Wilhelm Marc. Studied at the University of Munich and then at the Academy of Munich. Came to Paris in 1903, travelled in Greece, 1906. Second trip to Paris in 1907. Made friends with Kandinsky in 1910. They organised the 'Blaue Reiter' exhibitions together and published the famous 'Blaue Reiter' almanac. Third trip to Paris with Macke in 1912. Met Delaunay who greatly influenced him. Abstract works in 1913. Drafted in 1914, he was killed in front of Verdun, in 1916, leaving behind letters and a famous album of abstract sketches. Marc played a very important role in the compilation of the famous 'Blaue Reiter' almanac. The idea came from Kandinsky, but Marc found the publisher and helped Kandinsky along during the whole enterprise, both with the exhibitions and the publications. All Marc's force of conviction expresses itself in the words: "Traditions are beautiful, but only when one creates them, not when one lives on them." Through the representation of animals in natural life, Marc developed a style which slowly withdrew him from the object, until he attained pure abstraction in a few works painted in 1913 and 1914. (*Formes en lutte, Formes cassées, Petites compositions*, etc...) Retrospective exhibitions of Franz Marc's work have taken place in Germany, Holland, Belgium, and Switzerland. — *Bibl.* Dreier: *Modern Art* (New York 1926); Barr: *Cubism and Abstract Art* (New York 1936); Seuphor: *L'Art abstrait, ses origines, ses premiers maîtres* (Paris 1949); *Collection of the Société Anonyme* (New Haven, 1950); *Catalogue of the retrospective exhibition 'Der Blaue Reiter'* (Munich 1949); *Catalogue of the Franz Marc exhibition* (Munich 1950); Raynal: *De Picasso au Surréalisme* (Paris and Geneva 1950); *A Dictionary of Modern Painting* (Methuen, London 1956).

MARCUS Gert (b. Hamburg, 1914). A painter and a worker in mosaic. Exhibited a series of works called *la Croix d'espace* at the Franco-Swedish gallery, in Stockholm (1952) and contributed geometrical compositions to a group-show at the Norrköping Museum, Sweden, 1956. One-man exhibition at the Galerie Colette Allendy, Paris 1956. Lives in Stockholm.

MARELLI Giulio (b. Velletri, Italy, 1907). Took a diploma at the J. Romani Art School (1928). Took part, as a sculptor, in various exhibitions in Italy and elsewhere. From 1947 on, devoted himself completely to abstract painting. Included in the 'Arte astratta e concreta in Italia' show, Rome, 1951. Lives in Rome.

MARGO Boris (b. in Russia, 1902). Studied at the Analytical Art Institute in Leningrad, under Filonov. In the United States, 1930. Many exhibitions in America from 1939 on, particularly at the Betty Parsons Gallery, New York. Lives in New York. Abstract paintings reminiscent of surrealism; one recognizes also characteristic forms of Max Ernst and Tanguy. But these forms are achieved through the projection of 'cellocut' against the surface of the canvas, a technique akin to that of Dubuffet's works in plastic. — *Bibl.* Janis: *Abstract and Surrealist Art in America* (New York 1944); *Catalogue of the Boris Margo exhibition,* Betty Parsons Gallery (New York 1955).

MARLE Felix del (b. Pont-sur-Sambre, France, 1889; d. Paris, 1952). Studied painting in Brussels and in Paris. Friendship with Kupka in 1920 and with Mondrian in 1925. For a short time, took over the plastic direction of the review *Vouloir,* in Lille. Painted in the futurist and in the neo-plastic manners. Reverted to realism for a few years. After the Liberation, the emphasis in his compositions was on architecture and colour in space. General Secretary of the Salon des Réalités Nouvelles since 1946. One-man show at the Galerie Colette Allendy, 1949. Founded with André Bloc the group 'Espace' (1950).

MARTIN Kenneth (b. Sheffield, England, 1905). Studied at the Royal College of Art, London. Taught painting in a number of London schools. In 1951, published with Victor Pasmore *Broadsheet n⁰ 1* completely devoted to abstract art in England. Organized an exhibition of abstract art at the A.I.G. Gallery, London, with Robert Adams,

FRANZ MARC. ABSTRACT DESIGN. 1914.

Adrian Heath, Anthony Hill and Victor Pasmore. Lives in London. — Bibl. *Nine Abstract Artists* (London 1954).

MASON Alice Trumbull (b. Litchfield, Connecticut, 1904). One-man shows at the Museum of Living Art, New York 1942, and at the Rose Fried Gallery, New York 1948. Included in group-shows in France and in the United States. A member of the "American Abstract Artists" association. Lives in New York.

MATHIEU Georges (b. Boulogne-sur-Mer, 1921). Studied law and philosophy. Took a degree in English literature. Began to paint in 1942. Settled in Paris in 1947. Exhibited at the Salon des Réalités Nouvelles and the Salon des Sur-indépendants. Organized with Bryen and others, various exhibitions of an abstract art claiming to be 'lyric', 'psychic' and 'in a spirit of reaction against abstract formalism'. In close sympathy with the ideals of the American neo-expressionist painters. One-man show at the Galerie Drouin in 1950. Took part in many group-shows. Exhibited at the Kootz Gallery, New York, 1954. Wrote a manifesto addressed to the American avant-garde painters. One-man show at the Galerie Rive-Droite, Paris 1954 and 1956. — Bibl. *Art News* (New York, Feb. 1955).

MAUKE Rudolph (b. Magdeburg-on-the-Elbe, 1924). Studied at the Fine Arts School in Berlin from 1949 on. One-man shows in Berlin 1954 and 1955. Included in the German abstract painting exhibition at the Cercle Volney, Paris, 1955. A great simplicity of planes and lines, soft colours. Lives in Berlin.

MAUSSION Charles (b. Nantes, France, 1923). Settled in Paris, 1946. Studied at the Institute of Art and Archaeology. Attended the studio of Lhote, and then of Léger. Abstract painting since 1949. Worked at the Dewasne-Pillet academy the same year. Included in the

MATHIEU. CAPETAN ENTELECHY. 1954.
D. H. Clark Collection, New York.

Salon des Réalités Nou-
velles in 1951, 1952, and
1953. One-man show
at the Galerie Arnaud
in 1952. Lives in Paris.
Supple geometrical abs-
traction; very precise
stains and lines on a
white background, com-
bined like a piece of
music consisting of clear
rhythms.

MEERBERGEN Ru-
dolf
(b. Antwerp, 1908).
Studied at the Fine Arts
School in Antwerp
(1926-1930). Stayed in
Paris and in the South
of France, 1932. Then

MENDELSON. RECITATIVE. 1954. *A. Niels Collection, Brussels.*

visited Germany, Holland, Spain, and Italy.
Many one-man shows in Belgium. Launched into abstraction in 1951. Sober compositions with large and stripped forms.
Lives in Antwerp.

MEISTERMANN Georg (b. Solingen,
Germany, 1911).
Studied at the Academy of Dusseldorf.
Devoted himself for a few years to painting
on glass. Reverted to free-style painting
after 1943 and came progressively to abstraction. Many exhibitions in Europe,
India, New Zealand, Japan, America. A
professor at the School of Fine Arts in
Frankfurt since 1953. Included in the German abstract painting exhibition at the Cercle
Volney, Paris 1955. Lives in Frankfurt-
am-Main.

MELE Juan N. (b. Buenos Aires, 1923).
Attended the Fine Arts Academy
in Buenos Aires. Tackled abstract art in
1945, and the following year, exhibited with
the 'Arte Concreto' group. Travelled to

Europe 1948-1949. In Paris, met Vantongerloo, Pevsner, Domela, Herbin, Seuphor.
Made the acquaintance of Max Bill and of
the Italian abstract painters. When he
returned to the Argentine, figurative compositions reappeared in his work. But he
reverted to pure abstraction in 1952. Retrospective exhibition of his works at the
Meeba gallery, Buenos Aires, 1952. Lives
in Buenos Aires.

MENDELSON Marc (b. London, 1915
of an English mother
and a Belgian father). The founder of the
Belgian group 'Jeune Peinture Belge'.
Numerous exhibitions in Belgium and other
countries. Composed large abstract decorations for a restaurant in Brussels and for
the Kursaal in Ostend. One-man show
at the Palais des Beaux-Arts, Brussels 1955.
Took part in the Venice Biennale with about
ten canvases (1956). Each year Mendelson
spends a few months in Palamos (Spain),
where he has a studio, but generally lives
in Brussels. — *Bibl.* Séaux: *Marc Mendelson*
(Antwerp 1954).

MILO. SIKU ZOTE III. 1954.
Van Geluwe Collection, Brussels.

MESSAGIER Jean (b. Paris, 1920). Attended the National School of Decorative Arts in Paris, 1942. Included in the Salon d'Automne since 1947 and the Salon de Mai since 1948. Took part in a number of group-shows in Paris and in the main European countries. Travelled and studied in Algeria (1946) and in Italy (1948). His plastic works have affinities with those of the American painter Rothko. Lives in Paris. "Starting from nature, to re-group the various emotions, preserving all the while the utmost detachment. To waste none of the energy of a rage or passion. To pinpoint the great rhythms and then marshall them." (Messagier).

MICHEL (Michel Wulff) (b. Stettin, Germany, 1924). Studied typography at the School of Fine Arts in Hamburg (1946-1949) and worked for some time as a sub-editor in a printing-press. Came to Paris 1951. Took part a number of times in the Salon des Réalités Nouvelles and in other group-shows. Travelled throughout Europe as well as Asia Minor and North Africa. One-man show of collages and small pictures at the Galerie du Haut Pavé, Paris, 1956. Lives in Paris. Michel's collages are in the best tradition of Klee and Schwitters. They are held to be among the most refined in this genre.

MILO Jean (Émile van Gindertael) b. Brussels, 1906. Attended the Academy of Fine Arts in Brussels. Spent some time with the Etikhove group of Flemish painters, who took their name from the village they settled in. Travelled to Paris, London, Holland, and the Belgian Congo. A member of the 'Jeune Peinture Belge' group. Changed over to abstraction in 1950. Included in the Salon des Réalités Nouvelles in 1952. Numerous one-man shows in Paris and Brussels. He is the brother of the Parisian critic R. van Gindertael. Lives in Brussels. — *Bibl.* R. V. Gindertael: *Jean Milo,* Éditions 'Signe' (Paris 1953); Luc Haesaerts: *Jean Milo,* De Sikkel (Antwerp 1954).

MIOTTE Jean (b. Paris 1926). Studied in the non-institutional studios of Montparnasse. First abstract canvases in 1948. Travelled in Italy, Spain, England, and Algeria. Took part in the Salon des Réalités Nouvelles from 1953 on. Compositions high in colour and well articulated in design: they hang extraordinarily well.

MITCHELL Fred (b. Meridan, United States, 1923). Studied at the Carnegie Institute of Technology (1942-

1943) and the Cranbrook Academy of Art (1946-1948). Completed his studies in various schools in Rome (1948-1950). Taught in a number of colleges and academies, contributed to *Pictures on Exhibit,* exhibited in Pittsburgh, Rome, Minneapolis and New York (Tanager Gallery, Stable Gallery, Solomon R. Guggenheim Museum). Teaches at the Cranbrook Academy (Michigan).

MITCHELL Joan (b. Chicago, 1926). Studied at the Art Institute in Chicago. Was in France 1948-1949, then in New York where she had a number of one-man shows (New Gallery 1953; Stable Gallery 1953 and 1955). Returned to Paris in 1955. Friendship with Riopelle. Abstract-expressionist painting, roughly similar to that of Tworkow and Esteban Vicente.

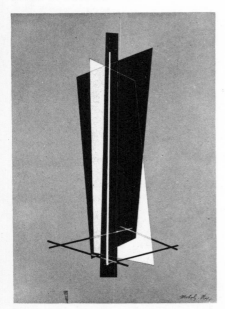

MOHOLY-NAGY. CONSTRUCTION. 1922-1923.
Jeanne Coppel Collection, Paris.

MOHOLY-NAGY Lazslo (b. Bacsbarsod, Hungary, 1895; d. Chicago, 1946), Studied law in Budapest. Was wounded in the First World War: during his convalescence, began to draw portraits. When the war was over, was attracted by Russian avant-garde art. In 1922, published *Buch Neuer Künstler,* the first anthology of world avant-garde art, with the Hungarian poet Kassak, in Vienna. From 1920 on, his work was completely abstract. Met Walter Gropius who appointed him a professor at the Bauhaus: from 1922 to 1928, he played an important role in the publications of the school as well as in its research work in new materials to be used in the applied arts. In Amsterdam, 1934. In London, 1935: he published a few books of documentary photographs and started on the paintings-sculptures he called *space modulators.* Was in the United States, 1937. When the new Chicago Bauhaus, of which he had become the director, had to fold up for financial reasons, he founded his own school (School of Design) which proved very successful. Published *The New Vision* in New York, 1946. There have been a number of retrospective exhibitions of his works in America. One of his books was published posthumously: *Vision in Motion,* Chicago 1947. His wife wrote a number of essays about him as well as a biography. — *Bibl.* Barr: *Cubism and Abstract Art* (New York, 1936); S. Giedion: *L. Moholy-Nagy* (Zurich 1937); Hitchcock: *Painting towards Architecture* (New York 1948); *Collection of the Société Anonyme* (New Haven 1947); 'Art d'Aujourd'hui' (Paris, Oct. 1951); *A Dictionary of Modern Painting* (Methuen, London 1956).

MOISSET Raymond (b. Paris, 1906). Attended the school of Applied Arts. Devoted himself to painting from 1954 on. Took part in the Salon de Mai every year since its creation (1945). One-man show at the Galerie Simone Heller,

Paris, 1956. Came to pure abstraction slowly, taking his departure always in a landscape theme. Lives in Paris.

MONDRIAN Piet (b. Amersfoort, 1872; d. New York, 1944.) Since his father wanted him to be a teacher, he obtained the two degrees needed to teach design in state schools. Entered the Academy of Amsterdam in 1892, and attended all its classes very regularly. Painted in the open air around Amsterdam. In order to make a living, gave drawing lessons, copied paintings in the museums, worked as an industrial designer. Friendship with the Dutch painter Jan Sluyters, then with Simon Maris whom he accompanied on a short trip to Spain (1901). Painted a whole year in the Dutch Brabant (1903-1904). Became a member of the main painters' associations in Amsterdam. In 1908, first stay in Domburg (Zeeland) where he met the painter Toorop, then very famous and the leader of an important group of painters. In Zeeland, painted in the divisionist manner, as a fauve, and as a disciple of Van Gogh, all in turn. In 1911, became a member of the Directing Committee of the Modern Art Club in Amsterdam: the club organized a number of important exhibitions, showing for the first time in Holland fauve and cubist painters. Was in Paris, 1912 to 1914. Exhibited at the Salon des Indépendants works influenced by cubism and yet almost completely abstract. Came to abstraction through an embellishment of his favourite themes: a tree, scaffoldings, the wall of a cathedral. First complete abstract paintings in 1913. Was on a visit to Holland when the war broke out: he remained there until 1919, kept on working, and after having met Van Doesburg, contributed to the creation of the 'De Stijl' movement. From 1917 to 1924, was one of the principal collaborators to its review. Returned to Paris and published *le Néo-Plasticisme,* a summary of his doctrine, at the Galerie de l'Effort

Moderne, 1920. During the following years, contributed a variety of articles to many Paris avant-garde reviews, while, in Germany, the Bauhaus published *Neue Gestaltung* (1925). Took part in many large international exhibitions of abstract art in Paris and in America. A member of the 'Cercle et Carré', then of the 'Abstraction-Création' groups. In London, 1938-1940. The bombings of London made him leave for New York. One-man show at the Valentine Gallery, New York 1942. His last exhibition, together with the Brazilian sculptor Maria Martins, was held at the same gallery in 1943.

The purely neo-plastic work of Mondrian is a kind of metaphysics of painting. One must approach it as one approaches icons which seek to express an immutable truth: that truth which, for the artist, is embodied in the dualism of horizontal and vertical, and glides towards us on black rails. These stark works, especially the square canvases of the 1929-1932 period, demand intellectual rather than visual contemplation. Later on, after the experience of New York, an unexpected lyricism pierces through the work (the *Boogie-Woogie* series). The rails fly up in splinters, black is banished as the last vestige of the 'tragic', a touch of exhilaration appears without, however, banishing the neo-plastic. Thus, a new abundance of inspiration is heralded (the *Victory Boogie-Woogie* remains unfinished), when death surprises the painter.

Retrospective exhibitions of his works were held at the Museum of Modern Art, New York (1945), at the Stedelijk Museum, Amsterdam (1946), the Kunsthalle, Bern (1947), the Municipal Museum, The Hague (1955), the Kunsthaus, Zurich (1955), the Whitechapel Gallery, London (1955), the Venice Biennale (1956) as well as in Rome and Milan (1956). — *Bibl.* Dreier: *Modern Art* (New York 1926); Barr: *Cubism and Abstract Art* (New York 1936); *Art of this Century* (New York 1942); Sweeney: *Mondrian* (New York 1948); *Catalogue of the retrospective exhibition in Amsterdam* (1946); Seuphor: *L'art abstrait, ses origines, ses premiers maîtres* (Paris 1949); Hitchcock: *Painting towards Architecture* (New York 1948); *Collection of the Société Anonyme* (New Haven 1950); 'Art d'Aujourd'hui' (Paris, Dec. 1949); *Catalogue of the Mondrian exhibition*, Sidney Janis Gallery (New York 1951); *Retrospective exhibition of the 'Stijl'* (Amsterdam 1951); *Magazine of Art* (New York, May 1952); Raynal: *From Picasso to Surrealism* (Paris-Geneva 1950); 'Art d'Aujourd'hui' (Paris, Feb. 1954); *A Dictionary of Modern Painting* (Methuen, London 1956); *XXᵉ Siècle*, n° 4 (Paris 1954); Zevi: *Poetica dell'architettura neoplastica* (Milan 1953); *Catalogue of the retrospective exhibition in The Hague* (1955); Seuphor: *Humanisme de Mondrian*, 'Aujourd'hui', n° 2 (Paris 1955); Catalogues of the retrospective exhibitions in Zurich and London (1955); Jaffé: *De Stijl, 1917-1931* (Amsterdam 1956); Seuphor: *De Stijl*, 'L'Œil' (Paris, Oct. 1956); Seuphor, *Piet Mondrian*, Dumont-Schauberg (Köln), Abrams (New York) and Flammarion (Paris), 1956.

MONNET Gianni (b. Turin, 1912). Co-founder, with Murani and Dorfles, of the 'Movement for Concrete Art', Milan 1949. Included in the 'Arte Astratta e Concreta in Italia' exhibition, Museum of Modern Art, Rome, 1951. Monnet is also an architect and an art-critic. Lives in Milan.

MONNINI Alvaro (b. Florence, 1922). Attended the Fine Arts Academy in Florence. One of the founders of the 'Arte d'Oggi' group. Took part in various exhibitions in Italy and in other countries of Europe and America. Lives in Florence.

MONTE M. G. dal (b. Italy, 1907). Was in Berlin, 1931. Contributed to the *Der Sturm* review. Then pursued his plastic researches in Paris, Prague, Geneva. Lives in Italy.

MONTHEILLET Pierre (b. Lyons, 1923). Studied Classics at the University of Lyons. Then devoted himself to painting. Exhibited in various Salons from 1939 on. Took part in all the displays of the 'Jeune Peinture Lyonnaise' group as well as in the Salon des Réalités Nouvelles and the Salon de Mai. Lives in Lyons.

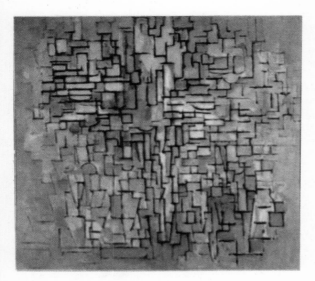

MONDRIAN. COMPOSITION NO. 7. 1913.
Guggenheim Museum, New York.

G. L. K. MORRIS. SPACE-RECESSION. 1954.

kubi and *Bokuzin* reviews, in which great space is devoted to American and European abstract artists. There are issues given over to Alcopley's drawings, to Bryen, to Tryggvadottir, to Seuphor. Morita is one of the artists who have worked most towards a rapprochement and mutual comprehension between Japanese and occidental artists in the field of abstraction. In his own works, he attempts to achieve significance through black patches, spread widely on the paper, having an interior vibration and a powerful tension of volume. — *Bibl.* 'Art Sacré' issue devoted to Japan (Paris 1954); Seuphor: *la Calligraphie japonaise,* 'Art d'Aujourd'hui' (Paris, Dec. 1954); Alechinsky: *Au delà de l'écriture,* 'Phases', n° 2 (Paris 1955).

MORENI Mattia (b. Pavie, 1920). Was educated in Turin. Included in various group-shows in a number of European countries. One-man shows in Turin (1946) and Milan (1947-1949). Lives in Bologna.

MORITA Shiryu (b. in Japan, 1912). Active since 1938 in the movement based on calligraphy considered as a plastic art form. Exhibited at the Institute of Calligraphy Shodo-Geijitsu in 1949. A member of the Bokuzin-Kai School in 1952. Included then in numerous exhibitions of calligraphy in the main Japanese cities, as well as in New York (Museum of Modern Art, 1954) and in Paris (Galerie Colette Allendy, 1955). Director of the *Bo-*

MORRIS George L. K. (b. New York, 1906). Studied at Yale. While still in college, began to paint in the academic tradition. First contact with abstract art in Paris, 1930. While studying at Léger's studio, met Arp, Hélion, Mondrian. Round the world tour 1933. Contributed to *Par-*

MORITA. BREAK FOR CONSTANT CREATION. 1954.

tisan Review in New York and the review *Plastique* in Paris. President of the 'American Abstract Artists' association until 1951. Numerous one-man and group-shows in New York and Paris. The most recent ones were held at the Downtown Gallery New York. Married to Suzy Frelinghuysen (cf. that name). Took part in the 'Abstract Painting and Sculpture in America' show, Museum of Modern Art, New York 1951. Lecture tour for UNESCO in Europe and Asia Minor, 1952. Lives in New York. — Bibl. *American Abstract Artists* (New York 1946); Ritchie: *Abstract Painting and Sculpture in America* (New York 1951); *What abstract art means to me* (Museum of Modern Art, New York, 1951); 'Art d'Aujourd'hui' (Paris, June 1951).

MORRIS Kyle (b. Des Moines, U.S.A., 1918). Studied at the Art Institute in Chicago (1935-1939). Then taught in a number of universities and colleges in the United States. Exhibited at the Walker Art Center (Minneapolis), the Whitney Museum (New York) and in the 'Younger American Painters' show at the Solomon R. Guggenheim Museum, New York, 1954. Lives in New York.

MORTENSEN Richard (b. Copenhagen, 1910). Worked for two years in an Academy in Copenhagen and then on his own. Contact with Kandinsky's work during a trip in Germany made him forcibly aware of his own approach. First abstract works in 1933. In Paris, 1937. Organised an exhibition of the abstract works of Paris painters in Copenhagen. Returned to Paris, 1947. A member of the Galerie Denise René group, with whom he exhibited regularly. In 1956, he assembled there a group of very large compositions simple in line and vivid in colour, one of which, *Opus Normandie,* was at least twenty-eight foot long. Lives in

Paris. "The power of Mortensen's painting is not immediately apparent, because of its great and perhaps cloaking refinement; refinement of articulation; refinement of spirit; the refinement, even, of restraint. The brilliance of this painting is almost always most vivid, but never brutal. The

MORTENSEN. JARGEAU. 1953.
Dr. Aronovitch Collection, Stockholm.

grasp is steel, not cast-iron" (Léon Degand). — *Bibl.* 'Art d'Aujourd'hui' (Paris, Dec. 1951); *Témoignages pour l'Art Abstrait* (Paris 1952); Catalogue of the Mortensen exhibition, Galerie Denise René (Paris 1956).

MOSER Wilfrid (b. Zurich 1914). Travelled extensively before he settled in Paris, 1945. Painted his first abstract works the same year. Exhibitions: Stockholm: 'Six Young Painters of Paris' (1951); Zurich: 'Dix Artistes de Paris' (1951); Paris, Galerie Jeanne Bucher, together with the painter Nallard (1952). One-man show in Zurich 1953. Lives in Paris.

MOSS Marlow (b. Richmond, Great Britain, 1890). Studied in London and in Paris. She was the first and purest disciple of Mondrian in Paris, about 1925. A member of the 'Abstraction-Création' group. Took part in group-shows in Paris, London, Holland, Switzerland, as well as in the Salon des Réalités Nouvelles. One-man show at the Hanover Gallery, London 1953. Is presently engaged in sculpture. Lives in Penzance (Cornwall).

MOTHERWELL Robert (b. Aberdeen, U.S.A., 1915). Studied in the Philosophy department at Harvard. University of Grenoble in 1938.

MOSER. PAINTING. 1955.
Galerie Jeanne Bucher, Paris.

School of Art and Achaeology at Columbia, New York. Travelled many times to British Columbia (1932, 1934, 1937), France, England (1938-1939) and Mexico (1941, 1943). Self-educated in matters of art; then studied engraving with Kurt Seligmann and S. W. Hayter. Taught at Hunter College, New York, 1951. Eleven one-man shows from 1944 to 1952 in American galleries and museums. At Wittenborn and Co.'s, New York, directed the *Documents of Modern Art* collection. A lecturer and essay-writer. Took part in the 'Abstract Painting and Sculpture in America' show at the Museum of Modern Art, New York, 1951. Numerous exhibitions at the Kootz Gallery, New York. Included in the 'Cinquante ans d'art aux États-Unis' exhibition at the Museum of Modern Art, Paris 1955. "One is to know that art is not national, that to be merely an American or a French artist is to be nothing; to fail to overcome one's initial environment is never to reach the human." — Bibl. *Fourteen Americans* (New York 1946); Ritchie: *Abstract Painting and Sculpture in America* (New York 1951); *What abstract art means to me,* Museum of Modern Art (New York 1951); 'Art d'Aujourd'hui' (Paris, June 1951); Hess: *Abstract Painting* (New York, 1951).

MULLICAN Lee (b. Chickasha, Oklahoma, 1919). Studied at the Oklahoma Art School and the Art Institute in Kansas City. One-man shows in a number of American cities and at the Willard Gallery, New York. Included, in 1951, in the 'Dynaton' exhibition, organized by Wolfgang Paalen at the San Francisco Museum of Art. — Bibl. *Dynaton 1951,* San Francisco Museum of Art; *Art News* (New York, Oct. 1953).

MUNARI Bruno (b. Milan, 1907). Took part in the futurist movement. A painter, an essaywriter and constructor of mobiles. Co-founder of the Milanese 'Arte Concreta' group, 1949. Included in many exhibitions in Italy, especially 'Arte Astratta e Concreta in Italia', at the Museum of Modern Art, Rome, 1951. Lives in Milan.

MURO José Antonio Fernandez (b. Madrid, 1920). Studied art in Buenos Aires. A naturalized Argentine citizen. First one-man show in 1942. Included in 1948 in the exhibition of Latin American Painting organized by the UNESCO in Paris. Abstract painting since 1943. Included in the 'Eight Argentine Abstracts' show at the Municipal Museum, Amsterdam, 1953. Husband of the abstract painter

MOTHERWELL. GRENADE. 1949.
Nelson A. Rockefeller Collection, Washington.

Sarah Grilo. Lives in Buenos Aires. Journey to Paris in 1957.

N

NAKAMURA Bokushi (b. in Japan, 1916). Took part in many exhibitions of abstract calligraphy in Japan and in other countries, particularly at the Museum of Modern Art, New York (1954), the Galerie Colette Allendy, Paris (1955) and the Musée Cernuschi, Paris (1956). Lives in Japan.

NALLARD Louis (b. Algiers, 1918). Educated in Algiers. Began to exhibit in Algiers at an early age. First exhibition of abstract painting in 1945. Settled in Paris, 1947. Travelled in Holland and in Spain. Took part in numerous exhibitions in Paris and abroad. One-man show at the Galerie Jeanne Bucher, Paris,

NALLARD. PAINTING. 1955.
Henri Perrenoud Collection, Paris.

1953. Took part regularly in the Salon de Mai. He often exhibited together with his wife, the painter Maria Manton. Lives in Paris. Supple variations of graphism within a restricted gamut of colours, sometimes limited to brown-ochres.

NATIVI Gualtiero (b. Pistoia, 1921). Studied Classics at the University of Florence. Devoted himself to painting at the same time. Was a co-founder of the 'Arte d'oggi' group, and signed the *Manifesto dell' Astrattismo,* Florence 1950. Took part in numerous exhibitions in Italy and in the other European countries. Lives in Florence. Compositions in rectilinear geometrical forms.

NAVARRO Pascal (b. in Venezuela, 1923). Studied painting and engraving at the Fine Arts Academy in Caracas (1938-1944). Was in Paris in 1947. Free-lance studies and travels in Italy, Spain, England, Belgium. Launched into abstraction as a result of the 'Premiers Maîtres de

l'Art Abstrait' show at the Galerie Maeght, Paris 1949. Worked in the Abstract Art workshop of Dewasne and Pillet (1950-1952) and took part in the Salon des Réalités Nouvelles. One-man show at the Galerie Arnaud, Paris 1952. Lives in Paris and Caracas.

NAY Ernst Wilhelm (b. Berlin, 1902). Attended the School of Fine Arts in Berlin (1925-1928). Travelled to Paris, 1928. Spent 1931-1932 in Rome. Kept on painting clandestinely under the Nazi regime. Was a student of Carl Hofer (1936-1937). Visited Edward Munch in Norway. Travelled abroad extensively. After having started from expressionism and neo-realism, he slowly progressed towards abstraction, which he attained about 1948. One-man shows in Munich, 1950 and 1952. Took part in numerous exhibitions in Germany and other countries, particularly "Peintures et Sculptures non-figuratives en Allemagne d'Aujourd'hui", at the Cercle Volney, Paris 1955. A member of the German group 'Zent' with whom he exhibited in Munich,

1955. Lives in Cologne. Nay's painting is often ebullient, but never beyond measure. This painter has retained from expressionism a love of vivid colours and striking oppositions. — Bibl. *Das Kunstwerk,* nº 8-9 (Baden-Baden 1950).

NEBEL Otto (b. Berlin, 1892). Studied architecture. Travelled extensively in Europe. After the First World War, he studied painting under Kandinsky. First one-man show in 1921. First abstract paintings in 1924: he called them 'architectures of light'. Contributed to the *Sturm.* Spent some time in Switzerland and in France. After further travels through Europe, he composed an album of caricatures (1931). Lives in Bern. Geometrical fantasies, rectilinear or curved, on a white background. A kind of game in space, reminding one now of Klee, now of Kandinsky. A text or title affixed to the bottom of the canvas, after the manner of Klee, always adds a poetical touch. — *Bibl.* Liebmann: *Der Malerdichter Otto Nebel* (Zurich 1935); *Almanach neuer Kunst in der Schweiz* (Zurich 1940); *Collection of the Société Anonyme* (New Haven 1950); Otto Nebel: *Worte zu Bildern* (Berne 1954).

NEGRI Nina (b. Argentine, 1909). Studied in France, Argentine, England, and Belgium. Travelled many times in Europe, Africa, South America. Took part in the Salon des Indépendants, the Salon des Réalités Nouvelles, and the Salon de Mai. One-man shows at the gallery 'Il Milione' (Milan) and the gallery 'Circle and Square' (New York). Took part in numerous group-shows in Paris. Lives in Paris. An experienced painter and engraver in whose works one can observe a fair proportion of science and mastery. The manner and the message fuse where the strictness of the composition yields to sudden discovery. The psychological intention of such an art is confident self-expression while keeping alert for the secret murmurs one must decode.

NEJAD Mehmed D. (b. Istanbul, 1923). Attended the Academy of Fine Arts in Istanbul, and was a student of the French landscape-painter Léopold-Lévy. Then studied the byzantine mosaics of Saint Sophia, arabic calligraphy, and Islamic abstract art. Was in Paris in 1945. His manner then altered completely. Travelled and studied in the main European countries. Nejad is the son of Princess Fahr-el-Nissa Zeid (cf. that name). One-man shows at the Galerie Lydia Conti (1950), Galerie de Beaune (1951), Studio Facchetti (1953) and

NEBEL. THE SONG OF THE PILOT II. 1951.
Galerie Simone Heller, Paris.

Galerie M. C. Coard (1956), Paris. Took also part in the Salon des Réalités Nouvelles and the Salon de Mai, as well as in group-shows. Lives in Paris. "In painting, I throw the whole of the work into question every time I take up my brush. One must break down, destroy, to the point of seem-ing insane. But that which seems madness is, at the very moment of creation, only the logic of the work of art, expanding into life like a plant, without our aid." (Nejad). In Nejad's works, whether black or coloured, sensibility and a despotic will come into violent conflict, sometimes fusing in a sudden and exceptional euphoria. — *Bibl.* Boudaille and Lassaigne: *Nejad,* Coll. 'Ar-tistes de ce temps', Paris 1955.

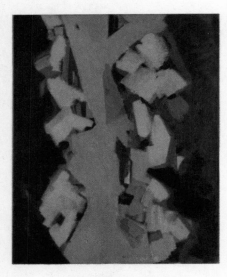

NEJAD. ALTITUDES I. 1955.

NEMOURS Aurélie (b. Paris, 1910). Studied in turn under Paul Colin, André Lhote, and Fernand Léger. Took part in a number of Salons since 1944. Published poems and contributed to the *Mercure de France.* Slowly progressed tow-ards total abstraction and took part in the Salon des Réalités Nouvelles in 1953. One-man shows at the Galerie Colette Allendy (1953), Galerie de Beaune (1954), both in Paris, and in the Galerie Saint-Laurent (Brussels) in 1955. Lives in Paris. Aurélie Nemours' work aspires to a 'primary geo-metry' which attains the very basis of sim-plicity, like that of Mondrian, Sophie Taeu-ber, and Klee. In her charcoal sketches of modulated blacks and greys, this voluntary paucity of rhythm seems, in her own words 'inseminated to the point of tears'.

"Having to face his own vision, each man is eternally Adam; a lifetime gives him ground to walk on, but he must beget him-self again and experience the whole trying process through his own flesh. Only then does he become humble and virile. Only then does painting become art, and art consciousness." (Aurélie Nemours).

NESCH Rolf (b. Oberesslingen, Ger-many, 1893). Studied under Ludwig Kirchner and Edward Munch. Later on developed towards abstraction, using a very personal technique of impres-sion on paper. Took part in many group-shows, particularly at the Petit Palais (1954) and the Cercle Volney (1955), both in Paris. Lives in Aal (Norway).

NEUBERTH Jean (b. Paris, 1915). Was first an aviator and and took part in various aviation meetings as an acrobatic parachutist. Then met the painter Closon who introduced him to painting. Began to take part in exhibitions of abstract art in 1937, while still a military pilot. Then turned toward the theatre. In 1941, he took up again his studies under Closon. A member of a symphony or-chestra in 1942. Played the piano in an American night-club, was a nightwatchman and a speaker on the Montpellier radio net-work. Devoted himself totally to painting

NEMOURS. PASTEL. 1955.
M. S. Collection, Paris.

in Germany in 1922. Met Kurt Schwitters and Moholy-Nagy. Settled in Paris, 1923. Spent 1928 in the South of France. Became friendly with Michel Seuphor who introduced him to Mondrian a little later. During the following years, oscillated constantly between representation and abstraction, choosing now one and then the other. Numerous one-man shows in Paris. Took part in the Salon des Réalités Nouvelles. Lives in Paris. "When things seen achieve a certain density in memory, transparencies, colours, and reflections detach themselves from the objects which first bore them and compose themselves, no longer as a representation or a figuration, but solely according to the intrinsic and unformulated laws of pure painting." (Lancelot Ney).

NICHOLSON Ben (b. 1894 near Uxbridge, England), the son of the painters William and Mabel Nicholson. Studied at the Slade School, London. Was later influenced by cubism.

from 1942 on. Was an organizer, together with Francis Bott and Michel Seuphor, of an exhibition of abstract art at the Museum of Nîmes (1949). Retrospective exhibition of his works held in Montpellier, 1950. Included in the Salon des Réalités Nouvelles. Lives in Montpellier.

NEWMAN Barnett (b. New York, 1905). Studied at the Art Students League. Published South American magazines and taught painting and drawing in various schools. Organised exhibitions of Pre-Columbian and Indian art. Included in numerous exhibitions in the United States. Lives in New York.

NEY Lancelot (b. Budapest, 1900). After secondary school, attended the School of Fine Arts in Budapest. Travelled

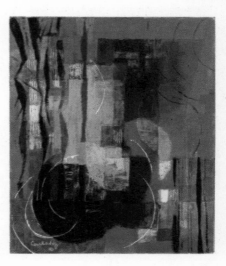

NEY. COMPOSITION. 1955.

Travelled many times to Paris. Composed abstract geometric reliefs as early as 1934. Visited Mondrian the same year. Included in many exhibitions in England and in America. A member of the 'Abstraction-Création' group, and then of the English 'Axis' group. During two years (1938-1940) was Mondrian's next door neighbour in Hampstead. After the Second World War, a whole group of young painters formed around him in Saint Ives, Cornwall. Exhibitions showing his complete work in Venice, Paris, Brussels, Zurich, Amsterdam. Lives in Saint-Ives.

In a now published letter to a friend, Nicholson relates how astonished he was by the atmosphere of Mondrian's studio when he visited the painter for the first time, in 1934. The English painter was then forty, the Dutch, sixty-two. One had already harvested the fruits of maturity, the other had gained enough assurance of personality not to be destroyed by the powerful example of his senior. There is indeed no work of Nicholson that is not totally his own. In his panels, both large and small, the nearest to neo-plasticism in his work, there is always a kind of lighthearted jauntiness which remains his characteristic imprint. "I think that so far from being a limited expression, understood by a few, abstract art is a powerful, unlimited, and universal language." (Nicholson). — *Bibl.* Barr : *Cubism and Abstract Art* (New York 1936); Nicholson and Gabo: *Circle* (London 1938); Summerson: *Ben Nicholson,* Penguin Books (London 1948); Read: *Ben Nicholson* (London 1948); Hitchcock: *Painting toward Architecture* (New York 1948); *A Dictionary of Modern Painting* (Me-

thuen, London 1956); 'Aujourd'hui', n° 1 (Paris 1955); *Ben Nicholson,* Museum of Modern Art (Paris 1955); Seuphor: *Léger and Nicholson,* 'Art Digest' (New York, April 1955).

NIGRO Mario (b. Pistoia, Italy, 1917). Took a diploma in mathematics. Self-educated in matters of art. Took part in numerous exhibitions in Italy. One-man show at the Salto Bookshop, Milan. Included in the 'Arte astratta e concreta in Italia' at the Museum of Modern Art, Rome 1951. Lives in Leghorn.

NOUVEAU Henri (b. Brasov, Transylvania, 1901). Studied music in Berlin. Was in contact with the *Sturm* group. Under the name of Neugeboren, composed abstract drawings as early as 1923. Settled in Paris in 1925 and composed abstract collages. Met Klee at the Bauhaus in 1928. Had his chamber music compositions produced in Paris, from 1928 to 1938. Took part at the same time in exhibitions in Zurich, Stockholm, and Berlin. After the second world war, he became friends with Picabia and took part in the Salon des Réalités Nouvelles. One-man show at the Galerie Colette Allendy in 1950. Travelling exhibition in Germany together with Francis Bott, in 1951. Lives in Paris. Henri Nouveau contributes to the great current of plastic fantasy inaugurated by Klee and Kandinsky. He is an inventor of rhythms and counterpoints which never lack a subtle and discreet humour.

O

OCAMPO Miguel (b. Buenos Aires, 1922). Began to paint in 1944. Travelled to Europe in 1948. One-man show in Paris and participation in the "Salon des Jeunes Peintres". Numerous one-man shows in Buenos Aires. Took part in the 'Eight Argentine Abstract Painters' at the Municipal Museum of Amsterdam, 1953. Lives in Buenos Aires.

OLIVE-TAMARI (b. La Seyne, Southern France, 1898). The General Secretary of the Salon des Réalités Nouvelles until 1954. Took part in numerous abstract art displays in Paris, the provinces, and the main European countries. Was appointed Director of the Fine Arts School of Toulon in 1955.

OMCIKUS Pierre (b. Rijeka, Yugoslavia, 1926). Attended the School of Applied Arts (1940-1944) then the School of Fine Arts (1944-1947) in Belgrade. Exhibited representational paintings in Belgrade, from 1949 to 1951. Slowly progressed towards abstraction. Was in Paris, 1952. Travelled to and exhibited in London. Included in the Salon de Mai, Paris 1955. The same year, exhibited abstract gouaches at the Galerie Arnaud. Lives in Paris.

ONGENAE Jozef Jan Marie (b. Antwerp, Belgium, 1921). Self-educated. Travelled in the United States, the Belgian Congo, Norway, and Asia. In 1945, worked in the Flemish expressionist manner, but the following year, came to

OMCIKUS. COMPOSITION. 1954.

abstraction. Later on, he launched into pure neo-plasticism. Exhibited in the main cities of Belgium and Holland. He executed mural paintings for the Municipal Museum in Amsterdam. Lives in Amsterdam.

ORIX. MINDSCAPE. 1955.
Sir Dinshaw Petit Collection.

ONSLOW-FORD Gordon Max (b. Wendover, England, 1912). After ten years in the Royal Navy, came to Paris and devoted himself to painting. Spent a short time in the studios of Lhote and Léger, in 1937. A member of the surrealist group in 1938. Organized an exhibition of surrealist art in London, 1940. Lectures in New York from 1940 to 1941. Retreated to an isolated village in Mexico (1941-1947). One-man show in San Francisco, 1948. There, also took part in an important exhibition organized by Wolfgang Paalen in 1951. His painting then lost all connection with surrealism. He is currently moving towards a kind of lyric plasticism both sparkling and profound.

Lives in Mill Valley (Calif.) — Bibl. *Dynaton 1951*, The San Francisco Museum of Art (U.S.A.).

ORIX Guillaume Hoorickx (b. Antwerp, 1900). Studied Medicine in Antwerp. A volunteer in the 1914-1918 war. Was attracted by painting about 1940. A member of the Resistance in Belgium, 1940 to 1942. Was deported by the Germans to the concentration camp of Mauthausen. After his return, he painted scenes of concentration camp life. Launched into abstraction in 1949. Took part in the Salon des Réalités Nouvelles from 1950 on, and was included in a number of group-shows in the South of France. He calls his paintings *ideograms* and *mindscapes*. One-man shows in Brussels, 1952, and London, 1955. Lives in Nice and in Paris.

OSAWA Gakiu (b. in Japan, 1890; d. in Japan, 1953). At first an elementary-school teacher, a poet, a novelist. Devoted himself to calligraphy from 1933 on. Studied under Tenrai Hidai (1872-1939), the precursor of the modern school of calligraphy. All his works prior to 1945 were destroyed in the bombings of Tokyo. But he started working again and took part in an exhibition of Japanese calligraphy at the Museum of Modern Art, New York, in 1954. "Perhaps because of his extreme freedom and a certain humour which he knew how to inject even into his most dramatic compositions, he ended his life after seeing one of his major works refused by the National Salon of Tokyo. In the middle of academism, dying and being born, it was the greatest honour that could have been conferred on him." (Pierre Alechinsky).

OSVER Arthur (b. Chicago, 1912). Studied at the Chicago Art Institute. Travelled in France and in Italy. Numerous one-man shows in New York. Took

236

part in an exhibition of American painting at the Galerie Jeanne Bucher, Paris 1953. Lives in New York.

OTANO Juan Andres (b. Buenos Aires, 1914). A painter and a sculptor. Abstract works since 1948. One-man shows in Buenos Aires. Composed mural paintings in collaboration with his wife, the painter Dustir. Lives in Buenos Aires.

OUBORG P. (b. Dordrecht, Holland, 1893; d. 1956). For many years, taught drawing in the Dutch West Indies. Returned to Holland in 1931. Abstract paintings since 1947. General exhibition of his work at the Municipal Museum, Amsterdam, 1954. A member of the 'Vrij Beelden' group in Amsterdam. — *Bibl.* Catalogue of the Amsterdam exhibition, 1954; Oudshoorn: *P. Ouborg,* 'Museum-journaal' (Groningen, Sept. 1956).

P

PAALEN Wolfgang (b. Vienna, 1907). Studied in France, Germany, Italy. Travelled extensively in Europe and in America. Lived in Paris until 1939, and then in Mexico. Became a Mexican citizen in 1945. One-man shows in various galleries in Paris, London, New York, and Mexico City. After having belonged to the 'Abstraction-Création' group (1932-1935), he became a member of the surrealist group (1936-1940). Organized an international exhibition of surrealism, together with André Breton, Mexico City, 1940. Left the surrealist movement in 1941, and founded the review *Dyn,* in Mexico City. In 1945, published *Form and Sense* (Wittenborn and Co.) in New York. In 1951, together with Gordon Onslow-Ford and Lee Mullican, organized the *Dynaton* exhibition at the San Francisco Museum of Art. The same year, returned to Paris. One-man show at the Galerie Pierre, 1952, and at the Galerie Galanis, 1954. Lives in Paris and Mexico City.

"It is the painting which, in turn, examines

PAALEN. BEATRICE LOST. 1953.
Private Collection, Paris.

and interrogates the spectator: what do *you* represent? Painting is not a trade, but a way of meditating on the world which makes and unmakes us." (Paalen). — *Bibl.* Regler: *Wolfgang Paalen* (New York 1946); *Illustrated catalogue of the Dynaton exhibition* (San Francisco 1951); *Cahiers d'Art* (Paris 1952).

PAJAK Jacques (b. Strasbourg, 1930). Attended the School of Architecture. First exhibitions of abstract paintings in Strasbourg, 1951. Then turned to applied arts. Exhibitions of drawings at the Galerie de Beaune, Paris 1955. Elegant and supple graphism, in black or in colour. Lives in Paris and Strasbourg.

PALAZUELO Pablo (b. Madrid, 1916). Began painting in 1940. Settled in Paris in 1948. Took part in the Salon de Mai and a number of group-shows. Exhibited in Lausanne, Zurich, Liège, and Toronto. Included in 'Tendance' at the Galerie Maeght, 1951 and 1952. One-man show at the same gallery, 1955. Lives in Paris. An artist's greatest hindrance may be his own abundance of talent. The conquest of personality begins by rejection of nearly everything in order to find the essential. Sobriety and restraint are the trump-cards of an artist like Palazuelo. A true harmonist suppresses everything of his internal struggle except the final victory. Behold, here are

lines and planes: music for two hands. Reduced to a few notes it will but serve better for the articulation of the rare.

PANTALEONI Ideo (b. Legnago, Italy, 1904). Took part in the Salon des Réalités Nouvelles from 1949 on. Was also included in 'Arte Astratta e Concreta in Italia' Museum of Modern Art, Rome, 1951. A number of trips to Paris. Abstract forms in supple compositions evidently influenced by Magnelli. Lives in Milan.

PARISOT Adriano (b. Turin, 1912). Attended the Academy of Fine Arts in Turin. One-man shows in Milan, Turin, and Paris. Since 1948, took part in numerous group-shows in Italy and in other European countries. The director-editor of *I 4 Soli,* Turin, a review welcoming all the trends of abstract art. Travelled many times to Paris. Abstract works with brisk dabs of colour assembled by instinct into a harmonious graphism. Lives in Turin.

PARISOT. SPACE, CONTINUITY, TIME. 1955.

PASMORE Victor (b. Chelsham, England, 1908). Spent his childhood in the country. London, 1927. Working as an employee of the London County Council until 1937. Painted in his spare time and attended night classes in drawing. At first attracted by the impressionists, then by the cubists. After a period of pure painting, returned to the study of Cézanne, Seurat, and Van Gogh. From there came back to his first sallies in abstraction in 1947-1948. Has since developed a very individual abstract style, where lines and planes are interwoven, sometimes with the addition of collages. Took part in a number of group-shows in England. One-man show at the Institute of Contemporary Arts, London 1954. Taught at the University of Durham. He is at present mainly concerned with reliefs and mobiles. Lives in London.— Pasmore is, after Ben Nicholson and Paule Vézelay, the first English artist to tackle the problems of abstract art resolutely. After having shown definite talent in impressionist painting, talent which would certainly have brought him success in Great Britain, Pasmore chose the less easy way and became the undisputed leader of the London abstract group. — Bibl. *Victor Pasmore,* 'Penguin Books' (London 1945); Sylvester: *Victor Pasmore,* 'Britain to-day' (London, Dec. 1950); Alloway: *Nine Abstract Artists* (London 1954).

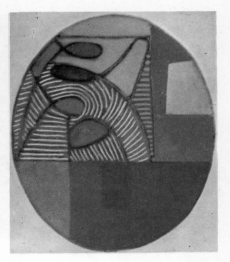

VICTOR PASMORE. OVAL MOTIF IN OCHRE, BROWN AND PINK. 1951.

of 1922. Met Walden, Gabo, Marinetti, Moholy-Nagy, and Prampolini. Took part in a number of abstract art displays in Belgium and gave up painting for about twenty years. Lives in Antwerp.

PEETERS Jozef (b. Antwerp 1895). Attended the Academy of Fine Arts in Antwerp. Progressed rapidly towards geometric abstraction, which he attained in 1921. The same year, one-man show in Antwerp. Actively contributed to a Congress of Modern Art, in Antwerp, 1921, and in Bruges, 1922. In 1922, Seuphor asked him to take part in the direction of the review *Het Overzicht* in which he published pithy articles about a 'community' art. Visited Paris the same year and called on Mondrian. Travelled to Berlin with Seuphor at the end

PEREIRA Rice (b. Boston, 1907). Studied at the Art Students League, New York. Then worked in Paris, Italy, North Africa, England. Since 1933, one-man shows in many museums and art galleries throughout the United States. Retrospective exhibition at the Whitney Museum, New York, 1953. Pereira has taught in various schools in New York from 1935 to 1943. Lives in New York.
"I employ the abstract idiom in painting, rather than more traditional forms of expression, because it offers me a wider range for experimentation. In these pictures I have endeavored to explore the formal possibilities of painting, with special emphasis

on constructional ways of expressing space and on experimenting with new use of materials such as glass and parchment, and new pigments. The paintings on glass are executed in a number of planes in spatial opposition. In these I have tried to produce an integrated picture using actual light as part of the painting." (Rice Pereira). — Bibl. *Fourteen Americans*, Museum of Modern Art (New York 1946); Hitchcock: *Painting toward Architecture* (New York 1948); Ritchie: *Abstract Painting and Sculpture in America* (New York 1951); Rice Pereira: *Light and the New Reality*, 'The Palette' (New York 1952).

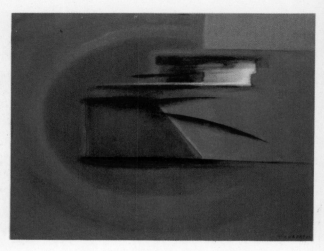

PIAUBERT. VORACIOUS BLUE. 1955.

PERI Laszlo (b. Budapest, 1889). At first a brick-layer in Budapest. Composed expressionist drawings from 1918 to 1920. After 1921, joined the constructivist movement in Berlin, together with his compatriot Moholy-Nagy. From 1924 to 1928 worked as an architect for the Berlin City Council. During this period, he contributed reproductions of abstract art, mostly in black and white, to almost all the avant-garde reviews of Central Europe. His work, a very sober constructivism, achieved a monumental quality through surprisingly simple means. Peri abandoned abstract painting in 1928. He emigrated to London in 1933. "Peri called his compositions of 1920-28 *Space Constructions*. The credo of the Constructivists to whom he then belonged was to see the world through the prism of tech-

nique. The Constructivists do not want to give an illusion by means of color on canvas, but work indirectly in iron, glass and related media." (Alexandre Dorner). — Bibl. *Het Overzicht*, n° 17 (Antwerp 1923); *Jahrbuch der jungen Kunst* (Leipzig 1924); Arp and Lissitzky: *Les Ismes de l'Art* (Zurich 1925); *Collection of the Société Anonyme* (New Haven 1950).

PERILLI Achille (b. Rome, 1927). Took part in many exhibitions of Italian abstract art, particularly 'Arte Astratta e Concreta in Italia' at the Museum of Modern Art, Rome 1951. A predilection for contrasting dynamic and static forms in space. Lives in Turin.

PETURSSON Valtyr (b. Iceland, 1919). Studied under the painter H. Bloom in Boston. Spent a long time in Florence and in Paris. Included in the Salon de Mai, Paris, in 1950 and in 1951; included as well in numerous exhibitions in France and Scandinavia.

PFRIEM Bernard (b. Cleveland, Ohio, 1916). Studied in Cleveland. Painted first in the academic manner. Was in Mexico from 1940 to 1942. In the armed forces 1942-1946. Gave lectures at the Museum of Modern Art, New York. Contributed articles on art to the American review *Interiors*. Settled in Paris in 1951. Many group-shows in America. One-man show at the Hugo Gallery, New York, 1951. Sensual and subtle work at times very much indebted to Gorky's influence (cf. that name).

PIAUBERT Jean (b. Pian, South-West France, 1900). Attended the School of Fine Arts in Bordeaux. Came to Paris in 1922. Designed materials and stage-costumes for the 'couturier' Paul Poiret. First one-man show in 1932; was included for a few years in the Salon des Tuileries. Slowly moved away from representation from 1940 onwards. One-man shows in Paris: 1932, 1946, 1947, 1951. In 1950, he published Jean Cassou's *XXXIII Sonnets* illustrated with thirty-three large lithographs where he proved brilliantly the potentialities of black and white (Librairie La Hune, Paris). Took part regularly in the Salon de Mai and numerous exhibitions in Paris and abroad. One-man show of paintings and tapestries, Paris, 1955. Lives in Paris.

"Piaubert is one of those chosen from birth for the task of creating style or symbol. Among contemporary painters, he is the one who, to my mind, has broken with all compromise and created the plastic world closest to the idea governing contemporary thought. Space is no longer defined as a volume with three dimensions, but is conjugated with a fourth: time. Thus, in Piaubert, the object becomes thought, thought movement, and movement a characteristic of space." (H. Bing-Bodmer). — *Bibl.* Cassou: *Piaubert* (Paris 1951). Elgar: *L'univers prophétique de Piaubert* (Copenhagen 1957).

PICABIA Francis (b. Paris, 1879; d. Paris, 1953). Attended the École des Beaux-Arts and the School of Decorative Arts. Composed impressionist works from 1903 to 1908. Travelled extensively in Spain before he visited America (Feb-April, 1913) to take part in the 'Armory Show'. Returned to America in 1915. Collaborated in the *291* review with Marcel Duchamp. Went to Barcelona in 1916; published the first number of the review *391* which he sustained the same year in New York, again with Marcel Duchamp. In Lausanne, 1918, was introduced to the Zurich dada group. After a short stay in Zurich, he returned to Paris, kept on working on *391* and organized a great dada festival (1920). He published *Jésus-Christ rastaquouère,* composed the ballet *Relâche,* contributed to the surrealist reviews. After composing remarkable abstract works from 1912 to 1913 and inventing the series of the *ironic machines,* Picabia reverted to represen-

PICABIA. COMPOSITION. 1948.
M. S. Collection, Paris.

tational art for more than twenty years. He lived mostly in Cannes at the time. When he came back to Paris in 1945, he tackled abstraction again. Retrospective exhibition at the Galerie Drouin, Paris, in 1949. On this occasion, he published a single issue of a *491* review. The same year, at the Galerie des Deux-Iles, he exhibited a series of paintings solely composed of points. A retrospective exhibition of his work was held at the Galerie Furstemberg, Paris, 1956.

"Life for an artist should lie in working for himself without considering the results of his work in the eyes of merchants, critics, amateurs, only the joy that accomplishment gives. A marvellous curiosity about oneself, never quite satisfied, and every day renewed. . ." (Picabia). "Francis Picabia is a Christopher Columbus of art. No one has his detached philosophic indifference, his creative abundance, his assured craftsmanship. He journeys without compass." (Arp). — *Bibl.* Barr: *Cubism and abstract art* (New York 1936); *Art of this Century* (New York 1942); Seuphor: *L'Art abstrait, ses origines, ses premiers maîtres* (Paris 1949); *Collection of the Société Anonyme* (New Haven 1950); Raynal: *De Picasso au Surréalisme* (Paris-Geneva, 1950); *The Dada Painters and Poets* (New York 1952); Seuphor: *Épitaphe à Picabia,* 'Preuves' (Jan. 1954).

PICELJ Ivan (b. Okucani, Yugoslavia, 1924). Attended the Academy of Fine Arts in Zagreb, 1943-1946. In 1948, together with the architect V. Richter and the painter A. Srnec, formed a committee for the organisation of art exhibitions in Yugoslavia and abroad. Launched out into abstraction in 1951; the same year, together with the architects Bernardi, Bregovac, Radic, Rasica, Richter, Zarahovix and the painter Srnec, founded the 'Exat 51' group (experimental workshop 51). Included in the Salon des Réalités Nouvelles, Paris 1952 and in the 'Exat 51' group-shows in Zagreb

and Belgrade, 1953, as well as in the Salon 54 (exhibition of contemporary Yugoslavian art in Rijeka). Travelled and studied in Stockholm, Vienna, New York, Chicago, Venice, and Paris. Lives in Zagreb.

PICHETTE James (b. Châteauroux, France, 1920). Self-educated in matters of art. Was wounded in the war, 1940. Painted in a representational manner until 1945. Took part in the Salon des Réalités Nouvelles in 1950 and 1951. One-man shows in Paris: Galerie de Beaune (1951), Galerie Dina Vierni (1955). Travelled and exhibited in Italy, Switzerland, Belgium, Holland. Lives in Paris. Compositions of curves and straight lines among coloured planes of great clarity. Certain poetic elements in Pichette's recent work suggest a movement back towards representation.

PILLET Edgar (b. Saint-Christoly-de-Médoc, South West France, 1912). Was at first a sculptor. Attended the Fine Arts School in Bordeaux, then in Paris. Spent seven years in Algeria. Returned to Paris in 1945 and contributed to the *Gazette des Lettres*. Was the chief editor of the review *Art d'Aujourd'hui* (1949-1954). One-man show at the Galerie Denise René, Paris 1951. Took part in numerous group-shows in Paris and in Scandinavia. Directed, with Dewasne (cf. that name), the Abstract Art Workshop (1950-1952). Produced films on Magnelli and Laurens. Executed large mural decorations in a printing-press in Tours (1952). Spent some time in Finland the same year. Produced an abstract film called *Genèse*. A number of one-man shows at the Galerie Arnaud, Paris. Travelled and exhibited in Switzerland, Belgium, and Italy. Was in the United States, 1955-1956. Lives in Paris.

Together with Dewasne, Pillet greatly influenced the young painters who attended

ble rather fanciful gardens: a whole alphabet of symbols in colour constituting a total effect now harmonious, now disparate.

PLOMTEUX Léopold (b. Belgium, 1920). Attended the Academy of Fine Arts in Liège (1940-1946). Took part in numerous Salons and group-shows in Belgium since 1945. A member of the 'Art Abstrait' group. Lives in Liège.

the Abstract Art Workshop, from 1950 to 1952. His own work shows exact technique and brilliant colour. Sometimes planes are interwoven or smoothly overlap, sometimes a heavy linear display composes a calligraphic symbol of a voluntary simplicity. — *Bibl.* Alvard: *Edgar Pillet* (Paris 1952); Pillet: *Idéogrammes,* préface by Seuphor (Paris 1954).

PINK Lutka (b. Warsaw, 1916). Attended the Academy of Fine Arts in Warsaw, 1930-1937, then the Academy of Cracow. Travelled in Italy. Was in Paris, 1939. The work she did in Poland was completely destroyed by the Nazis. Took part in a number of group-shows in Paris. One-man shows at the Galerie Jeanne Castel in 1952 and the Galerie Arnaud in 1954. Was in the United States 1952-1953. Lives in Paris. After having undergone the influence of Bonnard and Vuillard, Lutka Pink deduced from her masters the abstract lesson contained implicitly as well as explicitly in their works. She has never ceased to progress towards an always increasing subtlety. Her more recent paintings resem-

POLIAKOFF Serge (b. Moscow, 1906). Studied in Moscow and travelled extensively in Russia before the revolution. Stayed in Constantinople, Sofia, Belgrade, Berlin. Was in Paris, 1924. Studied painting in autonomous academies. Attended the Slade School in London from 1935 to 1937. Returned to Paris, exhibited in a number of galleries and slowly progressed towards abstract art. In 1938, met Kandinsky, Delaunay, and Freundlich. From 1938 to 1945, exhibited every year at the Salon des Indépendants and once at the Salon d'Automne. From 1946 on, he took part in the Salon des Réalités Nouvelles and the Salon de Mai. One man exhibition at the Galerie Denise René, Paris 1947 and 1949. Showed at Copenhagen in 1948 and took part in many group exhibitions in different countries. One-man show at the Galerie Bing, Paris 1956. Lives in Paris.

A certain rudimentary series of forms, usually geometric, form the basis of Poliakoff's abstract work. At the same time, the manner almost always retains some

POLIAKOFF. COMPOSITION. 1953.
Pierre Brache Collection, Paris.

primitive boisterousness which provokes the spectator to an almost physical appreciation of the substance of the painting. A warm inwardness plays in the relationship of colours; one sometimes detects naive discordances. This painting remains voluntarily rough against a background of well assimilated western culture. When the formal conflicts are reduced by the harmonies of dull colours, Poliakoff's painting can achieve strikingly spontaneous successes. A spontaneity full of secret and unexplored intelligences. "In a certain way, Poliakoff could be regarded as a painter of the same family as Juan Gris. They have nothing in common in matters of form, but they show the same concern for starkness, they exercise the same economy of means, they are both emotive in spite of the character of their paintings." (Michel Ragon). — *Bibl.* 'Art d'Aujourd'hui' (Paris, Dec. 1951); *Témoignages pour l'Art Abstrait* (Paris 1952);

Premier bilan de l'art actuel (Paris 1953); Ragon: *L'Aventure de l'Art abstrait* (Paris 1956).

POLLOCK Jackson (b. Wyoming, U.S.A., 1912; d. Southampton, New York, 1956). Spent his childhood in Arizona and North California. Came to New York about 1929. Studied at the Art Students League. Travelled a number of times throughout the States in order to draw landscapes. Tackled abstract art about 1940. First one-man show 'Art of this Century', New York 1944, followed by a number of others in America and in Europe: Betty Parsons Gallery, New York, 1948 and 1951; Studio Facchetti, Paris 1952; Sidney Janis Gallery, New York 1952 and 1955. "My painting does not come from the easel. I hardly ever stretch my canvas before painting. I prefer to tack the unstretched canvas to the hard wall or the floor. I need the resistance of hard surface. On the floor I am more at ease. I feel nearer, more a part of the painting, since this way I can walk around it, work from the four sides and literally be *in* the painting. This is akin to the method of the Indian sand painters of the West. I continue to get further away from the usual painter's tools such as easel, palette, brushes, etc. I prefer sticks, trowels, knives and dripping fluid paint or a heavy impasto with sand, broken glass, other foreign matter added." (Pollock).

But the violence of Pollock's work is mostly exterior. In reality this aggressive painting is very slowly and seriously executed. I see no provocation in this painter, but a real need to do what he does, as he does it; in a word an intimate union between the man and the work. It is pleasant to stress the fact that this painting now, so influential in the United States, is diametrically opposed to the precise and balanced art of Mondrian, which has been no less influential in the same country. "Compared to Pollock, Picasso, the little gentleman who troubles the sleep of his colleagues with the eternal nightmare of his destructive enterprises, becomes a placid conformist, a painter of the past." (Bruno Alfieri). — *Bibl.* Janis: *Abstract and Surrealist Art in America* (New York 1944); *Possibilities I* (New York 1947); Ritchie: *Abstract Painting and Sculpture in America* (New York 1951); *Catalogue of the '15 Americans' exhibition,* Museum of Modern Art (New York 1952); *Catalogue of the Pollock exhibition,* Studio Facchetti (Paris 1952); Seuphor: *La Peinture aux États-Unis,* 'Art d'Aujourd'hui' (Paris June 1951); Catalogue of the *'15 years of Jackson Pollock'* exhibition, Sidney Janis Gallery (New York 1955).

PONS Jean (b. Paris, 1913). Studied at the École Estienne. First exhibited at the Salon d'Automne, Paris 1940-1944, then in the major abstract Salons. One-man shows in Paris: Galerie Suzanne Michel (1954) and Galerie Colette Allendy (1955). Lives in Paris.

POUSSETTE-DART Richard (b. Saint-Paul, Minn. 1916). Self-educated in matters of art. Lived a long time in New York where he had a number of one-man shows since 1939. Lives at present in Eagle Valley (New York).

PRAMPOLINI Enrico (b. Modena, 1896; d. Rome, 1956). Studied at the Academy of Rome. Joined the futurist movement very early. Took part in the running of the *Casa futurista* in Berlin in 1922. Great friend of Marinetti, accompanying him on several journeys in Europe. Was a co-signer of many futurist manifestoes, particularly *l'Art mécanique* (1923). Took an active part in the Futurist Congress in Milan (1924) for which he drew the abstract insignia borne by each different regional delegation. Was in Paris from 1925

to 1937. During that time, contributed to various avant-garde reviews, designed stage-decors, took part in exhibitions. A member of the 'Cercle et Carré' group (1930), then of the 'Abstraction-Création' group (1932). Had already been a member of the 'Novembergruppe' in Berlin, 1913. Worked very seriously on the futurist review *Noi.* In Paris, Prampolini made friends with Dermée, Mondrian, Vantongerloo, Seuphor. Once back in Rome, like the other futurists, he followed the politics of fascism and his relations with Paris were broken off. Since the war, Prampolini has once more taken part in all the important exhibitions of Italian abstract art and published many essays on modern art. Prampolini's painting only finally broke away from representation in his last years. The works of his final phase

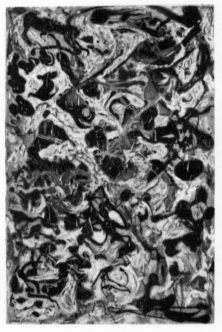

POLLOCK. SEARCH. 1955.
Sidney Janis Gallery, New York.

PRASSINOS. THE RED STONES. 1954. *Galerie de France, Paris.*

are from a pure painting point of view the best of his output. — *Bibl.* Carmelich: *L'art de Prampolini,* 'L'Effort Moderne', Paris, March 1926; Sartoris: *Esaltazione di Prampolini,* 'Origini', Rome, July 1939; Pfister *Enrico Prampolini,* 'Arte moderna italiana', n° 34, Milan 1940.

PRASSINOS Mario (b. Constantinople, 1916). Greek by birth. Volunteered in the 1939-1940 campaign and became a naturalized French citizen. Numerous exhibitions of paintings and engravings in Paris, New York, Brussels, Antwerp, Turin, Amsterdam. Exhibited regularly at the Galerie de France and contributed every year to the Salon de Mai, Paris. Has illustrated numerous literary works, particularly Sartre's *Le Mur,* the *Bestiaire* of Apollinaire, the *Journal d'un Fou* of Gogol, and Poe's *Corbeau.* He designed decors and costumes for a number of ballets, notably for Paul Claudel's *Toby et Sara.* Came gradually to abstraction through the way in which his painting transcended its basis of natural impressions. A herd of bulls or a forest-fire become the themes of purely plastic improvisations in which the emotion of the visual impact subsists, integrated in the composition. Lives in Paris.

PRATI Lidy (b. Resistencia, Argentine, 1921). Studied art in Buenos Aires. In 1944 took part in the avant-garde movement centred around the review *Arturo.* Exhibited regularly with the Argentine group 'Arte Concreto', since 1946. Has been married to Maldonado. Lives in Buenos Aires.

PRÉAUX Raymond (b. Paris, 1916). Studied in the free academies of Montparnasse. Then, worked on his own. First abstract works, in the constructivist manner, 1947. Took part in the Salon des Réalités Nouvelles since 1948. After 1953, progressed towards a more supple style of painting, where spontaneous sensibility is reintegrated. Lives in Sartrouville, near Paris.

PROBST Joseph (b. Vianden, Luxembourg, 1911). Studied in Luxembourg, Brussels, and Vienna. Composed various mural paintings. At first influenced by Matisse and Léger. Progressed towards abstraction from 1948 on and accepted it fully in 1951. Took part in numerous group-shows in Paris, Lyons, Luxembourg, Liège, Menton, Amsterdam, as well as in the Sao Paolo Biennale, 1953. Lives in Junglister, Luxembourg.

PUNI Ivan (better known under the name of Jean Pougny; b. in Finland, not far from Saint-Petersburg, in 1894; d. Paris, Dec. 1956). Was in Paris, 1912-1913. Exhibited abstract works with the constructivist and suprematist painters in Saint-Petersburg, in 1915 and the years following. Left Russia for Berlin in 1921 and exhibited at the *Der Sturm* gallery. Then settled in Paris; he returned to representational art and became a sophisticated successor of Vuillard in paintings usually small in size. — Bibl. Umanskij: *Neue Kunst in Russland* (Potsdam 1920); *Collection of the Société Anonyme* (New Haven 1950); *A Dictionary of Modern Painting* (Methuen, London 1956).

Q

QUENTIN Bernard (b. Somme, Northern France, 1923). Attended the School of Decorative Arts for four years. Travelled in Switzerland, Belgium, Sweden, Germany, Italy, Spain, England. Took part in many exhibitions at the Galerie Maeght, Paris, from 1947 on. Included in the Salon de Mai and Salon d'Automne in 1951 as well as in the "Nouvelle École de Paris" show in 1952. His first abstract canvas is dated 1947. "In order to reach this point, I underwent the influence of Klee, whose work I discovered in Switzerland. It was mainly architecture, however, that gave me feeling for proportions and structure: from arabic design, I derived inspiration for the graphic side of my work." (Quentin).

Later on, progressed toward a more lyrical painting. Lives in Paris.

QUENTIN. COMPOSITION. 1955.

R

RADICE Mario (b. Como, 1900). Self-educated in matters of art. One of the first promoters of abstract painting in Italy (1930). Worked with many architects and contributed to Italian art reviews. Took part in exhibitions of abstract art in Italy and in Scandinavia. Lives in Milan.

RADOU Othello (b. Monte Carlo, 1910). Prepared the entrance examinations for the École Polytechnique and the École des Mines, then studied painting and drawing under various instructors, particularly Jean Lombard. Took part in the major Parisian Salons from 1943 on. Exhibited his first abstract canvas at the Salon de Mai in 1946. Modulations of supple lines and planes. Radou lives in Paris and takes part every year in the Salon des Réalités Nouvelles.

RAY Man (b. Philadelphia, 1890). Dropped his studies of architecture and engineering in order to devote himself to painting (1907). First one-man show in 1912. The 'Armory Show' in 1913 sharpened his interest in abstract art. Together with Marcel Duchamp and Picabia, founded the New York dada group. In 1920, the co-organiser of the 'Société Anonyme' with Katherine S. Dreier and Marcel Duchamp. Came to Paris in 1920. In the following years was very much involved with the dada group, then the surrealist group. Contributed to *Sturm* (Berlin) and *De Stijl* (Holland). About 1922, he developed a new technique of photography and became one of the leading composers of photograms and a producer of surrealist films. Was in Hollywood from 1940 to 1951. He then returned to Paris where he is still living.

Although it belongs mainly to surrealism, Man Ray's work can be considered on the

MAN RAY. THE TIGHT-ROPE DANCER ACCOMPANIES HERSELF WITH HER SHADOWS. 1916. *Museum of Modern Art, New York.*

limits of abstraction in a certain number of compositions where no identifiable representation remains. With his works painted in 1915 and 1916, he became one of the first abstract painters in his country, a creator of strange and highly individual forms. — Bibl. *Art of this Century* (New York 1942); *Collection of the Société Anonyme* (New Haven 1950); Ritchie: *Abstract Painting and Sculpture in America* (New York 1952).

RAYMO Leopold (b. Botucatu, Brazil, 1912). A doctor in Sao Paolo. Began painting on his own and without previous art education, in the cubist manner. In 1950, attended the Abstraction Workshop of the painter Flexor, and has remained a member of the Sao Paolo abstract group with which he still exhibits. Lives in Sao Paolo.

RAYMOND Marie (b. La Colle-sur-Loup, in the Alps, 1908). Studied in autonomous academies in Nice and in Paris. Representational painting (portraits and landscapes) until 1938. Without knowing the works of Klee, Kandinsky, and Mondrian, she came to abstraction through the revelation of freedom she found in the works of Picasso. Settled in Paris in 1943. Took part in the Salon des Réalités Nouvelles, the Salon de Mai, and various group-shows. One-man shows at the Galerie de Beaune, Paris, 1950 and 1951. Included in exhibitions in Holland, Italy, Germany, Switzerland, Japan, and Brazil. The wife of the Dutch painter Klein, Marie Raymond has been for some years the Paris correspondent of the Dutch review *Kunst en Kultuur*. Lives in Paris. "Colour, the symbol of life, must attain the maximum of expression and through its harmonies constitute in some fashion the image of a whole to which thought can cling." (Marie Raymond). — *Bibl.* 'Art d'Aujourd'hui' (Paris, Dec. 1951); *Témoignages pour l'Art Abstrait* (Paris 1952).

REBAY Hilla (b. Strasbourg, 1890). Studied in Dusseldorf, Paris, Munich. Took part in the 'Secession' in Munich, 1914-1915. A member of the 'Novembergruppe' in 1918. Exhibited at the Salon des Indépendants, the Salon des Tuileries, and the Salon d'Automne. Through expressionism and cubism, her work slowly worked toward abstraction. Her canvases are often aggressively lyrical. Her collages, the best part of her work, have a highly individual imprint. Thin strips of coloured paper shape a fluid and delicate style. Madame Rebay has taken an active part in the foundation (1937) and the direction of the Museum of Non-Objective Painting, New York, which is mostly devoted to the works of Bauer and Kandinsky (it is now the Solomon R. Guggenheim Museum). Has taken part several times in the Salon des Réalités Nouvelles in Paris. Lives near New York. — Bibl. *Art of Tomorrow* (New York 1939); Catalogue of her exhibition at the Museum of Non-Objective Painting (New York 1948); Catalogue of the *Bauer-Kandinsky-Rebay* exhibition at Lakeland (Florida) 1955.

REGGIANI Mauro (b. Modena, Italy, 1897). Educated in Florence. The co-signer, with Bogliardi and Ghiringhelli, of the first Italian abstract art manifesto, Milan 1934. One-man show, with a preface by Alberto Sartoris, at the Galleria del Milione, Milan 1936. Took part in many exhibitions throughout Italy. Lives in Milan. Highly whimsical geometries, vigorously conceived and composed in swathes. Bright colours. — *Bibl.* Nello Ponente: *Mauro Reggiani,* 'I 4 Soli' (Turin, Nov. 1955).

REICHEL Hans (b. Wurzburg, 1892). Met Klee in 1919, Kandinsky in 1924. Was in Paris 1928. Numerous one-man shows, particularly at the Galerie Jeanne Bucher (after 1930). Lives in Paris.

Reichel's work is the creation of an imaginary world, like Klee's, but emphasizing tenderness more. He is only abstract, properly speaking, in a minute fraction of his work. "I do not believe that the nightingale, after having sung, says, at night: I have worked. Neither can my little watercolours properly be called *works*. They are rather songs, prayers, little tunes in colour which have given joy to many, no more, no less." (Reichel). — *Bibl.* Bissière et Morlet: *Reichel* (Paris 1953).

REICHEL. WATER-COLOUR. 1954.
Galerie Jeanne Bucher, Paris.

REINHARDT Ad (b. Buffalo, New York, 1913). Studied at Columbia (New York). Self-educated in matters of painting. Exhibited with the 'American Abstract Artists' group from 1939 to 1946. First one-man show in New York, 1945. Numerous shows at the Betty Pars-

ons Gallery, New York. Travelled in Europe in 1952 and 1954. Famous in the United States for his cartoons on the history and the present situation of art in his country. These last years, his painting has progressed towards the horizontal-vertical principle and dull harmonies. Lives in New York. — *Bibl.* Ritchie: *Abstract Painting and Sculpture in America* (New York 1951); Hess: *Abstract Painting* (New York 1951); *Modern Artists in America,* Wittenborn (New York 1951).

RENDON Manuel (b. Paris, 1894). He was the son of an Ambassador of Ecuador in Paris. First exhibition at Zborowsky's, Modigliani's friend (Paris 1925). In 1927, entered the Galerie de l'Effort Moderne (Léonce Rosenberg) and contributed to its review. Exhibitions in Guayaquil and Quito, in Ecuador. Then, again in Paris: Galerie d'Art du Faubourg (1949), Galerie Ariel (1951). Adopted completely the abstract manner which he had been approaching for a number of years and exhibited in Washington (Pan American Union) and in Paris (Galerie de Berri) in 1955 and 1956. Lives in Guayaquil.

RESSE Guy (b. Châtillon - sur - Indre, France, 1921). A painter and a ceramist. Studied at the School of Fine Arts in Tours and Lyons, then at the School of Decorative Arts in Paris. One-man shows in Paris: Galerie Saint-Placide (1947) and Galerie La Roue (1954). First abstract work in 1949. The director of the Galerie La Roue. Lives in Paris.

RETH Alfred (b. Budapest, 1884). After some time in Italy, settled in Paris in 1905 and worked in various autonomous Academies. From 1908 to 1910, his work was marked by Hindu influences. Took part in the Salon d'Automne and the Salon des Indépendants in 1910. In 1913, completely engaged in cubist painting; exhibited at the Galerie Berthe Weill, Paris, with Metzinger, and at the Gallery Der Sturm, Berlin. In 1926, in a retrospective exhibition of cubists anterior to 1914, he was represented by about ten canvases. Then exhibited in numerous Paris galleries, his paintings always testifying to new studies. A member of the 'Abstraction-Création' group in 1932. Took part in the Salon des Réalités Nouvelles from 1946 on. Was in Sweden 1952. Retrospective exhibition at the Galerie de l'Institut, Paris 1955. Lives in Paris. Reth has for a long time devoted himself to the study of materials (sand, pebbles, coal, ground brick, egg-shells, cement, etc. . .) which he incorporates in his compositions with perfect mastery. No one has investigated the possibilities of new techniques more thoroughly. — *Bibl.* Seuphor: *L'Art abstrait, ses origines, ses premiers maîtres* (Paris 1949); *Témoignages pour l'Art Abstrait* (Paris 1952); Waldemar George: *Alfred Reth* (Paris 1955).

RENDON. THE DAWN. 1954.

RETH. COMPOSITION. 1955.

RETS Jean (b. Paris, 1910). A member of many modern art groups in Belgium. Numerous exhibitions in Liège. Attained complete abstraction and exhibited his works at the Galerie Ex-Libris, Brussels, 1953. Lives in Liège.

REVOL Jean (b. Lyons, 1929). Took part in a number of group-shows in Lyons and Paris. One-man shows at the Galerie Creuze, Paris, 1952 and 1955. Neo-expressionist abstract paintings, with twisted symbols violently interwoven. Lives in Paris.

REZVANI Serge (b. Teheran, 1928). Came to France as a child. Attended the Académie de la Grande Chaumière. First exhibited at the age of seventeen. First abstract canvases in 1947. Included in group-shows at the Galerie Maeght. One-man shows in Paris: Galerie Arnaud (1950) and Galerie Berggruen (1953). Took part in the Salon de Mai and the Salon des Réalités Nouvelles. Lives in Paris. Highly coloured work, completely oriental in its warmth, but bathed in a sensibility born of the atmosphere of Paris, such as can be found also in Delaunay's *Fenêtres*.

RICHTER Hans (b. Berlin, 1888). First became acquainted with modern painting through the *Blaue Reiter*, 1912. Then influenced by Cézanne and cubism. First one-man show in Munich, 1916, where he exhibited works 'created in a vegetative manner'. The review *Die*

RICHTER. COMPOSITION. 1952.

Aktion devoted one whole issue to him. In 1916, Richter also joined the dada group just formed in Zurich. First abstract works (in black and white) in 1917. In 1918, met Eggeling, and the following year, composed on a large *rouleau* (reel or roll) a series of abstract designs developed like a musical theme. Met van Doesburg and contributed to *De Stijl*. First abstract film in 1921: *Rythme 21,* now a classic of avant-garde moving-pictures in the same way as Eggeling's films of the same period. From 1923 to 1926, the co-editor of the German review *G* (Gestaltung). Went to America in 1941. Appointed professor at New York City College and Director of the Film Institute. Produced a film *Dreams that money can buy* containing many abstract sequences in colour. In 1950, one-man show of paintings and abstract *rouleaux* at the Galerie des Deux-Iles, Paris, and the Galerie Feigl, Basel. Other one-man shows at the Galerie Mai, Paris, and the Municipal Museum, Amsterdam, in 1952. Lives in New York.

The blacks and whites of Richter, Arp, and Janco are the most typical plastic works of the Zurich period of the Dada movement. Later, Richter tried to apply in films the horizontal-vertical principle so much advocated by the *Stijl* painters. But his most remarkable works are probably the large *rouleaux* he composed during and after the war. They are rather like gigantic papyri composed of conflicting forces; among the disturbance and the swirls, unexpected delicacies appear. They testify to an enthusiastic temperament, both lyric and violent.

RIGHETTI Renato (b. Rome, 1916). First exhibition in 1934. First abstract works in 1937. Numerous one-man shows. Takes part every year in the Salon des Réalités Nouvelles. Lives in Paris. The work of Righetti is imbued with great freshness. His colours are vivid and his compositions charm by their almost child-like simplicity.

RIOPELLE. COMPOSITION. 1955. *Jean Larcade Collection, Paris.*

Most painters desire to be a force of nature integrated into nature, and to lose control in order to gain a certain explosive vigour, a constant source of masterpieces. The memory of Van Gogh haunts them. But no one can choose his rightful drama, nor decide his own spiritual density. — *Bibl.* Duthuit: Preface to the exhibition at the Galerie Rive-Droite (Paris 1954); Pierre Schneider: *Riopelle,* 'L'Œil' (Paris, June 1956).

RIOPELLE Jean-Paul (b. Montreal, 1924). One-man shows in Paris ever since 1947, particularly at the Galerie Creuze (1949), the Studio Facchetti and the Galerie Pierre (1952), the Galerie Rive-Droite (1954), and the Galerie Jacques Dubourg (1956). Exhibits regularly at the Salon de Mai; lives in Paris. Riopelle paints large monochromatic or polychromatic symphonies. The colour fizzles, sparks, splutters, spangles, radiates, falls into place, breaks loose again, surrenders. A kind of aerial impressionism, extremely fickle, adapting its fury to the capacity of the executor, and ruling it in powerful rhythms.

RITSCHL Otto (b. Erfurt, Germany, 1885). Self-educated in matters of painting. At first a writer, he turned to painting about 1919: he then burnt all his books and manuscripts. Worked until 1922 in the manner of Kokoschka and of the

RITSCHL. COMPOSITION 54/53. 1954.

'Brücke'. Was in Paris, 1928. Very much under the influence of French painting (Cézanne, Matisse, and cubism), he slowly progressed towards abstraction. Great retrospective exhibition at the Museum of Wiesbaden in 1955. Ritschl's work does not pay allegiance to the abstract neo-expressionism so characteristic of modern German art. His work of recent years shows him to be much closer in spirit to certain Paris painters, like Dewasne and Vasarely. He is an isolated figure in his own country, although widely esteemed. Lives in Wiesbaden. "Ritschl has suppressed the object not merely aesthetically through a play with forms, but rather ethically, through a philosophical by-passing of the objective world, which is to be considered as fiction." (Kurt Leonhard). — *Bibl.* Domnick: *Abstrakte Malerei* (Stuttgart 1947); Catalogue of the retrospective Ritschl exhibition at the Museum of Wiesbaden, 1955.

RODCHENKO Alexandre (b. Saint Petersburg, 1891). Attended the Academy of Kazan. First abstract works made with a pair of compasses in 1914. The founder of the non-objectivist movement in Moscow, 1915, a movement akin to, although at first competing with, Malevitch's suprematism. Exhibited with Malevitch and Tatlin from 1917 to 1922. The three movements were then generally grouped under the same name of constructivism. After 1922, Rodchenko devoted himself entirely to the applied arts. Lives in Moscow. — *Bibl.* Barr: *Cubism and Abstract art* (New York 1936); Seuphor: *L'Art abstrait, ses origines, ses premiers maîtres* (Paris 1949).

ROITMAN Wolf (b. Montevideo, 1930). Was in Buenos Aires in 1936. Was forced into studying architecture. Published poems and contributed to the review *Poesia Buenos Aires*. Was in Paris, 1951. Became friendly with Arden Quin whom he joined in the Madi movement. Since 1952 has taken part in all the Madi displays in Paris. One-man show at the Galerie de Beaune in 1955. Lives in Paris.

ROTHFUSS Rid (b. Montevideo, Uruguay, 1920). A professor of drawing and painting at the Industrial School and the Teachers College of Uruguay. Co-signer of the *Madi* manifesto in 1947. Took an active part in all the 'Arte Madi' shows in Buenos Aires and contributed to the Madi review. Numerous exhibitions in Montevideo and Buenos Aires. Sent paintings to the Salon des Réalités Nouvelles, Paris, in 1948. Lives in Montevideo.

ROTHKO Mark (b. Dvinsk, Russia, 1903). Emigrated to America in 1913. Studied under Max Weber at the Arts Students League. One-man shows from 1933 on, especially at the Betty Parsons Gallery, New York. Painted in an expressionist representational manner until 1939. First abstract works in 1945. Included in 1951, in the 'Abstract Painting and Sculpture in America' show at the Museum of Modern Art, New York. Included also in 'Cinquante Ans d'art aux États-Unis' at the Museum of Modern Art, Paris, in 1955. Lives in New York.

Ashy colours, a dulled pink, an ochred yellow spread and melt away and vibrate through the mere fact of their existence, of their unexpected expanse. A more orange yellow makes a splash or some blue is less generously laid on: there is the relation—or harmony—which is the whole object of the composition. A soft wind breathes over this desert. It is the innocence of art. — *Bibl. Possibilities I* (New York 1947); 'Art d'Aujourd'hui' (Paris, June 1951); Ritchie: *Abstract Painting and Sculpture in America* (New York 1951); Hess: *Abstract Painting* (New York 1951); *Art news annual* (New York 1951).

ROTHKO. NUMBER 10. 1950.
Museum of Modern Art, New York.

RUDULPH Rella (b. Livingston, Alabama, 1906). Attended the Chapelle School of Art in Denver, 1928. Was in New York, 1933. Studied at the Art Students League. Travelled in Peru, Ecuador, Chile, Mexico. One-man shows in Birmingham (Ala.), 1940; in New York, 1941; in Los Angeles, 1945. Was in Paris, 1948. First non-representational works in 1949. She feels an artistic affinity with Soldati. One-man show at the Galerie La Roue, Paris 1955: large geometrical compositions on aluminium. Lives in Paris.

RUSSELL Morgan (b. New York, 1886; d. Broomall, Penn., 1953). Studied painting under Robert Henri and Henri Matisse. Founded the synchromist movement with MacDonald-Wright (cf. that name) in Paris, 1912. Included in the Salon des Indépendants in 1912 and 1913. Exhibited in Munich with MacDonald-Wright and sent some paintings to the 'Armory Show' in New York. Exhibited his 'synchromies' with MacDonald-Wright in Paris, 1913, and New York, 1916. A little later he reverted to representational painting (still life and portrait). Lived a long time in isolation in the French provinces. Returned to America in 1946. Retrospective exhibition of his abstract work at the Rose Fried Gallery, 1950. Included in the 'Abstract Painting and Sculpture in America' show at the Museum of Modern Art, New York (1951), with major works from the years 1913 and 1914.

"Color is form; and in my attainment of abstract form I use those colors which optically correspond to the spatial extension of the forms desired." (Morgan Russell). Russell's 'synchromies' are distinguished from those of MacDonald-Wright by their more precise forms, and a certain quest for mass, akin to the cubist preoccupation, but in a quite different register of colours. — *Bibl.* W. H. Wright: *Modern painting, its tendency and meaning* (New York, 1915); Seuphor: *L'Art abstrait, ses origines, ses premiers maîtres* (Paris 1949); 'Art d'Aujourd'hui' (Paris, June 1951); Ritchie: *Abstract painting and sculpture in America* (New York 1951).

RUVOLO Felix (b. New York, 1912). Spent his childhood in Sicily. Was in Chicago from 1926 to 1948: studied at the Art Institute. First exhibition in 1947. Then exhibited in numerous galleries and academies throughout America. Composed a number of mural decorations in Chicago. Lives in Walnut Creek (Calif.).

S

SANTOMASO. COMPOSITION. 1955.

SALVATORE Nino di (b. Verbania Pallanza, Italy, 1924). One-man shows in Italy since 1944. The director of the School of Fine Arts in Domodossola since 1949. Took part in the Salon des Réalités Nouvelles in 1951, and in numerous exhibitions of Italian abstract art. Lives in Domodossola. A combination of curves and straight lines forming coloured planes.

SANDIG Armin (b. Hof-an-der-Saale, Germany, 1929). Studied naturalist painting. Was in Munich, 1949-

1950. Took part in numerous group-shows. One-man show in 1951. Lives in Hamburg.

SANFILIPPO Antonio (b. Partenne, Italy, 1923). Studied at the Academy of Fine Arts in Florence. Co-signer of the *Forma I* manifesto in 1947 and contributor to the *Forma I* review. Took part in the main abstract art displays in Italy, as well as in the Venice Biennale. Also included in group-shows abroad. Lives in Rome.

SANS Klaas (b. Sappemeer, Netherlands. 1927). Educated in Groningen, Travelled to Canada and Paris, where he frequented the Académie Ranson. Took part in group-shows in Holland and in Paris. Started by painting portraits and landscapes. Discovered modern painting in the museums of New York and Chicago. Sans leads a wandering life, but spends most of his time in Paris. Abstract works at the Galerie Olga Bogroff, Paris, and the Salon des Réalités Nouvelles in 1955. Lives in Paris and in Holland.

SANTOMASO Giuseppe (b. Venice, 1907). Attended the Academy of Fine Arts in Venice. Began to exhibit in 1928. After some time spent in Holland and in Paris, he tried to 'mature personal experience on the universal level'. Since 1940, numerous one-man shows in Italy as well as in Paris (Galerie Rive Gauche) and London (The Hanover Gallery). Has illustrated Éluard's *Grand Air* with twenty-seven original drawings (Galeria Santa Radegonda, Milan 1945). About 1952, his painting attained abstraction without completely abandoning the natural visual pretexts which pure painting integrates and transforms in its autonomous themes. It is a supple art, of great poetical charm. Santomaso lives in Venice. "His personality is best expressed—writes Giuseppe Marchiori—in the invention of a coloured atmosphere in which each form strives towards a visual incantation, a harmony where painting and music truly blend." — *Bibl.* Venturi: *Otto pittori italiani,* De Luca editore (Rome 1952); Read: *Santomaso,* The Hanover Gallery (London 1953); Marchiori: *Santomaso,* Alfieri (Venice 1954); Venturi: *Santomaso,* De Luca editore (Rome 1955).

SAUER Greta (b. Bregens, Austria, 1909). Attended University in Germany. Emigrated to France (Paris) in 1937. Abstract gouaches and collages since 1939. Included in group-shows in Paris, Marseilles, Copenhagen, San Francisco, and Turin. One-man shows in Paris: Galerie du Montparnasse (1947); Galerie de Beaune (1950); Galerie Arnaud (1951 and 1952). Lives in Paris. Direct projections of a wild, restless mind. There is a refined delicacy in the nuances of the collages.

SAVELLI Angelo (b. Pizzo-di-Calabria, Italy, 1911). Took part in various exhibitions of Italian abstract art. Studies in simple rhythms and great contrasts in colour. Lives in Rome.

SAVERYS Jan (b. Petegem, Belgium, 1924). The son of the painter Albert Saverys. Attended the Academy of Fine Arts in Ghent (1943-1946), then non-institutional academies in Paris (1946-1948). First abstract paintings in 1949. Calligraphic works of ordered elegance. A member of the Belgian 'Art Abstrait' group. Included in group-shows in Brussels, Knokke, Antwerp, Charleroi, (Belgium), in Bergen (Norway), and in Edinburgh. Lives in Petegem.

SCHANKER Louis (b. New York, 1903). Studied in various art-schools in New York. Lived in France and in Spain, 1931-1933. First one-man show in New York, in 1934. In 1944, published an album of wood-cuts in colour (Wittenborn). Since 1943, teaches the technique of wood-engraving at the New School for Social Research, in New York. Numerous one-man shows at the Willard Gallery New York, since 1944 (paintings and engravings). Lives in New York.

SAUER. COLLAGE. 1955.

SCHATZ Bezalel (b. Jerusalem, 1912). The son of Professor Boris Schatz, the founder of the first Fine Arts Academy in Israel. Studied in Paris and New York. Took part in exhibitions in the United States, London, Paris, and Israel. Abstract compositions in a free-style calligraphy influenced by his numerous contacts with modern Western artists.

SCHILLING Albrecht (b. Bremen, Germany, 1929). Began to paint on his own in 1946. After a cubist period, he came to pure abstraction about 1950. Travelled and studied in Italy and Switzerland (1951). Was in Paris in 1952. Lives in Bremen.

SCHMELZEISEN Gustav Klemens (b. Dusseldorf, 1900). Studied under von Wessel. A doctor in Law and professor of the history of German law. Came to abstraction in recent years. Lives in Hechingen (Germany).

SCHMIDT Gerhard Michael (b. Lesten, Silesia, 1922). An office worker in Berlin. Began to paint at the end of the war. Attended the Fine Arts school in Hamburg (1948-1952), under Willi Breest. Took part in numerous group-shows in Germany from 1952 on. Spent some time in Paris in 1952 and 1955. Together with Dieter Benecke and Jutta Benecke-Eberle, exhibited abstract works at the Librairie Didier, Paris, 1955. Lives in Hamburg.

SCHNEIDER Gérard (b. Sainte-Croix, Switzerland, 1896). Spent his childhood in Neuchâtel. Was in Paris in 1916. Attended the School of Decorative Arts, then the École des Beaux-Arts (under Cormon). When his studies were completed, returned to Switzerland where he took part in numerous exhibitions after 1920. Came back to Paris in 1924; by putting into practice his knowledge in matters of decoration he made a living restoring paintings. Starting from various subjects (figures and imaginary landscapes) he painted his first abstract canvas in 1944. Took part in the Salon d'Automne and the Salon des Surindépendants. After 1946, exhibited at the Salon des Réalités Nouvelles and the Salon de Mai (of which he is a co-organizer). One-man shows in Paris: Galerie Lydia Conti (1947); Galerie Galanis (1955). Sent some works to the Venice Biennale in 1948. Took part in group-shows at the

SCHNEIDER. CÉRAK. 1955. *Raymond Mindlin Collection, New York.*

Galerie Carré (Paris and New York) in 1950 and 1951 as well as in important displays in America, Germany, Scandinavia, Italy, Belgium, Japan, etc. One-man show at the Kootz Gallery, New York, in 1956. Lives in Paris.

His paintings looks as if they had been shaped by thrusts of a sickle, volatile in appearance, but perfectly conceived and composed. Among European abstract painters, Schneider is probably the closest to Japanese abstract calligraphy. Brief and deliberate symbols of a graphism where the significant spirit of the whole surpasses the effect of each letter. "There has not really been a brutal break between representational and non-representational art, but rather a logical development, a continuous enrichment since impressionism, which was the first move towards abstraction of the motif on behalf of a sensual impact based solely upon atmospheric relations. The cubists also worked toward abstraction when they imagined *a priori* forms, structures, and new relations between objects. We find abstraction again in the Fauvist tendency to draw clear orchestral harmony from the motif, with the help of intense colours. So many attempts to liberate painting from servile reproduction of the object broke the ground for an independent art, for an autonomous painting existing only for and in itself." (Schneider). — *Bibl.* 'Art d'Aujourd'hui' (Paris, June 1951); *Propos de Schneider sur l'Art Abstrait,* 'Les Amis de l'Art' (Paris, Jan. 1952); Brion: *Schneider,* 'I 4 Soli' (Turin, Jan. 1955). Schneider has also illustrated Ganzo's *Langage* with twelve abstract lithographs, ed. Lydia Conti (Paris 1948).

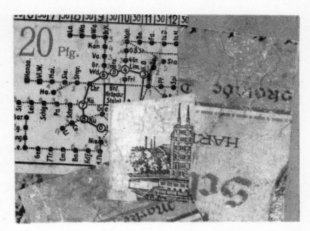

SCHWITTERS. COLLAGE IN BLUE AND WHITE. 1926.
Private Collection, Paris.

SCHULZE Bernard (b. Schneidemühl, 1915). Attended the School of Fine Arts in Berlin and Dusseldorf. Travelled in France in 1945 and 1953. Took part in exhibitions in Paris, London, and the United States. 'Informal' painting striving toward confused and ambiguous states. Lives in Frankfurt-am-Main.

SCHWITTERS Kurt (b. Hanover, Germany, 1887; d. Ambleside, England, 1948). At first an academic painter. Studied six years at the Academy of Dresden: painted portraits. During a stay in Munich was influenced by Franz Marc and Kandinsky. About 1918, his work was in the line of Picasso's cubism. Returned to Hanover in 1919 and founded his own sector of the Dada movement: *Merz,* and for a number of years published a review of that name. Met van Doesburg in 1922 and accompanied him on a 'dada' tour in Holland. About the same time, composed his famous verbal symphony *Lautsonate.* Contributed regularly to the review *Der Sturm.*

For years he 'constructed' the interior of his house with abstract compositions, into which he incorporated hundreds of various objects, sometimes even picked up in the street. A member of the 'Cercle et Carré' group in Paris 1930, and then of 'Abstraction-Création', 1932. In 1933, left Germany for Norway. Settled in England in 1941. In Ambleside, started on a new *Merz* construction inside a farmhouse. He died before he could complete the work (1948).

"Emerging from dada, Schwitters' paintings and his *Merz* constructions are among the most evident achievements of modern art. He collates accidental scraps of everyday life into compositions of great plastic beauty, thus affirming the superiority of spirit over matter. Through his humility a new purity is born. Schwitters' collages are as mystical and delicate as Taoist paintings." (Charmion von Wiegand). — *Bibl.* Arp and Lissitzky: *Les Ismes de l'Art* (Zurich 1925); Dreier: *Modern Art* (New York 1926); Barr: *Cubism and abstract Art* (New York 1936); *Art of this Century* (New York 1942); Moholy-Nagy: *Vision in Motion* (Chicago 1947); an article by Edith Thomas in *L'Art Abstrait, ses origines, ses premiers maîtres* (Seuphor, Paris 1949); *Collection of the Société Anonyme* (New York 1950); Hitchcock: *Painting toward Architecture* (New York 1948); *The Dada Painters and Poets* (New York 1951); *Catalogue-Album of the Schwitters exhibition*, Galerie Berggruen (Paris 1954).

SCOTT William (b. Greenock, Scotland, 1913). Studied in Belfast and in various Royal Academies. From 1937 to 1939, travelled in France and in Italy. One-man shows in London in 1942, 1948, 1950. Lives in London. — *Bibl.* Alloway: *Nine abstract artists* (Tiranti) London 1954).

SEKIYA Yoshimichi (b. in Japan, 1920). Studied at the Teachers College in Gifu. Exhibited at the Institute of

SEKIYA. CALLIGRAPHY. 1954.

calligraphy considered as an art-form (Shodo-Geijitsu-In) and the Japanese Academy of Fine Arts (Nitten) from 1949 to 1951. A member of the Bokusin-Kai School from 1952 on. Included in the exhibition of 'Present-day Fine Arts' (Kobe, 1953); in the Modern Art Fair (Osaka); in the exhibition of Japanese calligraphy at the Museum of Modern Art, New York; as well as in the Bokusin-Kai show in Tokyo, Kyoto, and Kobe, in 1954. Lives in Japan.

SEKULA Sonia (b. Lucerne, Switzerland, 1918). Was in the United States in 1934. A naturalized American citizen. Studied under Kurt Roesch and Morris Kantor. First exhibition at the 'Art of this Century' show, New York, 1946. She exhibits regularly at the Betty Parsons Gallery, and takes part in numerous art-displays throughout America. Lives in New York.

SERPAN Iaroslav (b. Prague, 1922). Was in France, 1929. Began to paint about 1940. At first a member of the surrealist group, with which he exhibited at the Galerie Maeght, Paris, in 1947. Then worked towards 'the realisation of a dynamic pictorial space', and took part in numerous group-shows, in Paris, Vienna, Berlin, Prague, London, and Rome. Published also theoretical and critical essays in various reviews, particularly in Italy. Lives in Paris. A graphism in brief slight strokes, commas or squiggles, gathered in compact masses or scattered across the canvas in galaxies. Serpan's works are highly strung in aspect.

SERVRANCKX Victor (b. Dieghem, near Brussels, in 1897). Attended the Academy in Brussels from 1912 to 1917. First one-man show in Brussels, 1917. Since 1932, a professor at the School of Industrial and Decorative Arts in Ixelles. He was the first Belgian painter to launch into abstraction. After the First World War, was a member of the 'Effort Moderne' group (Léonce Rosenberg) in Paris. Numerous one-man shows in Bel-

gium, in Paris, and in the main European countries. His work was first introduced in America by the 'Collection Anonyme' in 1926. Important retrospective exhibition at the Palais des Beaux-Arts, Brussels, in 1947. Takes part regularly in the Salon des Réalités Nouvelles; lives in Brussels.

The first part of Servranckx's work shared the aesthetic of the machine advocated by the futurists, but in a very individual and entirely abstract way. Then the painter progressed toward studies in imitation of substances, more akin to the ambiguous conceptions of surrealism. His recent work clearly indicates a return to compositions in simple elements, sometimes very close to neo-plasticism. — Bibl. *Het Overzicht,* nº 21 (Antwerp 1924); *Catalogue of the retrospective exhibition* (Brussels 1927); Seuphor: *L'Art abstrait, ses origines, ses premiers maîtres* (Paris 1949); *Collection of the Société Anonyme* (New Haven 1950).

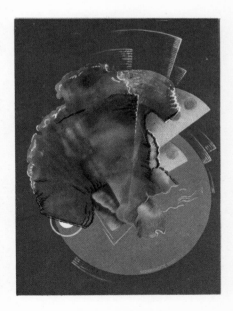

SERVRANCKX. PAINTING. 1920.

SEVERINI Gino (b. Cortona, Italy, 1883). Came to Rome in 1901 to study painting. Met Balla and Boccioni about 1904. In Paris, 1906. Had a studio in Impasse Guelma where Utrillo, Braque, and Dufy also had theirs. Met Modigliani and Max Jacob. Co-signer of the first futurist manifesto in 1910. In 1912, took part in the momentous futurist exhibitions in Paris, London, Berlin, etc. Married the daughter of the poet Paul Fort in 1913. His futurist work of the time bears the imprint of cubism as well as of the impressionism of Seurat. A series of paintings dated 1913 and 1914 (*Danseuses*) can be considered as pure abstractions. Severini reverted then to representational, and even academic, art for many years. In Italy after 1933. In Rome during the Second World War. Composed numerous mosaics and frescoes for churches in Switzerland and in

SEVERINI. THE MODISTE. 1911.
Joseph Slifka Coll., New York.

Italy. In 1946, published the first volume of his memoirs *Tutta la vita di un pittore* (Garzanti, Rome). In recent years, Severini has sporadically returned to abstraction. Exhibition of mosaics at the Galerie des Cahiers d'Art, Paris 1952. Retrospective at the Galerie Berggruen, Paris 1956. Severini has regularly contributed to the principal art Salons in Paris, and also showed some of his works at the exhibition "Art Abstrait, les Premières Générations", which was held at the Musée de Saint-Étienne in 1957. Lives in Paris where he directs a school of mosaics in the ancient Ravenna technique. — *Bibl.* Carrieri: *Pittura e scultura d'avanguardia in Italia* (Milan 1950); *A Dictionary of Modern Painting* (Methuen, London 1956); Seuphor: *Le futurisme . . . hier,* 'L'Œil' (Paris, Feb. 1956). Catalogue-Album of the Berggruen Exhibition (Paris 1956); Catalogue of the Saint-Étienne Exhibition (1957).

SHINODA. TRISTESSE. 1954.

SHAW Charles G. (b. New York, 1892). Studied in London, Paris, and the Art Students League, New York. First one-man show at the Valentine Gallery, New York 1934. Exhibited with the 'American Abstract Artists' from 1937 on. Lives in New York.

SHINODA Toko (b. in Japan, 1912). A member of the 'Institute of calligraphy considered as an art-form' since 1950. Took part in exhibitions of Japanese calligraphy at the Stedelijk Museum in Amsterdam, the Kunsthalle in Basel, the Musée Cernuschi in Paris, in 1955 and 1956. The author of a book: *How to learn the new calligraphy in twelve months*. Lives in Tokyo. Supple and velvety designs with delicate shading of greys.

SINEMUS Wilhelmus Friedrich (b. Amsterdam in 1903). Attended the School of Fine Arts in The Hague. Worked in France from 1928 to 1944. Devoted himself to abstract art since 1937. A member of the Dutch group 'Vrij Beelden'. Lives in The Hague.

SINGIER Gustave (b. Warneton, Belgium, 1909). Came to Paris in 1919 and was naturalized a French citizen. Until 1936, worked as a designer-decorator (installations of shops and apartments). During this period, he painted from Nature. Met Charles Walch, who advised and encouraged him and introduced him to pure painting. Included in the Salon des Indépendants, the Salon d'Automne, the Salon des Tuileries, and since 1945, in the Salon de Mai, of which he is a co-founder. Exhibition at the Galerie Drouin, Paris 1946, together with Le Moal and Manessier, followed by one-man shows at the Galerie Billet-Caputo (1949 and 1950) and the Galerie de France (1952 and 1955). Lives in Paris.

Sometimes close to that of Manessier, Singier's painting is yet lighter in appearance, and often decorative. Outstanding successes in the harmony of blues. His ready gift could easily tend to make this painter somewhat precious; but he strives to break away from such charm in large canvases where the tension of forms can be more amply realised. — *Bibl.* Bourniquel: *Trois Peintres (Le Moal, Manessier, Singier)*, (Paris 1946); Marester: *Singier et la sérénité*, 'XXe Siècle' (Paris 1952).

SKULASON Thorvaldur (b. Bordeyri, Iceland, 1906). Studied at the School of Fine Arts in Oslo. Travelled in Italy, Switzerland, Belgium, Netherlands, England. Was in Paris from 1931

SINGIER. ESTUARY. 1955
Galerie de France, Paris.

to 1933 and from 1938 to 1940. First abstract works (rectilinear geometry) in 1938. Took part in numerous exhibitions in Scandinavia, as well as in Brussels, New York, and Rome. One of the first exponents of abstract art in Iceland. Lives in Reyjavik.

SMADJA Alex (b. Mostaganem, Algeria, 1897). Exhibited at the Salon d'Automne ever since 1929. After the Liberation, his work became completely abstract; one-man show at the Galerie Breteau, Paris 1948. He took part in the Salon des Réalités Nouvelles, the Salon de Mai, and exhibited in Copenhagen. Lives in Paris. Smadja's recent works are very rhythmical compositions in supple lines, mostly in foggy greys, with light and joyful stresses of colour.

SMITH Leon Polk (b. in Ada, Oklahoma, 1906). Studied at Oklahoma State College and in New York. Taught in Oklahoma high schools from 1934 to 1939. Travelled in Europe in 1939. Then taught in various colleges in the United States. Was in New York from 1945 to 1949. One-man shows in a number of American cities since 1940. A professor in Winter Park, Florida. Compositions of a great geometrical precision, akin to Mondrian's neo-plasticism.

SOLDATI Atanasio (b. 1887 and d. 1953 in Parma, Italy). Took a Diploma in Architecture in 1920; then turned to painting. His first one-man show was held in Parma, 1922. Slowly, through a number of influences, particularly Klee's and Kandinsky's, Soldati progressed toward total abstraction, which he attained in 1949. One-man shows in all the main cities of Italy. Took part in group-shows in Italy, in Switzerland, and in Paris. A clear architecture in joyful, almost naive, colours was always Soldati's main concern. In recent years (1951-1953), his works are more simple and more powerful. — *Bibl.* Dorfles: *Soldati,* 'Arti visive' (Rome, Dec. 1952); Venturi: *Soldati,* Galleria Bergamini (Milan 1954).

SONDERBORG K. R. H. (b. in Sonderborg, Alsen Island, Denmark, in 1923). At first a shop-assistant in Hamburg. Interned in the Fuhlsbüttel concentration camp (1941-1942). Attended the Fine Arts School in Hamburg from 1947 to 1949. Travelled in Italy and spent some time on Stromboli Island. Worked under Hayter in Paris, 1953. A member of the group 'Zen 49'. Took part

SONDERBORG. 3-XI-54—11.5 a.m. to 12.10 p.m.
André V. Naggar Collection, Paris.

in many exhibitions of German abstract art, particularly in Amsterdam (1954) and in Paris (1955). Lives in Hamburg.

SOTO Jesus Raphael (b. in Ciudad Bolivar, Venezuela, 1923). Studied at the School of Plastic Arts in Caracas (1942-1947). Was then appointed director of the School of Plastic Arts in Maracaibo. Was in Paris in 1950. Took part every year in the Salon des Réalités Nouvelles. Was also included in a number of shows at the Galerie Denise René. At the same time, exhibited his abstract works in Venezuela, particularly in Caracas (1951) and in Valencia (1955). Lives in Paris. Soto composes 'cinetic structures' with elements close to suprematism and neo-plasticism.

SOULAGES Pierre (b. Rodez, South-West France, in 1919). While attending school in his home-town, he began to paint, completely unaware of any modern painting, but greatly attracted by prehistoric and romanesque art, of which there are numerous remains in that part of France. During a few months in Paris, in 1938, he got acquainted with the younger school of painting. Then, he worked on his own in Rodez. Settled in Paris in 1946, and the following year, exhibited for the first time at the Salon des Surindépendants. After that, he exhibited many times in Paris, in Germany, in Belgium, in Denmark, etc. Has taken part in the Salon de Mai since 1949. Costume and set-designer for a number of plays, including Vaillant's *Héloïse et Abélard* at the Théâtre des Mathurins, Paris 1949, and Graham Greene's *The Power and the Glory* at the Athénée, Paris 1951. Exhibitions at the Kootz Gallery, New York, 1954 and 1955, and at the Galerie de France, Paris 1956. Lives in Paris.

Black painting, in heavy lines, where an essential symbol summarizes the graphism. A certain gradation of greys or the clear

SOULAGES. PAINTING. 1954.

tints of the background produce by contrast a powerful dramatic effect. The sobriety of the forms, the reduction of colours to only black chords, attain their utmost significance through cleverly distributed lighting. Soulages' best canvases testify to an accomplished knowledge of *chiaroscuro*. The symbol rules, but it is conceived as a structure and the structure tries to become a force. — Bibl. *Premier Bilan de l'Art actuel* (Paris 1943); 'La Table Ronde', nº 77 (Paris, May 1954); Ragon: *Soulages,* 'Cimaise' (Paris, January 1956).

SPENCER Vera (b. Prague, 1926). Came to England in 1936. Took English nationality. After a period of expressionist painting (under the direction of Kokoschka), she studied for three years at the Slade School, London. First abstract paintings in 1950. One-man show at the Galerie Arnaud, Paris, 1952. Contributed collages to group-shows in England, in France, and in New York. Lives in London.

SPILLER Jurg (b. Basel, 1913). Lived in England, in France, and in Germany while attending university and studying painting. His first paintings were expressionist. Later on, the French influence became noticeable in Spiller's tendency towards a constructive realism. Before the Second World War, he exhibited in London and in Berlin, then in Basel, Zurich, Paris, and Copenhagen. Travelling exhibition in Germany, in 1950. Spent some time in Mexico (1951-1952). In company with the Swiss artist Bodmer, at the Galleria del Milione, Milan, 1949, exhibited abstract works often marked by a search for horizontal-vertical rhythms but always with a lyrical quality reminiscent of Paul Klee (Entre Jour et Nuit, 1947). Lives in Basel.

SPRINGER Ferdinand (b. in Berlin, 1907). Studied philosophy and art history at the University of Zurich. Came to Paris in 1928. Worked at the Académie Ranson under Bissière (cf. that name), then at S. W. Hayter's 'Atelier 17'. One-man shows in Paris, Basel, and New York, from 1935 to 1937. Drafted in the French army in 1939, he retreated to Switzerland when the Germans invaded Southern France (1942); lived in forced residence in a village near Bern, in the Oberland, until 1945. Then settled in Grasse. Illustrated numerous books with engravings testifying to an exceptional gift for adopting various styles: one can quote *The Symposium of Socrates* (London 1937), *Eupalinos* by Valéry (Paris 1947); *le Mythe de la Caverne* (Paris 1948). He came to abstraction with seventeen etchings for the *Tao-te-King*; afterwards the French Government commissioned four tapestries. Took part in various Paris Salons. His painted or engraved works have been exhibited in the United States, in Great Britain, in Germany, and in Switzerland. Lives in Paris and in Grasse.
— Bibl. *Das Kunstwerk,* heft 8-9 (Baden-Baden 1950); Springer: *Der Kupferstich ein Technik der Gegenwart,* 'Werk' (Winterthur, Jan. 1950).

STAËL Nicolas de (b. Saint-Petersburg, 1914; d. Antibes, 1955). Studied classics and attended the School of Fine Arts in Brussels. Travelled in Holland in 1930. In Paris, 1932, he made a living as a decor-painter. Travelled in Spain in 1935. The following years, he spent some time in Italy and North Africa. Returned to Paris in 1940. Met and became friendly with Braque. One-man show at the Galerie Jeanne

SPRINGER. PERSIAN THEME. 1954.

Bucher, Paris, 1945. After 1950, he exhibited mainly at the Galerie Jacques Dubourg, Paris, and took part regularly in the Salon de Mai. He had a number of exhibitions in New York. "The brush, and more often the trowel, organizes the surface in light panels with few nuances. The palette welcomes flashy reds, quiet blues, golden ochres, and amethysts; Staël can even make black luminous by charging it more and more heavily." (R. Van Gindertael). He reverted

DE STAËL. THE FOOTBALLERS. 1952.
Estorick Collection, London.

imperceptibly to representation from 1953 on and found himself in a cul-de-sac. He committed suicide by throwing himself from the window of his studio in Antibes. Staël's lyrical and brilliant painting had a marked influence over many young Paris painters about 1950. A generous and ardent nature, with a tendency to exaggeration, Staël seems to have been defeated—during the last two years of his life—by apparently insoluble problems. His tragic end remains as mysterious as that of Van Gogh, with whom he had evident affinities in character. One of his last canvases (*les Mouettes*, 1955) recalls irresistibly *Paysage aux Corbeaux*. His most beautiful works, both powerful and harmonious, are still those he painted between 1950 and 1952 : the abstract composition built up in large planes and free architecture *Grands Footballeurs* will probably remain as a masterpiece of modern art. Then, this fire, a token of a great wisdom, settled down little by little until it flickered out completely in representational works in grey. Did Staël burn himself out with the too violent ardour of his temperament ? Did the return to traditional painting seem to him too heavy a load to carry ? We shall never know the real cause of his fatal flaw. A large retrospective exhibition of his work was held at the Museum of Modern Art, Paris, 1956. — *Bibl.* Duthuit: *Nicolas de Staël* (Paris, 1950); Gindertael: *Nicolas de Staël* (Paris 1951); Courthion: *Peintres d'aujourd'hui* (Geneva 1952); *Cimaise*, nº 7 (Paris, June 1955); Catalogue of the retrospective exhibition at the Museum of Modern Art (Paris 1956).

STAMOS Theodoros (b. New York, 1922). Began as a sculptor. Spent three years at the Stuyvesant High School, New York. Then, turned to painting and took up many trades in order to live. First one-man show in 1943. Has exhibited regularly at the Betty Parsons Gallery, New York, since 1947. Took part in the 'Jeunes Peintres' show as well as in 'Cinquante ans d'Art aux États-Unis', both at the Museum of Modern Art, Paris, 1955. Lives in New York. — Bibl. *Contemporary American Painting*, San Fransisco 1950; Ritchie: *Abstract Painting and Sculpture in America*, Museum of Modern Art, New York 1951.

STILL. PAINTING. 1951.
Museum of Modern Art, New York.

STARITSKY Anna (b. Poltava, Ukraine, 1911). In Moscow, attended classes of drawing taught by Tolstoy's daughter. Studied at the School of Fine Arts in Sofia, Bulgaria. Was in Brussels from 1932 to 1947. Worked as a designer in a printing-press. One-man shows in Brussels, Antwerp, Paris, Nice, etc. Has taken part in the Salon des Réalités Nouvelles since 1951. She is married to the painter Orix (cf. that name). Lives in Paris and in Nice. Paintings of pure effusion, very rich in substance.

STARK Gustl (b. Mainz, Germany, 1917). Educated

in Wurtzburg and Nuremberg. Studied in Sylt and in Paris, where he spent some time. Took part in numerous group-shows in the main cities of Germany as well as in the Salon des Réalités Nouvelles. Combinations of elementary graphism and coloured planes. Lives in Mainz.

STERNE Hedda (b. in Rumania, 1915). Came to America in 1941, after having studied in Paris, Bucharest, and Vienna. Exhibited at the Betty Parsons Gallery, New York, since 1947. Took part in numerous group-shows in the United States. Is married to the American cartoonist Steinberg. Lives in New York.

STILL Clyfford (b. Grandin, North Dakota, 1904). Educated in Alberta (Canada); worked his way through Spokane University (Washington) by working on a farm during vacations. Taught at Washington State College (1933-1941) and at the California School of Fine Arts (1946-1950). One-man shows: San

STARITSKY. COMPOSITION. 1955.

268

Francisco Museum of Art (1941); 'Art in this Century' (1946), Betty Parsons Gallery, New York (1947, 1950, 1951). Took part in the exhibition 'Cinquante ans d'Art aux États-Unis' at the Museum of Modern Art, Paris, 1955. Taught at Hunter College, New York, and Brooklyn College, New York. Lives in New York.

"From the most ancient times the artist has been expected to perpetuate the values of his contemporaries. The record is mainly one of frustration, sadism, superstition, and the will to power. The anxious find comfort in the confusion of those artists who would walk beside them. The values involved, however, permit no peace, and mutual resentment is deep when it is discovered that salvation cannot be bought. We are now committed to an unqualified act, not illustrating outworn myths or contemporary alibis. The artist must accept total responsibility for what he executes. And the measure of his greatness will be in the depth of his insight and his courage in realizing his own vision." (Still). Large monochromatic surfaces of shredded forms. Often a red smear scorches the broadly spread black, a thick living black peculiar to Still. He must be considered among the American painters who have created an autonomous style owing little to the European tendencies of the last fifty years.— Bibl. *Fifteen Americans*, Museum of Modern Art (New York 1952); Greenberg: *American-type painting*, 'Partisan review', nº 2 (New York 1955).

STRZEMINSKI Wladislas (b. 1893 and d. 1952 in Poland). One of the leading Polish painters of the school of pure abstraction; took a very active part in the review *Blok*, founded in Warsaw in 1924. He was a close friend of Henri Stazewski who was included in the 'Cercle et Carré' exhibition in Paris, 1930, and whose whereabouts are now unknown. In the same Polish group were Berlewi,

Zarnowerowna, Szezuka, Kobro, Krynski. It seems that they were all very much influenced by Malevitch when he came to lecture on suprematism in Warsaw, in 1924. Moreover, Berlewi introduced in the group the neo-plastic conceptions which van Doesburg had directly imparted to him in Berlin, 1922.

SUGAÏ Kumi (b. in Kobe, Japan, 1919). He came from a family of classical musicians. Attended the School of Fine Arts in Osaka (1927-1932). Had a studio

SUGAÏ. CRACKER. 1954.
Galerie Craven, Paris.

in Kobe until 1951. Was a poster-designer. Was in Paris in 1952. One-man show at the Galerie Craven, Paris 1953. Took part in group-shows in Brussels, New York,

London, and Pittsburgh. He is attached to the concepts of Zen buddhism. Abstract compositions where oriental refinement fuses with a western sense of order. A very quiet and restrained emotion corrects the rigour of the integrated rule.

SZENÈS Arpad (b. in Budapest, 1900). Came to Paris in 1925 and worked under Lhote, Léger, Bissière. Exhibited at the Salon des Surindépendants from 1932 to 1938. As early as 1932, his work was very close to abstraction. Lived in Brazil from 1939 to 1947 with his wife Viera da Silva. One-man shows in Lisbon, Rio de Janeiro, and, a number of times, at the Galerie Jeanne Bucher, Paris. Took part in the Salon de Mai. Lives in Paris. Szenès was for a time on the borders of surrealism. His recent and abstract work is quite an individual phenomenon: a snowy world which reveals its story in melting white expanses. This affirmed paleness, these hardly perceptible tracks in the white are the vocabulary of a painter very sure of his meaning, but who whispers it and cares little about being heard. Besides, he thinks, one only speaks to those who already know and who can take a hint.

SZENÈS. COMPOSITION. 1955. *Galerie Jeanne Bucher, Paris.*

T

TABUCHI Yasse (b. in Japan, 1921). Attended the University of Tokyo. Took part in exhibitions in Tokyo from 1947 to 1950. Settled in Paris in 1951 and took part in numerous abstract art displays. One-man show at the Palais des Beaux-Arts, Brussels, in 1955. "The mainspring of Tabuchi's art is probably not the antagonism of the elements—real or imaginary—but their secret complicity under the vigilant control of man, who is not for all his special position, however, allowed to mislead." (Édouard Jaguer).

TAEUBER-ARP Sophie (b. in Davos, Switzerland, in 1889; d. in Zurich, 1943). Educated in Switzerland, in Munich, and in Hamburg. From 1916 to 1929 was a professor at the School of Arts and Crafts in Zurich. Entered the dada movement in Zurich with Arp whom she married in 1921. Composed mural paintings and stained glass windows in Strasbourg. In Strasbourg also, in 1928, she worked together with Arp and Theo van Doesburg on the remarkable interior decoration of the 'Aubette' *café dansant* (the decorations have since been destroyed). Settled in Meudon, near Paris, with Arp, from 1927 to 1940. Was a member of "Cercle et Carré' and then of 'Abstraction-Création'. Also a member of the Swiss group 'Die Allianz'. In Meudon, from 1937 to 1939, directed the review *Plastique*. Was in Grasse from 1941 to 1943. There she composed lithographs in collaboration with Sonia Delaunay, Arp, and Magnelli. She died accidentally in Zurich.

"Sophie Taeuber belongs already to the second generation of abstract artists: her

ARP AND SOPHIE TAEUBER-ARP.
COMPOSITION. 1942.

first works, dated 1916, water-colours and coloured crayon drawings composed of rectangles, no longer have the experimental and haphazard characteristics of the works of the preceding generation, 1900-1912. One can no longer discern the least trace of the troubled struggle for victory over the object. With logical calm, Sophie Taeuber already combines in her first works the rectangular form or rhythmical element derived from cubism, with pure colour or the melodic element, established by Delaunay. The fusion of formal rhythm and coloured melody—with an evident predominance of rhythm — characterises all the work of Sophie Taeuber. The progress of her work was but the development of the same themes, untroubled and continually enriched." (Georg Schmidt). — *Bibl.* Schmidt and others: *Sophie Taeuber-Arp* (a monograph, Basel 1948); Seuphor: *L'Art abstrait, ses origines, ses premiers maîtres* (Paris 1949); Arp: *On my way* (New York 1948); *Onze peintres vus par Arp* (Zurich 1949); Arp: *Jalons,* chez l'Auteur (Meudon 1951); *Catalogue of the Sophie Taeuber-Arp exhibition,* Sidney Janis Gallery (New York 1950); 'Art d'Aujourd'hui' (Paris, May-June 1950; December 1951; December 1953); Seuphor: *Mission spirituelle de l'art* (Paris 1953); *A Dictionary of Modern Painting* (Methuen, London 1956).

TAL COAT. SIGN AND RETURN. 1952.
Galerie Maeght, Paris.

TAL COAT Pierre (b. Clohars-Carnoët, Brittany, 1905). His parents were fishermen. Under the influence of the French and foreign painters who frequented the fishing-village where he was born, his vocation was awakened early. Worked in a pottery factory in Quimper. Came to Paris at the age of nineteen. Spent some time in Burgundy and in Provence. Had a number of one-man shows at the Galerie de France, after 1943; at the Galerie Maeght in 1954. Lives in Paris or in Aix-en-Provence. Tal Coat has many times revealed undeniable affinities with Picasso. In recent works, he has drawn the best of his inspiration from Cézanne. Glistening lines, voluntarily hesitant, furtive, seeking only to skim lightly but surely, seeking not to ring out but to sharpen hearing by a whisper of such quality that it will last. — Bibl. *Derrière le Miroir,* Galerie Maeght (Paris, April 1954).

TANAKA Shu (b. Tokyo, 1908). Attended the École Normale Supérieure. Then, travelled in England, Belgium, China, Egypt, Italy, and Holland. Took part in exhibitions in Japan and in Paris. Lives in Paris.

TANCREDI (b. Feltre, Italy). Academic schooling in Italy. For some time he practised the 'automatic' painting advocated by the surrealists. One-man show in Venice, at the Gallery Sandri. A member of the Italian 'Pittori spaziali' group. Lives in Venice.

TAPIES Antonio (b. Barcelona, 1923). Broke up his law studies in order to devote himself to painting. In 1948, a co-founder of the review and the group *Dau al set,* in Barcelona. Was in Paris in 1950 and 1951 and travelled in Belgium and in Holland. Spent a short time in New York in 1953, while his works were exhibited at the Martha Jackson Gallery. Numerous one-man shows in Spain. First Paris one-man show at the Galerie Stadler,

1956. Lives in Barcelona. From various influences more or less absorbed (Miro, Dubuffet) Tapies has been able to evolve an intense and deeply dramatic art, incantatory in effect. — *Bibl.* Michel Tapié: *Antonio Tapies et l'œuvre complète,* Galerie Stadler (Paris 1956).

TATAFIORE Guido (b. Naples, 1919). Attended the Art Institute in Naples. Many one-man shows in Naples. Included in the 'Arte Astratta e Concreta in Italia' exhibition, at the Museum of Modern Art, Rome 1951. Lives in Naples.

TESTA Clorindo (b. Naples 1923). He emigrated to Argentine at an early age. First travelled and studied in Europe from 1949 to 1951. First one-man show in 1951, in Buenos Aires, followed by many others in the main cities of Argentine. Included in 1953 in the 'Eight Argentine Abstract Painters' show at the Municipal Museum in Amsterdam. Lives in Buenos Aires.

THIELER Fred (b. Königsberg, East Prussia, in 1916). Studied medicine (1937-1941) and began to paint. Attended the School of Fine Arts in Munich (1946-1948). Was in Paris in 1951 and 1952. One-man shows in Amsterdam, Galerie Le Canatd (1951); in Paris, Galerie Suzanne Michel (1953); in Munich, Ophir Gallery (1953); in Oslo, Gallery of Modern Art (1954). A member of the 'Zen 49' group. Included in the exhibition 'Peintures et Sculptures non-figuratives en Allemagne d'Aujourd'hui' at the Cercle Volney, Paris, 1955. Lives in Munich. Abstract neo-expressionism expressed in turbulent visions of a universe in violent disintegration. "Thieler is one of the few post-war artists to have attained a substantial place in the artistic life of modern Germany." (J. A. Thwaites).

TINGUELY Jean (b. in Basel, 1925). Attended the School of Fine Arts in Basel (1940-1944). At first a painter, but from 1944 on, devoted himself to the study of movement in space. One-man show of mobiles, Galerie Arnaud, Paris 1954. Took part the same year in the Salon des Réalités Nouvelles. A member of the group 'Espace'. Was extensively represented in the exhibition 'Le Mouvement' at the Galerie Denise René, Paris 1955. Lives in Paris.

TOBEY Mark (b. in Centerville, Wisconsin, 1890). A self-educated painter. Came to New York in 1911: spent half his time in New York and half in Chicago. Was in Seattle in 1923: taught two years at the Cornish School. Then travelled

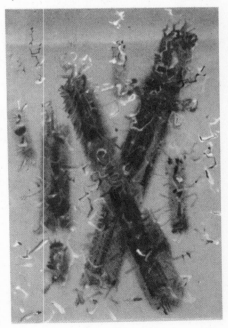

TOBEY. COMPOSITION. 1955.
Galerie Rive Droite, Paris.

to Europe and the Near East. Returned to Seattle in 1927. Was in England from 1931 to 1938. Travelled throughout Europe, in Mexico, in Asia. Studied chinese calligraphy in China. Between all these travels, his fixed residence was in England. In 1939, he returned again to Seattle where he is still living today. First exhibition at the Knoedler Gallery, New York, in 1917. Since 1944, he exhibited regularly at the Willard Gallery, New York. In 1951, took part in the 'Abstract Painting and Sculpture in America' exhibition at the Museum of Modern Art, New York. The same year, a retrospective exhibition of his works was held at the Whitney Museum, New York. Was in Europe in 1954 and 1955. Took part in various exhibitions, particularly at the Galerie Rive Droite and the Museum of Modern Art, Paris. One-man shows in London and Paris (Galerie Jeanne Bucher, 1955).

One may wonder why some works of small format — gouaches, water-colours, drawings—of Klee or Tobey, seem much more convincing to us than the vast compositions of Riopelle, Mathieu, Pollock, or Sam Francis. It must be because inflated language overreaches its goal and lacks zest. The spectacle of animal power, even magnificently endowed physically, always leaves us with a nostalgia for perfume, for inwardness, in spite of the spell of pure size. The restraint of Tobey or Klee touches us more because true eloquence comes from the heart, and the heart is a seed slow to mature.

"Our ground today is not so much the national or the regional ground as it is the understanding of this single earth. The earth has been round for some time now, but not in man's relations to man nor in the understanding of the arts of each as a part of that roundness. As usual we have occupied ourselves too much with the outer, the objective, at the expense of the inner world wherein the true roundness lies. America more than any other country is placed geographically to lead in this understanding, and if from past methods of behavior she has constantly looked toward Europe, today she must assume her position, Janus-faced, toward Asia, for in not too long a time the waves of the Orient shall wash heavily upon her shores. All this is deeply related with her growth in the arts, particularly upon the Pacific slopes. Of this I am aware. Naturally my work will reflect such a condition and so it is not surprising to me when an Oriental responds to a painting of mine as well as an American or a European." (Tobey).— *Bibl.* Janis : *Abstract and Surrealist Art in America* (New York 1944); *Fourteen Americans* (New York 1946); Hitchcock: *Painting towards Architecture* (New York 1948); *40 American Painters, 1904-1950* (U. of Minnesota, 1951); Ritchie: *Abstract Painting and Sculpture in America* (New York 1951); Catalogue of the Tobey exhibition at the Whitney Museum (New York 1951); Hess: *Abstract Painting* (New York 1951); Barr: *Masters of Modern Art* (New York 1954); Alvard: *Tobey, 'Cimaise'*

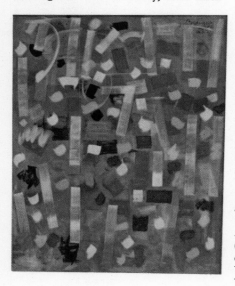

TOMLIN. NUMBER. 4. 1952.

(Paris, May 1955); Flanner: *Tobey, mystique errant,* 'L'Œil' (Paris, June 1955).

TOMLIN Bradley-Walker (b. Syracuse, New York, 1899; d. New York, 1953). Attended the University of Syracuse. Spent some years in Europe after 1921. Taught for about ten years in a New York college (1932-1941). One-man shows since 1924, particularly at the Rehn Gallery and the Betty Parsons Gallery, New York. After having painted a long time in the cubist manner, Tomlin turned toward the calligraphic style characteristic of his work about 1946. The work he left, which is very close in spirit to Tobey's, although somewhat less *intimate,* somewhat less restrained, will always remain very significant. The surfaces covered with dancing signs, both precise and supple, are feasts of the free spirit which, plastically, vocalizes, alliterates, invents, associates, organizes. — *Bibl.* Ritchie: *Abstract Painting and Sculpture in America* (New York 1951); Hess: *Abstract Painting* (New York 1951); *Fifteen Americans* (New York 1952); Barr: *Masters of Modern Art* (New York 1954); *50 ans d'art aux États-Unis,* Museum of Modern Art (Paris 1955).

TRIER Hann (b. Dusseldorf, 1915). Attended the School of Fine Arts in Dusseldorf (1934-1938). The brother of the art-critic Edouard Trier. Travelled in France, Holland, Italy, Switzerland, Spain, Colombia. A member of the German group 'Zen 49'. Took part in numerous art displays in Germany. Lives in Cologne. "Sceptical, but very open and eager for new experiences, Hann Trier is by no means an artist who paints according to set rules. The contours vibrate and each form is pregnant with unexpected possibilities. This instability in composition may reflect the spiritual situation of our time, where objects and concepts change every day; for us, indeed, reality is no longer constant, but a dynamic process." (Gert Schiff).

TROKES Heinz (b. Hamborn, on the Rhine, 1913). Worked under Johannes Itten and Georg Muche at the Bauhaus of Dessau. One-man shows in Amsterdam, Zurich, Paris, Brussels, Berlin. Lives in the Balearic Islands.

TRYGGVADOTTIR. PAINTING. 1955.

TRYGGVADOTTIR Nina (b. in Seydisfjordur, Iceland, 1913). Attended the Royal Academy in Copenhagen (1935-1939), and spent some time in Paris. Returned to Iceland and took part in a number of exhibitions in Reykjavik. Was in New York in 1943 in order to complete her art studies. She worked under Fernand Léger and Hans Hofmann. First one-man show at the New Art Circle, New York, 1945. Married the American painter Alcopley (cf. that name) in 1949. Was in Paris in 1952. One-man show at the Galerie Colette Allendy, Paris 1954, in Brussels (Palais des Beaux-Arts), and in Copenhagen. Took part in the Salon des Réalités Nouvelles and in numerous other group-shows. Lives now in Paris. Nina Tryggvadottir's art is sober and powerful. She composes cyclopean walls, from which the weight melts into colour; from which even, occasionally, the stones themselves escape into the sky. One also knows her collages, with their multiple and strong black veins, which could be cartoons for unexpectedly archaic stained glass windows. She is without question the most striking personality of her country in the field of plastic arts.

TSINGOS Thanos (b. Eleusis, Greece, 1914). Began to paint at the age of seventeen. In 1936, received a diploma in architecture and engineering from the Polytechnical School in Athens. Was an architect in Greece up to the war. From 1939 to 1946, fought in the Greek army. Joined the allied Armies on the El Alamein front. After the war, he settled in Paris and took up painting again. One-man show in Paris, Studio Facchetti, 1952. He took part in the Salon des Réalités Nouvelles and numerous other group-shows. Lives in Paris. A black lyricism, lineary effusions cut deep in the mass of fresh paint. In his recent work, Tsingos shows a desire for clarity and organization.

TSUJI Futoshi (b. Gifu, Japan, 1925). Exhibited at the "Institute of Calligraphy considered as an art-form" in 1950 and with the Kei-Sei-Kai school in 1952. A member of the Bokubi and Bokusin group of modern calligraphies (Shiryu Morita).

Took part in all the exhibitions organised by the group in various Museums of Europe (Amsterdam, Basel, Paris) and at the Museum of Modern Art, New York. Lives in Japan.

TURAN Selim (b. Istanbul, 1915). Attended the Academy of Fine Arts in Istanbul. Travelled in Germany, France, England, Greece, Italy, Turkey. One-man show at the Galerie Breteau, Paris, 1950. First non-representational canvas in 1945. Took part in the Salon des Réalités Nouvelles since 1947. Lives in Paris.

TURCATO Giulio (b. Mantua, Italy, 1912). Was a member of the 'Forma I' group and took part in numerous group-shows in Italy and various other countries. Lives in Rome.

TWORKOV Jack (b. Biala, Poland, 1900). Came to the United States in 1913. Attended Columbia University 1920-1923. Spent some time at the Art Students League and the National Academy of Design. Exhibited at the Dudensing Gallery, New York, from 1931 to 1935, at the Egan Gallery, New York, since 1947. Took part in numerous group-shows throughout America. Taught at various colleges since 1948. Lives in New York. Abstract impressionism in a harsh and sometimes very violent style. — *Bibl.* Hess: *Abstract Painting* (New York 1951); *Art News* (New York, May 1953).

U

UBAC Rodolphe Raoul (b. Malmédy, Belgium, 1910). At first wanted to become a Forestry Inspector. Came to Paris in 1929, entered the Classics Department at the Sorbonne, but soon deserted the University in order to attend the Grande Chaumière in Montparnasse. Travelled extensively in Europe. Practised surrealistic photography for some time. A member of the surrealist group in 1934; but about 1942, abandoned surrealism and photography, and devoted himself exclusively to painting and drawing, progressing more and more towards abstract art. From then on, one of his favourite materials was cut and engraved slate. One-man shows at the Galerie Maeght, Paris 1950 and 1955. Lives in Paris. — *Bibl.* Frenaud: *Une peinture tragique,* 'Derrière le Miroir', nº 34 (Paris 1950); *Premier bilan de l'art actuel* (Paris 1953); *Raoul Ubac,* 'Derrière le Miroir', nº 74-75-76 (Paris 1955); Frenaud: *La peinture tragique de Raoul Ubac,* 'XXᵉ Siècle' (Paris, June 1956).

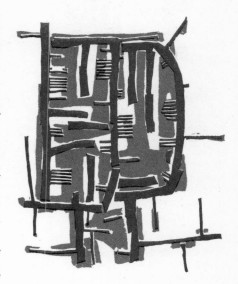

UBAC. WOODCUT. 1956.

V

VAÏTO Agathe (b. Hungary, 1928). Attended the School of Fine Arts in Budapest. Came to Paris in 1949. Took part in the Salon des Surindépendants (1951 and 1952), in the Salon de Mai and the Salon d'Octobre (1954), as well as in a group-show at the Galerie de France, in 1956. Lives in Paris.

VALENSI Henry (b. Algiers, 1883). The founder and the director since 1932 of the 'Association des Artistes Musicalistes', in Paris. Travelled extensively in Europe and Africa. Included in the Salon des Indépendants since 1907. Organized twenty-three Salons of 'Musicalist painting' in Paris, in the provinces, and

VALMIER. THE FIVE SENSES. 1931.
Galerie Saint-Augustin, Paris.

abroad. He is the Vice-President of the Salon des Réalités Nouvelles. Lives in Paris. Allegorical compositions in bright colours.

VALMIER Georges (b. Angoulême, · France, 1885; d. Paris, 1937). Attended the École des Beaux-Arts in Paris in 1905. Afterwards worked on his own. Was drafted in the 1914-1918 war. Exhibited in Paris in 1921. Designed a number of decors for Marinetti's futurist plays. An excellent musician, he made a living as a choir-master. His last works were decorations for the Exposition Universelle, Paris 1937. Starting from cubism, and henceforth from objective reality, Valmier's work is often transposed as far as abstraction. Among his best compositions one must count those now at the Solomon R. Guggenheim Museum in New York. They

were painted between 1919 and 1923 and most of them have musical titles (*Fugue, Scherzo, Improvisation*).

VANBER Albert (b. Lestre, France, 1905). Studied at the School of Fine Arts in Paris, under Cormon and Pierre Laurens. One-man show of abstract works at the Galerie Suzanne Michel, Paris 1953. Took part in the Salon des Réalités Nouvelles the same year. Lives in Paris.

VANNI Sam (b. Viborg, Finland, 1908). Attended the School of Fine Arts in Helsinki (1927-1928). Studied under the sculptor W. Aaltonen in 1930. Travelled many times in France and in Italy. Numerous one-man shows in Finland. Abstract painting since 1948. Took part in group-shows in Paris, Rome, Stockholm, Oslo, Copenhagen, and Reykjavik. Lives in Helsinki.

VANTONGERLOO Georges (b. Antwerp, 1886). Attended the Academies of Antwerp and Brussels. At first a sculptor. Was drafted in the Belgian army in 1914, and imprisoned in Holland after the fall of Antwerp. Met Theo van Doesburg in 1916. Co-signer of the *De Stijl* manifesto and a contributor to the *De Stijl* review during the first years of its publication (1917-1920). Was in Menton from 1919 to 1927, then settled in Paris. Friendships with Mondrian and Seuphor, later with Max Bill and Pevsner. Took part in the 'Cercle et Carré' exhibition in 1930. The founder with Herbin of the 'Abstraction-Création' group (1931). After having for a long time followed—as well in his painting as in his sculpture—the fundamental horizontal-vertical principle of *De Stijl*, Vantongerloo adopted the curve about 1935, and from there turned to the study of the 'indeterminate'. Nevertheless the basis of his works remains almost always mathematical, sometimes elaborately so. More than sixty of his works were exhibited in 1949 at the Kunsthaus of Zurich together with works by Pevsner and Max Bill. Lives in Paris. — *Bibl.* Vantongerloo: *L'art et son avenir* (Antwerp 1924); Barr: *Cubism and Abstract Art* (New York 1936); Vantongerloo: *Paintings, Sculptures, Reflexions* (New York 1948); Seuphor: *L'Art abstrait, ses origines, ses premiers maîtres* (Paris 1949); Catalogue of the Zurich exhibition (1949); Catalogue of the retrospective *De Stijl* exhibition (Amsterdam 1951).

VARAUD Serge (b. near Lyons in 1925; d. in Toulon, 1956). First abstract works in 1948. Exhibited in Toulon in 1948 and in Paris in 1949. He founded a group of abstract painters in Toulon and organised exhibitions in his own studio to encourage them. "To the calm of the horizontal, to the spirituality of the vertical, join the two sources of life: the curve with its feminine gentleness and the diagonal with its masculine purpose. Out of the coloured life of harmonies, contrasts, and dissonances, create a work where feeling expression can gain completeness with a minimum of constraint." (Varaud).

VARDANEGA G. (b. Possagno, near Venice, 1923). Attended the School of Fine Arts in Buenos Aires. In 1946, became a mem-

ber of the Argentine group 'Arte Concreto-Invencion'. Travelled in Europe 1948-1949. Spent a year in Paris and returned to Buenos Aires where he continues to investigate painting on glass and construction in space. Lives in Buenos Aires.

VASARELY Victor (b. Pecs, Hungary, 1908). Was enrolled at the School of Medecine in Budapest but classes in anatomy of the nude, at the Podolini-Volkman Academy, attracted him more. In 1929 he entered the Bauhaus of Budapest: the 'Mühely' of Bortnyik. He attended lectures by Moholy-Nagy and was introduced to the works of Malevitch, Mondrian, Gropius, Kandinsky, Le Corbusier. Settled in Paris at the end of 1930. A member of the Galerie Denise René group since its foundation in 1944. Took part in the Salon des Surindépendants, the Salon des Réalités Nouvelles, the Salon de Mai. One-man shows in Budapest (1930, 1933), in Copenhagen (1950), in Stockholm (1952),

VASARELY. YELLAN. 1950. *Galerie Denise René, Paris.*

in Brussels (1954), and at the Galerie Denise René, Paris (1944, 1946, 1949, 1952, 1955).

"The ways of abstract painting are not easy ones. One does not create a new universe overnight without abandoning tender sentimental habits: I mean, without regret for a representational training. One has to harden oneself, learn a way of life for which there exists no tradition, foster affections between unknown forms, invent a world of emotions without previous example, and never, never lose grip. This is the climate in which Vasarely casts off his old self, with that brilliant austerity which endows his compositions with a characteristic note of heroism." (Léon Degand). — Bibl. *Témoignages pour l'art abstrait* (Paris 1952); Dewasne: *Vasarely,* Presses Littéraires de France (Paris 1952); Catalogue exposition Galerie Denise René, 1955.

BRAM VAN VELDE. COMPOSITION. 1955.

VEDOVA Emilio (b. Venice, 1919). Self-educated. Began to exhibit in 1936. His painting passed through periods of cubism and expressionism before it attained abstraction. He travelled across Italy, living among the workers and the poor. Hostile to Fascism, he took part in the battles of the Liberation. Was the promoter in Venice of the New Front of the Arts (1946). One-man shows in all the main cities of Italy as well as in New York (Viviano Gallery) and in Munich (Gallery Günther Franke). Took part in the Venice Biennales and numerous other Salons in Italy, in France, in Germany, in South America. He travelled to Paris, Brazil, Vienna, Germany. Lives in Venice.

"For Vedova, painting is a conception of the world, the very image of the eternal conflict between being and non-being, good and evil. It is not the primary forces of the cosmos which fuse and explode in his paintings, but the deep impulses of the human soul." (Giulio Carlo Argan). — *Bibl.* Mazzariol: *Appunti sulla poetica di Emilio Vedova,* 'I 4 Soli' (Turin, Nov. 1955).

VELDE Bram van (b. Zonderwonde, Holland, 1895). A very difficult early life in Leyden and The Hague. A house painter, then a decorator in a luxury-shop. His employer helped him to get to Paris (about 1924) so as to study painting. Spent some time in the Balearic Islands. Returned to Paris in 1936. Included in the Salon des Indépendants and the Salon des Surindépendants. One-man shows at the Galerie Mai (1946), the Galerie Maeght (1952), and the Galerie Warren (1955). Lives in Paris. Supple forms integrated into each other; a sinuous line (baroque) but without anguish. The colour is light (blues, greens, whites) and seems to float in a timeless, limpid, atmosphere, deeply fraught with human sensibility. — Bibl. *Derrière le Miroir,* nº 11-12 and 43 (Paris 1948 and 1952).

VEDOVA. SKETCH FOR "RÉVOLTE". GOUACHE. 1951. *Private Collection.*

VERONESI
Luigi (b. Milan, 1908). In 1934, a member of the 'Abstraction-Création' group in Paris. One-man shows in Milan and Paris in 1939. Produced abstract films. Took part in various abstract art displays in Italy, particularly at the Galleria del Milione (as early as 1935). Lives in Milan.

VELDE Geer van (b. Lisse, Holland, 1898). Brother of the preceding painter. Came to Paris in 1925. Exhibited at the Salon des Indépendants in 1926 and 1930. First one-man show in London, Gallery Guggenheim Jr., in 1938. From 1939 to 1945, was in Cagnes-sur-Mer. One-man shows at the Galerie Maeght, Paris 1946 and 1952. Took part in the Salon d'Automne, the Salon des Tuileries and the Salon de Mai. Exhibited at the Kootz Gallery, New York, together with his brother, in 1948. He has had and still has a great influence upon younger painters. Lives in Paris. Playfully rigorous compositions, the principal element of which is a sure knowledge of the harmony of nuances. "Van Velde's gay colours and Impressionist taste for gentle diffused tones often recall the painting of Villon" (Frank Elgar). — Bibl. *Derrière le Miroir,* nº 11-12 and 51 (Paris); *Premier Bilan de l'art actuel,* Paris 1953.

VEZELAY Paule (b. Southern England, 1893). Educated in London. At first illustrated books for English publishers. First exhibition in 1921, at the Gallery Dorian Leigh, London. Was in Paris from 1923 to 1939; first abstract paint-

GEER VAN VELDE. COMPOSITION. 1953.

ing in 1928. A member of 'Abstraction-Création' in 1934. Included in the Salon des Surindépendants from 1929 to 1939 and in numerous exhibitions of abstract art. On the committee of the Salon des Réalités Nouvelles. Main one-man shows: Galerie Jeanne Bucher, Paris 1928, 1932, 1934, 1937, 1946; Galerie Lefevre, London, 1936, 1942; Galerie Colette Allendy, Paris 1950; Gimpel fils Gallery, London 1950. Lives in London. Few artists illustrate as well as Paule Vézelay the many-sidedness of art. She has practised painting, sculpture, collages, compositions with stretched strings, drawing, engraving. Her work has a discreet charm, a childish and yet very elegant purity. — *Bibl.* 'Art d'Aujourd'hui', Paris, December 1954.

VICENTE Esteban (b. Spain, 1906). From 1928 to 1935, exhibited in Madrid, Barcelona, Paris, London. First exhibition in New York, 1937, at the Kleeman Galleries. Took part in numerous group-shows in various New York galleries, as well as in 'Aspects de la Peinture Américaine', Galerie de France, Paris 1952. Lives in New York. Surfaces freely organized by a lyricism of colour. The improvisation is only on the surface; there is a true discipline in the combination of lines, forms, and colours. Vicente has composed collages possessing a surprising density of forms and colours. — *Bibl.* Hess: *Abstract Painting* (New York 1951).

VIEIRA DA SILVA Maria Elena (b. Lisbon, 1908). Came to Paris at the age of nineteen to study sculpture under Bourdelle and Despiau. Then attended the studios of Friesz and Léger, and Hayter's engraving workshop. In 1930, she married the Hungarian painter Arpad Szenès. Travelled extensively in Europe. Was in South America during the Second World War. Came back to Paris in 1947. One-man shows at the Galerie Jeanne Bucher since 1933, at the Galerie Pierre since 1949. Numerous exhibitions in London. She

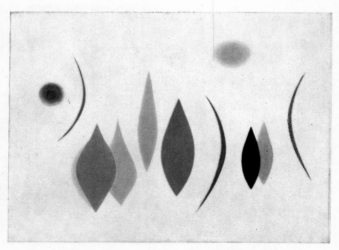

VÉZELAY. COMPOSITION. 1954. *M. S. Collection Paris.*

takes part regularly in the Salon de Ma. Lives in Paris.

Little by little, through embellishment of her familiar theme, Vieira da Silva has created an exceptional art, a rare type of painting. Something is there that was never expressed before: a space without dimensions, both limited and boundless, a hallucinating mosaic where each element is endowed with an inner power transcending its own matrix. Each touch of paint is charged with restrained dynamism, but the whole canvas reveals potency. The art of Mondrian was pure style, that of Van Gogh pure anguish. In Vieira da Silva, style and the cry of the heart are simultaneously present in each work, closely involved in each minute of it. It is a hymn of restraint and invention: rigour and freedom in an exalting marriage. — *Bibl.* Descargues: *Vieira da Silva* (Paris 1949); Seuphor: *Promenade autour de Vieira da Silva,* 'Cahiers d'Art', n⁰ 2 (Paris 1949); Grenier: *Vieira da Silva,* 'L'Œil' (Paris, Feb. 1956); Guéguen: *Vieira da Silva,* 'XXᵉ Siècle' (Paris, June 1950).

VILLALBA V. (b. Canary Islands, 1925). Attended the Academy of Fine Arts in Buenos Aires. Has taken part in the group-shows of 'Arte Concreto - Invencion' since 1946. Lives in Buenos Aires.

VILLERI Jean (b. Oneglia, Italy, 1898). Came to France in 1906. At first an impressionist painter in the South of France. A member of the 'Abstraction-Création' group in 1932. Took part in the Salon des Tuileries, the Salon des Réalités Nouvelles, the Salon de Mai. One-man show at the Galerie Maeght in 1948. Included in a number of group-shows in Germany, Belgium, Brazil, and the United States. Lives in Cagnes-sur-Mer (on the Riviera) and travels frequently to Paris. Villeri is a painter of great culture. His work, like that of most painters, is torn in the constant contradiction between improvisation and the desire for structure. His most successful canvases are those where the struggle remains visible.

VIEIRA DA SILVA. SPACE ASLEEP. 1954. *Galerie J. Bucher, Paris.*

VILLON. RACEHORSE. 1922. *Galerie Louis Carré, Paris.*

VILLON Jacques (b. Damville, Normandy, in 1875). His real name is Gaston Duchamp; he is the brother of the sculptor Raymond Duchamp-Villon, and of Marcel Duchamp. Attended the École des Beaux-Arts and studied under Cormon about 1894. For a long time he contributed cartoons to the comic papers of the period. A member of the Salon d'Automne. First exhibited with Duchamp-Villon in Rouen, 1905. Joined the cubist movement in 1911. It was in his studio in Puteaux that the group 'Section d'Or' assembled: the principal members were Léger, Picabia, La Fresnaye, Metzinger, and Gleizes. Was mobilised during the First World War. First abstract paintings in 1919, Included in the exhibitions of the Société Anonyme, in New York, from 1922 on. From 1921 to 1930, to make a living, he engraved a series of coloured reproductions of modern paintings, often very remarkable. New period of abstract painting from 1931 to 1933. In the United States in 1935. Took part in the 'Réalités Nouvelles' exhibition at the Galerie Charpentier, Paris 1939. Since the Liberation, he has exhibited regularly at the Galerie Carré, Paris. Lives in Puteaux, near Paris.

As with Klee, only a fraction of Villon's work belongs to abstract art, but more than Klee's, each of Villon's works is on the way to abstraction. He has written: "Modern painting is a painting of creation, a painting of rhythms and volumes. In order to satisfy the exigencies of this painting, one must extract rhythms and volumes from the subject, as one extracts a diamond from its matrix." Villon's painting may seem light, puny, superficial. But the quick look is more mistaken than ever: here is a compact and measured world of which the painter has counted all the riches, probed all the dimensions, without overlooking the most secret. A world both solid and supple, like a tree—as vibrant and dense as a tree. — *Bibl.* Barr: *Cubism and Abstract Art* (New York 1936); *Art of this Century* (New York 1942); Paul Éluard et René Jean: *Jacques Villon ou l'Art Glorieux* (Paris 1948); 'Art d'Aujourd'hui' (Paris, Dec. 1949); *Collection of the Société Anonyme* (New York 1950); Raynal: *De Picasso au Surréalisme* (Paris-Geneva 1950); *A Dictionary of Modern Painting* (Methuen, London 1956); Seuphor: *Klee et Villon* 'Preuves' (Paris, June 1955). Catalogue of the exhibition at the Musée de Saint-Étienne, 1957.

VISEUX Claude (b. Paris 1927). Studied architecture at the École des Beaux-Arts in Paris. First non-representational paintings in 1950. Took part in numerous Salons and group-shows in Paris and abroad. Lives in Paris. "I envisaged a kind of landscape-portrait, like a crowd where everyone shouts at the top of his voice; an infinite paroxysm, blinding the very one who thought he could see." (Viseux, in an interview with Julien Alvard).

VORDEMBERGE- GILDEWART Friedrich (b. Osnabrück, Germany, in 1899). Studied architecture and sculpture in Hanover. Was a constructivist painter from the beginning (1919). Since 1924, a member of the 'Sturm' (Berlin) and the 'Stijl' (Holland). Was in Paris 1925-1926. Returned to Paris in 1929 and had a one-man show at the Galerie Povolotsky. Took part in the exhibition 'Cercle et Carré', Paris 1930. A member of 'Abstraction-Création' (1932). Was in Berlin 1936-1937; in Zurich the following year, then in Amsterdam. Became a Dutch citizen. Included in numerous avant-garde exhibitions in Europe and the United States, and in the 'Premiers Maîtres de l'Art abstrait' show at the Galerie Maeght, Paris 1949. One-man shows in Cologne and Ulm (1955), in Zurich and Rio de Janeiro (1956). Since 1955, a professor at the Hochschule für Gestaltung in Ulm.

Lives in Ulm. He has written many books, particularly an album on Kandinsky (published by Duwaer, Amsterdam).

VOSSEN André van der (b. Haarlem, Holland, 1893). First studied lithography. Attended a school of Industrial Art in Haarlem. Began to paint in 1928. At first an impressionist, then progressively came to abstraction. His work is non-representational since 1946. Took part in numerous group-shows in Amsterdam, The Hague, Brussels, in the Salon des Réalités Nouvelles (Paris). Lives in Overveen, near Haarlem.

VULLIAMY Gérard (b. Paris, 1909, of Swiss parents). Studied advertising, decoration, stage-designing, engraving. Began to paint in 1928 (landscape and still life). Spent three years at the Academy Lhote. Launched into abstraction in 1932 and joined the 'Abstraction-Création' group. First one-man show at

VORDEMBERGE-GILDEWART. COMPOSITION NO. 180. 1950.
Th. Bally Collection, Montreux.

VULLIAMY. PAINTING. 1953. *Galerie Benador, Geneva.*

ature can have their say in that mode." Joined the Swiss group 'Die Allianz'. One-man show at the Galerie Jeanne Bucher, Paris 1948. Reverted to a fresco-technique while studying graphic and spatial movement. Took part in the Salon des Réalités Nouvelles and the Salon de Mai. Exhibited in Bern and in Basel (1949) together with Gérard Schneider. One-man show at the Galerie Roque, Paris, 1952. Lives in Paris. Very luminous abstract impressionism: the colours vibrate in space, yellow often predominating like a rioting sun. Vulliamy eschews black, even sombre colours. — *Bibl.* Gindertaël: *Propos sur la peinture actuelle* (Paris 1955).

the Galerie Pierre, Paris 1953; abstract canvases the technique of which recalls that of fresco-painting. Then attracted by surrealism. He left the movement in 1937. "I think then that there is no real opening for painting in surrealism; only poetry and liter-

WARB Nicolaas (b. Amsterdam, 1906). Her actual name is Sophie Warburg. Studied at the Academy of Amsterdam. In Paris in 1928. Frequented various academies in Montparnasse. For some time, she was very much under the influence of Vantongerloo. She moved away from it and progressed toward a constructivism to which she added elements of her own invention which gave it sometimes a poetic and spontaneous touch. Took part in the Salon des Réalités Nouvelles since 1946. One-man shows at the Galerie Creuze (1947) and the Galerie Colette Allendy (1954). Took part in numerous exhibitions of abstract art in France, Holland, and other countries. Lives in Paris. — *Bibl.* Warb: *Aperçus et pensées sur la peinture abstraite* (Paris 1942).

WEBB Marie (b. Sydney, 1901). Attended a non-institutional school of painting in Sydney, about 1930. Took part in various exhibitions in Australia from 1936 on. First one-man show in Sidney, 1945. Was in London in 1947. In Paris, 1949, she launched out into abstraction. One-man shows at the Galerie Colette Allendy (1950) and the Galerie Suzanne Michel (1953). Exhibited many times at the Salon des Réalités Nouvelles as well as in various Parisian displays. Lives in Paris.

WEBER Hugo (b. Basel, 1918). Studied in Basel and in Paris: painting and sculpture. Moholy-Nagy appointed him a professor at the Institute of Design in Chicago (1946). Afterwards, a professor at the Illinois Institute of Technology. Numerous exhibitions in the United States, Canada, France, Switzerland, Norway, Lebanon. Lives in Chicago. "I like to call my approach to painting 'energetic'. I work fast in a semi-automatic manner, with a feeling for the total expanse of the flat area. I attempt a balance of physical and psychic sensation, like a dancer might do. The results are open forms, fluid spatial structures; vision in flux." (Weber).

WEBER Max (b. Bialystok, Russia, 1881). Came to the United States in 1891. Attended the Pratt Institute from 1898 to 1901. Studied in various Paris academies from 1905 to 1908. He studied under Henri Matisse, together with Bruce and A. B. Frost, about 1907. Included in the Salon des Indépendants and the Salon d'Automne. Returned to the United States in 1908. First one-man show at the Haas Gallery, New York, in 1909. Greatly influenced by cubism, Max Weber attained complete abstraction in a series of paintings dated 1915, the inspiration of which comes from the landscapes and the atmosphere of New York. After 1918, he reverted to representational painting. Lives in New York. — *Bibl.* Cahill: *Max Weber* (New York 1930); *Collection of the Société anonyme* (Yale University 1950).

WELLS John (b. Penzance, Cornwall, 1909). Studied medicine. Was a doctor until 1946. Then, devoted himself exclusively to painting. Was greatly influenced by the sculptor Gabo, while the latter lived in England. One-man shows in London (1948) and in New York (1952). Lives in Saint Ives (Cornwall).

WARB. MYSELF SECRET. 1955. *Mills Collection, Paris.*

WERKMAN. TYPOGRAPHICAL COMPOSITION.
1928.

WENDT François Willi (b. Berlin, 1909). Studied philosophy and art history at college from 1928 to 1934. First non-representational paintings in 1932. In Paris since 1937. Studied six months in Léger's studio, took part in a group-show and met Kandinsky, Delaunay, Freundlich, Hartung, Poliakoff. Included in the Salon des Surindépendants, the Salon des Réalités Nouvelles, the Salon d'Octobre, and in numerous other group-shows. One-man show at the Galerie Colette Allendy in 1951. Lives in Paris. Wendt's work is varied, but always marked by a concern for balance and quiet distinction. There is more discipline than effusion, more style than anguish. The colours are generally light, but not aggressively so. The light is diffuse, more interior than dazzling. — *Bibl.* Gindertaël: *Propos sur la peinture actuelle* (Paris 1955).

WERKMAN Hendrik Nicolaas (b. Leens, 1882; d. Groningen, 1945, in Holland). At first a journalist, then a printer in Groningen, Werkman began to paint at the age of thirty five. About 1923, he began using typographical material in printed abstract compositions. At first, he composed his works on large sheets of paper, with blacks and greys. Then, after 1925, he began to use the larger typographical characters (wooden poster characters) as abstract motifs in multicoloured compositions. An exhibition of these works was held at the Galerie Sacre du Printemps, Paris, 1927. At the same period, Werkman published a review of dadaist inspiration,

WENDT. PAINTING. 1955.

The next Call, which he printed himself. He reverted to representational art after 1938. He was shot by the Nazis a few days before the Liberation of Groningen (April 1944).

Werkman was one of the most enterprising minds in Holland between the two wars. His monotypes are those of an artist who does not shrink from adventure, shirks no encounter and always remains receptive. A constructivist influence can be recognized in his first impressions and a certain impressionism softens his later work; but the accent remains highly individual and the spirit uncompromising. — *Bibl.* Catalogue of the H. N. Werkman retrospective exhibition at the Municipal Museum of Amsterdam (Dec. 1945); 'Art d'Aujourd'hui' (Paris, February-March 1952); Catalogue de l'Exposition à la Librairie La Hune (Paris 1952).

WERNER Lambert (b. Stockholm, 1900). Educated in Paris and Berlin. Took part in the Salon des Surindépendants, Paris. One-man shows in Stockholm (Gallery Farg och Form); Paris (Galerie Creuze); Basel (Gallery of Modern Art); Berlin (Gallery Bremer); Brussels (Galerie Apollo); Lucerne (Galerie d'Art National). Lives in Stockholm.

WERNER Theodor (b. near Tübingen, Germany, 1886). Attended the Academy of Stuttgart (1908-1909), travelled extensively, and spent some time in Paris every year. Settled in Paris from 1930 to 1935, then in Potsdam. Werner is one of the most active and most pure exponents of abstract painting in Germany since 1945. Numerous one-man shows in Germany, and in Paris (Galerie des Cahiers d'Art, 1950). A member of the German group 'Zen 49'. Woty Werner, his wife, attended non-institutional academies and studios in Berlin, Munich, and Paris. She is mostly known for the remarkable abstract designs on printed material which she ex-

hibited in Germany and in Paris. Both Theodor and Woty Werner were included in the 'Peinture et Sculpture non-figurative en Allemagne d'Aujourd'hui' exhibition at the Cercle Volney, Paris 1955. They live in Berlin-Charlottenburg. — *Bibl.* 'Art d'Aujourd'hui' (Paris, August 1953); catalogue of the exhibition at the Cercle Volney (Paris 1955).

WESTPFAHL Conrad (b. Berlin, 1891). Studied in Berlin under Orlick (1910-1912), then at the Academy in

THEODOR WERNER. INK DRAWING. 1949.
Private Collection, Paris.

Munich. Stayed extensively in Paris, in Italy, North Africa, and in Greece. Took part in numerous exhibitions of abstract art;

has also published art criticism. Lives in Munich.

WIEGAND Charmion von (b. Chicago, 1900). The daughter of the journalist Karl H. von Wiegand, then the senior American correspondent in Europe. She took an active part in journalism and art criticism. Knew intimately the avant-garde milieu in New York from 1920 on. Met Hartley, Max Weber, Stella, Stuart Davis, etc. Began to paint in 1926, at first in a primitive and fanciful manner. Became a friend of Piet Mondrian when the latter came to New York (1940), and under his direct influence, she launched into geometrical abstraction, after having dropped painting for about a year. One-man shows at the Rose Fried Gallery, New York (1947 and 1948); at the Saidenberg Gallery, New York (1952). A number of other one-man shows in the United States. Since 1947, she took part in the exhibitions of the 'American Abstract Artists' group of which she was elected president in 1951. Travelled in Europe and in Mexico. Lives in New York. — *Bibl.* Seuphor: *La Peinture aux États-Unis,* "Art d'Aujourd'hui" (Paris, June 1951); *The world of Abstract Art,* Wittenborn (New York, 1957).

WINTER Bryan (b. London, 1915). Studied at the Slade School, London. A number of exhibitions in London; exhibited also in Germany, in France, and in New York. A professor at the Bath Academy of Art. Lives in London.

WINTER Fritz (b. Altenbögge, Germany, 1905). Attended the Dessau Bauhaus from 1927 to 1930. Studied under Schlemmer, Kandinsky, and Klee. While he was staying in Berlin, he met and made friends with the constructivist sculptor Gabo. Travelled extensively in Switzerland and in France. Friendship with Kirchner. Gave lectures at the Halle-Saale academy. Was under a Nazi ban while Hitler was in power: his works, classed as 'degenerate art', were taken from the German museums and sold in Zurich (1934) and in London (1938). Made a prisoner in Russia in 1945. When he returned to Germany, he retreated to Diessen-am-Ammersee where he now lives. "We are working on objects and pictures the beginning of which goes back thousands of years. And our present action is addressed to the future. Like obedient servants, we link the beginnings of time to the millenia of the future according to the law of an order directly superior to ours. In painting, form and colour are the expression of consciousness. A new art demands a knowledge and a continuity which the artist must be able to guarantee. He must broaden his inner range. The compass of knowledge makes the grandeur of the style." (Winter). — *Bibl.* Domnick: *Abstrakte Malerei* (Stuttgart 1947).

WOLFF Robert Jay (b. Chicago, 1905). Attended Yale University. Worked as a painter and a sculptor in London (1927), in Paris (1929-1931), then in New York and Chicago (1932-1942). Since 1935, has devoted himself entirely to painting. Numerous one-man or group-shows in New York, Chicago, San Francisco, etc. Took part also in exhibitions in Paris, Munich, Rome, and other European cities. Moholy-Nagy's collaborator in the foundation of the Chicago School of Design (now Institute of Design). Drafted during the Second World War. Then appointed a professor of drawing at Brooklyn College. Now spends half his time in Brooklyn and half in Ridgefield (Connecticut) where he has a studio. Lyrical composition in brief multicoloured touches, a sort of fireworks assembled by an optimistic and sensitive mind.

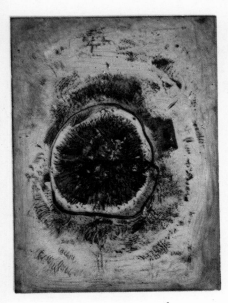

WOLS. PAINTING. 1946.
Jean Paulhan Collection, Paris.

WOLS (b. Berlin, 1913; d. Paris, 1951). His real name was Otto Alfred Schulze Battman. Took the name of Wols in 1937. Spent some time at the Bauhaus, in Dessau, and went to Paris (1932) where he met Miro, Max Ernst, Tzara and Calder (whom he tutored in German). In Spain (1933) he made photographs to earn a living. Returned to France, had an exhibition of photographs and was appointed official photographer for the Exposition Universelle, Paris. At the beginning of the Second World War, was imprisoned for about a year as a German citizen. Once liberated, he kept on painting in the South of France. Became a close friend of Pierre-Henri Roché in Dieulefit. Back in Paris, he met Sartre and Simone de Beauvoir who encouraged him. One-man show at the Galerie Drouin, in 1947. Took part in numerous group-shows in Paris and in Italy. One-man show at the Hugo Gallery New York, in 1950.

When Wols goes beyond literary allusions (the *Villes* series) and lasciviousness (drawings with suggestions of expressionism and surrealism) and attains pure abstraction, his work may sometimes show a great density of nervous energy and exude an extraordinary magnetism. The large paintings composed of an incalculable number of little touches forming one single mass, both changing and homogeneous, are probably among the most powerful and rare works of abstract art. Organized deliriums, states of intellectual ecstasy which seem to have consumed the painter, for he falls back after that into a woolly indecision. Wols also wrote poems: his natural anarchy found a favorable climate in Chinese mysticism. — *Bibl.* Bryen et Roché: *Wols,* Galerie Drouin, (Paris, no date); Guilly: *Wols,* Galerie Drouin (Paris 1947); *I 4 Soli,* no 5 (Turin, Sept. 1955). Wols also illustrated books by Kafka, Artaud, Paulhan, Sartre, etc.

X.Y.Z

XCERON Jean (b. Isari, Greece, 1890). In the United States, 1904. Attended the Corcoran Art School (Washington) from 1910 to 1916, then various New York art-schools. Was in Paris from 1927 to 1937. During that time, he took part in numerous exhibitions in Paris and in various European countries. First one-man show in New York in 1935, followed by many others in a number of cities throughout the United States. One-man shows at the Sidney Janis Gallery, New York, in 1950, and at the Rose Fried Gallery, New York, in 1955. Lives in New York. Xcéron's style is highly individual. His work is strongly built, yet without excessive rigour; there is always a touch of playfulness in the composition which is pleasing to the eye and the mind.

YOUNGERMAN Jack (b. in the United States, 1925). Came to Paris in 1947. Attended the École des Beaux-Arts for a year. Took part in the Salon de Mai, the Salon des Réalités Nouvelles, and the exhibition 'Les Mains éblouies' at the Galerie Maeght, 1950. One-man show at the Galerie Arnaud, Paris 1951. In 1952, took part in a group-show at the Galerie Denise René. Lives in the United States. Free geometries in discreetly coloured swathes.

YUNKERS Adja (b. in Riga, Latvia, 1900). Studied art in Leningrad, Berlin, Paris, and London. One-man shows in the main European and American cities. Taught at the New School for Social Research, New York (1947-1954) and

ZACK. COMPOSITION. 1954.

ZAO-WOU-KI. EARLY OCTOBER. 1955.

summer sessions at the University of New Mexico in 1948 and 1949. Spent 1954-1955 in Europe (Paris and Rome). Yunkers's works are impressions obtained through superimposing wood-cuts: sometimes a great number of colours are attained. His work is rooted in expressionism, but it blossoms out in a skilful and sometimes subtle abstract organization.

ZACK Leon (b. Nijni-Novgorod, Russia, in 1892). Studied classics at the University of Moscow. Attended at the same time schools of painting and design. Was in Italy from 1920 to 1922. After spending a year in Berlin, where he designed sets and costumes for the Russian Romantic Ballets, he came to Paris and settled there (1923). Exhibited at the Salon d'Automne, the Salon des Indépendants, the Salon des Surindépendants (of which he is a founder), and, after 1952, at the Salon de Mai. One-man shows in various Paris galleries since 1926. He took part in many exhibitions in the main European countries. His art passed through various representational periods before it slowly made its way to abstraction. One-man shows of abstract paintings at the Galerie des Garets, Paris (1949), at the Centre Saint-Jacques (1953), and at the Galerie Kléber (1956). Lives in Paris. Monochromatic compositions of very simple geometrical figures and touches, sometimes isolated in the middle of the canvas. A complete stripping of the spirit which tends sometimes toward Malevitch, and sometimes toward a direct expression of sensibility centred around the disposition of the spots.

ZAO WOU-KI (b. Peiping, 1920), Entered the National School of Fine Arts in Hanchow at the age of fifteen. Taught at the same school from 1941 to 1947. Came to Paris in 1948. One-man shows at the Galerie Pierre, Paris, since 1950, and at the Galerie Cadly-Birch, New York, since 1952. Takes part regularly in the Salon de Mai. Lives in Paris. Zao Wou-Ki's work, at first representational and sometimes marked with a certain preciosity, has progressed in recent years toward pure calligraphy. When abstract, it becomes more transparent to the mind, and henceforth more significant.

ZARITZKY Joseph (b. Borispol. Ukraine, 1891). Until 1914, studied at the Academy of Fine Arts in Kiev. Settled in Israel in 1923 but came to Paris in 1927 in order to complete his studies. Once back in Israel, he organized an Association of painters and sculptors and was a co-founder of the group *New Horizons*. Took part in the Venice Biennale. One-man show at the Municipal Museum in Amsterdam, 1955. Zaritsky's painting is a supple and light improvisation. His work, full of discoveries and shades, testifies with great elegance to an infinitely subtle sensibility. Lives in Israel.

ZEID Fahr-el-Nissa (b. Prinkipo, Turkey, 1903). In 1920, entered the Sénaï-Néfissé Academy. Came to Paris in 1928. Attended the Académie Ranson. Returned to Turkey the following year, and travelled extensively throughout Europe. Was in Berlin in 1937; in Budapest 1939-1940. One-man show in Istanbul in 1941. Back again in Paris in 1948. Launched resolutely into abstraction and exhibited at the Galerie Colette Allendy (1950) and the Galerie de Beaune (1951). Took part in the Salon des Réalités Nouvelles and the Salon de Mai, with large abstract compositions, veritable symphonies with countless bright and sprightly facets. She is the mother of the painter Nejad (cf. that name). Lives in London or in Paris. — Bibl. *Témoignages pour l'Art abstrait* (Paris 1952).

ZIMMERMAN Leo (b. Pennsylvania, U.S.A., 1924). Attended the Kentucky School of Fine Arts. Came to France with the American armed forces (1944-1946). Took part in group-shows in Kentucky in 1948. Came back to Paris the same year. Took part in the Salon des Réalités Nouvelles in 1949 and in an exhibition at the Galerie Denise René in 1952. Returned to the United States in 1953. Lives in Louisville, Kentucky.

Bibliography of Abstract Art

I. General Works.

Willard Huntington Wright: *Modern Painting, Its Tendency and Meaning*, New York, John Lane, 1915.

Willard Huntington Wright: *The Future of Painting*, New York, B. W. Huebsch, 1923.

Herwarth Walden: *Einblick in Kunst*, Berlin, "Der Sturm", 1925.

Katherine S. Dreier: *Modern Art*, Société Anonyme, New York, 1926.

J. Bendien : *Richtingen in de Hedendaagsche Schilderkunst*, Rotterdam, 1935.

Herbert Read: *Art Now*, London, Faber & Faber, 1933. New Edition 1950.

Alfred H. Barr Jr.: *Cubism and Abstract Art*, New York, Museum of Modern Art, 1936.

Christian Zervos: *Histoire de l'Art Contemporain*, Paris, "Cahiers d'Art", 1938.

Art of This Century, Edited by Peggy Guggenheim, New York, 1942.

Sidney Janis: *Abstract and Surrealist Art in America*, New York, 1944.

American Abstract Artists, The Ram Press, New York, 1946. (Albers, Gallatin, Léger, Moholy-Nagy, Knath, Mondrian, Morris).

Ottomar Domnick: *Die Schöpferischen Kräfte in der Abstrakten Malerei,* Müller und Kiepenheuer, Bergen, 1947.

Henry-Russell Hitchcock: *Painting Toward Architecture,* New York, 1948.

Charles Biederman: *Art as the Evolution of Visual Knowledge,* Red Wing, Minn., 1948.

Michel Seuphor: *L'Art Abstrait, Ses Origines, Ses Premiers Maîtres,* Galerie Maeght, Paris, 1949. New Edition 1950.

Collection of the Société Anonyme, Yale University Art Gallery, New Haven, Conn., 1950.

Michel Ragon: *Expression et Non-Figuration,* Paris, 1951.

Andrew Carnduff Ritchie: *Abstract Painting and Sculpture in America,* New York, Museum of Modern Art, 1951.

Thomas B. Hess: *Abstract Painting* (Background and American Phase), The Viking Press, New York, 1951.

Charles Biederman, *Letters on the New Art,* Red Wing, Minn., 1951.

Témoignages pour l'Art Abstrait, Editions Art d'Aujourd'hui, Paris, 1952.

Pierre Courthion: *Peintres d'Aujourd'hui,* Geneva, 1952.

Modern Artists in America, Wittenborn, New York, 1952.

Michel Tapié: *Un Art Autre,* Paris, 1952.

A Dictionary of Modern Painting, Hazan, Paris, 1954; Methuen, London, 1956.

Lawrence Alloway: *Nine Abstract Artists,* London, 1954.

Alfred H. Barr, Jr.: *Masters of Modern Art,* New York, Museum of Modern Art, 1954.

Charles-Pierre Bru: *Esthétique de l'Abstraction,* Privat, Toulouse, 1955.

Michel Ragon: *L'Aventure de l'Art Abstrait,* Laffont, Paris, 1956.

Léon Degand: *Langage et Signification de la Peinture,* Architecture d'Aujourd'hui, Paris, 1956.

H. L. C. Jaffé: *De Stijl, 1917-1931,* Meulenhoff, Amsterdam, 1956.

Marcel Brion and Arnulf Neuwirth: *L'Abstraction,* Gründ, Paris, 1956.

Marcel Brion: *Art Abstrait,* Albin Michel, Paris, 1956.

Alberto Sartoris: *Encyclopédie de l'Architecture Nouvelle,* (3 vol.), Hoepli, Milan, 1957.

The World of Abstract Art, Wittenborn, New York, 1957.

Jean Bouret: *L'Art abstrait,* Club Français du Livre, Paris, 1957.

II. Periodicals Directly Connected With Abstract Art.

Der Sturm, Berlin, 1910-32.   Editor: Walden.

De Stijl, Leyden and Paris, 1917-28.   Editor: Van Doesburg.

Dada, Zurich and Paris, 1917-20.   Editor: Tzara.

Het Overzicht, Antwerp, 1921-25.   Editor: Seuphor (F. Berckelaers).

Ma, Vienna, 1922.   Editor: Kassak.

Manomètre, Lyons, 1922-28.   Editor: Malespine.

Merz, Hanover, 1923-25.   Editor: Schwitters.

G. Zeitschrift für Elementare Gestaltung, Berlin, 1923-25.   Editors: Hans Richter and Lissitzky.

The Next Call, Groningen, 1923-25.   Editor: Werkman.

Vouloir, Lille, 1924-27.   Editor: Del Marle.

Zenith, Belgrade, 1924-26.   Editor: Mitzich.

Bulletin de l'Effort Moderne, Paris, 1924-27.   Editor: Léonce Rosenberg.

Cahiers d'Art, Paris, founded 1926.   Editor: Zervos.

Bauhaus, Vierteljahr-Zeitschrift für Gestaltung, Dessau, 1927-32.

Documents Internationaux de l'Esprit Nouveau, Paris, 1927. One issue only. Editors: Dermée and Seuphor.

Internationale Revue i 10, Amsterdam, 1927-29. Editor: A. Müller-Lehning.

Transition, Paris, The Hague and New York, 1927-38. Editor: Eugène Jolas.

Cercle et Carré, Paris, 1930. Three issues only. Editor: Seuphor.

Art Concret, Paris, 1930. One issue only. Editor: Van Doesburg.

L'Art Contemporain, Paris, 1931-32. Three issues only. Editors: Grabowska and Brzekowski.

Abstraction-Création, Paris, 1932-36. Five albums. Editors: Herbin and Vantongerloo.

Axis, London, 1935-36. Editor: Myfanwy Evans.

Plastique, Paris, 1936-39. Five issues only. Editors: Sophie Taeuber and César Domela.

Réalités Nouvelles, Paris, 1947-56. Album published annually for the Salon des Réalités Nouvelles.

Art d'Aujourd'hui, Paris, 1949-54. Editor: André Bloc.

Numero, Florence, founded 1949. Editors: Vigo and Sartoris.

XXᵉ Siècle, Paris, founded 1951. Editor: San Lazzaro.

Arte Visive, Rome, founded 1952. Editor: Colla.

Cimaise, Paris, founded 1952. Editors: Galerie Arnaud.

Phases, Paris, founded 1954. Editor: Jaguer.

Bokubi, Kyoto, Japan, founded 1951. Editor: Shiryu Morita.

Bokuzin, Kyoto, Japan, founded 1951. Editor: Shiryu Morita.

I 4 Soli, Turin, founded 1954. Editor: Parisot.

Aujourd'hui, Paris, founded 1955.   Editor: André Bloc.

Quadrum, Brussels, founded 1956.   Editors: Palais des Beaux-Arts.

L'Œil, Paris, founded 1955.   Editor: Bernier.

III. Works by Practising Artists.

See under artists' names in the Biographical section—in particular: Kandinsky, Van Doesburg, Mondrian, Malevitch, Moholy-Nagy, Arp and Herbin.

IV. Works Dealing With Artists.

See under artists' names in the Biographical section.

V. Exhibition Catalogues (containing texts or information of interest).

Die Erste Ausstellung der Redaktion der Blaue Reiter, Munich, 1911-12.

Internationale Tentoonstelling van Moderne Kunst, Amsterdam, 1911.

Moderne Kunst Kring.   Catalogue of paintings, Amsterdam, 1912.

L'Art d'Aujourd'hui, Paris, Catalogue, 1925.

Catalogus 2ᵉ Tentoonstelling A.S.B., Amsterdam, 1929.

Tentoonstelling Abstracte Kunst, Stedelijk Museum, Amsterdam, 1938.

Almanach Neuer Kunst in der Schweiz, Die Allianz, Zurich, 1940.

Masters of Abstract Art, Helena Rubinstein's New Art Center, New York 1942.

Austellung Moderne Malerei, Gstaad, 1943.

Konkrete Kunst, Kunsthalle, Basle, 1944.

Art Concret, Galerie Drouin, Paris, 1945.

Allianz, Kunsthaus, Zürich, 1947.

Peinture d'Aujourd'hui, Cannes, 1947.

Exposition de Peintures et Sculptures Contemporaines, Avignon, Palais des Papes, 1947.

Albers, Arp, Bill, Herrmann Gallery, Stuttgart, 1948.

Zürcher Konkrete Kunst, Lutz und Meyer Gallery, Stuttgart, 1949.

Antoine Pevsner, Georges Vantongerloo, Max Bill, Kunsthaus, Zürich, 1949.

Der Blaue Reiter, Retrospective Exhibition, Munich, 1949.

Advancing French Art, Louis Carré Gallery, New York, 1950.

Contemporary American Painting, California Palace of the Legion of Honor, San Francisco, 1950-51.

40 American Painters, 1940-1950, University of Minnesota, 1951.

De Stijl, Retrospective Exhibition, Stedelijk Museum, Amsterdam, 1951.

Dynaton 1951, San Francisco Museum of Art, 1951.

Arte Astratta e Concreta in Italia, Roma, 1951.

15 Americans, Museum of Modern Art, New York, 1952.

Art Abstrait Contemporain, Cannes, Toulon, Aix-en-Provence, 1952.

Regards sur la Peinture Américaine, Galerie de France, Paris, 1952.

Grupo de Artistas Modernos de la Argentina, Viau, Buenos Aires, 1952.

12 Peintres et Sculpteurs Américains, Musée d'Art Moderne, Paris, 1953.

Catalogue of the *Espace* Group, Biot, 1954.

Younger European Painters, Sol. R. Guggenheim Museum, New York, 1954.

Younger American Painters, Sol. R. Guggenheim Museum, New York, 1954.

Arte Nuevo, Buenos Aires, 1955.

Artistas Abstractos de la Argentina, International Circle of Art, Buenos Aires, 1955.

Peintures et Sculptures Non-Figuratives en Allemagne d'Aujourd'hui, Cercle Volney, Paris, 1955.

50 Ans d'Art aux États-Unis, Musée d'Art Moderne, Paris, 1955.

Divergences 3, Galerie Arnaud, Paris, 1955.

R. V. Gindertael: *Propos sur la Peinture Actuelle,* Paris, 1955.

Vanguard 1955, Walker Art Center, Minneapolis, 1955.

Divergences 4, Galerie Arnaud, Paris, 1956.

La Calligraphie Japonaise, Musée Cernuschi, Paris, 1956.

L'art abstrait — Les premières générations (1910-1939), Musée de Saint-Étienne, 1957.

50 ans de Peinture Abstraite, Galerie Creuze, Paris, 1957.

The main catalogues of individual exhibitions are listed under artists' names in the Biographical section.

VI. Articles of Importance and Special Numbers of Periodicals.

Buch Neuer Künstler, publ. *Ma,* Vienna, 1922.

Die Neue Welt, publ. *Das Werk,* 1926.

L'Art Abstrait, Galerie Maeght, " Derrière le Miroir", May 1949.

Painting in Paris, Magazine of Art, New York, 1950.

Das Kunstwerk, Baden Baden, Heft 8-9, 1950.

Punto dell'Arte Non Obiettiva, Spazio, Rome, Jan.-Feb., 1951.

Thomas B. Hess: *Introduction to Abstract,* Art News Annual, New York, 1951.

Tendances Actuelles de la Peinture Française, in *XXᵉ Siècle,* New Series, No. 1.

John Begg: *Abstract Art and Typographic Format,* Magazine of Art, New York, Jan. 1952.

Michel Seuphor: *Il n'y a pas de Repos,* "Derrière le Miroir", Oct. 1952.

De Hedendaagse Schilderkunst in België, "Die Meridiaan", 5-6, Brussels, 1954.

Michel Seuphor: *Algèbres et Géométries,* "Cimaise", Paris, May 1954.

Léon Degand: *Défense de l'Art Abstrait,* "Le Point", Mulhouse, 1954.

Michel Seuphor: *Le Style et le Cri en 1955,* "Aujourd'hui", Paris, June 1955.

Michel Seuphor: *Au Temps de l'Avant-Garde (en Russie),* "L'Œil", Paris, Nov. 1955.

Michel Seuphor: *De Stijl,* "L'Œil", Paris, Oct. 1956.

Cimaise, issue on art in the U.S., Paris, Nov.-Dec. 1956.

VII. Museum Catalogues — Miscellaneous.

Collection Internationale d'Art Nouveau, Lodz Museum, 1932.

Gallatin Collection, Philadelphia Museum of Art, 1940.

Art of Tomorrow, Guggenheim Foundation, New York, 1939.

Anatole Jakovski: *Erni, Schiess, Seligmann, Taeuber-Arp, Vulliamy,* Paris, Abstraction-Création, 1934.

Anatole Jakovski: *Arp, Calder, Hélion, Miro, Pevsner, Seligmann,* Paris, undated.

Alexander Dorner : *The Way Beyond Art,* Wittenborn, New York, 1947.

Possibilities I, Wittenborn, New York, 1947-48.

Vrij Beelden, Group of Modern Dutch Artists, Amsterdam, 1948.

What Abstract Art Means to Me, Statements by Morris, de Kooning, Calder, Glarner, Motherwell, Davis. Museum of Modern Art, New York, 1951.